GRANT LEWI

By far the most original and innovative astrologer of this century, Grant Lewi abandoned a Dartmouth professorship to pursue full time the ancient science of the stars. His readings were practical, his interpretations unique and insightful. Those who sought his advice were amazed by the scope of his powers. More than a year before he died, Lewi himself presaged the event. The heavens had held for him that final answer which all men contemplate but seldom dare to seek.

ASTROLOGY FOR THE MILLIONS

Grant Lewi

Fourth Revised Edition

ASTROLOGY FOR THE MILLIONS
*A Bantam Book / published by arrangement with
Llewellyn Publications*

PRINTING HISTORY
*Doubleday, Doran & Co. edition published 1940
Grant Lewi edition published 1950
Llewellyn Publications edition published 1969*

Bantam edition /February 1978

*Chapter I ("Why I Believe in Astrology") and Chapter V
("Fate and Free Will") and some of the tables for finding
the planets' places in Chapter X have appeared in* Horoscope
Magazine, *and are used here by the kind permission of its
publisher, Dell Publishing Co.*

*Bantam Books are published by Bantam Books, Inc. Its trade-
mark, consisting of the words "Bantam Books" and the por-
trayal of a bantam, is registered in the United States Patent
Office and in other countries. Marca Registrada. Bantam
Books, Inc., 666 Fifth Avenue, New York, New York 10019.*

Contents

Introduction   ix

I   Why I Believe In Astrology   1

II   The Everlasting Quest   7
Man's Search for Himself

III   The Pattern of Life   12
How Astrology Provides it in the Vitasphere

IV   What is Prophecy?   21
The Projection of the Vitasphere

V   Fate or Free Will?   26
Astrology's Answer

VI   Strong Men of Destiny   32
*Hitler, Mussolini, Stalin, Napoleon,
Kaiser Wilhelm*

VII   Strong Men of Destiny: America   62
*The Strange Cycles of the Presidents.
Lincoln, Wilson, Theodore Roosevelt,
Franklin D. Roosevelt*

VIII   Ordinary Mortals   78
*Individual Stories Checked Against
Planetary Patterns and Planetary
Movements*

IX   Self-Destruction   103

*Suicide, Insanity, Psychosis & Neuroses,
Dipsomania, Claustrophobia, Fixations,
Obsessions, Genius, Sudden Death*

X   Your Vitasphere of Birth   111

*The Sun, how to find it, how it
  moves in the Signs*   112
The Moon, how to find it in the Signs 135
Your Dominant Planet   162
Mercury, Tables, in the Signs   163
Venus, Tables, in the Signs   184
Mars, Tables, in the Signs   202
Jupiter, Tables, in the Signs   219
Saturn, Tables, in the Signs   236
Uranus, Tables, in the Signs   249
Neptune, Tables, in the Signs   261
Pluto, Tables, in the Signs   270

XI   Planetary Influence in Your Life 273

How to Find Transits   273
Transits in your Vitasphere   274
How to Place the Sectors (Houses) 277
Interpretation of Influences   279
*Planets' Places to Approximate
  Degrees*   280
Neptune Transits   285
Uranus Transits   294
Saturn Transits   304
Jupiter Transits   319
Mars Transits   326

XII   The Grand Strategy of Living   335

Nature and Meaning of the Planets 335
The Timing of Action and Passivity 348
*Cycology—Judging the Future by
  by the Past*   355

Supplemental Material   358

Astrology for the Millions
  Horoscope Blanks   end of book

Index to Tables of Planets' Places

Sun	132-134
Moon: 1870–1999	136-148
Mercury: 1870–1999	171-182
Venus: 1870–1999	191-200
Mars: 1870–1999	211-218
Jupiter: 1870–1999	226-235
Saturn: 1870–1999	246-248
Uranus: 1870–1999	259-260
Neptune: 1870–1999	268-269
Pluto: 1870–1999	272

Index to Birth Chart Readings

	Pars.	Pgs.	
Sun through the Signs	1–12		115-131
Moon through the Signs	13–24		153-163
Mercury through the Signs	25–36		164-170
Venus through the Signs	37–48		184-190
Mars through the Signs	49–60		202-210
Jupiter through the Signs	61–72		219-225
Saturn through the Signs	13–84		236-245
Uranus through the Signs	85–96		251-258
Neptune through the Signs	97–108		261-267
Pluto through the Signs	109–120		270-271

Index to Transit Readings

Transits through the Sectors (Houses)	Pars.		Pgs.	
Saturn		121		284
Uranus		122		284-285
Transits of Neptune	123–138			285-294
Transits of Uranus	139–157			294-304
Transits of Saturn	158–177			304-319
Transits of Jupiter	178–192			319-326
Transits of Mars	193–211			326-334

World History Charts

Napoleon	52	Roosevelt, F. D.	69
Kaiser Wilhelm	53	U.S.A.	149
Hitler	55	U.S.S.R.	183
Mussolini	59	Nazi Revolution	201

Astrology for the Millions . . . is the first book to enable readers to investigate Astrology for themselves, to watch the year-by-year workings of the planets in their own lives, to see with their own eyes how and under what circumstances they respond to planetary influences.

GRANT LEWI

MR. HALLEY: But I don't believe in Astrology!
SIR ISAAC NEWTON: I have studied the subject, Mr. Halley, you have not.

Introduction

Astrology for the Millions is more than the title of this book—it was the ideal for which Grant Lewi wrote.

Astrology is no longer one of the esoteric sciences of which knowledge and practice is limited to the privileged few. Today astrology *is* "for the millions"; it is in the vanguard of the movement bringing all the esoteric sciences out into the open and making them accessible to all.

While astrology itself is ancient—some claim it to be the first science—this popularization is new, it is truly Aquarian Age! We astrologers argue among ourselves as to the time when the Piscean Age ends and the Aquarian Age begins, but all recognize that no matter what the actual date of the new beginning is, there is a period of several hundred years marking the transitional phase between the two Great Ages of approximately 2,000 years each.

Some astrologers mark the transitional influence of Aquarius in the very early part of the 20th century, noting the founding of Llewellyn George's astrological publishing business in 1901. Llewellyn's annual *Moon Sign Book* first appeared in 1905—making it the oldest astrological periodical in the Western Hemisphere—and it was in 1904 that Aleister Crowley received *The Book of the Law,* which he proclaimed the key to the New Aeon.

Others have marked the Aquarian influence as early as 1860, others as late as 1972, and others insist that we have to wait until 2200 or so for our first glimmerings. These arguments are largely subjective at one extreme, and very technical at the other. But it remains true that of the esoteric sciences, astrology is the most widely known and accepted.

The 1930's marked a period in which astrology became "mass-marketed" for the first time—with the appearance of the newsstand astrological monthlies. And it was in the 1930's that Grant Lewi's two books were written. First came *Heaven Knows What,* and then *Astrology for the Millions.*

But Grant Lewi's books are more than the popularization of astrology. What Grant Lewi sought, and *accomplished,* was the means *to make astrology accessible to the millions.* These books are not "about" books, but real "do-it-yourself" and "learn-by-doing" guides.

With the advent of these two books, anyone who could read and do simple calculations could quickly start drawing accurate-to-the-day horoscopes within 15 minutes, and learn to project them into the future for guidance over the balance of this century. That's really "astrology for the millions"!

And Grant Lewi's books are true "Aquarian Age astrology" for they don't tell you what a wonderful fellow their author is, or how movie stars plead to have him "read their stars," or that you must go to a professional astrologer in order to benefit from the wonderful science that astrology is, etc. What these books do is tell the reader how to *do* astrology at a practical level, by-passing needless complications. With these books, astrology is no longer left in the hands of the experts, the authority figures, but is given to the people.

The horoscope is a tool for both self-understanding and self-development. Contrary to the common misunderstanding, astrology is not fatalistic, for it really says that, once you understand the dynamic forces at work in your life, you can use your knowledge to "take destiny into your own hands." All the esoteric sciences say the same thing: that it is ignorance that is fatalistic; knowledge is power! With knowledge, the mind becomes the point upon which the wheel of life turns: the mind imposes decision between the forces of the universe and the forces at work within the individual life.

Astrology for the Millions and *Heaven Knows What* both work on the premise that you learn best by doing, and that once you are familiar with the actual process of relating interpretations to real lives, then you are in a better position to learn the details of calculation, the particular symbols, the rules of application, etc. It's the same way we learn most things in life: the way we learned to talk and write and handle words—we learned the rules of grammar and spelling long afterwards as a means of refinement and mastery. Think how difficult it is for most of us to learn a foreign language—yet we learned our native language as infants!

And I do urge you to go more deeply into the study of astrology. If you don't already have *Heaven Knows What,* you certainly should. These two books work side by side. And after using these two books, you can go more deeply into the study of astrology, and learn the details of horoscope construction and astrological refinement with Noel Tyl's *The Principles and Practice of Astrology.* And there are daily applications in which you will find the annual *Moon Sign Book* and *Llewellyn's Astrological Calendar* all very helpful.

* * *

The first edition of *Astrology for the Millions* was published in 1940, and in bringing out this fifth revised edition we have tried to keep in mind several principles that we feel reflect the spirit of Grant Lewi's work as an astrologer.

First, we have brought the tables up through the balance of the 20th century. When we brought out the fourth edition, we updated it to the year 1980 and added other material that had not been included in the original edition. And now we are adding still more material to make this edition complete.

During Grant Lewi's lifetime, Neptune was never

in Sagittarius, Capricorn, Aquarius or Pisces, and Pluto was only discovered in 1930. With no personal observation to guide him, Lewi was not inclined to write something just to complete the book. But we have had time to make many observations since that original writing, and we have included new material in the previous edition of this book, and now we add still more to it—completing the picture that Grant Lewi started.

Grant Lewi was a most unusual man, and he was an honest astrologer. Not only did he refuse to write about things he was not in a position to observe, but he stood by the predictions he made, even when time proved him in error. He felt that one has to learn by mistakes, and it is only by exposing mistakes that one can see the source of the error.

When he was ready to bring out a second edition of this book, he decided to include his original predictions for this reason. He wrote:

Another reason—a very simple one—weighed heavily in our decision to let everything stand. The method of chart analysis and prediction (or as it is more properly called, *projection*), set forth here for the first time, is sound. The basic theory works in practice, as you will discover when you apply it to your own life. It is not our predictive hits that make it work, though they do help demonstrate its soundness. And, by the same token, the misses do not condemn the system in the eyes of any right-thinking person who tests it in his own life and who understands that this book represents *a wholly new combination of old truths,* a combination which *Astrology for the Millions* presents to the world for the first time. It is a system rapidly being accepted by astrologers and laymen alike; and with increasing numbers of people investigating it and adding data to it, new truths will emerge from a study of its initial errors perhaps even more than from triumph over its initial hits. For this reason the errors must be preserved, for knowing where and how errors were made in the beginning cannot fail to help those who are adding each day to its perfection. To know what interpretation is *wrong* eliminates at least one possibility in the search for the right one.

Astrology for the Millions presents a system of prediction by transits, i.e., the passing over a planetary position in the birth horoscope by a planet at a future time. Grant Lewi preferred to call this technique "projection."

Before writing this book, he had investigated the force of transits for 14 years, and he published his first findings in *Horoscope* magazine in 1936 under a pen name, Michael Bogan, in a series entitled "You and Today's Planets." In 1938 and 1939 he continued publication of this material in *Horoscope* in a series called "Why I Believe in Astrology," and one article entitled "The Transits That Made Hitler." Additional material (written by Edward Wagner, then editor of *Horoscope*, who had worked with Grant Lewi) that was originally published in *Horoscope* has been included in this edition, along with further material by Llewellyn astrologers Marylee Satren and myself.

In every case, we have used the model that Grant Lewi established, and in our publishing work in the field of astrology have followed his ideal of making it truly "for the millions."

Astrology for the Millions and its companion volume, *Heaven Knows What*, are practical do-it-yourself textbooks that enable you to learn astrology the right way—*by seeing it at work in your life and the lives of people you know.*

You can read all the books you want, but unless you apply astrology to your daily life and observe it at work, you will never be a real astrologer.

And you should become an astrologer! You should be enough of an astrologer to benefit from the commonsense application of planetary cycles to the timing of your actions in daily living. You should be enough of an astrologer to better understand your life and the things that happen to you because you understand the pattern of the life-forces at work in your birth chart. You should become enough of an astrologer to apply this understanding to help your marriage, your profession, and your guidance of your children.

This is true *even though you consult a professional astrologer*. You consult a physician about your health, but you still have to watch your own diet, hygiene, etc., and be able to care for your minor cuts, injuries, burns, etc., by yourself. You consult a lawyer, but you still have to apply what you know of the law every day yourself.

This book is designed to enable you to apply astrology on the same day-to-day basis. You need no other book, but as your experience grows you will broaden your horizons and may even be able to make original contributions to this aspect of astrology.

There are a great many astrologers practicing today that got their start from these two books. This is what one writes:

> I'm a professional astrologer presently counseling and teaching here in Austin, Texas. I've used many of the works you publish for some time now, and find that among the outstanding books, *Astrology for the Millions* and *Heaven Knows What* rank as two of the foremost astrological works of our century. It seems that people are astounded that works written in excess of 35 years ago can still be applicable today, and be so precise while being so general.

A girl from Canada once told me that *Heaven Knows What* saved her life! She, as many of us today, needed to know that life did indeed have meaning, and that she could play a purposeful role—why else continue living? She was given a copy of the book, and that was her answer! It not only saved her life, but changed it totally, for the insight she gained became the foundation for new psychological and spiritual growth.

And that's the real reason every person should study astrology: to become a more fulfilled person, to be able to fulfill more of the potential of the life that has been given to you, and to contribute more to the life of the world within which we live. Knowledge—*gnosis*—is power: the power to become, to grow, to evolve, to add to life.

To study astrology is to continue growing and learning, for people who otherwise might stop growing and learning when they "grow up." I don't suggest that everyone should become a professional astrologer, doing the horoscopes of other people for a living. But no matter how much you know of astrology, you will never know enough not to benefit from consultation with another astrologer; and the more you know of astrology, the more benefit you will give to another person, even to another astrologer in consultation with him. Astrology becomes a language of communication, and of relationship, between people.

The study of astrology becomes a lifelong pursuit, for once you start with your own horoscope and your relationship with the transiting planets, you are discovering your personal destiny and working to come to terms with life. In one sense you are waking up! For until you begin to understand yourself and know more about the inner nature of the world in which you live, you are only half-alive, only partially conscious.

The message of *Astrology for the Millions* could be: *Wake up! Tune in! Live!*

The study of astrology enables you to participate in the life of the Universe as you consciously identify with the planetary cycles and the forces of Nature. It's like using Llewellyn's annual *Moon Sign Book* as a guide to planting. We learn to work *with* the life cycles, in harmony with Nature. We become more at one with Nature, working in rhythm with one another as well, like a crew of oarsmen all pulling together for maximum power.

In *Astrology for the Millions*, Grant Lewi says:

The basic principle of astrology is that man can choose to develop his good and constructive qualities, rather than to indulge his bad and destructive ones; and that he can choose his times for action and his times for inaction, rather than remain passive before the tides of circumstance.

He called this the "Grand Strategy of Living" and it is the culminating chapter in the book, with complete directions and tables for charting the cycles —by means of transits to the birth horoscope—in any person's life and understanding their effect. The point is that the birth chart is not something forever fixed, like *fate,* but is only a map of a beginning. The birth horoscope is only a picture of the solar system at that moment of time, seen from that particular place. It is a map of the forces of the universe, the *macrocosm,* and it is reproduced within the person, the *microcosm.* It is a description of the world into which one is born, and all the forces that exist in that environment.

The birth chart is the base from which we evolve. And knowing the positions of the planetary factors in the birth chart enables us to predict when future planetary influences will operate. This enables us to plan living strategically, so that by doing the right thing at the right time, and not doing the wrong thing, or doing it at the wrong time, we can succeed and find happiness and fulfillment.

Yes, the study of astrology in this manner—a truly lifelong study and practice—is extremely practical, for it helps the individual attain success and happiness. But it's more than ordinary practicality, for it is this *living practice of astrology* that brings about the fulfillment of the promise of this particular life. Through conscious cooperation with the "weavers of fate," as it were, man takes his past, his *karma,* and transforms it into *dharma,* purposeful living.

Today astrology *is* for the millions! It is for everyone; it is no longer limited to the few—to the priests and the kings, as it was in ancient times; it is no longer confined to professionals; it is no longer dependent upon the mastery of the technology of chartcasting. With this one book, the entire practice of astrology is opened up to the ordinary person; not in the form of "popular" astrology, which is mainly entertaining, but as a real person-centered, life-fulfilling, consciousness-expanding science in which knowledge is applied to living.

Perhaps it is equally true to say that astrology was reborn, in a new body, for the Aquarian Age with the appearance of Grant Lewi's two books that suddenly enabled the reader to ride the shoulders of a giant into a new world. "Do-it-yourself" astrology was born, for the reader now can easily and accurately attain that which was available to him before only as a client, or with long years of study and apprenticeship. Suddenly, anybody could become an astrologer.

That's my view of astrology. With this book, I have been able to look back upon my life and understand the elements of the past better, and learn more from them. Life has ceased to be directionless; it has revealed a pattern that I have learned is truly mine, one that I seek now to fulfill.

And that's how I urge you to use this book. Use the tables to go back over your life and find the important periods when the different portions of your birth horoscope were being activated, and construct a diary-in-reverse. What happened to you at these important times? Analyze your life-events in terms of your personal pattern of energies, and learn from this analysis the nature of your own reactions to the changing pattern of energies in the universe around you. Learn to understand yourself. Put the past into perspective. Be able to say to yourself: "Now I understand, now I know why this happened."

Then you will be able to construct your diary-into-the-future, charting the coming important periods, and, with the aid of this book and the analysis of your past and the continual study of the present, project into the future—and plan ahead.

Llewellyn George called astrology the study of "life's reactions to planetary vibrations."

Astrology is really the study of life itself, for the whole universe is alive, filled with vibrations, pulsing, being expressed in cycles, and astrology brings us into awareness of the awesome intimacy of our place in this universe. Energies radiate outward from every center, from every being, and touch every other being. I am a solar system, whose Sun is my heart, and whose energies reach out to touch the most distant part of the universe. That's what astrology can do for you—you need no longer be a passive receiver of life-forces, but with your awareness you can become an active center of life-force yourself.

CARL L. WESCHCKE, AMAFA

I

Why I Believe In Astrology

Astrology, bar sinister in the escutcheon of astronomy, maintains a unique and lonely position in human thought. It is "believed in" by a lot of people who know practically nothing about it; and it is "disbelieved in" by even more who know *absolutely* nothing about it.

Of no other art or science can this be said.

Astronomy, the haughty scientific offspring of astrology, has developed through the centuries into a science of celestial measurement. It has developed even further than the lay mind can comprehend, into a sort of metaphysics of time, space and motion which only initiates can talk about, let alone comprehend.

Mathematics, intimately related to astronomy both through astrology and through the developments of centuries, has, like astronomy, grown with the ages into a part of the taken-for-granted language of our thinking.

Only the most stubborn and bigoted skeptic would think of standing up and saying, for example, that he "did not believe in" the Einstein theory, which is the most abstruse boundary to which astronomical and mathematical philosophy has reached. Such a skeptic would be promptly, and rightly, reprimanded by a more reasonable person, who would remind him that he was unequipped by information either to believe in, or disbelieve in, the Einstein theory.

Similarly, few will be found who have the temerity to "disbelieve" in the law of gravity, Avogadro's hypothesis, Newton's laws of motion, the multiplication table, the effect of sugar injected into the spinal column, Archimedes' principle, or the result of grafting sheep glands onto guinea pigs. These are not matters to "believe in" or "disbelieve in," but things to know about. Once you know, it is not necessary to believe; they are verifiable by experiment, and subject thereafter to the workings of law.

Astrology's position in human thought develops from the fact that it is frequently the subject of the most violent controversy, militantly carried on in the presence of practically no knowledge whatsoever.

Ask your doctor, for example, if he believes in astrology. Ten to one he will shake his head deprecatingly and say, "Of course not!"

If you ask him "Why not?" he will probably eye you suspiciously and reply something like, "Don't tell me that an intelligent person like you believes in astrology!"

At this point you must avow that you do not believe in astrology, you just were wondering about it. Thereupon, if he runs true to form, he will launch into a long discussion of why astrology must on the face of it be nonsense.

He will admit that, once upon a time, most of the world believed in astrology, but that was long ago, in the heyday of ignorance, before the dawn of science and the systematic search for truth. He will point out that astrology believes that the fate of men can be read in the stars; and he will go into a fine frenzy of righteous indignation that any modern could even consider such poppycock.

Listen carefully to everything he says. See if you can detect one sound, scientific reason or proof that astrology is false. See if you can discover, among all the people you can find who "don't believe in astrology," anyone who has a scientific or even a logical reason for not believing.

Three chief reasons are generally advanced for

not believing in astrology: (1) It is superstition because it was believed in a superstitious age. This is not a superstitious age; therefore we should not believe in astrology. (2) It is perfectly ridiculous to believe that the planets can influence human beings. What! Those things millions of miles away? Why, it's absurd! (3) The Great Wizard Magipocus read my horoscope at a summer resort, and it was all wrong.

These are virtually all the arguments you will hear on the subject, so let's look at them carefully.

(1) It is superstition because it was believed in a superstitious age, etc. The great principles of mathematics and physics, none of them false, were laid down in the age of the world's youth and "superstition." Large portions of the *materia medica* were discovered by the ancients. The advanced astronomy of the Egyptians and Babylonians is well known: their calculations have been proved of phenomenal accuracy. These same intellectual and accurate ancients believed in astrology: surely this should be no part of the argument against it! The beliefs and findings of these same ancients which co-existed with their belief in astrology, and which have since been given the benefit of modern verification, have been proved amazingly true. It is plainly illogical to dub astrology *ipso facto* false because it was evolved by those same ancients who gave us the beginnings of astronomy, mathematics, physics, navigation, chemistry and medicine.

(2) It is perfectly ridiculous to believe that the planets could influence us! Now nothing, in itself, is "perfectly ridiculous to believe"—except something that goes against a known law of nature. The planets could affect us without violating any law of nature. In fact, all the laws we have of the solar system, with which astrology is concerned, tell us that it is quite logical to believe that every body of the solar system exerts a measurable, if small, influence on every other body. Thus it is not "perfectly ridiculous" at all to believe that the planets affect us. It is perfectly ridiculous to believe anything on faith alone; but it is equally ridiculous to disbelieve it on un-faith alone. Both faith

and un-faith must bow before knowledge, of which, alas, woefully few people have any where astrology is concerned!

(3) Astrology must be false because so many astrologers are fakers. Well, if this were so, the law would be false because many lawyers are crooked; and medicine would be false because so many doctors are quacks and fee splitters. Architecture would be false because the Tower of Pisa leans; and art would be false because Diego Rivera painted Lenin instead of J. P. Morgan in Rockefeller Center.

There are many poor astrologers. There are many dishonest astrologers. There are many ignorant astrologers. There are many people reading and selling horoscopes who are not astrologers at all, but promoters, hack writers and petty racketeers.

Yet this argument, like 1 and 2, is a phony, as any logical person can see.

Now in pointing out that these arguments—the classics generally used against astrology—are not really arguments at all, I have not, of course, proved the truth of astrology. Far from it. I have merely tried to clear away the smoke of prejudice and confusion, in order that we may examine the subject on its own merits. It is the fashion today not to believe in astrology, just as long ago it was the fashion to believe in it.

Yet today, or yesterday, or tomorrow, intelligent people neither believe nor disbelieve something of which they are in total ignorance. When such a subject crosses their minds, they say, "I don't know anything about it, and therefore can't have an opinion." Then they are in a proper frame of mind to learn about it and thus acquire, not an opinion, not a belief, but a body of knowledge, from which the truth may appear.

Thus far, I have never heard of anyone who has investigated astrology and who has come away from his investigation dubbing it false. I should earnestly like to hear of such a person.

Richard Garnett, one-time curator of the British Museum, and a man of keen scientific bent, decided to study astrology to see what was in it. For his findings, I quote the 11th Edition Encyclopedia Britannica, Dr. Morris Jastrow's article on astrology:

> *Dr. Garnett insisted that it was a mistake to confuse astrology with fortune-telling, and maintained that it was a "physical science just as much as geology," depending like them on ascertained facts, and grossly misrepresented by being connected with magic.*

Isaac Newton, father of modern physics, reprimanded Mr. Halley who said to him, "I don't believe in astrology" with, "You have not studied the subject, sir; I have"; and Dr. Jastrow concludes the Britannica article:

> *It is at least conceivable that some new synthesis might once more justify part, at all events, of ancient and medieval astrology.*

Men of good will, and of scientific bent, have thus far never been able to declare it false, have indeed seen in it the truth which eludes the mere skeptic whose knowledge of it is limited to a "belief."

My reasons for "believing in" astrology are extremely simple. I have studied it, I have put together known facts of people's lives with known planetary influences, and I have observed, in thousands of cases, correspondences which are laws. I have watched these laws operate in the lives of individuals——of clients, of those close to me, of great men whose biographies are known or whose stories appear from day to day in the press of the contemporary world. I have watched Hitler and his chart, Roosevelt, Mussolini, Stalin; studied the careers and the charts of Napoleon, Bismarck, the old Kaiser, Lincoln, Washington, Wilson; as well as thousands of lesser individuals who, like yourself, respond to planetary action quite as much as do the great, the near-great, and the pseudo-great who for better and for worse make the headlines. The response of human beings to planetary stimuli is among the most amazing of all the natural phenomena capable of being observed.

I "believe in" astrology for the same reason that you "believe in" the multiplication table or the intoxicating effect of alcohol. It works: and it is the purpose of this book to show you how it works, and to enable you to test its workings in your own life.

II

The Everlasting Quest
Man's Search for Himself

Everything else, however lofty, however universal, is dwarfed by the crusade of the individual seeking for peace on earth. History is the history of this search of man, as he has prowled up and down the earth in war and in peace—of his efforts to relate himself more satisfyingly to the conditions of his existence. These efforts have produced religion, science, art, literature, metaphysics—in a word, what we call civilization and culture. At the center of them all stands man himself, who in all ages, on whatever deity he may rely, always finds himself forced, for the ultimate solution of his perplexities, back into the mystery that is himself.

As if by inescapable instinct, each individual seems to know that he carries in himself the root and germ of all that he is and may become. He seeks for knowledge and acquires it; he struggles for power and gains possessions; he rants aloud at the unfairness of circumstances or blesses the gods for what he calls luck. Yet deep beneath all this he knows that the final and irreducible sum total of his happiness lies in the secret of himself; and that any means by which he may approach the mystery of self-understanding is the most important thing in the world.

Because of this, the human race is lavish in heaping honors on the head of the poet, the philosopher, the psychoanalyst—on those men who are devoted to the study of man himself. They are man's foremost friends and servants, for whatever assists man in the achievement of self-knowledge, and therefore of self-mastery and happiness, belongs in the permanent treasure house of human possessions.

The endurance of astrology is one of the surest indexes of the value man places on himself and his destiny. Its roots are planted five thousand years ago, in the lore of Israel; and its branches include every race that has a history. The Egyptians, Babylonians, Chinese, Assyrians, Chaldeans, Persians, Indians, all had their astrology. The Greeks acquired it from the East, and the western world inherits it today. First carefully guarded, it was part of the Hermetic doctrine of the priests of Isis, by which they ruled the masses of the Egyptians. Later it became the luxury of kings and captains, a means of determining propitious moments for victory and of guarding against or slaying enemies.

From esoteric and private uses, it evolved, till today we have it for what it is: a science dealing with inner, and ultimate, causes behind human conduct. It has escaped from the airs of mystery, the odors of sanctity, that surrounded it when priests used it to frighten and subjugate their flocks.

It is eluding the grasp of charlatans who would exploit it as a mystic rite for which the uninitiated must pay a fancy price. It is rapidly wearing away the stigma attached to fortune-telling, and emerging in the psychology-minded twentieth century as an essential cog in the machinery of man's understanding of himself.

The roots of human conduct are always hidden from the eye, and must be come upon by stealth, if not indeed by force. There is no way of proving anything about the inner nature of the spirit of man, and thus no examination of the soul is ever strictly scientific. Whatever we study or read, we are forced to accept much on faith, or at best on the say-so of some individual in whom we have faith.

The human spirit, its motives and aims, eludes absolute detection. The best we can do is to observe, with the sharpest vision, what the human spirit does, probe as we may beneath the surface of its activity, and discover, if we can, in the well-nigh impenetrable darkness with which it is surrounded, what makes the wheels go round, and what makes the engines purr or choke in that complicated machine called man. For this examination, no tool has yet been developed that lays open the secret places of the heart and exposes them so that we may say, with absolute certainty, "There, you see with your own eyes, is the nerve sheath which causes this man to hate"—or love, or aspire, or fail.

In the very nature of the search, it is reasonable to suppose that no such tool ever will be devised, no such method of examination ever will be discovered. For we deal not in forces that can be weighed and measured, but in the very intangibles of life itself, when we deal with the human spirit and its ways and foibles; and dealing as we do in intangibles, we are forced to rely, for our researches, on other intangibles: on logic, on common sense and sympathy and understanding, by a combination of which we may hope to reach some degree of understanding about the central core of our world—man himself.

If we are to brand as "superstition" every advance of the human mind that cannot be set up in steel or stone, or measured with a pair of calipers, we shall rule out the highest and most inspired of human achievement. All religion will go into the discard, followed swiftly by all philosophy: none of it can be proved, save as one follows, with an understanding heart, the windings of an inquiring mind through the maze of human problems. All metaphysics would follow—all speculation into the ultimate nature of things —by which tortuous path we sometimes arrive at some small piece of knowledge that is of the utmost importance to the increase of the total of human understanding.

Furthermore, many things now understood to be "scientific" must go into discard if we are to insist on full material demonstrations of the whys and wherefores. Perhaps the foremost scientist of today is Professor Albert Einstein; few have the temerity to question that what he puts forth is scientific. Yet a mere handful of people understand the workings of his theory of relativity, or the doctrine that time is a function of space, or the almost metaphysical statement that "space is finite but curved," or the notion that the universe is not universal but merely a function of a larger universe, which in turn is probably not universal. These are high and fearful things, the ultimate reaches of our science, to be sure, approaching the boundary of metaphysics, where what is physically demonstrable merges with what is intuitively and logically perceptible, in that borderland of bright mists where the spirit of man takes its birth and has its being.

The study of the human spirit, of which astrology is such an integral part, has led along devious, and sometimes terrible, paths. The Witch of Endor, whom Saul in his agony sought, called up the dead to reveal their secrets to the living. The mystics of the East practiced, and still do, dreadful rites of immolation, self-torture and self-destruction in their effort to liberate the spirit from the trammels of the flesh. In various parts of the world individuals who appeared to possess understanding too great to be assigned to the forces of good were said to be in league with the devil and were put to death in a variety of horrible ways.

Today, however, we are kinder to those who devote their lives to the study of ours. We are not only kinder, but we are more ready to believe what they tell us. In consequence, analysts of the human spirit are among the highest paid of the medical profession: men whose study and knowledge are devoted to the secret corners of our minds and hearts, into which we, being too close, cannot probe without the aid of a trained outsider. Psychoanalysis (that is to say, spirit analysis, soul analysis, mind analysis) rests solidly, in the twentieth century, on a foundation of faith, a very triumph of the spirit of man over the forces of materialism. More and more, from the hurly-burly of *things,* we come back, by little and little, into the center of the universe which is ourselves; and more and more, in this renewed sense of the need of self-understanding, we are forced to realize that though electricity may move mountains or probe the ultimate of material depths, only the mind of man can probe the deeps of himself. He must do it virtually without tools; in a very real sense, he must go unaided by hand, eye or ear down into the depths of his own spirit and by the logic and precision of his own mental processes raise himself into the light of self-knowledge.

For this process man has evolved various techniques by which he surprises himself into recognizing more about himself than his mind would let him if left to its own secretive habits. Religion is such a technique. Psychoanalysis is another. Various cults and methods of self-improvement, part religion and part psychology, are others.

And, though just at the beginning of its career along these lines, astrology is one of the most important techniques by which man can pursue the elusive spirit that is himself to its hiding place and discover, in the secret corners of his own heart, the means by which he may be happy and successful.

III

The Pattern of Life
How Astrology Provides it in the Vitasphere

Man is born into certain conditions that he has had no say about. From his parents and ancestors he inherits physical and mental characteristics. Quite without volition he comes into an environment that existed before him, independent of him. The equipment with which he comes into the world and the world into which he brings his equipment are both, at the moment of birth, fixed quantities, in the creation of which he, the individual, has had no hand or part.

A proper understanding of this hereditary equipment, working in the mold of the environment, lies at the root of all psychological research and practice. Everything that a man has to work with lies within the scope of these two conditions under which he starts his existence. All success and all happiness come from properly using and combining the numerous components of these two factors, which in their simplest form are One's Self and One's World.

Contrariwise, all failure, all misery, spring from the misuse of inherited possibilities and from the misapplication of one's talents to the world in which they must find expression.

In the presence of a "sick mind" the first task which the contemporary psychologist sets himself is the discovery of basic factors in the patient's nature. He probes his past and his ancestry. He strives to bring out of his patient memories of experiences en-

12

countered early in life; he goes back, as much as he can, to the basic pattern from which the patient's life has developed, in an effort to discover from what essential factors the malady springs.

Astrology's value to the science of man, his problems and success, rests securely on the fact that it provides a permanent record of *what surrounded life at its beginning*. The record of the moment of birth, stating the conditions that surrounded birth, provides the student with a clear statement of those things for which analysts and individuals working along other lines probe laboriously and long, only to emerge at the end with a less-than-certain result.

This record of what surrounded life at its beginning we shall call the *Vitasphere* (*vita,* life; and *sphere,* a ball, or surrounding). Generally represented as a flat surface, it is in reality the representation of a globe, with the earth at the center and the heavenly bodies around, above and below, as they were at the moment of birth. The Vitasphere, then, is the universe of life. At the center stands the precious human nucleus, with the forces of heredity and environment impinging on it from all directions, right, left, above and below, at the moment of its emergence into human existence.

The Vitasphere provides a blueprint from which the following may be read:

1. The hereditary (physical, mental, psychic) equipment with which the individual is born.
2. The environmental pattern into which the individual with his equipment is born.
3. How (1) and (2) react and interact to produce a new personality, a new life, and thus a new and unique career.

The Vitasphere contains all the major bodies of the solar system: the Sun, the Moon and the planets Mercury, Venus, Mars, Jupiter, Saturn, Uranus and Neptune. It shows their relationship to the earth, and to that which came into being at the specific point of time for which the Vitasphere is recorded. In it are contained all the attributes that make up the human being, and all the forces which, translated through the human being, make up life.

The Vitasphere records these factors in all their implications. First and foremost, it provides an index to the physical inheritance of the individual: his physical body, his mental qualifications, his psychic and psychological biases, as inherited from his father and mother. On the basis of these fundamentals, it records the channels along which sensory and emotional impressions will be transmitted from the outer world to his inner nature, and it shows how his nature will respond to, and make use of, these impressions. It provides an index to the flow of his energies and the direction they are likely to take. It indicates how he will react to experience as it clashes around him during life and how he will set up and use those defenses which, in our complex life, so greatly complicate nature's first law, of self-preservation. Below all these, in the psychic pattern, it indicates the deep psychic bias which is his ancestral and racial inheritance, and how this will express itself, creatively or destructively, as he seeks that individualism which distinguishes mankind from the other animals.

All this is recorded in the Vitasphere, in the disposition of the members of the solar system at the moment of birth.

The nature of the physical body, including the brain as a physical organism, and of the psychic nature as it is a product of organic functioning, are indicated by the Sun and the Moon.

1. The masculine ancestry, and that which is inherited from it, is represented by the Sun. This in general includes the external nature of the individual, his physical attributes superficially considered, his expressiveness, his extraverted qualities, and the manner in which they will assert, or fail to assert, themselves in contact with life. The Sun also represents the physical organ of the brain; and thus has relationship to brain soundness and brain strength. It does not re-

late primarily to intelligence, but merely to the physical soundness of the brain as an organ. It is possible to have a sound brain but not much intelligence, imagination, flexibility, etc. Consequently, it is possible to have a weak, unstable brain in the presence of considerable understanding and intelligence. The Sun also relates to the physical structure of the nervous system, the sympathetic nervous system, the glands; and all that is physical, either on the surface of the body or deep within it. In the glandular system, the Sun relates to the pituitary, the gland of continued effort; and especially to the posterior lobe (nerve cells, involuntary muscle cell, brain and sex tone).

2. The feminine ancestry, and that which is inherited from or through it, is represented by the Moon. This in general indicates the inner nature of the individual and the uses to which, within himself, he will put the physical attributes as indicated by the Sun. It provides an index to psychic and mental qualities, particularly as these arise from the functioning of physical (brain, nerve, gland) attributes as indicated by the Sun. It indicates the inner nature, and how it will assert itself in the world, or drive itself back into introversion. It represents intuition, understanding, inceptivity, the extent to which external impressions are assimilated into the intelligence, the directions which impressions take within the intelligence, and, conversely, the route and direction they will take when, having been absorbed, they emerge from the intelligence in thought, speech and action. As the masculine principle relates to the physical brain as to its soundness and strength, so the feminine principle relates to the understanding, the intelligence, the perceptive and inceptive qualities and abilities of the mind, as distinguished from the physical organ of the brain. Since the mind relates to, and is influenced by, the nerves, the sympathetic nervous system and the glandular system, the feminine principle relates to the functioning of these. In the glandular system, the Moon relates to the thymus, gland of childhood; and later to the testes (male) and ovaries (female).

The paths by which impressions reach the physical body for use by the brain are indicated by the antennae, Mercury and Venus.

3. Mercury stands for the perceptive functions —the sense, or sensory antennae of human life: sight, hearing, smell, taste, feeling. This antenna of existence, interpreted in the Vitasphere, gives the clue to the kind of perceptiveness that the individual will develop, on the basis of his physical body, brain, and nerve system (the Sun) and his mental, intuitive, inner understanding (the Moon). From this antenna and its attributes in the Vitasphere we discover whether one will be acute or dull in his perceptions; mundane or idealistic in his outlook; practical or flighty, brilliant or slow. The same impressions fall upon all alike, and each one receives them differently, senses them differently. The same smell is sweeter to some than to others; the same noise louder; the same music more appealing. The attributes of the antenna Mercury, recorded in the Vitasphere, indicate these differences of reception to sensory perception. These in turn reflect back on the brain (Sun) and the mind (Moon) for their final interpretation. In the glandular system, Mercury relates to the pineal as the gland of brain development, and also to the parathyroids in relation to their function in the excitability of muscle and nerve.

4. Venus stands for the sex-love-emotion principle in the Vitasphere and in human life, and has to do with *emotional perceptivity* much as Mercury has to do with *sensory perceptivity*. Since these perceptivities cross and recross each other in the complex human machine, the antennae Venus and Mercury must be interpreted in terms of each other, as well as in their relation to the indices of Sun and Moon—body and soul. By its relationship to other attributes of the Vitasphere, Venus may relate to sexual activity; but more basically it relates to the individuals's reception to emotional impulses, his reactions to that which is not reasoned but felt. It is the ear and eye of the brain. The relative prominence of the two will indicate if the individual is "brain-minded" or "heart-minded"; and the disposition of Venus will tell, specifically, with

what kind of attention the individual receives the emotional opportunities that are put before him. In this way it is the index of human relations, indicating how the native is attuned to human contacts and how he will react to stimuli rising from them. Since sex is the most basic of human contacts, Venus is one of the prime indices of the place of sex in the individual life. In the gland system it relates especially to the thyroid gland, controller of the growth of specialized sex organs and tissues; and to the pineal gland in its function of sex development, adolescence and puberty.

The next three bodies in the Vitasphere relate especially to the relation of the individual to the outer world: energy production and consumption, and reactions to experience.

5. Mars represents the energy principle in the Vitasphere and in life, relating thus to the thyroid as the gland of energy production. The disposition of Mars indicates the nature of energy production in the individual and the constancy and direction of its flow; its tendency to persist or to flag, to be steady or intermittent, to be well directed or ill directed, its usefulness to the individual, and the uses to which he will put it. Mars in the Vitasphere gives a preview of the utility of energy, and indicates how the energy will be assisted or retarded by the other functions of the body, psychic and physical. Since energy is basic to human life and progress, Mars and its interpretation are of fundamental importance to any proper understanding of the Vitasphere and of life. Because of Mars's close affiliation with Venus, especially in relation to the thyroid gland, Mars is sometimes thought of as a sex planet, for the expression of energy along emotional lines is frequently what sex is. However, Mars is primarily energy, and becomes sex only when the energy is directed along that specific line. In the glandular system Mars relates to the thyroid as indicated above; also to the adrenal glands in their function of producing energy for emergency; and to the parathyroid glands as they function in relation to nerve and muscle excitability.

6. Jupiter represents the absorptive and assimilative qualities in the Vitasphere. As Mars represents the outpouring of energies and the direction they take going out of the individual, so Jupiter represents the indrawing of energies and the effect that things in the outer world will have as they impinge on the inner nature. This sixth principle of the Vitasphere indicates less how an individual will exert himself than how he will use what is thrown in his path—the interpretation he will place on experience, as it were, and the use he will make of it. It is an auxiliary antenna, conditioned to receive, not sensory-mental-emotional impressions, but experience impressions directly. For this reason, Jupiter has been said to be the planet of luck—luck, the things thrown in our path for good or bad. It does not indicate the nature of what will come, but rather how one will absorb and assimilate and make use of what does come. Jupiter represents, not the knock of opportunity at the door, but the nature of the response that the knock meets from the inside. In the glandular system, Jupiter relates to the pancreas, the controller of sugar metabolism.

7. Saturn represents the first law of nature: self-preservation: the defense mechanism of the individual which he puts up against himself, other people and the world in general. This principle of the Vitasphere is as basic as the first law of nature which it represents, and is of fundamental importance to the understanding of the Vitasphere and the life it stands for. Because progress and success are only the extensions of the law of self-preservation into active life, so this principle of the Vitasphere indicates ambition, or its absence, and what the individual will do about it. But essentially it is the defense principle in nature which in extraverts takes the form of ambition, progress, success or fame. In the glandular system, Saturn relates to the pituitary as the gland of energy consumption and utilization (continued effort); also specifically to its anterior lobe, controlling the growth of the skeleton and supporting tissue. It also relates to the parathyroids in their function as controllers of lime metabolism.

The last two bodies of the Vitasphere, Uranus and Neptune, relate to the super- and sub-consciousness of the individual, the flow of his psychic and creative energies, and the extent to which he can draw upon his hereditary and racial past for practical expression and use in life.

8. Uranus relates to the neuromentality, and thus has a relationship to the Sun, which represents the physical nerve structure. Uranus bears, however, on the reactions of the neuromentality rather than on its physical structure, especially to the sympathetic nervous system and to involuntary reaction, physical and mental. It has to do with creative force, originality and action; in its best form it is genius; in its worst, crankiness, eccentricity, violence, and destruction. It must be interpreted strictly in terms of the preceding seven attributes of the Vitasphere, for it will not of itself produce any effect at all except as it heightens qualities already established. It stands for the mental-artistic-intellectual-political creative principle—not the bio-creative principle; and indicates the extent to which the individual is endowed with originality, creative powers, genius. An understanding of its action gives a clue to why it is said that "genius and insanity are separated only by a hair line," for it is Uranus that is responsible for the fact that so many creators in all fields are said to be "high-strung" and "unpredictable." Uranus gives a quickness of perception, a speed of logical application, the results of which seem eccentric to those who can't follow so fast. It is not intuitive, but logical, in its actions; but its logic works so fast that it appears to be intuition. Uranus represents the extension of perception into the realms of the superconscious mentality. It does not bear directly on any gland, but on the entire nervous and sympathetic nervous systems, which in turn are related to the functioning of all the glands.

9. Neptune represents the psychic mentality, and thus has a relationship to the Moon. It relates to that which, in the depths of the unconscious and subconscious, is taken for granted by the inner nature, and

which is projected through the other attributes unconsciously or subconsciously. Thus it can contribute to the highest reaches of exalted genius or to the lower depths of inherited degeneracy, or to both in the same individual. It is the index of racial and inherited psychic traits; and thus its effects are established and permanent, subject to almost no possibility of change. For the deepest understanding of the Vitasphere, this attribute must form the primary base of analysis, even though, except in very highly aware individuals, its influence never penetrates the censor to rise into the realms of consciousness. It may represent thus genius or insanity, inherited wealth or inherited poverty, hereditary brilliance or stupidity or anything between. It relates also to all activities of the subconscious, and therefore has a bearing on inspiration, intuition, dreams, hallucinations, delusions, and all functions of the conscious and subconscious that are not primarily related to rational thought or logic. Like Uranus, it bears on no special gland, but influences them all by its action, through the Moon, on the mind and general intelligence.

which is projected through the other attitudes unconsciously or subconsciously. Thus it can contribute to
the highest reaches of self in either progressive types

IV

What Is Prophecy?

The Projection of the Vitasphere

With the Vitasphere interpreted before us, we know
the nature of the individual, whose life is of utmost
importance to him. We know the nature of his physical body and of his mentality, as he inherits them. We
know the interpretation he is going to put on sense
impressions as they come to him during his life. We
know the efficiency of his energies, the reaction he will
have to experience, the means by which he will seek,
through life, for self-fulfillment and progress. We
know the extent of his creative powers, if any, and
the direction they will take in practice; we know the
bearing which racial and ancestral libidos will have on
his mental, emotional and physical reactions. We have,
in short, a blueprint of the human spirit—of the outer
and inner man whose progress through life we wish to
assist with as much foreknowledge as possible.

In Chapters VI and VII, where we interpret the
Vitaspheres of great figures of the past and present,
you will see with what accuracy their known psychological traits and physical activities line up with the indications of their charts. You will be able also to apply
this method of interpretation to your own life and to
discover how you are the product of your heredity and
environment as indicated in the testimony of the Vitasphere recorded for the moment of your birth.

Knowing as we do the basic and primary traits
and characteristics of a human being, how can we

project this knowledge to determine what, from this starting point, he will become?

It should be borne in mind at the outset that there is nothing metaphysical or mystical about the idea of looking into the future. The idea of "prophesying" is so shrouded in the mumbo-jumbo of oracles and mysticism that we lose sight of the fact that "prophesying" in various forms goes on all the time.

Our political commentators are always forecasting what is going to happen, and with considerable accuracy. They do this by several methods. They have their ears to the ground, in the first place, and acquire thereby certain knowledge that the rest of us do not have. They take polls of what people think, and how they are going to vote; they take soundings; they have spies and scouts sending in reports. Thus, before the election returns are in—sometimes many weeks before the people go to the polls—they "prophesy" the outcome. Jim Farley prophesied that Roosevelt would carry forty-six states in 1936, and named the two he would not carry: Maine and Vermont. This was neither accident nor evidence of second sight: it was simply the putting together of known facts, carefully collected and integrated toward their normal outcome.

Long before Germany and Russia signed their explosive non-aggression pact, we were told they were headed toward an alliance. It was prophesied, against all surface indications, and the prophecy was borne out in the facts. Obviously, the prophets knew things which we did not know; had sources of information not available to us, because such knowledge is the very *sine qua non* of prophecy, which is nothing more nor less than the *projection into the future of a known body of facts, known to be progressing along a determinable line*. These facts, because of their nature, and the direction they are taking, are bound to arrive at a certain goal. The pointing out, in advance, of this goal is prophecy. There is nothing mysterious or strange about it. Doctors prophesy all the time—about the course of an illness, the chances of recovery, the time of crisis and the like. Experience has taught them that when certain conditions and symptoms exist, certain other conditions and symptoms will follow and a certain end will be reached. Knowledge enables them to do this; our lack of knowledge makes it appear wonderful to us. But in reality it is not wonderful: it is merely logical and inevitable.

Prophecy, then, is merely *the projection of the line of logic into the future*. It is the *extension of events along the line which they are already traveling, toward a goal which experience has led the prophet to expect*. Eliminating the mystics, of whom I know nothing, the "prophet"—be he political commentator, military expert, diplomatic emissary, doctor, or astrologer—is only an individual who has knowledge and experience and who by combining these can project a line of action past the boundaries of the immediate present.

Everyone, to some degree, is a prophet in everyday life. The child who returns from a motor trip and says, "Lassie will be happy to see us" is a prophet. The child knows (a) the disposition of the family dog, (b) the conditions in existence—the family has been away from home, (c) how the dog has acted under similar conditions in the past; and the child's prophecy will be proved correct.

You prophesy about your friends in somewhat more complicated matters. You say, "Gene will like that movie" because you know (a) Gene's likes and dislikes, (b) the quality of the movie; and from knowing these things, you know how Gene will react to the movie. You'll generally be right in this kind of prophecy; most of us are, and feel very well pleased with ourselves when we are proved so.

Even in more involved problems, we sometimes display remarkable prophetic insight. We say, "We want Ben and Sadie to meet; they're sure to like each other, and who knows . . ." And when they get married, we say, "I told you so" and decorate ourselves with the Order of Cupid. What we have done is simple enough: we have put together our knowledge of Ben and our knowledge of Sadie, and we have projected the line of their lives in the light of that knowledge. This is the very essence of prophecy; and forecasting from the testimony of the Vitasphere is no more mystical than that: *we deal in known quantities, following a known line of activity, from a known phase; and we project the line of such activities into the future.* We know the basic and inner nature of the individual; we know the field of his operations in life. As we follow the movement of the planets in the Vitasphere from the moment of his birth onward, we see how his initial tendencies develop in contact with the outer world. We see how his perceptions are influenced and changed by time; how his emotions evolve, and what experiences he encounters to quicken or dull or sensitize or desensitize them. We see his response to experience, the workings of his originality, the flow of his energy, the struggles he goes through to achieve his place in the world and to defend himself against the incursions of society and circumstance. We witness the development, for good or ill, of the primitive and racial urges of his subconscious; and we follow him up hill and down dale, at every turn noting his development as it is recorded in the initial and the projected Vitasphere. We know this individual intimately—more intimately than it is possible to know him by any other means. We know what kind of opportunity he will seek, and how he will handle it when he gets it. We know what experience he will accept and make an integral part of himself, and what he will reject as useless to his peculiar inner purposes. We know what he *says* he wants, what he *thinks* he wants, and what he *appears* to strive for: but more important, we know what he *really* wants—which may be more than he knows himself. We are not fooled by appearances, for we are looking always at the man as he is, deeply, and not at the masks and defenses which he puts up for purposes of fooling himself and others. Thus, with this knowledge, we are able to project his life into the future, along the line it is known to be following, and in this way to forecast; or, if you will, to prophesy.

In the latter half of this book you will be given a chance to test your own Vitasphere and to observe how *in the past* you have responded as prescribed to the movements of the planets. You will find this fascinating, for though the tests given are elementary, you will be surprised by the accuracy with which periods of your life are described. What happened to you, and how you felt and reacted to it, are confirmed in the testimony of the Vitasphere. You will also be given a chance to *project your own line into the future* for a period of ten years, and subsequently to watch developments, fending off the worst possibilities and developing the best as they come up in clocklike response to the line indicated by the projected Vitasphere.

V

Fate or Free Will?

Astrology's Answer

No question is raised more often in the life of an astrologer than the age-old one of fate and free will. He is continuously bombarded with queries like this:

> Doesn't astrology say that you're fated to a certain life, and that there's nothing you can do about it?
> If astrology tells this, what's the use of it? What good does it do to know what your fate is, if you can't help it?
> And if astrology isn't fatalistic, how can it be accurate? Of what use is it, if it doesn't tell what's going to happen to you?
> And of what use is it if it does, if your fate can't be avoided?

These are perfectly fair queries, which astrologers —and, for that matter, all students of man and of life —must answer, even if the answer is difficult.

It does no good to hedge and to say that astrology prophesies, but not positively. That "the stars incline but do not impel" is a modern doctrine of western astrology that does not return a satisfactory answer to the sincerely inquiring mind.

For the sincerely inquiring mind, if it has given the matter any thought, must have arrived at the conclusion that life itself appears to be a curious compound of fate and free will—a compound in which the

26

individual is subjected to the dictates of an inexorable fate on the one hand, and appears free, godlike, untrammeled in his control over life on the other hand.

Surely we are "fated" with our ancestry, our hereditary and racial traits, our physical body with all that it implies of nervous and glandular systems. We come into the world surrounded by and bound to a tradition, a family, a legacy of intellect or stupidity, education or no education, money or no money. For good or for bad, we came pre-equipped with certain things over which we have no control, and this much is *fated to us* quite definitely. We may believe that all men are created equal with respect to their political rights. But we cannot overlook the fact that all men are not born equal with respect to the equipment with which they come into the world and the environment into which they bring it.

One's fate is to a large degree bound up with the simple matter of one's physical body. Take, for example, a little man of five feet four, weighing at twenty-one about a hundred and fifteen pounds. We would say offhand that the man is definitely *fated,* by his bodily limitations, from ever becoming, for example, a piano mover, a stevedore or a freight handler. He has limitations which close certain fields to him, and these limitations over which he has no control are his fate.

On the other hand, a boy is born who at five has exhibited extraordinary gifts at school. At ten he is even more brilliant. Quite obviously that boy was fated with an exceptional mind; and in all probability that piece of good fortune will hold his head up through life and cause him to be successful. He is, as it were, fated to success, because of the equipment with which he came into the world.

We find no difficulty accepting and believing in these aspects of fate, because they are matters of common knowledge. Neither do these fated matters eliminate in our minds the possibility of free will, and it is right that they should not.

Our little man is fated never to become a truck driver. But there is no fate attached to what he *may* become. He is physically limited from stepping beyond certain boundaries. But within the limits of his fate, he may become any one of a million things. All kinds of fields are open to small men. So far as his bodily limitations are concerned—so far as his "fate" is concerned—he may be anything from a peanut vendor to Napoleon. There is plenty of scope for free will, even within the "fated" limitations.

Similarly our boy with the brilliant mind. His outer, extreme limit appears, on the basis of his mentality, to be tremendous in scope. But there is nothing to say he will reach it. He may fall woefully short of living up to the bright promises of his childhood and youth. Here, again, free will has room to operate: by its exercise, he may make the most of himself, or he may decide (consciously or subconsciously) not to. Free will operates in the decision.

The Vitasphere indicates with what limitations, and with what capabilities, the individual comes into the world. Under ordinary circumstances, without the benefit of astrology, the individual usually uses up a good part of his life discovering either or both of these truths about himself. Heartbreaking years are spent barking up the wrong tree, trying to do something that should never have been attempted in the first place, puzzling to fit square pegs into round holes.

The Vitasphere provides the index by which this waste may be avoided: provides the only objective clue to the inner nature of the individual, the only empiric check on his capacities and limitations which does not depend on long and wasteful trial and error. In the end, through trial and error, he might arrive at the same conclusions. In the end, we are forced to believe, he would fulfill, in a general way, his "destiny" without the aid of the Vitasphere. For we cannot, by astrology, alter the fundamental pattern of life nor change its ultimate end. We cannot make silk purses out of sow's ears, change geniuses into morons, poets into soldiers or sinners into saints. The limits of a man's life are fixed, whether by the planets, by God, or by his physical and nerval make-up. We cannot alter these.

But we can, through astrology, tell a good stone-mason not to waste his time trying to be a bookkeeper; we can tell a potentially useful clerk not to waste his time trying to write plays; we can tell an excellent poet not to waste away because he can't save the world from Fascism; we can tell a loving mother not to aspire to be chairman of the board of aldermen.

On the other hand, we can encourage a down-hearted youngster not to be content with soda jerking when he can do something more satisfying to him. We can indicate to men and women that they are really better than they believe themselves to be and can conquer larger fields than they dare dream of.

We cannot make them *other* than they are; but we can assist them to the discovery of *what* they are, and save them long years of struggle in finding themselves by the hit-or-miss business that makes up ordinary undirected experience.

Within their limits, men and women are capable of infinite variation. We cannot make everyone great, for the limits of most are fixed somewhere short of greatness. But we can indicate to everyone what he may aspire to; we may encourage him to develop to the utmost limit of his capabilities; and we may tell him when he has reached the limit beyond which all his best efforts will be merely nerve-racking and fruitless.

If every man developed automatically to the limit of his possibilities and knew when to stop, there would be no use for astrology. The sad fact is that few of us develop as far as we can. We leave vast possibilities untouched, either through not seeing them or through doubting our own capacities. It is in the task of encouraging men and women to go as far as possible within the mold of their possibilities that astrology fulfills one of its most useful functions.

Also, in the case of very ambitious people, astrology fulfills an equally useful function in warning them when they are approaching or have reached the point of diminishing returns: that is, the point beyond which they cannot profitably force themselves.

Thus, our conclusions. We cannot alter the pattern of life or redefine the limits of abilities. But we can *define* these in advance, and thus give men and women a working basis, a direction, and a field in which to exercise their will and their energies. No amount of will power can take them outside their limits, which are predetermined by conditions over which they have no control. But there is nothing in most people which insists that they live up to their capacities. The gods seem perfectly willing to let people live and die, even if they never achieve the best that is in them. And many, through ignorance of their abilities, through lack of self-confidence, need a push and a definition, if they are to go on to maximum happiness and success. Astrology does not give unlimited scope to an individual, but it can give him a field in which to operate, accurately defined by the analysis of the Vitasphere.

The strict constructionist of the doctrine of fate will say that every man does live up to his limits: that, by definition, whatever he does *is* his limit. To this there is no logical reply. We are forced back to a paraphrase of Voltaire when he said, "If there were no God, it would be necessary to invent him." Similarly, we say, "If there were no free will, it would be necessary to invent it and assume its existence."

But we may—indeed, must—invent it within rational limits. Man's scope, as an individual, is limited. He cannot exceed certain boundary marks: there are frontiers beyond which the individual may not pass, no matter what his will power. But few of us ever come within eyeshot of those frontiers. Most of us mill around somewhere in the center of our possibilities and never even explore the outer fringes.

Precisely here free will enters: we may by free will proceed to the uttermost limits of our possibilities. Or we may—by no-will, by inertia—lazily relax, with many available worlds unconquered, and never live up even to our own limited possibilities.

The value of astrology lies in its ability (a) to fix our limits and define our capacities by a study of the Vitasphere; and (b) to tell us how to achieve the most with the equipment we have, by a study of the projections of the Vitasphere.

And the Vitasphere is the only objective index of these matters known to man at the present time.

The man who relaxes before reaching his limits is a failure and unhappy; while the man who explores the limits of his capacities is a success and happy no matter to what small compass he may be restricted. In a very literal sense he leads a *full life,* and this is success, is happiness. It is not limitations that eat out the heart, but inaction, the knowledge of powers not used, the sense of having failed to develop to the utmost. The overcoming of fate is not the overcoming of limitations: that is impossible. It is the exercise of free will, the assertion of the full self, expanding to its utmost with the tools at hand, in the circumstances that are set. Astrology, through the interpretation of the Vitasphere, assists men to the achievement of their maximum by indicating to them the lines along which their will may be most progressively applied, the goals to be sought, and the individual means by which each one may arrive at the outermost boundaries of his world.

VI

Strong Men of Destiny

Hitler, Mussolini, Stalin, Napoleon, Kaiser Wilhelm

"What can be avoided whose end is purposed by the mighty gods?" asked imperial Caesar, and walked forth to assassination. He was heedless of the Soothsayer's warning, not because he scorned it, but because his faith in prophecy and his own destiny was excessive. He "rode loose in the saddle of Fate," trusting his mount even as it bore him to treachery and death.

Alexander consulted the Oracle, and, when he could not untie the Gordian knot, cut it, so that none after him might rule more of the world than he had mastered.

Napoleon knew his horoscope and, according to the story, lost Waterloo and his empire through ignoring the advice of his astrologer.

In the Fall of 1939, Nicholas Murray Butler came back from Germany with the story, which he said was well authenticated, that Hitler has five astrologers, each of whom reports to Der Führer independently. Hitler takes a cross-section of their opinions and findings and decides what to do, being thus assured that no individual or collective astrologer can betray him. We shall hear more of Hitler's astrology, and also of his fear of betrayal.

Strong men stride across the world like the incarnation of manifest destiny. Their spectacular rise, their

32

intuitive foresight, their superlust for power and their uncanny ability to get it, the heroic stature to which they draw themselves up, for good or bad—all these contribute to the effect they give of being in some way fated to the role they play. Supergood, or superbad, they "are not in the role of common men"; like Owen Glendower, each in his turn believes that

> At my nativity
> The front of heaven was full of fiery shapes,
> Of burning cressets, and at my birth
> The frame and huge foundations of the earth
> Shak'd like a coward,

and, by the scope and pace of his actions, awes men into something approaching the same belief.

In no place do the workings of the planets become more nearly visible to the naked eye than in the careers of these strong men of destiny. We sense that they are supported on the waves of the world's strife by some peculiar Thing. We may call it genius, or destiny, or psychopathic drive, and whatever we call it, we are sure to be uneasily aware of its existence. If, trying to explain his power, we examine the Vitasphere of the strong man, we shall approach close to the heart of the secret of his strength. For we find that the strong man of destiny is simply living up to the movement of the planets through his Vitasphere with astonishing accuracy. The sense of ego, of the will, that dominates all strong men is apparently a delusion of nature, a trick played on those who are the special agents of fate, whom fate slyly flatters with the chimera of will power that they may the more completely play out the role assigned to them. For, throughout the course of their entire lives, these great of the world never do anything but respond, precisely on time, to the influences brought to bear on them by Neptune, Uranus, Saturn and Mars in their implacable march through the sectors of the Vitasphere.

They ride the full tide of their natures, upward and downward. They start obscurely, rise meteorically, and fall spectacularly. Their sole function appears to be to cling to the hands of the universal clock and to perform their individualistic antics to the regular "Cuckoo! Cuckoo!" that times the rhythm and pace of their lives. Standing at the midnight point, they proclaim their will to be, and catch the hour hand as it swings up the circle from obscurity to fame. Still proclaiming their individual pre-eminence, they stand for one fearful hour at the noon point, and then, orating about their indomitable will, they have not the will to let go of their fate, but, clutching the indicator with death grip, sweep with it down the slope to darkness.

To follow this indicator through the lives of those who have ridden it to the full is to see the very wheels of life go round before your eyes. It is to understand that, as Carlyle said, "History is the biography of great men." It is, indeed, to go beyond this, and to discover that the biography of men, great and small, is the product of what they come into the world with (the Vitasphere of birth), played on through life by the movement of planets through the chart (the projected Vitasphere).

The chart on the facing page is the skeleton of the Vitasphere chart, which, when it contains the proper signs around the circle and the planets in their places, is the Vitasphere itself. In this skeleton chart is contained the basic principle of projection (prophecy) which we are going to trace through careers great and small.

The essence of this principle is contained in the arrows around the outside of the chart. These show *the direction in which the transiting planets move through the Vitasphere.* The planets of birth (natal planets) are fixed forever somewhere in the twelve sectors. But the planets from day to day—the traveling, or transiting, planets—move through the sectors in the direction given by the arrows. Thus, starting at the 1st sector (Ascendant) a planet moves downward through 2 and 3 to 4; upward from the cusp of the 4th sector (N) through 4, 5 and 6 to the 7th cusp; and on upward to the cusp of the 10th sector (M.C.— Lat., Medan Coeli, middle of heaven, Mid-heaven).

From here it moves on downward through 10, 11 and 12 to 1 again, and so on.

The principal planet we shall follow through this course is Saturn, which takes twenty-eight to thirty years to complete the circle, and which is the chief indicator to which men great and small cling. In following this mainspring of the clock of destiny, we shall see how men follow an inescapable rule. *They rise to, or assume, their maximum power, as Saturn comes up to the 10th sector. They reach a second peak of some kind as Saturn comes to their 1st sector. They recede from fame, or success, as Saturn moves downward through the 1st, 2nd and 3rd sectors.* By the

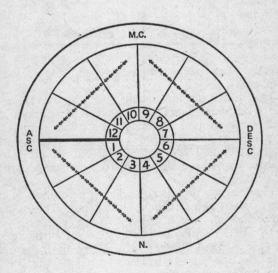

time it comes to the 4th sector (N) they either fade completely from the picture, or take a new start in life, depending on their age and other considerations of the complete Vitasphere.

We shall see presently how this works as we trace

the planets through the charts of Hitler, Kaiser Wilhelm and Napoleon. Later we shall apply it to Roosevelt and other Americans. Finally, in Chapter XI, you will apply it to your own life.

First, however, two more simple rules, symbolized in the charts below, which still deal with the transits of the all-important Saturn. Chart A indicates the relation of the transiting Saturn to the natal (fixed) Sun. Here a second rule: *When Saturn contacts the*

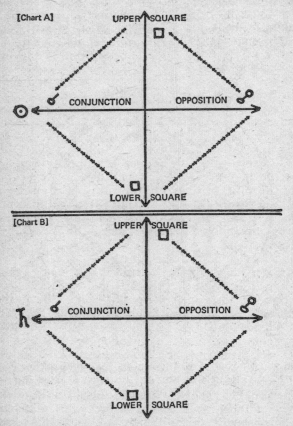

place of the Sun (Saturn tr. conj. Sun) the career climaxes for good or bad. The career is blocked when Saturn opposes the Sun (Saturn tr. opp. Sun): temporarily or permanently, major obstacles intervene. A new start comes at the Lower Square (Saturn tr. sq. l. Sun); while some kind of an accretion of power comes at the Upper Square (Saturn tr. sq. u. Sun). These four arms are activated at intervals of about seven years and account for the legendary "seven years' good luck" or "seven years' bad luck."

Chart B indicates the relation of the transiting Saturn to the place of the natal (fixed) Saturn. *When Saturn contacts his own place (Saturn tr. conj. Saturn) a wiping out of the past occurs, with a new lease on life for the future. When Saturn opposes his own place (Saturn tr. opp. Saturn), climaxing developments occur* along the line laid down at the time of the conjunction fourteen years before. At the squares, halfway between the conjunction and the opposition, lesser, but still important, developments take place.

Before you go on to see how these things have worked in your own life, watch the developments in the life of Hitler who, as we are told, has five astrologers working independently in order that none may use the planets to betray him—and who for all these precautions has been unable to forestall the "betrayal" which the planets made sure of in the first place by planting it within himself.

Der Führer's fear of betrayal is a very important factor of his psychology, clearly indicated in his Vitasphere and accurately portrayed in his life. Fear of treachery is a direct symptom of paranoia (delusions of persecution). The neurotic (or psychotic) personality, out of tune with the world, imagines that, like Ishmael, the hand of the world is against him. He seeks at once to avenge and vindicate himself by dominating the world he fears, which he imagines seeks his destruction. Fear (of betrayal, of persecution) constantly shows through his armor of arrogance. He feels himself constantly surrounded by danger, and, to prove to himself that he is no coward, courts it, lives dangerously, tempting fate, and thus actually seeking destruction. The psychotic urge of the dictator is to dominate and die—and to die is just as important to him as to dominate. Hitler's history is full of hysterical suicidal outbursts. He promised to kill himself if the Saar coup failed. He has repeatedly said he would take his own life if fall or capture were imminent. Dramatically he named his successor before departing, quite unnecessarily, for the dangers of the Polish front. The idea of death, of death by violence, by treachery or by his own hand, is never far from his thoughts. Between the lust for power and the urge to self-destruction, the borderland is shrouded in mists: to the neurotic or psychotic mind, the search for immortality-on-earth (power, fame) and immortality-in-eterno (death) becomes much the same thing. To the power urge belongs the will to rule; to the self-destruction urge belong the recklessness, the ruthlessness and the cruelty which are always part and parcel of this particular type of "great" man.

The Vitaspheres of all dictators bear this out, as we shall see. In all, the self-destructive urges (8th sector, Mars) share rulership with the self-preservation urges (10th sector, Saturn). In all, the Moon attributes (spiritual and imaginative values) are limited in scope, cramped by Saturn limitations or by sector position, or by both.

Hitler's Vitasphere is full of this unhappy testimony. The Moon is cramped into Saturn's sign, Capricorn, in the very limited 3rd sector, where the favorable conjunction with Jupiter grants temporal, but denies spiritual, power. At the top of the dial, we find Saturn, the self-preservation urge, dominant in the 10th sector (fame, power) in the dramatic self-conscious Leo. This is the defense mechanism of the individual (Saturn) working in the sector (10) that controls his desire for fame, power and authority. The close link with the self-destructive urges is seen in Saturn's close square (90° aspect) to Venus, his ruler, and his emotional responses, which in turn is exactly conjunction

Mars, his energies, working through the self-destructive (8th) sector. Thus Hitler's "will" is in essence to defend and preserve himself (Saturn) by acquiring power (10th sector), even if (nay, especially if!) the acquisition of power leads to death (Mars and 8th sector). The first part of this "will"—the power—has already been accomplished; and we may rest assured that the planets will not deny him the accomplishment of the second part as well. Hitler will kill himself, psychologically, if he does not actually die by his own hand: that is, he will drive himself against the spears of fate until he achieves what in his eyes will be the equivalent of crucifixion and therefore his ultimate vindication before the world that would, but could not, persecute him.

When did this urge for self-vindication before the world take hold of Hitler in active form? At the end of the World War, we are told, when Germany, and Hitler himself was at fortune's low ebb. This was 1919, when Hitler made his political debut by joining the German Workers' Party.

Two things were occurring in his Vitasphere. (1) Saturn had returned to his own place for the first time. Hitler was thirty years old and was living under the cyclic influence explained by Chart B, page 36. (2) Perhaps even of more importance, because of longer duration, Neptune, planet of the instinctive inner ego, the primal urges, the deep subconscious instincts, had climbed to the top of the dial—10th sector—and was creeping up to contact Saturn.

Thus came the awakening of Germany's man of destiny, whose intimations of immortality came exactly on the stroke of the indicator. From the outset, as all along the line, the iron will of the world submitted inescapably to the will of the planets.

He was not to succeed at once—had, indeed, to wait fourteen years (1919–33) before he became chancellor and finally president, too. Fourteen years is exactly half of one Saturn cycle—the time it takes for Saturn to move from the conjunction of his own place to the opposition of the same. The *birth of awareness*

of power came in 1919 as the self-preservation principles (Saturn) were activated by Saturn's cyclic return
to his own place, and by the imprint on these urges
of the inner, subconscious forces (Neptune) brought
into line at the same time. The *results* of this personal
renascence came as these urges and instincts were
brought to fruition by Saturn's simultaneous contact
(see rules, page 34). This development was thoroughly
with the 4th cusp, and opposition to his own place
predictable, since planetary positions are known long
in advance, and their action in any given position of
the Vitasphere is a matter of record. Chapter X gives
you positions and readings in your own life that enable
you to look ahead. So far as Hitler is concerned, the
fact that Neptune and Saturn arrived simultaneously at
his 10th sector and on his Saturn accounts for much
of his uncanny power. Of such celestial accidents—
such fortuitous timings in the Vitasphere—are "great"
men made!

In the meantime, from 1919 to 1933, while Hitler waits for fame and fame waits for Hitler, what
happens? Saturn moves from 10th to first and down
to 4th. According to our rule (page 34) this should
bring some increase of power and aggression as Saturn
comes to 1st; then obscurity in 1, 2, 3; finally a new
start at 4. We shall see.

Hitler makes his first speech to the party (February 24, 1920), thus starting a series of February and
March events which will appear later. Jupiter is by
now in the 10th sector, bringing opportunity and his
response to it. Also Mars opposes his own place, suggesting that things begun here will not work out as
well as hoped.

True to form, our man of destiny moves from
here inexorably toward November 8, 1923—the Munich beerhall putsch. This must have been before the
days of the five astrologers, for any one astrologer in
his right senses would have told the fledgling dictator
to cool his heels for some time yet. On this ill-chosen
date Saturn was on Hitler's Ascendant opposing his
Sun—a doubly bad influence!—and as Mars came to-

ward that place in November 1923 the itch to do something at whatever cost grew too strong for the strong man of destiny. On the click of the New Moon of November 8, directly activating Hitler's most daring, reckless and self-destructive instincts, he struck.

The results of the strike are well known. Having refused to bide his time willingly, as all must do when Saturn opposes Sun, he was forced to bide his time unwillingly, which is to say in jail. There he languished from April 1 to December 24, 1924, while Saturn continued to hover around the opposition to his Sun and the conjunction with his Ascendant. During all this time, too, Mars hovered in his 4th House, held to this one spot of obscurity and new starts by retrograde motion. Here, locked up by the world, held by force from action, feeding upon and nursing all his delusions of persecution, he formed his final and definitive plan of action and wrote it down in *Mein Kampf*.

The fact that *Mein Kampf* was written in jail, under these planetary conditions, is an important psychological commentary on Der Führer. For here we have, starkly symbolized, the sharp picture of the mind which for so long has been the lash and terror of the world. The motive of his plan, the singleness of purpose that has enabled him to stick to it fanatically, the will power to carry it through to success despite all obstacles, are all contained in the Vitasphere of birth, plus the testimony of the transiting planets at this critical juncture.

Hitler had tasted success, and it had turned to failure. He had brought himself to the leadership of a cause, and the cause had failed. Saturn in 10th on its own place had started the chain; Saturn passing beneath the 1st cusp had brought to setback. Napoleon, Kaiser Wilhelm, Roosevelt, all experienced the same sequence. So does everyone. But Hitler in jail was, to himself, more than the discredited leader of a lost cause. He was, in his own eyes, a persecuted individual who had identified himself with other persecuted individuals—the entire German nation, persecuted by the Treaty of Versailles. He was someone whom the world would down if it could, who was determined that it should not. It was failure of the self-preservation urge to gain power quickly that landed him in jail, and it was while he was in jail, and thus confined, that his fear (of persecution, of failure) broke out in *Mein Kampf,* which, whatever else it may be, is the blueprint of Hitler's determination to impress himself on the world—to vindicate the Saturn urge to self-preservation in the grandest style which his limited imagination can grasp; temporal power on a huge scale.

To this we must add the testimony of Mars, representing, as we have seen, the self-destructive urges in Hitler's Vitasphere of birth. And it is interesting here to point out that very similar indexes in the Vitasphere account for both self-destruction and claustrophobia (fear of closed spaces), both of which appear to be neurotic symptoms of the same fear complex as it finds different expression. Hitler's psychosis found articulation in jail—when he was locked up and held down. When he was persecuted, he found voice for his plan to make further persecution of himself impossible. When others tried to destroy him, he enunciated the plot whereby the further efforts to do so would be foiled.

The pathological well-spring of this work is found in the fact that Mars—Hitler's self-destructive urge, his fears, his cruelty, his recklessness—was, like the man himself at the moment, "locked up" in his 4th sector, playing on the underpinnings of Hitler's life with all its energy hampered and all its neurotic factors working overtime. What happens to those with delusions of persecution and fear of closed spaces when they are locked up is well known. The maniacal fear that possesses them endangers life itself. Literally, they cannot endure confinement. In extreme cases they die of exhaustion or of heart failure due to fear. Hitler did not die. He lived. But the rebellion of spirit against the confinement and failure that he dreads gave rise to the literary monstrosity which ever since has haunted him, dominated him and unnerved the world.

From the evidence of the Vitasphere, *Mein Kampf* represents the time when the jailed Hitler chained himself forever to his evil demons of fear and made himself their permanent slave, deluded (Neptune in 10th) by the belief that he was mastering the world through the power of his will.

Thus Hitler emerged from jail a man obsessed. Just as Jupiter returned to his own place, and Saturn opposed his Mars and Venus from the 2nd sector, he resumed the leadership of his party (February 27, 1925)—another February date to remember later. Mars is on his own place, with the Moon there on the given date. From here on, Saturn moves through 2 and 3, the obscure period, in which progress is slow but sure; and it receives no setback till power is achieved. This is the classic "obscure" period, as noted on page 34. In it, success will not flash out spectacularly, but must be courted by patience and the firm building of foundations. We shall find it so in the other charts studied. In this period the Nazis made steady gains at elections throughout the Reich, and further "consolidated" their domestic position by a policy of terror. The Brown Shirts did the dirty work for the man who was holding himself in readiness. On April 10, 1932, he was defeated for president in the general election. But the apparent defeat, with Jupiter in 10th, was paving the way for an even greater victory, which did not overtake the strong man of destiny till Saturn got ready for it.

Saturn was ready only after it passed the cusp of his 4th sector and started the climb on the other side. And this did not happen till January 1, 1933. After this it did not take the man of destiny long to catch the indicator for the upward sweep—four weeks, to be exact. On January 30, 1933, following the New Moon on the cusp of 4th by only four days and Saturn's favorable position by only four weeks, Hitler forced the aging Von Hindenburg to make him chancellor.

The "obscure" period, which began on time as he went to jail, ended on time as Saturn gave him a new start—not one day before, and not many days after.

> But man, proud man,
> Drest in a little brief authority,
> Most ignorant of what he's most assured,
> His glassy essence, like an angry ape
> Plays such fantastic tricks before high heaven
> As make the angels weep.

Now, in addition to working under Saturn's movement *upward* in his chart, Der Führer is further aided by Uranus, emerging from his 6th sector of work and drudgery, entering his 7th (public relations) and moving to contact his Sun. Under this expansive influence he quickly completes his domestic consolidation and moves onward. Saturn in 4th keeps his attention at home, which the 4th sector rules, and this work is completed just as Saturn leaves the 4th, in the bloody Roehm purge of June 30, 1934, when Hitler caused to be killed Ernst Roehm, his best friend, and some sixty others suspected of less than complete loyalty. This came on the click of Uranus' first contact with Der Führer's Sun, emphasizing at one and the same time (1) his delusional dread of betrayal and (2) his conquestual urge which now takes the center of the stage in his mind.

With the Saar plebiscite, January 13, 1935, the borders of the Reich begin to expand, and he begins to fulfill the obsessions of *Mein Kampf:* a greater Germany. He has, of course, been fulfilling all along some of the other major obsessions: fear and cruelty in the persecution of the Jews, in which he who fears persecution inverts his fear by visiting it on others; and his fear of treachery in the Roehm purge.

The January 13th plebiscite which returned 90 per cent for Hitler came with the Moon in his own sign, Taurus. Mars was in Libra on his Ascendant, where it was at the time of the ill-fated Munich beerhall putsch. But with this essential difference: that while the Munich event was ill-fated because of Saturn's opposition to the Sun, the Saar works out well because Saturn is now climbing *toward* his Sun, which is additionally supported by Uranus. Saturn is not to arrive at the Sun till 1939–40, but the power begins to accumulate. The expansion which now begins with the remilitarization of the Rhineland (March 16, 1935) and the scrapping of the Versailles Treaty leads inexorably to the conquests of Austria, Czechoslovakia, Poland, and war with the western democracies —begun precisely as Saturn hit the place of Hitler's Sun for the first time.

Hitler's astrologers apparently began advising him about this time, for with March 16, 1935, begins a long sequence of dates having many astrological factors in common and presenting certain puzzles that appear incapable of solution until the testimony of the Vitasphere is brought to bear.

The plebiscite awarded the Saar to Germany as of March 1, 1935. Why, then, did the Führer wait two full weeks, till March 16th, for his triumphal entry? A similar question will arise later: why, after the Soviet pact was signed, did he wait several days to strike at Poland? To the astrologer, there is a clear answer to these questions in the date finally chosen. Much of the mystery and inscrutability of Der Führer's public life becomes clear in the light of this answer. We know why, for example, he let Schuschnigg wait till (as the last Chancellor of Austria told his friends) "exactly the stroke of noon." We know why he delayed his entrance into Vienna, which waited two days to "welcome" him. We know why he launched the "peace offensive"—and we are able to assure you that it was not because he wanted peace. The system by which he acts is no mystery when you know the answer. That he is systematic we know, if only by the precision with which he follows the obsessions of *Mein Kampf* and of his own mind. A creature of passion, of fury, he is not a creature of impulse. Every move he makes is planned, and from every evidence that can be gathered all major moves have been timed to a nicety to the rhythm of the planets, ever since he came to power and has been able himself to dictate the timing of events.

The move into the Saar was neatly arranged. The Moon was in Leo, his 10th sector, on his Saturn, and two days from the full. This condition occurs once during each year, sometime between February 20 and March 20, and it clears up the mystery of why he moves so often at this time of the year. The Sun in Pisces, where it is annually between these dates, hits off nothing special in his chart. But only at this time is the Moon most favorably disposed when it passes through Leo, his 10th sector. The Moon is then two days from the full, when things develop fastest and best; and to get this favorable timing, plus the Moon in the right place in his own chart (10th sector), requires actions in February–March, of which the first was the delayed remilitarization of the Rhineland. Other factors favored this move also. Venus helped, and Der Führer waited till it had passed the opposition of Mars to insure the passivity of France. There was nothing slipshod about the astrology that timed this maneuver!

Furthermore, the astrologers apparently told Der Führer to lie low after this initial venture. At this point Saturn enters his 5th sector and opposes Neptune, and throughout this period (March 1935–January 1938) only internal consolidation of Germany goes on.

The man of destiny waited till the planet of destiny came to his next angle of destiny before exerting his indomitable Aryan will.

Saturn entered Aries (Hitler's 6th–7th sectors) January 15, 1938. Mars joined him there February 1. On February 4th, with the Moon activating their conjunction in the 6th sector (inferiors, servants), came the purge of the army officers who, as it turned out, had opposed the impression of Austria into the Reich.

On Saturday, February 12, came Kurt Schuschnigg, the last Austrian chancellor, to Berchtesgaden—with the Moon two days from the full again, and again high in Der Führer's chart, at the end of Cancer and the beginning of Leo. By March 11 Austria was German.

Why did not Der Führer enter Vienna as expected that night? He waited for the same solar-lunar setup that shone on his conquest of the Saar—also for Mars to be exactly on his Sun. His astrologers did a good job on that one, too!

Goering is said to have twitted Hitler for not taking Czechoslovakia in May of the same year. Everything was set for it, said Goering: why did the iron will of Germany back down before the Czechs? The iron will had probably been advised by his astrologers to wait, and for good and sufficient reasons. The Czech president Beneš and the French premier Daladier were both born in Gemini. In May 1938 Mars and Venus were in Gemini—and when, according to Goering, "everything was ready," Czechoslovakia's leadership and France's leadership were at the peak of their fighting bent. Why should Hitler attack Beneš when Mars on his Sun would cause him to fight like a tiger, and when Venus there would bring in his friend France, who was also geared to fight like a tiger?

Quite prudently Hitler waited. In August 1938, when the full Moon in Leo-Aquarius maximized his strength, he started the war of nerves that was to end in Munich. Mars was now in Leo, in his 10th and on his Saturn. Also, this Mars in Leo opposed Jupiter in Aquarius—the explosive aspect that started the first World War (August 1914) and *was not repeated at any time till August 1938*. Time was ripe for war, as Hitler's astrologers evidently told him. Also, Hitler was ripe. He was able to time it himself, and did so in such a manner that, if it came, it would come when the planets caught him at his peak and his enemies off their balance.

And it came—for nothing will ever convince this writer that war did not break in Europe until August 1938, and that Munich was not a peace, but the backdown of England and France in the first encounter.

Subsequent events bear this out. Economic war between England and Germany, following Munich, led to Poland: the declarations of war in 1939 were more the statement of a *fait accompli*—war—than news. The war has been going on since August 1938 and will not stop yet awhile. The apparent stalling on the western front is not a stall: it is a willful military stalemate in which England and France have voluntarily engaged in order to carry on the war that started with the peace of Munich—the war to starve out Germany. It was the effect of this war, after it had run only a year, that drove him into the arms of the Soviet, forced his recklessness in Poland, and started the ball rolling for the military conflict which never was destined to come till 1940.[1] Hitler had nothing to lose by going into Poland; he had already lost the peace of Munich in which, as it now seems, Der Führer dug a pit into which he himself has fallen.

For Hitler signed at Munich with his tongue in his cheek. Why not, with Moon square Neptune? Someone is always fooled under this aspect. Hitler, with Mars and Neptune then transiting his 12th sector, of secrecy (and also, by the way, related to delusions and fears), signed with many mental reservations. Because he dealt primarily with Chamberlain he was able for the moment to hornswoggle the peace-loving Briton, for Chamberlain worked under the extreme disadvantage of Neptune and Mars opposing his Sun.

But Chamberlain did not have to wait long to be unfooled. Came March 1939, and Hitler swallowed what was left of Czechoslovakia. This looks like the first slip of Hitler's astrologers. Or perhaps Der Führer is getting careless. Saturn rushes up toward his Sun, which it reaches in July 1939, and the ego is swollen to the bursting point. Men of Hitler's stomach

---

[1]This worked out. The dogs of war were not unleashed till Saturn returned to Taurus, March 20, 1940, and after he did so return, they were unleashed at once—that is, on the next New Moon, April 7, 1940, when Norway was attacked. The astrologer also noted with interest that New Moons—of May and June—witnessed the launching of the attacks on the Low Countries and France respectively.

do not have the restraint to moderate their pace at this time. The treachery planted in them by the planets at birth goes to work here. The moderation, the system, that has supported them is lost in a bewildering sense of infallibility. The disease of the world carries its own cure in the head of the diseased one. The scourge of humanity cannot fail in the end to scourge himself to his finish. It is the one compensation which a cynical nature grants mankind, to atone for making dictators in the first place.

Hitler's astrologers told him last summer that he had to get what he wanted before September 15, 1939. Why? Because by this date Saturn would be retrograding away from Hitler's Sun in Taurus, and after that his aggressiveness would fail. Saturn actually did not leave Taurus till September 22. Hitler's astrologers may have said September 15 because it was an even date—middle of the month. Perhaps it flattered Hitler to be thus linked with Caesar, who had to beware of the ides of March, another 15 date famous in conqueror prophecy.

Knowing his time was short, why did Hitler wait till September 1 to move on Poland? The Nazi-Soviet pact was complete days before. He waited for the favorable conjunction of the Moon with Jupiter and then he annihilated Poland. Before Saturn left Taurus, the conquest was over and the peace offensive begun. There was not one really good date between the signing of the Soviet pact and the date finally chosen. There is even significance in the weird hour when the offensive began: 5:45 A.M., somewhat too complex to go into here. Truly, he got what he wanted by September 15! *Heil Astrologie!* It should be put to better uses—it is too keen a knife to be in the hands of maniacs.

Does he know that he is finished? Have his astrologers dared to tell him that?[2]

---

[2]Two years later, with Hitler still (so far as we know) alive, it may seem metaphysical to stand by the implication that he was "finished" by late 1939 and early 1940. Yet we still feel this to have been true. See note on pages 51–52.

There is some reason to think that he knows he is nearing the end of his rope. Lately he has spoken publicly of death and named two successors. He has spoken of retiring to paint. His flamboyant rush to the Polish front, clad in his old uniform, which he swore to take off "only in victory or in death," looked suspiciously like a suicide gesture. The paranoiac, having forced his instinct of self-preservation to a conquestual height, seeks his final escape. But his bullet did not find him; the glory of a conqueror's death was denied. So he must continue in one way or another to court danger, for death by violence must come at the hands of an enemy, preferably also an enemy of Germany, with whose persecution he has identified himself. Such death will vindicate the delusions of persecution which have through life animated his self-assertive, self-preservative mechanism. His struggle with the world that refused him work in Vienna, that killed his mother, that gave him a father he despised, that forced upon him the charity of Jews and kicked him around the gutters and poorhouses of Bavaria—this must end with the ineluctable proof that he is persecuted, as he has always told himself, which tale has been the breath of his conquestual flame. The German nation's sense of betrayal at Versailles found proper spokesman in this neurotic underdog. Hitler is Germany—the worst of Germany—the brute, the inferior, the violent, the psychopath. He is not Germany the home-loving, the *gemütlich,* the musical, the scientific. In him, as in his Germany, the sweet things of life must take second place to the delusion of persecution. He has set his foot across a line, and there is no turning back, for in turning back is defeat, and defeat is the one thing that is intolerable to the defeated. Better to persist to the last bourne of defiance, the last outpost of recklessness, than to admit that the persecution of the world has succeeded in downing you. Better, in the struggle, destroy yourself, bring yourself to annihilation, than consent to be persecuted. This is Hitler, and this is the Germany of which he is the evil genius, being himself the slave of his own evil genius.

Is it necessary after this specifically to "prophesy" for Hitler? Is not his fate contained in himself, in his past, in what we now know about him? Is it necessary to point out that in 1940, when Saturn returns to Taurus (March 20, see footnote 1 above), and conceivably just before that, the dogs of war will be unleashed in greater fury—either by his armies, or by those of his enemies which he has caused to be held in readiness? Is it necessary to point out that when his self-preservative urges (Saturn) run into his aggressive and self-destructive urges (Mars-Venus) he will fall? Saturn moves to the place of his Mars-Venus conjunction in August 1940, retrogrades, and comes to it again by May 1941, which is the ultimate date to which Hitler can endure; and it seems to me that, in the light of what we know, this "prophecy" becomes as inevitable as that tomorrow shall follow today.[3]

When Hitler came in, the Nazis boasted that he was founding a structure that would last a thousand years. Lately, men have been shaking their heads sadly and saying that it won't do any good to do away with Hitler, because Hitlerism will march on without him. What can we make of this in the light of the Vitasphere? Simply that what Hitler built will scarcely outlive him by a single year. The square of Mars to Saturn in his chart insures this. In public figures and private lives the truth is made clear: *men and women*

---

[3] "May 1941, which is the ultimate date to which Hitler can endure." This prediction occasioned much comment, seemed quite wrong, but is proved to have been based in a correct astrological theory: that *Saturn transmitting Mars in the chart of one "on the aggressive" is bound to work his ruin.* Hitler did endure past the second contact of Saturn to his Mars—May 1941. But as this is written (January 6, 1942) he is not enduring so well the final approach of Saturn to this place. For as Saturn retrograded toward the last contact with his Mars came the Russian offensive, and the retreat from Moscow is a classic example of the defeat which astrology describes for one who pushes his luck too far as Saturn transits his Mars. The three successive transits of Saturn to Hitler's Mars tell their own story. (1) August 1940: end of conquest in the west, failure of the blitz to knock out England. (2) May 1941: Saturn's second contact with his Mars: flight of Hess with whatever that meant of internal cracking of his Reich. It is not believed that Hess's flight was connected with the Russian war, launched six weeks later, leading to (3) the

with Mars square or opposition Saturn do not leave
behind them a legacy of any importance—that which
they have set their hearts on is gone before they are,
or immediately thereafter. They build their lives on

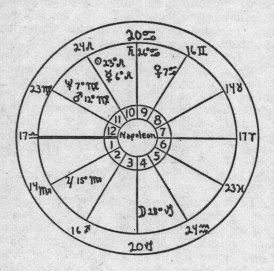

a false premise, and it collapses beneath them. I could
cite numerous life histories of Vitaspheres with Mars

retreat from Moscow under Saturn's return by retrograde motion to
Mars' place. . . . It should be noted that the nature of the action of
Saturn on Hitler's Mars was correctly judged: it did account for
setbacks and lead to increasingly great defeats. January–February
1942, with Saturn close as he gets to Hitler's Mars, write the final
word of how thereafter he is going to endure. The error of placing
the major crack at the second, instead of the third, contact appears
of less consequence than the vindication of the theory that *Saturn*
transiting Mars will, before the end of the transit, wear down
and destroy any unsound, overextended, or overaggressive elements
in the life of the individual. Thus the retreat from Moscow links to
setbacks of the past. It also links to the necessity of pushing Japan
into war with the United States and to the war between the United
States and Germany, and appears to be the signal of Hitler's end
coming, as it theoretically should at the completion of Saturn's contact with his Mars, which has all along been pointed to as the
fateful condition of 1941 because of which he was doomed.

square Saturn to prove this point. One is contained in
the discussion of Roosevelt, in the next chapter (not
his own chart, but that of his chief adviser). Another
is the chart of a man whose fictionized biography was

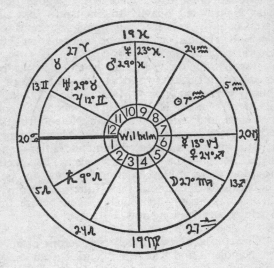

the basis for my novel, *Star of Empire*. He was a mil-
lionaire and land operator whose desire, as he expressed it, was to leave a farm and a fortune to every
one of seven grandchildren when he died. For a while
it looked as if he might do it; yet he died penniless,
and not one cent or one acre survived him or descended
to benefit anyone. He built too high, and without
sound foundations. It is the invariable record of Mars
square Saturn, which never can found an empire, personal, national or international.

Empire founding requires other things. Thus
Queen Elizabeth, in whose "spacious days" England
began to grow great, shows Saturn conjoined with
Uranus and trine Neptune. Victoria's chart, in whose
reign England's domain expanded further, shows
Neptune and Uranus conjoined, in trine to Mars and

Venus; while her imperialistic Prime Minister, who envisioned the Suez Canal and gave her India as an anniversary present, Disraeli, had Saturn conjoined with Uranus and sextile to Mars.

On the other hand, George III, whose pigheadedness contributed heavily to England's loss of her greatest colony, America, had Saturn square Mars and opposition Uranus, with Moon conjunction Uranus in Capricorn, and square Mars.

But Washington, who calmly aided in the establishment of our great world power, had Saturn conjunction Venus and trine Mars; while Lincoln, who saved it at a crisis, had Saturn conjunction Neptune, trine Venus, and unrelated to Mars. No enduring structure of history has been built under Mars square Saturn; and since this aspect dominates Hitler—and is, really, Hitlerism—the world may relax. The specter of a thousand years of Nazism sweeping away the culture of the world is only another of Hitler's delusions. Nazism dies with him—conceivably even before him—and neither survives long now.

The charts of two other conquerors of modern times, Napoleon and Kaiser Wilhelm, appear on pages 52–53, with Hitler's on page 55. Note the similarities:

(1) All have powerful activation of the 10th sector.
(2) All have Mars in negative signs.
(3) All have Mars in signs or sectors related to delusions of persecution. Hitler's is in the 8th—self-destruction, paranoia; Napoleon's in 6th sign, Virgo, which sign is on 12th sector, delusional, Kaiser Wilhelm's in 12th sign, Pisces, dominating the chart from the 10th.
(4) Napoleon and Kaiser Wilhelm both have Mars conjunction Neptune, the conquestual delusion par excellence, appearing also in Stalin's Vitasphere.
(5) Hitler and Kaiser Wilhelm both have Saturn in Leo, apparently Germany's negative genius; Napoleon's Sun is in Leo. Mussolini's Sun is

also in Leo, and so, according to tradition, was Julius Caesar's.

(6) All have violently activated 8th sectors: self-destruction as the end of delusions of persecution. Hitler has Mars and Venus there square Saturn. Kaiser Wilhelm has Sun there, opposing Saturn. Napoleon has Uranus there, opposing Jupiter.

(7) All were born in fixed signs: Kaiser Wilhelm, Aquarius; Napoleon, Leo; Hitler, Taurus. (The other fixed sign, Scorpio, apparently never produces a dictator, because when this sign develops a perverted psychology the self-destruction takes a more personal, direct and introverting form.

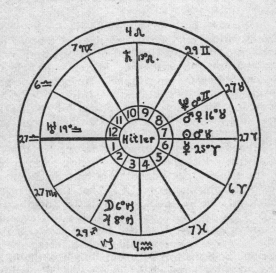

The consideration of the fixed signs and their production of dictators brings up an interesting parallel. The struggle between ideologies going on in the world today is really the struggle between the fixed signs (dictators) and the mutable signs (democracies). Here is the line up:

FIXED SIGNS	MUTABLE SIGNS
(Taurus, Leo, Scorpio, Aquarius)	(Gemini, Virgo, Sagittarius, Pisces)

Hitler: *Taurus*

Mussolini: *Leo*

Chamberlain: *Sagittarius*

Eden: *Gemini*

Daladier: *Gemini*

Beneš (Ex-Pres. Czechoslovakia): *Gemini*

Schuschnigg (Ex-Chanc. Austria): *Sagittarius*

Pilsudsky (Poland's founder): *Sagittarius*

Smigly-Rydz (Poland): *Pisces*

The puzzle is—you've guessed it—Stalin, and the puzzle is further complicated by the fact that we don't know his birth hour. His Sun is in Sagittarius—and for a long time the world thought he would fight Germany, with England and France. He now appears on the side of the dictators, swayed by Hitler's Mars conjunction his Mars and Neptune, which has submerged the democratic mutable sign Sagittarius in favor of his conquestual (Mars-Neptune) urges.[4]

Franco, too, once supported by the dictators and looking like a dictator himself, belongs, astrologically, with the democracies, since he is born in Sagittarius. Also, Mussolini, dictator (Leo), has three planets in Gemini, of the democracies. It is my opinion that Franco (Spain) and Mussolini (Italy) will eventually line up with the democracies, swayed into that camp by the power of their mutable-sign planets; and that Hitler will hold the fort substantially alone. Stalin himself is none too sure where he belongs.[4] Probably he would be willing to support Hitler if he could work with him along the line of their only real contact— military (Mars) support. But when this appears impossible, as it will when the Russian people understand

---

[4]This worked out. Stalin, of the mutable-sign, democratic Sagittarius, has found himself on the side of the democracies.

vhat's going on, there will be an end of the alliance.
Despite all appearances to the contrary, and despite
all character faults which I have no desire to minimize,
Stalin (Sagittarius) belongs ideologically with the democracies and will find himself there in the end, if not
much before it.

Both Hitler and Mussolini (fixed signs) have
often castigated the vacillations of the democratic process (mutable signs). The difference between the totalitarian state and the democratic state becomes
apparent in light of the difference between the signs
of their rulers. The totalitarian leadership is fixed—
stubborn, egotistic, dramatic, hardheaded, decisive.
The democratic leadership (mutable) is reasonable,
frequently to the point of vacillation; the democratic
process itself is talkative, discursive. It muddles
through, by head work, instead of charging through
by main strength and ignorance like the bull (Taurus)
or the rampant lion (Leo).

Remember this when we come to the United
States, in the chart of which Gemini rises; and to
President Roosevelt, whose Sun the fixed sign Aquarius
makes him look like a dictator, but who combines
with this the democratic quality of his rising Virgo
(mutable) and his dominant Mars in Gemini (mutable).

The careers of Napoleon and Kaiser Wilhelm follow, like Hitler's (and, in fact, like everyone's), the
march of Saturn through the sectors of the Vitasphere.

When (astrologically) Hitler was nursing his
grievances against the world and feeling down and out
under Saturn's contact of his own place, the young
Napoleon was similarly set back on his heels and
forced back into himself, there to find the means by
which he could vindicate his grievances on an un-
friendly world.

Disgraced and dismissed from his command as
Saturn contacted his own place, Napoleon came out of
the depths and rode at once the crest of Saturn in his
10th sector. The spectacular Italian campaigns ("Beyond the Alps lies Italy!") and the conquest of Egypt

("Soldiers! Five thousand years are looking down upon you!") crowned dramatically the affront which the
proud and sensitive young officer nursed, and made
into the scourge of the world that opposed him. By
the time he returned to France to take over the Consu-
late (November 10, 1799) Saturn was on his Sun in
Leo, and the world was at his feet. (Cf. Roosevelt,
who became President as Saturn contacted his Sun.)
Here, too, was Saturn at the Battle of Marengo (1800),
which led to the consolidation of his power when
the Deputies made him Consul for life, and he
swept aside the Pope (December 2, 1804) to crown
himself emperor with his own hand. Mars was on his
Sun; Saturn and Uranus were joined on his Ascendant:
the delusion of grandeur was complete, and he went
from here to what historians call "the climax of his
career": Friedland (June 14, 1807). Saturn and Uranus were both still in his Ascendant (1st sector) and
his height of power was reached. From here as Saturn
moves down the slope from 1 to 2 and 3, into 4, he
loses ground. He abdicates in 1814, as Saturn contacts
his Moon in 4th and opposes his own place.

He tries to stage a comeback (the hundred days)
and meets his Waterloo. Finally he leaves the world
stage for St. Helena, just one half of a Saturn cycle
after his return from Italy, and exactly to the click of
the indicator of the clock of destiny. Saturn, which
forced a new start in contacting his own place, which
brought him to power in his 10th sector (1797–99)
and triumph when it swept across his Ascendant (Aus-
terlitz, imperial power, Friedland—1805–06) swept
him downward to oblivion when it transited the obscure sector. The iron will followed the will of Saturn.
It always does.

Similarly the Kaiser, the war lord, whom God
was with, and then was with no more. He came to the
throne, and to refurbished intimations of power, as
Saturn contacted his own place (1888). He precipi-
tated the World War as Saturn came to his 12th (delusional) sector, and as Uranus contacted his Sun.
(Cf. Hitler expansion as Uranus contacted his Sun.)

He had apparent victory swiftly, for Uranus and Jupiter both supported his Sun and his armies at the outset, and he was able to hang on as Saturn remained above the 1st sector. Then with American troops arriving in France (June 1917), began his collapse, as Saturn came back to his own place and opposed the Sun at the same time. (Identical to the conditions under which Hoover was defeated by Roosevelt, 1932.) And one exact Saturn cycle after he ascended the throne of power (1888), he left it forever (1918). Again the down sweep of Saturn through 1 to 2, 3 and 4 brought oblivion. In the "obscure" sector came obscurity. The iron will obeyed the will of the planets. His St. Helena is at Doorn. Where will Hitler's be? In death it seems, and soon, for to Hitler we can say, "It is later than you think!"

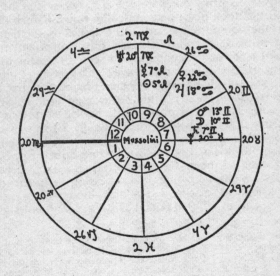

Mussolini began feeling his oats before Hitler, for when the World War broke in 1914, Saturn was contacting his Saturn, and Mussolini was already a force in the Italian press. The "oats" he felt at this time were democratic oats, stressed as Saturn was empha-

sized in the democratic Gemini. Mussolini was socialist editor of *Avanti,* and fought to keep Italy out
of the imperialist war. But as Saturn got out of Gemini,
Mussolini got out of his high principles. As Neptune
approached Leo to go over his Sun, the Neptunian delusions took hold in the Leo (dictator) nature of the
future Duce. As Neptune contacted his Jupiter and
Venus, French gold, it is whispered, found its way
into the pocket of the young socialist (cf. George
Seldes, *Sawdust Cesar*) and suddenly *Avanti* screamed
for, and got, Italy to go to war with the Allies. As the
war drew on, Saturn went over Mussolini's Sun and
planted the Leo (Sun) dictator urges in place of the
Gemini (democratic, socialist) urges of earlier years.
Through the postwar years Mussolini built his party
and his power steadily, through Saturn's contact with
10th to Saturn's contact with 1st, when the March
on Rome took place and Mussolini ruled. Saturn dived
into the "obscure" period, Mussolini consolidated domestic matters and bided his time impatiently. He
talked a lot about conquest, but couldn't seem to get
one started; and he had to leave to his German imitator
the glory of giving England and France the first slap
(Saar: March 1935) while he awaited destiny. Why?
Because Saturn had passed Hitler's 4th cusp, but not
Il Duce's. As soon as it did, he sallied forth to conquer Ethiopia, which he started at a bad time, and
which has not been the glory he had hoped for. Since
then, he has been the tail of Hitler's kite, because
Hitler's Vitasphere finds Saturn rising in it ahead of
Mussolini's. Mussolini has a brief hour of glory coming to him in 1940–41[4] and Hitler's death will signal-

---

[4] There wasn't any brief hour of glory for Il Duce in 1940, and now
(December 3, 1941), it doesn't look as if he'll have one in 1941
either. This "miss" links with Note 3 and derives from the same
error in calculation that accounted for that one. Misjudging the
force of Saturn on Hitler's Mars, I translated that error into Il
Duce's chart for this second "miss" on the same calculation. I
judged that *if* Hitler collapsed under those influences, the power
would pass to Mussolini briefly. But Hitler didn't; rather, the weight
of it fell on his ally (Hitler's Mars in 7th) Mussolini, who became,
astrologically, the whipping boy for the blows that I judged would
punish Der Führer.

ize a forward push for Il Duce, for the same transit that ends Hitler brings renewed vigor to Mussolini. But for all that, he will not outstay 1943-44.[5]

---

[5]Here's a very interesting one to puzzle over. In 1942 Saturn contacts his own place in Mussolini's chart and becomes static on his Mars. Now remember that Saturn was static on Hitler's Mars in August 1940 and that it was this aspect that led me to think he would collapse by May 1941—which, as we have seen, he did not do. Mussolini now comes under the same condition, also in his 7th House—as Hitler had it—and remember it fell on Hitler's ally, not on Hitler himself so much. How, then, shall we judge this in Il Duce's chart? What does 1942 hold for him? Saturn rises, as it did in Hitler's chart, offsetting (as we believe) the doom of Saturn on Mars. Shall we judge a similar offsetting, a similar postponement of doom for Il Duce? I think not. The reasons are complex, involved as they are with Saturn's second contact with his own place (see Paragraph 173 especially the last part of it starting on page 314). Il Duce hasn't, in our opinion, "lived right" enough to go through this with impunity. And since both Saturn and Uranus are out of Taurus where they have supported dictators, and in Gemini where they support democracy, it can well mean curtains for Il Duce in 1942.

VII

Strong Men of Destiny: America

*The Strange Cycles of the Presidents. Lincoln.
Wilson. Theodore Roosevelt. Franklin D.
Roosevelt and What Lies Ahead of Him*

The presidents of the United States provide enough
astrological material for a book of their own, for the
study of their Vitaspheres in connection with their
rise, power and fall (or retirement) would provide a
complete course in the astrology of public figures. Here
is one of the dramatic and salient facts.

Of the seventeen presidents from Lincoln to
Franklin D. Roosevelt, inclusive, *only one has man-
aged to get elected and serve out a term under Saturn's
transit of his own place.* It seems impossible to survive
in public service this condition which accounted for
the fall of the Kaiser and Napoleon, and which takes
its toll regularly of the hopes of America's leaders.
"Let's look at the record"—to quote Al Smith, who,
by the way, succumbed to this transit (1931–32) and
despite previous popularity was forced to back off the
political scene. Look at this table carefully—there is
more in it than meets the eye, and some of what is
there is not, for reasons of policy, going to be explained. But the facts are there. Remember two things.
(1) The one president who got re-elected under this
transit was Woodrow Wilson. This occurred in 1916, in
the presence of a European war, and Wilson's Saturn
is in the 9th sector of foreign relations, which conditions stressed. Nevertheless Wilson, though re-elected,
was completely broken by his second term, pushed

around at the Peace Conference, discredited by his own Senate, defeated at every turn. (2) Franklin D. Roosevelt's Saturn returns to its own place in 1940–1941. Roosevelt's Saturn, like Wilson's is in the 9th House. Also, there is now a European war. With this hint in mind, look closely at the following table. It, plus the two steers above, provides all the evidence you need to prophesy on the much-mooted question of the third term. From it you can answer definitely the question "Should he seek it?" and almost as definitely, "Will he get it?" And by this time you will understand why nothing more definite than this is being uttered here. But this much we can say, and leave you to figure the reasons: Mr. Roosevelt will not serve three terms.[1]

The few who have been in the White House through this transit or just prior to it have earnestly wished they weren't; and happy have been they who got out from under, even if in defeat!

The United States, since 1900, has picked its presidents from a small and esoteric section of the population. High born or low born, rich or poor, whether from North, South, East, or West, all have been born under conditions that unite them in a common bond, invisible to the naked eye, or to ordinary classifiers, but crystal clear to anyone who takes even a casual look at their Vitaspheres. Theodore Roosevelt, Woodrow Wilson, Warren G. Harding, Calvin Coolidge, Herbert Hoover, and Franklin D. Roosevelt, *all have the Sun and Saturn, and the Moon and Mars, in similar relation.* Taft shows only one of these two conditions—but then he was only half president: the other, and dominant half, was chief justice of the Supreme Court, he being the only man ever to hold both offices.

---

[1]We made this statement in this form in the first place for reasons of our own and leave it here for the same reasons which the time is not yet ripe to explain.

WHAT HAPPENED TO PRESIDENTS UNDER SATURN'S RETURN TO HIS OWN PLACE IN THEIR VITASPHERES

	Saturn's return to his own place occurred	*What Happened*
Lincoln	1868	Re-elected, 1864, presumably to serve through 1868. Shot, 1865.
Johnson	1867	Came in, 1865, as Lincoln's successor. Impeached. (Cf. discrediting of Wilson in second term.)
Grant	1881	Retired, 1877.
Garfield	1890	Shot, 1881.
Arthur	1889	Retired, 1885.
Benj. Harrison	1892	First term ended here: did not get a second.
Cleveland	1896	Second term ended: retired.
McKinley	1902	Elected, 1900, to serve till 1904. Shot 1901.
T. Roosevelt	1917	Failed of election, 1912; was refused a World War command, 1917. Retired.
Taft	1916	Defeated, 1912, by Wilson.
Wilson	1916	The single exception: served through second term to be discredited and die a broken man.
Harding	1924	Elected, 1920, to serve till 1924. Died in office, 1923.
Coolidge	1931	Retired, 1928.
Hoover	1932	Defeated by Roosevelt after one term. Retired.
F. D. Roosevelt	1940–41	?[2]

---

[2]He was elected, like the single exception cited above, Woodrow Wilson, who had, like F.D.R., Saturn in 9th House of foreign affairs when he was the only President, except F.D.R., to be elected with Saturn's return to his own place—and Wilson, like Roosevelt, owed his re-election to the existence of a foreign (9th House) war. (It might be interesting to note here that in *Horoscope* magazine, September 1940 issue, in an article written in late June, I said that Willkie could not be elected and in the November issue, in an article written in late August, said unequivocally that Roosevelt would be re-elected.)

This means that, on a basis of simple arithmetical probabilities, we selected our last seven presidents from about 1/300 of the total population—for one person in three hundred will have both these conditions in his Vitasphere of birth. The characteristic earmark of American presidents of the last forty years is not Republican, Democrat, rich, poor capitalist, labor, North, South, etc.—it is Sun square Saturn-Moon conjunction Mars. The only dark horse on the political horizon with this configuration is Philip La Follette, ex-governor of Wisconsin, who has been out of the political picture since his ill-starred National Progressive Party (which was neither national nor progressive) hit the skids in 1938. Before this election, in *Horoscope* magazine for August 1938, in an article written in May, I pointed out that Governor Phil was stronger than the party which he had just launched, and that he should be watched in 1940. I repeat that here.

If you consider Garner a dark horse, you may be interested to know that his planets are in the tradition, but in a very unhappy part of it. He has Moon opposition Mars, instead of the classic conjunction. This doesn't necessarily rule him out. Theodore Roosevelt had it, and got to be president because McKinley was shot. Harding had it, got to be president, and died as a result.

Once there was a lot of talk about "the Roosevelt luck." It swept him to power, drew support to his side, and stood by him through the 1936 landslide. Then it left him. The Supreme Court fight was the first of a series of blunders that put his prestige definitely on the wane, where it would still be if the European situation had not intervened to give him a break.

What was "the Roosevelt luck"? Where did it come from in the first place? What happened to it? Will it ever come back, and what is the answer to the riddle of the President and what lies ahead for him, and for us?

Roosevelt is a strong man of destiny, and, like others, we find him responding to the movements of the planets through his Vitasphere, especially to Saturn. We find all the factors present: intimations of power, rise, setback, "obscure" period, new start, emergence and dizzy rise—all clicked off with the usual timeliness, all clearly indicated in the Vitasphere as its successive sectors are activated by Saturn, Uranus, Neptune and Jupiter. We have more data on Roosevelt's biography than on the others, and are thus able to take our start earlier in his life.

The first important event recorded is the death of his father, which all modern psychologists—Adler, Jung, Freud—agree is an event of deep psychological consequence in the life of a boy or man. It represents the time when the growing ego feels its growth as, through the loss, the young man becomes head of his family and, in his own thinking, master of himself and potentially of his world. It is the young man's *start in life on his own,* and is marked in the young Roosevelt's Vitasphere by contacts of Saturn, Jupiter and Uranus with the cusp of his 4th sector; while Neptune in the 10th on his Mars enables him to transmute these deep inner urges into ego expansion aimed toward power (10th sector). Thus, in 1900, the parent-home complex, always vital in men of genius, receives release into action, signalized by the death of the father and the simultaneous planetary activation. Roosevelt is then eighteen, and from this time onward he is on the rise, as Saturn goes upward in his chart from 4th to 10th. He has come through his first obscure period (Saturn from 1st to 4th) in school; now he is psychologically matured and feels the growing power within himself.

He is graduated from Harvard (1904), marries (1905), and goes on to law school. By the time he is graduated from law school (1907), Saturn has climbed from 4th to 7th, and is emerging into the sphere of public action.

Follows swiftly (1910) his election to the New York State Senate, where he goes in January 1911— just as Saturn returns to his own place—and we will remember that it was at such a time as this that Napoleon, the Kaiser and Hitler all took their first grip on things, and established in their own minds the "success" they were going to achieve.

This cycle of Roosevelt's life, in addition to bringing him first to public office, brought him also a contact of rare importance. In Albany in January 1911 he met Louis McHenry Howe, ambitious and shrewd newspaperman, who immediately recognized the genius of the young senator and became his friend, counselor and adviser till Howe died early in 1936.

The importance of Howe in the life of Roosevelt has been noted but not, it seems, sufficiently emphasized. Howe never aspired to publicity—he was content to be known esoterically as "the president maker" —and perhaps it has been impossible, without the testimony of the Vitasphere, adequately to estimate the importance of this small man who, according to his own words, had the appearance of "a medieval gnome."

He was born January 14, 1871. His pictures, his description of himself, and the character he is known to have had suggest that he had Capricorn rising, with the Sun and Saturn therein, giving terrific force of personality, a burning desire for power and success, but a desire that would be satisfied by *ruling the ruler,* which is precisely what he did. And the square of Mars to Saturn in his Vitasphere of birth is an apt picture of the kind of advice he would give and the effect it would have on the fortunes of his principal.

Naturally, the young Roosevelt took to him. Howe's Venus and Mercury are conjoined in Aquarius, near Roosevelt's Sun and Venus, all supported by the trine of Howe's Mars; while Howe's Jupiter is exactly on the cusp of Roosevelt's 10th sector. History credits Howe with much of Roosevelt's early "success"; yet only the interplay of planets in the two Vitaspheres tells to what an enormous extent Howe was Roosevelt's intuition, his genius for proper timing, and in many ways the Roosevelt luck itself, such as it

was. For the Vitasphere suggests strongly that Howe
was the guiding spirit behind what Hugh Johnson calls
"the First New Deal," of which all the major legislation went into the scrap heap before Howe died.
Howe's Vitasphere indicates a man "brilliant but unsound." The hair-trigger power accumulation of
Roosevelt's first months belongs more to Howe than
to Roosevelt. Howe had the Vitasphere of a dictator,
more even than Roosevelt. Howe had, also, that square
between Mars and Saturn which builds too swiftly a
structure that is bound to fall. Roosevelt had no such
unsoundness. That Howe's ideas and Howe's methods
found fertile soil in which to grow in the mind of
Roosevelt is true. Yet I submit for the researches of
historians the belief that Howe's influence on Roosevet
was a two-edged sword, cutting for him the path to
power and cutting also from under his feet the sound
bases for power with unsound recommendations which
the President, all too eagerly and trustingly, followed.

Now, however, Roosevelt is in Albany (1910)
getting his first taste of success, and meeting Howe,
who is to become an integral part of his success and
of his consciousness of power. From 1910 to 1920, as
Saturn goes down the slope from 10 to 1, Roosevelt,
true to form, improves his opportunities. He is re-
elected—to the State Senate (1912), made Assistant
Secretary of Navy by Wilson (1913), travels in Europe to wind up war matters (1918–19). Then, with
Saturn on his Ascendant, he runs for Vice-President
(with Cox, 1920) and meets his first defeat. As Saturn
goes under his Ascendant (into the "obscure" period),
he, like everyone else, goes into eclipse.

With Saturn still here, he is stricken (August
1921) with infantile paralysis. He does not, like
Hitler at a similar time, go to jail; nor, like the
Kaiser, into exile: nor, like Napoleon, down the
stretch to Waterloo. But physically he meets with
a setback apparently more conclusive and more dreadful.

Why is he able to survive this and to emerge with

increased mental and spiritual power? The answer lies in his Vitasphere of birth and in the fact that Jupiter was also in his Ascendant at this time, saving him from the ultimate of Saturn's weight there. The two, conjoined at birth, bring him now, despite physical handicap, renewed "intimations of immortality" as they conjoin in his Ascendant.

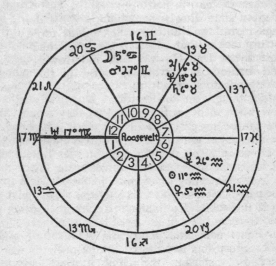

He emerges (as Hitler from prison) with his life plan complete—not written down in *Mein Kampf,* but indelibly impressed on his mind. As Saturn goes down through the 1st, 2nd and 3rd, he is a lawyer practising in New York. This is the "obscure" period. Through his illness and crisis, Howe has stood by him, never allowing him to forget that he is going on to greater things. And now this pertinacious and far-sighted man, while Roosevelt is still a crippled lawyer in New York, starts (1924), slowly and quietly, a Roosevelt-for-President movement. He writes people all over the country suggesting to them that young Franklin Delano Roosevelt is someone to watch.

What led Howe to do this in 1924? Prosperity was riding high, wide and handsome under Coolidge, and the Democrats were out; 1929 was still five years off, and we were plunging gaily into prosperity. What did the gnomelike Howe know that others did not know? True, in 1924, Roosevelt's Saturn was exactly opposing his natal place, and Jupiter had returned to the cusp of his 4th sector—excellent auspices under which to start, slowly, something important for long-range maturing. Did Howe know this? Was this the first instance of that uncanny intuition that was to become a byword? Or was this "intuition", then and later, backed by something else—some method of looking ahead, some means of seeing, behind the surface of things, the bigger forces at work, so that he knew when to begin things so that they would culminate at the proper time? However it happened, the first movement to make Roosevelt president was made by Howe in 1924, when Roosevelt was little known, but when all the planetary forces were lined up for the long pull, ready to support, in the invisible underpinnings of circumstance, exactly the slow, quiet start which the subtle Howe made for his recovering protege.

Four years later, Roosevelt is Governor of New York. Saturn has just passed the cusp of the 4th sector and is starting the climb upward. Roosevelt emerges—and loses the friendship of Al Smith, who is backing off the scene (though he doesn't know it) because Saturn is about to contact its own place in his chart. In the Vitasphere the hand of Howe is clearly visible in the Roosevelt-Smith feud. Smith, like Howe, was born in Capricorn—and the Capricorn Howe was not going to share his budding president with another ambitious man. Smith's Saturn on Howe's Venus made Howe look upon him as an enemy: Howe's Saturn on Smith's Sun, and Howe's Mars on Smith's Jupiter, enabled Howe to beat him in the battle for the mind of the Governor. Howe was jealous of Smith, and the interplay of planetary forces enabled him to translate this to Roosevelt. Howe won.

Roosevelt went back to Albany with Saturn starting the climb upward—the position in Hitler's chart when he became Chancellor in 1933. He is re-elected in 1930, with Saturn still in 4th, returned to the place it occupied at the death of his father thirty years before. The impression of superiority is complete: Saturn moves onward toward his Sun; and precisely as the contact is complete, Roosevelt the governor becomes Roosevelt the president. The work of Howe, begun in 1924, culminates just one quarter of a Saturn cycle later.

On July 1, 1932, at 9:33 P.M., Roosevelt is nominated by the Democratic convention in Chicago. Aquarius, Roosevelt's sign, rises, with Saturn, the planet that is sweeping him to power, close to the Ascendant. The Saturn cycle is clicked off by the cycle of Mars approaching his own place; and this in turn is activated (to index the day itself) by the Moon's return to the place of Mars.

Why does Roosevelt *fly* to the convention? Did he know that by so doing he would arrive at the precise astrological moment to make his acceptance most effective? Did Howe tell him to get there fast, or was this just another piece of the Roosevelt luck? Probably only the President could tell us. In any case, by flying, he was able to speak to the convention and the nation, with the Moon and Venus conjoined on his own Moon, in his 10th sector. The nation knew from that moment that Roosevelt was the next President, and sensed that he would be one of the most spectacular. He spoke not one minute before the Moon entered Cancer, where it was at his birth, and where each month it enables the personality to shine forth at its most characteristic.

Roosevelt now takes one of his vacations, which are to become famous. Nine days after his acceptance speech, instead of plunging into the campaign, he goes on a cruise. Not to Warm Springs, where health might lead him, but north, by boat. He sails and fishes. He went away just as the Moon went into his "obscure" sector, and we shall later see how his worst mistakes were made with the Moon in this sector—at which time now, by luck or design, he does nothing but fish. And he comes back—when? He comes back with the Moon in his own sign, Aquarius, and precisely as Venus turns direct on the place of his Mars. Any astrologer knows that when Venus is retrograde, issues should not be forced, and that the time to start big pushes is just after a planet turns direct. (Hitler, for example, started the Polish push just as Mars turned direct, and he is known to have five astrologers.) Any astrologer knows this—but how did Roosevelt know it? Maybe it was the Roosevelt luck that caused him to delay starting his campaign till this favorable influence took hold. But maybe, on the other hand, it was good management, of the subtle and wily Howe, who perhaps never even told his protege what the basis of his management was.

On November 8, 1932, Roosevelt was elected president. On March 4, 1933, at 1:06 P.M., he was inaugurated, exactly eight lunar months after the Chicago nomination, with the Moon back in his 10th sector; with Mars, Jupiter and Neptune in his Ascendant; and with Saturn precisely in the degree occupied by his Sun: 11 degrees Aquarius. The man of destiny arrives on the stroke of his hour, and at once gets more power than any peacetime President has ever had.

Before this, as President-elect, he was shot at (Miami, Florida, February 15, 1933). The Moon was in Scorpio—in the "obscure," least favorable sector, in square to Venus and Saturn on his Sun and Venus. He was saved, as from death by paralysis, by Jupiter on his Ascendant—and by Tony Cermak, mayor of Chicago, who died by the bullet that was meant for him.

Now follows (March 4–June 16, 1933) the period of New Deal legislation, virtually turning over all power to the President. The session of March 9 made him in effect a dictator. The Moon is here in Leo, his 12th sector of enmity, and surely the great power proved a boomerang. Followed in quick succession the CCC (March 31); the relief bill and the AAA (May 12); and the NRA (June 13). All these presents of power resulted from Saturn on his Sun and Mercury in Aquarius—and, as we shall see, the power of these laws did not survive after Saturn left Aquarius.

It is this group of laws, which eventually proved unsound, that are attributable to the unsound Marssquare-Saturn of Howe more plausibly than to anything in Roosevelt's Vitasphere. The period of Howe's last illness includes the two big reversals by the Supreme Court whereby the First New Deal died.

Howe was taken ill February 23, 1935.

The Supreme Court voided NRA May 12, 1935.

The Supreme Court voided AAA January 6, 1936.

Howe died April 18, 1936.

Howe's work did not survive him, and his death left the President, without his chief adviser and support, alone to face the rising enmity. And this support he lost as Saturn left his Sun sign February 15, 1935, and moved into his 7th sector of public enmity, where it moved to oppose his Uranus and the transiting Neptune. On the stroke of the first complete opposition, as the Moon in Pisces activated it, Howe died, and the opposition to the President—Saturn in 7th opposing his Uranus, his guiding genius—gathered steam.

It was not enough to defeat him in 1936. That it would not be was pointed out in an article in *Horoscope* written in December 1935, in print March 1936, entitled "The Planets Desert Mr. Roosevelt." In this I wrote:

> No, his stars are not going to desert him by causing his defeat in November. They are going to desert him by giving him such a hard row to hoe, after the November elections, that he may easily come to wish he "had not chosen to run."

This was proved true. The November 1936 landslide was hardly more than a memory when, on the ill-fated February 5, 1937, with the Moon in Scorpio-Sagittarius (the President's "obscure" sector, and his evil genius under which, in Howe's day, he had never started anything important), he sent his angry Supreme Court proposals to Congress. Mars was hastening to a static position opposite his Neptune, and before Mars turned direct, in June, the fight was lost in all but final surrender. This came with the death of Senator Joe Robinson and with the Moon again in the unlucky (for the President) Sagittarius—six lunar months to the day after the ill-fated message of February 5.

Surely the planets had deserted the President, or he had deserted them: it amounts to much the same thing. By November 1938 the New Deal was in the doghouse. An embattled electorate unseated scores of New Deal congressmen and replaced them with Republicans or anti-Roosevelt Democrats. States found themselves with Republican governors that had been Democratic since 1930. The President's working majority was cut to the bone.

Only the European crisis has made it possible for him to be considered for a third term. And this broke as Saturn entered Taurus (July 6, 1939) to contact the place of his natal Saturn. The first, and only, actual contact occurs May 8, 1940, but Saturn returns to a static position one and one-half degrees from the exact contact February 10, 1941. We have previously seen what happens to presidents who try to carry through this contact; and in this connection it is pertinent to quote again from "The Planets Desert Mr. Roosevelt," which you will recall was written in December 1935:

> There is a way out for the President. In fact, there are two ways, by which the President may avoid being caught in the dilemma of the planets. The first is for Mr. Roosevelt to change his viewpoint . . . which seems difficult to the point of impossibility.
>
> But there is a second way by which Mr. Roosevelt can change his fate—which is to say,

prevent the desertion of the planets from crushing his 'career. It is simple, but it is one which he will probably not adopt. It is merely not to be a candidate for re-election this year (1936). Not that he cannot win! He can win! But he will win an office which in the next four years, he will be better off without. He will win an office which, because of planetary vibrations during the next four years, will be unsatisfactory, to put it mildly.

Mr. Roosevelt should withdraw now [1936] *and tune his ear to the ground, thinking of 1940.* For then he can be again the man of the hour. But not if he serves the impending term from 1936 to 1940. The planets which desert him now come back to support him in 1940 . . . By 1940 America will need a leader, and he may well be Franklin Delano Roosevelt—not *still*, but *again.* . . . *If he spends those four years of stress and strain in the White House, in an effort to make compromises between irreconcilable forces, he will have little left to give his country in 1940; he will be personally exhausted; he may, very likely, have incurred the enmity of both lines of battle through being insufficiently part of either.*

But if, from a detached private life, he watches the course of events with that understanding of human needs which he so fundamentally has, then by 1940 he will know, as he knew in 1932, what the tempo of the people's thought and desire is. It will be a different thought, a different desire. But he is equipped by nature to catch it again—if he does not push his luck past normal limits now.

It must be said that it is extremely unlikely that Mr. Roosevelt will adopt either of the two methods necessary for him if he is to "change his fate."[3]

Thus the prophecy. He *was* elected. He *did* lose in prestige. He was, and is attacked for being insufficiently of either camp. Only the war makes it pos-

---

[3]Mr. Roosevelt took neither method of changing his fate and as a result did not change it.

sible for him to think of a third term. And now, when he might be the man of the hour, when he is needed to carry on, other bugaboos rear their heads, of tradition and the like, which would not be present if he had not chosen to run in 1936. Inevitable that he should have run? Yes; the prophecy itself agrees with that. Yet if, and if, and if . . .

Imagine he had not run in 1936. Imagine he had never gone off half cocked on the Supreme Court proposals, had retired before Congress wrangled around his head as it did in 1937, before Joe Robinson gave his life fighting that bitter fight, before the Reorganization Bill had caused him to be stamped would-be dictator, before the nation repudiated him and his candidates in the 1938 elections. Imagine him, since 1936, a quiet gentleman at Hyde Park, New York, quietly studying national and world affairs with his ear to the ground, his brain working diligently.

Imagine, then, that war in Europe had broken, and that we had Alfred M. Landon in the White House, with perhaps William Allen White for Secretary of State, to cope with Hitler, Stalin, Chamberlain, Mussolini, and all the tangle of European affairs. Imagine the diplomacy of Kansas pitted against Nazi and Communist and the wiles of Britain, instead of the suave, sophisticated, worldly viewpoint that had steered us through and kept our head up among the warring nations of the earth.

And imagine how in that case we would now be looking upon the quiet gentleman of Hyde Park unable, almost, to wait till November to send him back to Washington. For he is the only American on the scene who has the grip on international viewpoint to take us through the crisis which is not yet over but is just beginning. Even now, with the third-term bugaboo, we can see that somewhat. How much more clearly we would see it if we had to look only at Roosevelt and the situation, and if there were no such traditional sacred cow to stand in the way.

As the prophecy said, times have changed, and Roosevelt is—or should be—the man of the hour.

But having forced his hour when he should not have, in 1936, he meets his Nemesis within eyeshot of the third term—and that is not his tragedy alone, but America's also.[4]

_____

[4]If we had been rewriting any portion of this book, we would have changed this sentence to read ". . . he meets his Nemesis within eyeshot of being the first President to serve three terms, and that is not his tragedy alone, but America's and the world's also."

VIII

Ordinary Mortals

Individual Stories Checked Against Planetary Patterns and Planetary Movements

Strong men of destiny are the flashiest specimens of the *genus homo* to dissect under the microscope of the Vitasphere. Their fields are broadest, their reactions most vivid. They live up to the last ounce of their powers, straining forever at a pinnacle of success, a frenzy of drama, a depth of failure. Everything in their lives is clearly black and white, success or failure. Grays and half tones drop out. Their responses to planetary stimuli are swift, obvious and explicit.

Not everyone is a world or national leader, yet to each in due course comes Saturn's contact with his own place, his transit of the 10th sector, his approach to the 1st, his decline through the obscure part and his rise on the other side. Everyone does not gain a throne, go forth to conquer the world, or become president. The Vitaspheres of most of us do not contain these possibilities. Yet the unnoticed private goes over the same road as the strutting drum major, encounters the same ups and downs, the better and worse periods, the obscurity, planning, new start, rise, success and failure; and each in his own life and in his own sphere reacts similarly to the movement of the planets through his chart.

To observe how run-of-the-mill mortals react to the same stimuli that shake thrones, principalities and powers is to take your seat in the theater of souls, and to read with your own eyes the Magna Charta of the universal stage, of which the fundamental law is the democracy of the spirit. For to Saturn, Uranus and Neptune, wheeling forever through the shadows above the stage, the reputation of the actor is of no importance. To each in his part comes the same elation, the same awareness of merit, the same doubts, the same joys, the same sorrows. By comparative standards, the stage on which he plays may be large or small in his eyes, the role great or trivial. Yet because it fills his life, it is his maximum, the same 100 per cent sum total, no more and no less than the sum total of anyone's stage and anyone's role; and with the utmost impartiality, the designers of the scenery, the handlers of the lighting and sound effects, the prompters, the call boy, and the author and director himself, provide each with the same equipment, and lavish upon each individual production the same painstaking and impersonal care.

For many years I have been checking charts of individuals against the movement of the planets. I have suitcases and filing cases full of biographies of ordinary men and women who have sent them to me with their birth data so that I might check *known events* against *known planetary positions* and *known transits* in an effort to clarify and make more exact the laws of planetary influence. I have deduced exclusively from how the planets *do work*—not from how ancient texts say they ought to; and this takes astrology out of the realm of theory and metaphysical speculation and puts it into the realm of science.

To further this research, and also to provide *Horoscope* with a unique department, we started last August requesting "experience letters" from readers. They furnish the experience, and we add the astrology. We pay for each letter used, and for permission to publish it with or without the name of the writer, as he wishes. We have received thousands of letters, of all sorts of experiences, some sudden and dramatic, but for the most part straightforward recitals of lives more or less happy or unhappy, successful or unsuccessful. The writers naturally stress what has been important to them, with the time of its occurrence. Many of them begin: "I have often wondered what explanation astrology would have for—this experience" or "for my eventful life" or "for the hard luck that has followed me," indicating that these people, though readers of an astrological magazine, have no knowledge of the planets against which to check their lives and are, like most, bewildered before the circumstances that have baffled or elated them. They write us in the hope that we, through astrology, can solve their puzzles by applying the rules that we know and they do not. Knowing this, we approach these letters and these experiences with something like reverence, for here before us is the simple record of what has happened to people living naturally and without any self-conscious application of planetary laws. To their lives, to their spontaneously experienced joys and sorrows and triumphs, we are now going to apply the yardstick of the planets.

To what do the events measure that have impressed these people who write: "This was undoubtedly the worst year of my life" or "I shall always remember September of 1925 as the happiest month of my existence"? Invariably to a characteristic position of Saturn in the Vitasphere at the time of the event, plus some action of Neptune, Uranus, Jupiter or Mars. Listen to these, and remember that we have filing cases full of them:

September 1904, entered college through the kindness of five older brothers. Three weeks later I had an attack of infantile paralysis, and was told by the doctors that I would never walk again. (I did, though.)

Saturn at this time had just plunged below the Ascendant of this girl's chart (into the "obscure" period), where it at once contacted the Moon and Mars. (Cf. Roosevelt, who had this identical attack with Saturn thus going into his "obscure" sector.)

Another:

I have often wondered why life was so easy for some people, and why others must struggle

for even the barest necessities. . . . I believe
that 1931 was the blackest year of my life.

And again we find that, in 1931, Saturn had just
gone beneath the Ascendant of this girl's Vitasphere,
and was just entering the "obscure" sector, where it at
once contacted Uranus.

Another:

If you want a series of experiences to interpret astrologically, here's a swell bunch from
my life.

There follows a recital of deaths surrounding this
young man which is like classic tragedy as defined by
Aristotle, filled with "pity and fear." Two periods are
noted. The first accounts for a single death that made
perhaps the most profound impression, according to
the writer, and which checks accurately to a characteristic angle. The second period, of six months, con-
taining four deaths, including those of the father and
the mother, and one other disaster of a different type,
checks to another characteristic angle of Saturn and
Uranus. I am not identifying any further the indices
of these tragedies, because I don't want to frighten
readers who might find similar circumstances in their
own charts and might interpret them more alarmingly
than is necessary. It requires special natal conditions
to bring about this kind of mass tragedy, and few
Vitaspheres will respond in the manner of this young
man's, who now, happily, is past his worst period and
is moving on to better things as Saturn comes to his
10th sector this year.

Another:

The year of 1929 is a year I have written
down in my diary of happy experiences. If I
could choose, among all the years of my life,
just one to live over, this is the one I would take.
In June I graduated from high school, and then
what should turn up unexpectedly but a chance
to take a trip abroad!

There follows a description of a happy and glamorous month. Saturn was exactly on her Sun and Venus—a peak of achievement, identical with the influence that made Franklin Roosevelt president. This girl, in her sphere, reached her maximum—and since her Sun and Venus are in her 9th sector—of travel —she reached it in travel. The romance and glamor she describes come from the heady influence of Neptune transiting her 5th sector, clicked off during the thirty-three days of the cruise by the transit of Mars in the same place.

You can dive into that file at random, pull out a handful of letters, and they will all check. Some are more exciting, more dramatic, than others. The measure of what a person thinks exciting is the measure of the scope of his life. One lady wrote that the happiest moment of her existence was when she received from a newspaperman an autographed letter, replying to one she had written him. Others fix a meeting, a marriage, a vacation, a birth, a death, a legacy, a loss, an election, a defeat, a change of job. They all check out. Some lives have been drudgery and hardship, with occasional bright flashes which are outstanding. Some have been all lilies and roses with a few minor setbacks that looked like the misfortunes of Job. Whatever the lives may be, each in his sphere and each from his viewpoint reacts on time to the click of the indicator.

We used in *Horoscope* for January 1940 one long letter written with the beautiful simplicity of unselfconscious integrity. It was the story of a woman who started, and remained, obscure, who desired from life no more than to be quiet and peaceful and secure, to whom for the most part peace and quiet and security were denied. From her childhood of heavy responsibility, through false glimmers of happiness that faded quickly, through drudgery and betrayal and loss (but never defeat) to new hope and reaffirmed courage, this brave, stressful life followed with undeviating accuracy the click of the indicator as Saturn wheeled through the sectors of the Vitasphere.

A girl writes:

This was an amazingly good year for me. I had great success in writing—dramatic writing, poetry, etc., in college. I'd like to know astrology's explanation.

It is simple enough. Saturn was in the 10th sector in this "amazingly good year," and the girl in her sphere responded as Napoleon had done in his.

In the lives of people I know, I am able to follow events as they occur, to see the underlying circumstances leading up to the events, sometimes to ferret out, in the obscure workings of the human mind, how an individual has brought on himself something unfortunate for which he is unable to see his own responsibility, or why a piece of "luck" has really, in the careful analysis, been thoroughly logical and deserved. It is here that astrological study becomes most fascinating and most useful, as we are able to understand that nothing is accidental, that we get nothing that does not belong to us, and that, conversely, nothing that belongs to us, whether it be riches or happiness or success or failure, can long be denied us. There is a Justice at work in the world, and its even hand seldom slips. Sometimes, in tragic and sudden death, the blindness of Justice supersedes her equity. Yet in almost everything else it is possible to see the workings of the wheels that have thrown this one up for fortune and that one down for poverty; and to understand these laws of the planets, which clarify these workings, is to approach the secret by which mastery of life, and happiness, and success may be gained.

Case Histories

CASE 1 stresses one of the more philosophic ways by which to approach the "obscure" period and turn it to constructive, if unspectacular, use. When I met George, he was a successful but moody minor executive. Life had developed rapidly for him (as also for the next three cases who, like George, have Saturn near the Ascendant at birth). He accepted responsibility early and started to make his own way in the world. Not until he married the girl he adored did tragedy strike: she died almost at once, under Saturn's characteristic transit.[1] Swiftly George withdrew into himself, fulfilling the most negative phase of his rising Saturn in Pisces,[2] and of his Moon in 12th sector square Mars. His friends feared for his sanity and for what he might do to himself. He had unusually good friends, who stood by him, lived with him, watched over him, and by degrees brought him back more or less to himself. At the time I met him, he was progressing under Saturn's transit of 10th sector, but his progress was still blocked by emotional torment. A cloud hung over him; he remembered with frightening intensity and self-pity what he had had and lost, and, as if he were somehow responsible for it, this haunted him, made him feel a man apart, drove him more and more into himself. As Saturn by characteristic transit repeated the conditions that had accompanied the death of his wife, he felt that life was not worth living, and talked much of suicide. But the Vitasphere held the key to his salvation. As Saturn contacted his own place and cusp of the 1st sector, he quite suddenly remarried. He has entered his "obscure" phase happy. I haven't heard that he has made any spectacular business advances: he is substantially where he was when he reached his maximum seven years ago, under Saturn's transit of 10th. But who shall say that he did not achieve his personal (1st sector) maximum when he remarried, buried the past (Saturn transiting conjunction Saturn) in a new life, and went into the "obscure" period content to be blocked in business because he had achieved a contentment that made business success insignificant?

CASE 2. Joel Harman has a distinguished ancestry and started life with many advantages. He at-

---

[1] Throughout this book, aspects indicating death, suicide, nervous collapse and insanity are not specifically identified. The suggestion of these is too dangerous; and since readers of this book can check up on their lives for ten years ahead, the specific indices of these things are omitted, because of the danger of incomplete knowledge.
[2] You can amplify this and similar references by reading the proper paragraph in Chapter X.

tended a college where his family name was traditional, and he was by way of being a prodigy. (Adherence to family tradition and early mental development result from Saturn's position near the Ascendant at birth. See also cases 1, 3 and 4.) Joel zipped through college and emerged into a teaching career at twenty-one, as Saturn contacted his 10th. He was a brilliant teacher and soon broke away from small institutions to do university graduate work. His rise during the years when Saturn was going from 10th to 1st was spectacular. Everyone looked up to him and admired him and predicted a great career as teacher or novelist, or both. As Saturn neared 1st, he got a splendid break, moved to his best job and married. He held this job throughout Saturn's transit of 1st and his contact with his own place. Then—bango!—as Saturn passed into 2nd—the "obscure" sector—budgets troubled the college authorities, and Joel was let out. Saturn promptly opposed his Moon (2nd to 8th) and then his Sun, two of the most difficult transits of a lifetime, additionally difficult when, as in Joel's case, Saturn at the same time is in the "obscure" phase. He foundered. He could not find work. He could not even wholeheartedly look for work. He was unable to finish the book he was writing. He lived first with his wife's family, then with his own, unable to get a grip on himself. Finally he landed in a small town where a relative had a house he could rent cheaply, and there fell into a high-school teaching job. This occurred as Saturn approached the 4th—new start. From this he moved next year to a better job, in a better school, in a better locality, progress accelerating as Saturn got into the 4th sector. Around the cusp of this it now hovers, just about to start the climb on the other side, where it leads upward toward success. Will it take Joel to success, or will "success" be just something better than the worst of the past? Has he permanently lost his chance?

I doubt it. Surely Saturn struck him down in the "obscure" phase, brought him to his knees and gave him a bitter pill to swallow. But I think he still has high success before him, for his Vitasphere shows a powerful setup, with both Sun and Moon in Virgo (like Tolstoy), with Venus strong in 10th, and with Jupiter conjunction Saturn rising, which works slowly but invincibly. He had to go into that tailspin as Saturn ducked under the Horizon of his Vitasphere and opposed his Sun and Moon. And it seems just as inevitable that Saturn, plus his dogged Virgo character, will pull him up on the other side. Once he was selected by all who knew him to write the Great American Novel. His Vitasphere indicates to me that, despite all superficial evidence to the contrary, he is going to do it yet, and is probably now feeling a greater upsurgence of self-confidence and creative power than he has felt since 1935.

CASE 3. Anne with Saturn rising at birth stuck closer to home and elders than she wanted to. The "tradition" testimony of the rising Saturn in her Vitasphere is uncomfortably stressed by its square to Moon and Neptune in 4th which has a further, and more specific, bearing on parental ties. From the beginning Anne felt the heavy paternal influence, from which her older brother and sister escaped, but under which Anne and her mother continued to live. Her first intimations of "success" and independence came as she married, when Saturn approached 10th, and she knew her happiest years as Saturn went from 10th to 1st. Then, as he contacted her Ascendant and his own place, her mother died, and again the demands of her father weighed on her. Her husband's reverses made it practical for her to live with her father, where she was miserable; the renewal of this burden was brought by the "obscure" period. She still labors under it, though she has rejoined her husband for another four years.

Now here is an interesting point. Anne is Joel's (Case 2) wife. He is due for a rise now. But not she. This slows Joel's rise but does not stop it. Rather it may deepen and intensify it and make it sounder in the end. When Saturn enters Anne's 4th, to end the "obscure" phase, it also emerges into his 7th—publicity. Until this time he isn't likely to have any big public success. Between now and then he will work; he will feel the rise of self-assurance and the capacity to create within himself. He will produce. And in 1944 he will publish, when both his chart and Anne's are ready for the break which that year will bring them.

CASE 4. Richard Drew also stayed close to family tradition and to elders. He was something of a prodigy and was graduated from a family-founded college at the age of eighteen. Saturn was just emerging into his 7th (cf. Roosevelt) and, like all those born with Saturn near the Ascendant, he found himself shot out into the world before his eyeteeth were cut. For two years he marked time, tried to sell and write. Then his grandfather (enter the elders) made him an offer. "Go to the Iowa farm," he said, "run it for me, and I'll give it to you."

It looked like the chance of a lifetime. The three thousand acres had only a small mortgage which two good crops would clear. Though George knew nothing of that kind of farming, his grandfather, in whom he had unbounded confidence, thought he could do it. (Note that his confidence was not in himself, but in his elders, a characteristic quirk of Saturn above 1st cusp in 12th. His Saturn is opposed by Mars—elders influenced him and *were* his self-confidence.) With Saturn rising, in the 8th sector of big business and co-operative ventures, the boy of twenty took on the man-sized job that he was so badly fitted for. (The afflicted Mars noted above occupies the 6th house of work and elders—Saturn—pushed him into the wrong work—Mars in 6th.) His star (Saturn going from 7th to 10th) was mature, though he wasn't. He was moving faster than he was able to, borne treacherously along on Saturn's tide.

What looked like the chance of a lifetime never gave him as good as an even break, for despite the boom times (1924–25–26) the Iowa farm was a headache. He had treacherous help (Mars afflicted in 6th sector of servants). An uncle, by then the main prop of the family credit, died suddenly. Finally, as Saturn squared his own place, a hail storm ruined the crop that was to have saved him.

But he hung on. Pisces rising, Sun in Virgo, is a dogged combination. Saturn still climbed toward his 10th. He married as it reached there, and a year later had twin boys. It kept him going, but being an afflicted Saturn badly placed at birth, he was able to hold on only by accumulating a mountainous debt. (Virgo, for some reason or other, frequently runs to debt. So does Pisces.) Finally, as Saturn finished the transit of 10th and 11th and moved toward 12th to contact his own place, he lost the Iowa farm. The past was being wiped out (Saturn's first contact with his own place).

At this time the home farm was also in trouble. His mother held the deed and now turned it over to the bank for a small cash equity, with which she purchased at long distance twenty acres in California that someone told her was a good buy. Saturn was just emerging from the lower half of her chart into the 7th sector (marriage), where it at once contacted her afflicted Mars. She was beginning to feel released, as everyone does when Saturn goes from 6th to 7th, and now broke finally with her husband with whom she was not happy.

Just then Richard came home from Iowa with wife and twins and fell in with his mother's plans: she and her father and Richard and his family should all go out to the California twenty acres and start over. Richard was ready for a new start (Saturn conj. his Saturn) and had left the Iowa burdens behind him. But he could not, apparently, leave behind also the elders. Saturn conjunction Saturn always wants to wipe out the restrictive elements of the past and always offers a chance to do so. Coming around the age of thirty, it is one of the crucial places where free will operates, and fixes the path for many years. If one chooses to perpetuate the best in his past, he goes forward; and to do this, and eliminate restraints, always entails a wrestling match with deep inner forces. If one chooses to perpetuate the things that have blocked him, he blocks himself for some time to come. Richard chose to perpetuate what had blocked him. His confidence in his grandfather had led into the disastrous Iowa venture. Now, following his mother's plan, he went to the twenty acres in California, again marching behind the dubious aegis of his elders, and adding a wife and children to the parade, which was still led in spirit by the aging, patriarchal grandfather, whose bold, pioneering spirit had brought them all both riches and the loss of riches.[3]

It is worth while to look at this twentieth-century covered wagon as it sets out for California, for the similarities in their Vitaspheres bring out the way in which aspects, and therefore traits, character and destiny, are passed from generation to generation. Note how the Mars-Saturn afflictions run through the charts; and how the fixed signs (Taurus, Leo, Scorpio, Aquarius) are repeatedly, and importantly, activated.

The grandfather has Mars afflicting Saturn, with the Moon conjunction Mars and opposed to Saturn. His Sun is in Leo.

The mother has Mars afflicting Saturn, with Mars in Aquarius; Saturn dominates her chart from 10th sector.

Richard (the son) has Mars afflicting Saturn, in Leo-Aquarius, with Moon conjunction Mars and opposing Saturn.

His wife has Moon conjunction Mars in Aquarius; Saturn in Aquarius and square Venus in Scorpio.

(Another son, not dealt with, has Sun in Aquarius square Mars in Taurus. A daughter—Linda, Case 18—has Sun in Taurus [fixed], but escaped the bad Mars-Saturn involvement. She married and got out

---

[3]The story of Richard's grandfather is the theme of my novel *Star of Empire* (Vanguard, 1935), which, in addition to whatever merits as fiction it may or may not have, is a study in Mars opposition Saturn, and how this aspect worked in the life of a native of Leo who had all the magnanimity, aggressiveness and ambition of that powerful sign.

of the family troubles; and, adding an interesting note, the man she married came of a family through which Mars-Saturn afflictions ran for generations, and he, like Linda, escaped them, to marry a girl with a similar background to which her chart, like his, was a sport, an exception to the rule.)

The twins' charts show Moon, Venus, Mercury rising in Scorpio, fixed, with Mars the ruler weak in Cancer in 8th sector.

On the day they arrived in California, Saturn had returned exactly to his own place in Richard's chart. Neptune, Jupiter and Mars were all conjoined on his Sun in Virgo. Truly it was Saturn's new start, the timing clicked off to a nicety by the indicator—but what a start!

Nothing has gone right. The twenty acres were worthless; the house, a mere shack which they never could make really livable. The mother who had taken them there was heartsick. She and the grandfather found a place where they could take care of themselves and tried to remove the added burden of their care from Richard, but for all that he has had serious responsibilities.

The land would not pay, and Richard took a laborer's job for which he is ill fitted, though he is a prodigious worker, even against physical handicaps. For a while they struggled along in the little house in the fields. Then, after two years, Richard took a different job, and they were able to move to a nearby small city, where they had more conveniences and company, and things began to look better. The mother acquired a better piece of property through the good offices of friends, and by writing was able to care for herself and her father.

But Saturn was not through with them. In characteristic position, it took one of the twins. The next year the grandfather died, and the mother, stricken seriously, came back to live with Richard and his wife and the other boy. For a time it seemed that she too would die, but she is recovering slowly.

The hand of Saturn lay heavy on all these charts, to which the response in all cases has been precise.

What is the prognosis for Richard? His "obscure" phase began just after they went to California, and he has three years more to struggle along in it, before Saturn comes to his 4th cusp, as it does in 1943. He is living out the "obscure" period with great fortitude and moral courage, building his foundations as strongly as he can in the given circumstances with the opportunities that are at hand. No one can do more than this. He has not "winced nor cried aloud." And there is an upturn for him in 1943, which he is approaching in the way that insures his getting the most out of it. When the grip of Fate—"the fell clutch of circumstance"—once takes hold, it must be endured till it is ready to let go. Whether the clutch can be eluded in the first place is a question too complex to do more than hint at here. To most of us the problem is how to deal with it when it is a *fait accompli,* as it generally becomes before we are aware of it; and with the *fait accompli* of his life as of today, Richard Drew is dealing in what is probably the only practicable manner. He is "relaxed in the saddle of fate," doing what is required of him and keeping his ears cocked for the first sound of the bugle to advance.

CASE 5. A brilliant young man, nationally famous at a very early age, and generally thought to be going far fast, started going to pieces as Saturn contacted in rapid succession his Venus, Saturn and Sun. Pulled himself together periodically for fourteen years, during which he received important support from friends (moral rather than material) through many personal difficulties, all of which were brought on exclusively by himself. Through all these inner vicissitudes he held two excellent jobs (at the same time) for years. Finally lost them both as Saturn opposed his own place and the place of his Sun. An excellent example of the self-destructive instincts, touched off by Saturn's transits. Remember this case when you read the next chapter.

CASE 6. This is Alfred Emanuel Smith, one of America's most tragic political figures. A Scorpio ascendant gives him Saturn in the 3rd sector—O.K. for politics up to the state variety, bad for national. Uranus inhabits the 9th (religion) and, opposed by Saturn, lends support to his bitter conviction that religion stood between him and the Presidency. But Saturn also stood in the path. Al tried to buck the planets: he tried to expand as Saturn contacted his own place for the second time, and he couldn't do it any more than Napoleon could, or Kaiser Wilhelm, or Herbert Hoover, all of whom defied this influence and fell under it. When Al was defeated by Hoover, Saturn had already entered the "obscure" phase (1928), and when he couldn't even hold his own New York delegation in line (1932 at Chicago), Saturn was back at its own place. Even the brilliant record to which he pointed with justifiable pride couldn't beat the planets.

CASE 7 never tried to conquer the world as did Napoleon, or Kaiser Wilhelm; nor to be President of the United States as Smith or Hoover the second time. But he did try to expand his world as Saturn contacted the 4th cusp and his own place almost simultaneously, and gave up much for something that could not be attained. The difficulties of this case, like those of the more famous men similarly set back on their heels, are a good example of the false starts that can be avoided by interpreting and heeding the index of the Vitasphere.

CASE 8. A world-famous name, dealt with also in Chapter IX, an unquestioned genius whose life followed the path of Saturn: emergence from obscurity as Saturn went into 7th; height of fame with Saturn in 10th; holding and improving position as Saturn went from 10th to 1st; decline as Saturn went into the "obscure" sector, which he did in 1921. Since this time our genius, though comparatively young, has been heard from infrequently and inconsequentially. A chance at a new start comes 1940–41, which ends abruptly in 1943.

CASE 9. Oscar finished college and started teaching just as Saturn passed the cusp of his 4th sector. This career lasted till Saturn opposed the place of his

Sun, when both career and man went into a tailspin. Almost everyone does a tailspin in this period, but not all do it so thoroughly as Oscar, whose tailspin was a power dive in the general direction of hell. In rapid succession Saturn opposed Sun, Neptune, Mercury and Moon, and contacted his own place, and during the two and a half years covered by these fearful transits it was touch and go whether Oscar would ever amount to anything.[4] But despite the unhappy personal equation, Saturn kept rising in the chart from 4th to 7th. The depth of self-undoing, irresponsibility and despair came when the transiting Saturn, nearing its own place, was opposed by the transiting Mars. With amazing speed thereafter Oscar pulled himself together, got steady work (Saturn in 6th sector of work, and the routine of this period was his salvation), pulled together the erstwhile neglected strands of his life, and made up his mind to do what was expected of him even if he never amounted to anything in his chosen field. He wanted to be a writer.

As a result of this releasing of an intense desire, a curious thing happened. Just as Saturn contacted his own place, while Oscar was still working ten hours a day at a routine job unrelated to creative activity, he wrote, nights and Sundays, a book which found immediate publication. This happened just under Saturn conjunction Saturn, emerging into the 7th sector. It looked like a triumph, but it wasn't. The book sold all right, but was in many ways a bitter disappointment; the effort to expand under Saturn's contact with his own place took its toll. His faith in himself was shaken; he felt he would never write again, and for another two years he didn't.

But Saturn was still rising in his chart, from 7th to 10th. As Uranus touched the cusp of his 10th, he lost his job, and things looked black. No work; no money; 1943, and no job that would support the family, by now large. In desperation he went back to his

---

[4] The story of this is elaborated in my novel *The Gods Arrive* (Lippincott, 1937), especially Part II—The Wilderness—in which Karl Horton's subjective and objective experiences follow the pattern of the planetary influences indicated above.

publisher, who gave him a small advance to write another book. While doing so, another job popped up, in a new field where his talents as a writer acquired a new utility, and where he was able to make use of a body of knowledge he had acquired in private study, but of which he had never expected to make any public or commercial use.

Ever since, under Saturn's rise through 7th, 8th and 9th, he has continued to free-lance. He has four published books to his credit, and by the time this appears in print he will have another. What next? Saturn, Jupiter and Uranus animate his 10th sector in 1940–41 and move on to contact his Sun, Moon and Ascendant. Apparently he has eight years more to get what he wants, which he hasn't got yet by any means. Eight years before Saturn goes into the "obscure" sector. The prognosis is encouraging, if he doesn't let irrelevancies go to his head and distract him from his ultimate goal, which has never changed.

CASE 10. Nationally famous individual who slid downhill with Saturn in the "obscure" sector and lost an important position as he came to the cusp of the 4th, where he opposed Moon and Uranus. Without work for a year; then got another, quite satisfactory job along his regular line of work, which, in the late fifties, is quite an accomplishment for any man. It is accounted for by the rugged setup of the Vitasphere, plus the fact that Neptune activates his 10th now by transit. Saturn's contact with its own place in 1940 brings an important change which, we may hope, will not tempt him to an expansion of some sort which would be doomed to fail.

CASE 11. Edith left her natal environment to complete her studies in New York as Saturn contacted her 4th sector and opposed her Venus, Sun and Jupiter: a classic picture of striking out on your own and asserting the end of childhood and the beginning of maturity. Ambition, plus instinct, told this girl she would succeed best away from parents, and the evidence of an afflicted Mars in the 4th (home) sector bears out her intuitive conviction.

As Saturn moved through 4th, she completed college, worked in New York, met a man and married him as Saturn got into the 5th. With Saturn in 5th and 6th, domestic duties, including the birth of children, occupied her, but she continued fixedly to write plays. As Saturn wound up his transit of 6th, a producer contracted to put one on; and the actual production waited nearly two years, till Saturn got into her 7th, when the play was tried out and flopped before getting to Broadway. Saturn was also approaching the contact of his own place, and the expansion attempted under it failed. It set her back on her heels till Saturn conjunction Saturn (February 1935), which gave her a new start. Here she wiped out the less desirable things of the past, reaffirmed her faith in herself, and recaptured the zest for creation, under which she worked steadily as Saturn rose through 8th and 9th.

With Jupiter in 7th, with Uranus on her Sun and Jupiter in 10th, and with Saturn right on her Moon in 9th, she satisfied herself with a play and sold it. But this too was to be a disappointment. At a cyclic Mars period, with Uranus opposed to Mars, and with Saturn on her Moon, this play failed, to give her a second setback to her ambitions.

From this she emerged quickly and went to work again. What is the prognosis? Excellent! Edith's Vitasphere has inescapable success written all over it, and it will arrive in 1940–41. She has taken her setbacks seriously to heart, especially the last one which Saturn on her Moon made especially difficult and personal in its effect. But it was a deepening experience, not a permanent blockade, for it came with Saturn rising in her chart, toward the 10th cusp, where it, along with the transiting Jupiter, contacts her Sun in 1940 and 1941. This cannot fail to bring her what she has worked for, and though it may surprise Broadway as a nine-days wonder of "the girl who came back" with hair-trigger speed, it will not surprise the student of the Vitasphere.

CASE 12. Jim refused to finish college because he knew what he wanted to do and was eager to get out and do it. Saturn in his Vitasphere is high in the 9th, almost in the Napoleonic 10th, where it always gives the ambition to conquer the world fast in one form or another. Jim knew what part of the business world he wanted to conquer, and has never deviated from this aim, which became fixed at the typical time of Saturn's transit of his Sun.

Jim continued in college till Saturn got into 6th (work), and then he went to work. After three years, with Saturn still in 6th, and now contacting his Mars, Jim's health went bad on him, and he went West to spend six months on a ranch. At the end of this time he felt better, lit out and landed a job (still in his chosen line) in a big city where he was completely unknown, and "sold" himself and his talents cold. Saturn was emerging into his 7th, and Jim was feeling his oats. He licked the new job, gave it up and went back to New York, where despite much family pressure he held out for the one job he wanted and got it. Promptly he married and started raising a family, all with Saturn in 7th and 8th sectors.

By the end of 1930 he had arrived at a pretty fancy salary for one of his years, and, as Saturn in 8th opposed his Moon and Neptune in 2nd, got fired when his firm underwent a reorganization. Cf. Joel, Case 2, who also got fired when Saturn opposed Moon involving 2nd and 8th sectors. But note this difference: Saturn in Joel's chart was in the "obscure" sector, and to recover from his setback took four years. Jim's setback came with Saturn rising, and thus took him, as we shall see, upward and onward. The knock was a boost, though for a while it didn't seem to be. As Saturn moved to contact his own place, Jim found himself in an inferior job, at a poor salary (for him!), till finally, as Saturn came into his 10th sector, he was fired from this.

Ensued then a period of some difficulty through which Jim & Company rode with imperturbable equanimity. Jim's brother Felix was working and had a home to which Jim and family were invited. Four adults and four children pushed themselves into a seven-room nest in suburbia and prepared to struggle along on Felix's not so handsome salary till things broke for Jim. Jim was sure they would break, and everyone agreed that it would be felonious for him to sell his services for less than they were worth. Everyone, including Jim (nay, even, *especially* Jim), set the figure of his worth high, and all dug in.

Then Felix lost *his* job. The four adults and the four children under seven had no visible means of support after Felix's savings were gone, which was soon. Presently they were living on credit which was stretching rapidly to the breaking point. It now became Felix's turn to refuse to sell himself cheap. Both the men and their wives—the oldest of the four was thirty-two and the youngest twenty-six—had the sublimest confidence in themselves and in each other; and all scorned the idea that it was necessary to resort to desperate measures—by which they meant that Jim and Felix should not be forced to go to work for a miserable salary that would cramp their brilliant talents.

Before we see how it worked out, how can we account for this sublime self-confidence? By many things, of course, starting with the four Vitaspheres of birth. But most important was the fact that, in all four charts, Saturn at the time was well placed by transit, activating the rise sectors of all of them. In Jim's chart and Felix's wife's it was in the 10th. In Felix's and Jim's wife's, it was in the 7th. All were on the rise, felt it, and refused to be distracted by minor setbacks and discouragements.

Finally Jim took a job, to try out. Promptly Felix contracted to write a novel, and departed for points west to get needed data, using up thereby half of the small amount of money advanced to him by his publisher. No sooner had the dust settled after the departure of Felix's Greyhound than Jim's job blew up. Everyone felt that this news would distract Felix from the great work on which he was embarked, so they didn't write him about it. Jim felt he was equal to the task of taking care of two wives and assorted children, and did, by means of various free-lance jobs. Felix came back, sat down amid a totally bankrupt household, and went to work to deliver the novel which already was paid for, and therefore constituted a debt of honor, even if nobody ate.

The extent of Jim's self-confidence is best illustrated by the chilling fact that at this point he said no to a job at $75 a week, held out for two days for $100 and got it. When Felix and his wife heard this story they quaked and paled, but since it worked out all right, no one dared to say anything. The eight of them continued to live together till Felix finished his novel and got on his feet again, when Felix and his family moved to their own establishment, which they inhabit to this day.

Jim had got the $100-a-week job with Saturn in his 10th, clicked off by Mars in his 2nd. He held it two years, and exactly as Mars returned to the same place, got another and better job. While his business was thus improving, however, Jim was running afoul of personal difficulties. As Saturn opposed his Sun, his health wasn't good, and he didn't take proper care of himself. But he held and bettered his jobs through his personal trouble till he lost it five years after the Jim-Felix hook-up.

As Saturn got toward his 12th sector, things got hectic, but Jim's old genius for getting swell jobs sticks by him. At a low point of physical and moral fighting strength, he found himself without work, and within a week had two jobs waiting for him, each better than the one he had left.

He has a lot to offer. He has overcome the personal setbacks of Saturn opposing his Sun. What is the prognosis? Good. In the next four years (that is, before Saturn goes below his 1st cusp into the "obscure" sector), he is moving to build his self-confidence into his work itself, instead of keeping it up his sleeve as something to carry him through recurring crises. His sense of values is changing: he now takes more stock in security and less in the doctrine that sustained him so long, that "in skating over thin ice, your safety lies in your speed." In the next four years he will dig into his permanent lines. He will go into the obscure period safe in a good job, probably at a high salary, where his true genius will shine steadily and securely, and where he will not have to use it looking for something new. His self-assurance will be his greatest asset, but instead of using it to conquer new worlds in rapid succession, he will use it henceforth to conquer one world completely and to permanent purpose.

CASE 13. This girl broke with tradition and family background, when Saturn contacted 4th, by entering into an unconventional love affair which, while it lasted, amounted to marriage. The marriage phase started as Saturn joined Mars in her 4th sector, touched off by the transiting Mars in the same place; and it lasted a year and a half, till Mars got around to her 1st sector. At this time the engagement was broken by the man, living through the transit of Saturn opposition his Venus. This made him appear hard-boiled and shallow, and let the girl off with hurt pride instead of a broken heart. Her Sun, Venus and Mercury all conjoined in 5th (love) in square to Saturn brought her the experience and also gave her the character to go on from it into a happy and useful married life later.

CASE 14. This name has been in the white lights of musical comedy and light opera on Broadway—a very lovely and talented girl whose career ended abruptly as Saturn contacted its own place and went to the 10th sector. The Vitasphere suggests the correctness of her hunch that she had reached her peak and might as well retire and enjoy private life. She left the stage before she was thirty and hasn't been heard from since.

CASE 15. Well-known and popular figure in the publishing world who found himself an active executive in a big firm. According to the way he put it at the time, he wanted to make a move that would insure him an income when he couldn't be as active as he had been. With Saturn in the 4th opposing its own place, he had a choice of two changes. One meant going into business for himself, with a good partner who wanted him, which involved considerable risk. The other offered him a good place with an established firm. He took the latter, held it for three years, and then, as Saturn reached the lower square of his Sun, left. Saturn is rising in his chart—has been for three years. This is an interesting example of the double new-start that comes when Saturn clicks off two 4th-sector vibrations in comparatively rapid succession. This man is virtually assured of the success of his new venture on which he embarks under the favorable up-swing of all the major planets in his chart.

CASE 16. A big-shot executive who had saved some money and had the good sense to fulfill his life-long ambition: he shook the dust of New York from his feet, bought a small-town newspaper, and settled down in the rural ease he had always wanted to go back to. This seems to me a parable of New York, where almost everyone comes to fulfill a dream and then has to get away to fulfill a more important dream. This man did it under Saturn's opposition to his own place; he retrenched and made the correct move to security. Not everyone is so smart, and not every-one, by the same token, insures his ultimate content-ment by thus riding the rhythm of the planets.

CASE 17. This is Bruno Richard Hauptmann, executed for the kidnaping and murder of the Lind-bergh baby. Saturn is in the 10th at birth, with Mars, Venus and Mercury, with Sun conjunction Uranus close by, and all square Moon in 7th. At the time of the crime (March 1, 1932), Saturn was in his 12th sector, and Mars was on the cusp of his 1st in Pisces, opposing Neptune—a setup sure to bring out the worst in a psychopathic case such as Hauptmann. His secret remained intact as Saturn stayed in the 12th sector of secrecy. Then, as it emerged into his 1st, he was caught, tried and electrocuted, as Saturn opposed his Moon from the Ascendant, squared its natal place, and brought the end. Cf. Hitler, also with Saturn in 10th, also psychopathic, who also went to jail as Saturn came to his Ascendant. Hauptmann's "obscure" period brought the ultimate of obscurity from psychopathic causes similar to Hitler's. A whole book could be written on the astrology of the Lindbergh kidnaping.

CASE 18. Linda is the sister of Richard Drew (Case 4), and if you refer back to that case you will see how Linda's Vitasphere escaped the afflictions of her family inheritance and took her into a different life from theirs. Her only Saturn affliction is the square to Venus, a heavy enough cross which throughout her married life she has borne in a variety of uncomfortable ways, even though her Jupiter trine Saturn has protected her material well-being.

Linda married early, as Saturn opposed her Sun and emerged into her 7th sector, the event of the marriage clicked off by a static position of Mars on her Sun, and on the Venus of the man she married. She stuck to marriage through every conceivable kind of difficulty. Some pretty stormy early-married years apparently held her back, but through it all her loyalty built her character. Suddenly, as Uranus moved to contact her Sun, she emerged from silence and inaction into school and community work, in a new city which they moved to under Uranus' shift into her Sun sign. As Saturn contacted its own place soon thereafter, she eliminated the less constructive things of the past that had cluttered her thinking, forgot what had made her unhappy, and started fulfilling, publicly and privately, an admirable and increasingly important role.

Her Vitasphere is a classic of character and self-sufficiency, plus a generous share of charm and social grace. It is necessary that her progress should come from within herself, because her Sun and Mercury are conjoined in her 12th sector; and only by throwing back into herself was she able to find the best self that she wanted to be. She is a calm, charming, gracious wife and mother; her family (husband and six children) adore her. Her associates in community work regard her with affection, to which they add respect for her intelligence and admiration for the thorough and conscientious way in which she fulfills the many obligations which she voluntarily assumes.

Yet Linda started out with a dreadful inferiority complex. Even yet, I doubt that she ever expects to amount to anything. She has a wholehearted admiration for the clever people with whom she is surrounded, and has not one ounce of envy for what she calls their "success," which is to her something marvelous. It does not occur to her to compete with them in their fields; the residual inferiority makes it impossible for her to dream of being as bright as they are. Naturally, with this attitude, she builds everyone's ego, makes people feel consequential, encourages them to tell her their troubles, and always has a sane and soothing approach to them. One of her more nervous and jittery associates says that mountains of woe become molehills just by virtue of being told to Linda. Her husband, whom she admires with exaggerated admiration (while not being in the least deceived about his faults), depends on her for more than she would believe; thus, if in no other way, does she earn whatever may come to her as a result of the "brilliance" which she so genuinely, if excessively, admires.

There is a strange and just prognosis for this gracious girl who is so eager, and so content, to sit at the feet of "superior intelligence." Uranus, Saturn and Jupiter contact her Sun in the next two years. Thereafter they move on to contact her 1st sector. Five dynamic years lie ahead of her in which, moving graciously along the unobtrusive path she has set herself, she will find herself emerging more and more from the shadows of the stage and into a limelight which has never had a chance to shine on anyone who merited it more.

IX

Self-Destruction

*Suicide, Insanity, Psychosis and Neurosis,
Dipsomania, Claustrophobia, Fixations,
Obsessions, Genius, Sudden Death*

Self-destruction is a perversion of the self-preservation instinct which causes the individual to destroy some or all of himself in an effort, generally subconscious, to avoid assuming the full responsibilities of normal life.

In its extreme form, this becomes suicide. But every self-destructionist does not destroy himself completely. For every suicide there are thousands who give up in part, sacrificing some portion of the personality so that, as their perverse subconscious tells them, the rest may have an easier time. In the well-known mother fixation, the ego avoids connubial and parental responsibility by adhering exaggeratedly to the tie that represents the protection of childhood. The claustrophobiac (he who fears closed spaces), the altraphobiac (high places), the agoraphobiac (open spaces), all have destroyed a part of the normal personality for ends and purposes of their own, frequently buried in the subconscious. Perhaps it is to avoid responsibility; perhaps it is to get, by a trick, the center of the stage which others strive for more aggressively. The hypochondriac (who always has an ailment) destroys bodily vigor to get attention and avoid responsibility—and who has not heard the story of the bedridden harridan who leaped up to escape the fire? Suddenly in a crisis the genuine urge to self-preservation assumed command and routed the phony one that had ruled so long.

The dipsomaniac escapes into liquor, the "snow-bird" into dope, the sex pervert or sex excessive into sensation. All turn the normal law of self-preservation inside out. In their struggle to conquer the world they begin, invertedly, by destroying something, and persisting in its destruction, because the perverted subconscious tells them that by this curious inversion they are best serving their ends.

The study of the abnormal sheds essential light on both the normal and the supernormal. By knowing the bases of extreme cases, we are able to ferret out through the Vitasphere the minor quirks that plague otherwise normal individuals who are not really psychotic at all, but who have some vestigial residue of an escape mechanism to plague them. The autopsies of the cases that have proved fatal to some souls provide the means of saving others. And further, we are able to understand much of the best of the world by understanding more about this curious self-destructive sickness of the human mind that accounts for nearly all abnormality. For, as the sickness of the oyster in rare cases throws up the pearl, so the sickness of the mind, in rare cases, produces genius. Thus we find men of genius almost invariably exhibiting mental abnormalities or physical handicaps that have heightened neurotically their need for self-assertion. Caesar was an epileptic; so, probably, was Alexander the Great. Napoleon confessed to an exaggerated mother fixation, and had in addition a little-man complex which demanded that he become the greatest man of the world. Byron hated his mother and had a club foot which gave him a deep sense of physical inferiority. Keats's tuberculosis accounted in him for what Adler would call "organic inferiority." Mussolini labors under the conviction, perhaps delusional, that he is persecuted by hereditary syphilis, is an epileptic, and hates closed spaces. Hitler, as we have seen, has paranoia (delusions of persecution). The list could be extended indefinitely.

That there is an underpinning relationship in psychic abnormalities of whatever manifestation is agreed by psychologists. Nowhere does it become so graphic as in the Vitasphere. For here we see that all mental abnormalities, from suicide down to the simple jitters, are linked together in the chain of self-destruction, showing in greater or less degree. The critical planets are always found in specific sectors, in specific relationships.[1]

I have before me the charts of five conquestual dictators, four dipsomaniacs, four pseudo-dipsomaniacs, four suicides, five assorted neurotics, and the wives and husbands of those who are married.[2] In all of them, we find the self-destructive sectors (called H, D, L and J in the table on the following page) powerfully activated; and the planets called 2, 5, 7 and 8 prominent therein. The unknown neurotics who stew in their own juice, and the dictator neurotics whose self-destructive urge causes the world at large to stew in theirs, are all cut out of the same piece of cloth.

---

[1] What these sectors, planets and positions are is not sensible to specify. The human mind is a delicate instrument, and many are only too eager to find something "interesting" the matter with themselves. If it were written that the planet Janus in the sign Hippogriff led to delusions of persecution, suggestible persons, finding that their Vitaspheres contained Janus in Hippogriff, would promptly start acquiring this high-sounding scourge, and they and the world would be made no better thereby. The planets in this study are therefore indicated by numbers, and the sectors and signs by letters.

[2] The inclusion of wives and husbands of neurotics may seem odd. "The drunkard's wife, God pity her!"—what has her Vitasphere got to do with the drunk? Plenty! It tells much about her spouse. I have never seen the chart of the spouse of a serious neurotic whose Vitasphere did not show related conditions. Usually both husband and wife exhibit the same type of neuroses, perhaps in different degrees. The question then rises, Which came first, the hen or the egg? Did the serious neurotic make his mate that way, or get driven into it by mate's neurosis? The truth lies somewhere between the two horns of the dilemma. We attract to us certain people, certain experiences, and the type attracted shows in the Vitasphere. Where the neurosis of the spouse is indicated, the influence did not fall directly on the native, but caused him to select a mate who satisfied his neurotic temperament. The self-destructive urge took the form of marrying a man to reform him—i.e., self-sacrifice. One cure for incipient neurosis is suggested here: marry someone who is really neurotic, and be forced to pull yourself together in sheer self-defense.

One obvious connection between the dictator and the neurotic-psychotic will present itself to anyone who has had any experience with either. The dominance of the power urge in the dictator is apparent. It is just as dominant in the neurotic-psychotic, but it dominates negatively instead of positively. Any vic-

		H	D	L	J
Wives & Husbands of Cases 19-35	34 A	5, 2	9	8	4, 6, 7
	33 A	7	8	2, 3, 4, 6, 9	
	29 A	1, 3, 4	5, 9	7	6, 8
	26 A	6		4	
	25 A	7, 8	1, 3, 6		
	23 B	7	9	8	
	23 A		3, 4, 6, 8	8	1, 2, 9
	22 A	7, 8	7, 8		1, 3, 5
	20 A	8		3	2, 5
Assorted Neurotics	35	2, 5, 6	2, 5, 6	3, 7	9
	34		2, 9	3	8
	33	5	2		1, 2, 3, 4, 9
	32	8	2, 6, 9		
	31	5	5	7	1, 4, 6
Suicides	30	5	5	3, 4	8
	29	8		8	1, 3, 4, 7
	28	1, 2, 3, 9	1, 3, 9	2	
	27		1	5, 9	
Pseudo Dipso-Maniacs	26	6	1, 2	2, 3, 9	
	25	5, 8	1		5
	24	5	2, 9	6	
	23	1	2		4, 6, 7
Dipso-Maniacs	22	2, 8	4	3, 6	5
	21	2	9		3, 4
	20	2, 3, 8	2, 3		9
	19	2	1, 4		
Kaiser Wilhelm		1		5, 9	5, 9
Napoleon		6, 8	7	5, 9	7
Stalin		2, 7			1
Mussolini		2, 5, 7			8
Hitler		4, 5		8	7

tim of a neurosis, or anyone who has lived closely with one, knows there is no tyranny in the world like it. The neurosis is always in the driver's seat. The dipsomaniac is slave to his drink and rules his world through it. Similarly the claustrophobiac, the mother-attached, down the line. Their world, and the people in it, must conform to the neurosis, and therefore with the neurotic. It is the negative, and highly effective, expression of the power urge, and shows forth as such in the Vitasphere.

Look awhile at the table on page 106 and you will see how the coded sectors H, D, J and L are activated by the coded planets 2, 5, 7, 8 and sometimes others. Remember that there are 12 sectors in all, and that planets 2, 5, 7 and 8 might fall in any of them; but that in these charts they fall invariably in one of the self-destruction sectors. Remember also that planets 2, 5, 7 and 8 have classic relations in these Vitaspheres, which repeat themselves faithfully. For one example, planets 2 and 5 are always found in the charts of dipsomaniacs in fixed relation to each other, from the same sectors of the Vitasphere.

Case 35 of the table gives the coded positions of Lawrence of Arabia, included here because it provides a link between these self-destructive charts, and charts in which tragedy appears to descend from nowhere as early, sudden, accidental or criminal death.

Lawrence of Arabia was a curious man—a mystic adventurer whose sense of the cosmic required him to live swiftly and dangerously, always in a state of spiritual exaltation. In his philosophy, of which he left an exhaustive record, life and death merged invisibly, and it became his obsession to make the life-death transition swiftly, at high speed, and in the presence of danger. To this end he courted danger on the battle-field and in strange out-of-the-way places, but death was denied him: he emerged unscathed to take up the humdrum peacetime life of an English officer. But the mysticism, the exaltation, the obsession that he must embrace death magnificently did not leave him. He continued to live, in every way that peace offered him, forever at the brink of danger, till at last he cracked up on a motorcycle going ninety miles an hour, and went as he had wished to go to the eternity from which he had never felt himself separated by more than a short and sudden step.

Because we know of Lawrence both this and his Vitasphere we may be able to get an insight into the mental processes of less articulate mortals who left no record of their philosophy, but whose taking off was, like Lawrence's, apparently a tragic accident of destiny. For Lawrence did not destroy himself any more than hundreds of other individuals whose lives have been snuffed out by an accident. Yet their charts, like Lawrence's abound in the planetary positions found in the table on page 106 and are dominated by them. Normal death, or death late in life at a normal time, does not show very clearly in the Vitasphere. Apparently it is such a natural transition that, like graduation from school or the birth of children, it is not clearly or definitely indicated in planetary movement. But early, sudden or tragic death is not natural, and therefore we find it indicated both in the Vitasphere of birth and in the transits in force at the time.

For those same positions, which make psychotics and neurotics, carried upward one step make conquestual dictators. Carried one step further, they make Genius. And carried beyond this, into the realm of the pure of heart, they liberate the spirit swiftly into the eternity from which it never, in all probability, has felt much separated.

I think there is in this a confirmation of a truth that most people recognize instinctively. Poets in all ages have divined it. Two hundred years before Christ, the Roman Plautus wrote:

He whom the gods favor dies in youth.

Wordsworth knew it:

The good die first,
And they whose hearts are dry as summer dust
Burn to the socket.

Even the cynic Byron claimed:

> Heaven gives its favorites—early death,

and Shelley's "Adonais," mourning the untimely death of the brilliant and lovable Keats, is one long encomium of a spirit that earth was not good enough to chain.

Those who die young, violently, tragically, are all too likely to be the best that earth has given, and that this is more than a sentiment is borne out in the Vitasphere. For the positions and aspects that make great men are the very ones which, in the Vitaspheres of the early dead, have borne them beyond material and temporal greatness, into greatness of the spirit, frequently into genius, always into an exceptionally mature, sweet, lovable personality, showing great promise, perhaps already on the highroad to success. The forces of genius are there, brilliantly controlled, and since genius is the closest that the chained spirit of man gets to immortality during life, the transition is easy to make from what we call life to what we call death.

I think we may believe that those lovable souls who went on their way as we thought, too soon, did not embrace death with fear, but probably had within themselves that which made death to them, as to the mystic Lawrence, somehow the last adventure of life, and the greatest.

> No! let me taste the whole of it, fare like my peers
> > The heroes of old.
> Bear the brunt, in a minute pay glad life's arrears
> > Of pain, darkness and cold.
> For sudden the worst turns the best to the brave,
> > The black minute's at end,
> And the elements' rage, the fiend-voices that rave
> > Shall dwindle, shall blend,
> Shall change, shall become first a peace out of pain,
> > Then a light, then thy breast,
> O thou soul of my soul! I shall clasp thee again,
> > And with God be the rest.

Poets approach nearest the bourne of wisdom, and Robinson Jeffers envisions a great cosmic truth that

only a mystic or a student of the Vitasphere can fully
comprehend:

> Too great self-control is dangerous—
> It attracts hard events, as height does lightning.

Your quivering neurotic never has anything happen
to him in reality except what he causes to happen in
the fears and bogies of his own mind. He invents ter-
rors so frightful that his whole life is an effort to escape
from their danger; thus he avoids all positions, emotional and material, in which he might be harmed.
The great sudden things, tragic or ecstatic, are reserved for the disciplined, the controlled, whose spiritual stature "attracts hard events as height does lightning" and attracts also triumph and ecstasy unknown
to the fearful and the evasive. The back is fitted to
the burden, the spirit to the experience it attracts.
Only a great soul can feel cramped. Only one that
towers can be struck down, or, indeed, be aimed at at
all. And there is every reason for the instinct which
tells us that those who go early are "earth's best, who
learned their lesson here" and that, in going, they bear
a song in their souls.

Through life, and into whatever Beyond there
may be, the Vitasphere charts the path of the individual. Thus far you have had a brief—very brief—
summary of the findings of the Vitasphere. Each
chapter could be expanded into a book; and indeed,
every life, every Vitasphere, is in itself a volume. For
this reason, and because your own Vitasphere is more
important to you than that of the greatest man who
ever walked the earth, the balance of this book is
devoted to your own life as it is indicated in your own
Vitasphere. Some of what precedes this may be useful
to you in interpreting the movement of the planets
in your chart, which you can trace fifty years back
and ten years ahead in Chapter XI. And some of it
may be useful to you in interpreting your own natal
Vitasphere, to an important phase of which you now
proceed in Chapter X.

X

Your Vitasphere of Birth

Your Vitasphere of birth is the blueprint of your personality and character as indicated by the position of the Sun, the Moon and the seven planets on the date of your birth. A section of this chapter is devoted to each of these members of the solar system. In each of the nine sections you will read the one paragraph that relates to you, according to the sign occupied by the planet on the day you were born.[1]

Detach now, from the back of the book, one of the tabular pages, and get a pencil or pen. This sheet is divided into two sections. There is a narrow section at the left side headed "Birth Position of the Planets in My Vitasphere," and it is this narrow left-hand section that we use now. In it you will enter (1) the name of the sign occupied by each planet as you come to it, and (2) the paragraph reading that describes its influence on you. Except in the case of the Sun and Moon, ignore the degree occupied by the planet to which we will come later, in its proper place.

Go through this chapter from one section to the

---

[1]In the numbered paragraphs that make up your Vitasphere reading, the lowest numbers (1–12) correspond to the Sun readings and come first; while the highest numbers (109–120) correspond to the Pluto readings and come last. This order gives you the Vitasphere picture of character and personality in sequence beginning with the Sun and Moon and then moving out from Mercury to the farthest planet.

next, reading carefully the introductory page to each section, getting the sign of the planet carefully, reading and digesting the paragraph that applies to you, and proceeding to the next section, the next introduction, the next reading till you have read all ten, and have the complete picture of your planetary make-up according to sign positions.[2]

THE SUN

The Sun indicates the appearance you will present before the world and the psychological bias which will dominate your actions. What you seem, and why, are told in the reading for your Sun. In many ways the Sun is the dominant force in your Vitasphere and in your life. Other influences, especially that of the Moon, may modify the Sun's influence, but nothing will cause you to depart very far from the basic solar pattern. For this reason a whole literature and a whole business have grown up around Sun-sign astrology; and many people exist who think there is nothing more to the horoscope than knowing what "sign you were born in" and what the Sun in that sign means. This is a mistake, as you will discover when you have read the influence of the other bodies. But throughout your other readings, keep in mind always the basic influence of the Sun, and remember that all other influences must be interpreted in terms of it, especially in so far as other influences play a visible role in your life. You may think, dream, imagine, hope to be a thousand things, according to your Moon and your other planets: but the Sun is what you are, and to be your best self in terms of your Sun is to cause your energies to

[2]A note for those who have used *Heaven Knows What*, The Cast-Your-Own Horoscope Book. You may find some apparent discrepancies between the sign positions given in *Heaven Knows What* and in the tables in this chapter. USE THE SIGNS GIVEN HERE FOR USE WITH THESE READINGS. *Heaven Knows What* reads *aspects,* not sign positions, and thus the apparent place of some planets is shifted in *Heaven Knows What* to bring out the aspects in force. *Heaven Knows What* gives accurate aspects; this chapter gives accurate sign positions, and the positions given here should be used exclusively for purposes of these readings.

work along the path in which they will have maximum help from planetary vibrations.

How to Find Your Sun's Sign and Degree

A great many people know what sign they were "born under." By this they mean that they know what sign the Sun was in at the time of their birth. However, some confusion exists about the sign occupied by the Sun, because the Sun changes signs around the 20th of each month. The date on which it changes signs is not the same in March as it is in June. Nor is the date on which it changes signs the same in March 1903, 1904, 1905 and 1906. Therefore people born between the 17th and the 24th of any month are likely to be confused about what sign they belong to by virtue of the Sun's position.

To overcome this confusion and enable everyone to know the sign occupied by his Sun, a table has been prepared which will give, simply and accurately (1) the sign occupied by your Sun; and (2) the degree within the sign occupied by the Sun.

The table is on pages 132, 133 and 134 and you proceed with it as follows:

1. Divide the year of your birth by 4, and note the *remainder*. It will be either 1, 2, 3 or 0. *Example:* Born June 22, 1904. 1904 divided by 4 gives 476, even. The remainder is 0. *Example:* July 23, 1905. 1905 divided by 4 gives 476, and 1 over. 1 is therefore the remainder.

2. Taking June 22, 1904, as our example, and knowing the remainder is 0, go to the table. This is divided into three sections: Years before 1900, 1900 itself, and years after 1900. 1904 is after 1900, so we work in this section. Find the column corresponding to your remainder—0—and run down it till you come to the June section. In the June section, there are two X's in the *0 remainder column*. One of these is on the line with your birth date— June 22, 1904; and at the left, this shows that the Sun was in Cancer on June 22, 1904.

3. To find the Sun's degree in Cancer, go over this same line to the extreme right. Here it says, at the top, "To get degree of Sun in your sign"; and on the line you are following, it says, "Subtract 22 from birth date." Your birth date is 22—(June 22)—thus from 22 subtract 22, and you get 0. The Sun, therefore, on June 22, 1904, was 0 degrees Cancer.

Try June 22, 1907. 1907 divided by 4 gives 476, and 3 left over. Remainder 3, in years after 1900: down this column to the June area. The first X is on the line reading "Gemini—June 1–22." So the Sun was in Gemini. At the right, it says, to get the degree, add 7. 22 plus 7 equals 29. The Sun, therefore, was at 29 degrees Gemini on June 22, 1907.

Condensed Directions

1. Divide birth year by 4 and note remainder.
2. Find section in which you fit: before 1900—1900 itself—or after 1900. (If born in 1900, there is no remainder.)
3. Find in your proper section (before or after 1900) the column headed with the remainder you have found.
4. Go down this column to the section in your birth month. One of the X's there will be in a line with your birth date.
5. At the left of this line is given the sign your Sun is in.
6. At the right you find what to add to, or subtract from, your birth date, to get your Sun's degree in the sign.

Example: May 2, 1905. 1905 divided by 4 equals 476 and remainder of 1. 1 column, after 1900, shows "Taurus—May 1–21," including our date, May 2. At right, it says, "Add 8 to birth date," giving 10 degrees of Taurus as the degree of the Sun in the sign.

Example: March 23, 1870. 1870 divided by 4 equals 467, with remainder of 2. 2 column, before 1900—run down to March section. X falls on line showing "March 21–31: Aries." At right: "Subtract 21 from birth date." 23 minus 21 leaves 2, so the Sun is 2 degrees in Aries.

Example: May 10, 1908. 1908 divided by 4 gives 477, 0 remainder. 0 column, after 1900: May section gives "May 1–20, Taurus" at left. Sun is in Taurus. At right: "Add 9 to birth date"—10 plus 9 equals 19, so Sun is 19 degrees Taurus.

Example: January 12, 1874. 1874 divided by 4 gives 468, remainder of 2. 2 column, before 1900: down to January section: first X shows "Capricorn January 1–19" which includes our date, the 12th; therefore the Sun is in Capricorn. At right: "Add 10 to birth date." 12 plus 10 equals 22; therefore the Sun was 22 degrees in Capricorn on January 12, 1874.

Enter Sun's sign and degree in birth record. Enter also the paragraph number that applies to your Sun sign.

1. SUN IN ARIES

"Here lies Thomas Jefferson, author of the Declaration of Independence, of the Statute of Virginia for religious Liberty, and founder of the University of Virginia."
Self-written epitaph of Thomas Jefferson, born in Aries, April 13, 1743.

Aries' great independence is a symptom of vitality and physical energy and becomes intellectualized later in life, if at all. The highest type of Arian becomes capable of idealizing and universalizing his love of independence, which has its source in egocentricity. The first ambition of the Arian is to be first. He is an inveterate contestant, a professional competitor. His object is not so much the material stake as the glory of winning. He will never boast about coming in second; the also-rans he beats impress him less than the one fellow who beats him and thus steals his rightful place at the head of the procession. Literally as well as figuratively this first-ness shows. Your Arian walks one step ahead of his companions, goes through doors first (sometimes even before ladies), has the first word (and often the last) in any argument. He loves arguments, not as a means of arriving at truth so much as a means of demonstrating that he can come out in front. He often wins by sheer noise and vitality—that is, he makes the other fellow cry uncle. Aries is frequently original in his efforts to be first, and, when not original, is sure to be novel. Any Arian who doesn't understand the difference between *originality* and *novelty* should study the two words till he does. When an Arian is *original* he is a pioneer, an inventor, a great thinker. When he is only *novel,* he is putting *first his ego ideal to be first* and neglecting to make his ideas sound and his methods practical. He thus loses the benefit of his energy, his genius and his ambition. All the bugaboos of the ego beset the Arian, and he must beware of self-centeredness. This can make him arrogant, conceited, self-pitying, self-assertive, and in the face of opposition or restraint can lead to delusions of persecution in mild or acute form. To forget self, to become absorbed in mental matters, to put ideas first, and to make sure that originality (or novelties) rest on a sound basis of fact, to see the other fellow's point of view, and to regard the other fellow's needs, wishes, desires just as seriously as his own are the means by which Aries may emphasize his great good points, and insure that his desire to be first shall actually cause him to be first.

2. SUN IN TAURUS

"I propose to fight it out on this line if it takes all Summer."
Ulysses S. Grant, born in Taurus, April 27, 1822.

"In all movements, we bring to the front as the leading question in each case, the property question."
The Communist Manifesto of Karl Marx, born in Taurus, May 5, 1818.

"From each according to his abilities, to each according to his needs."
Karl Marx.

The singleness of purpose of the Taurean, his loyalty, his stick-to-it-iveness, spring from one source: his need for security. Self-preservation, the first law animating all nature in some degree, is the hub of the Taurean wheel of life; and the Taurean curls up and dies within himself when security—emotional or material—is denied him. Not likely to be grasping, sure to be the embodiment of the idealist form of love, Taurus may himself, or herself, be quite unaware of inner motives, for self-analysis is rarely important to this sign. Instincts are powerful and generally right—*always* right in so far as they serve the perhaps unarticulated motives of the Taurean, who, while not selfish in the ordinary material sense, sees to it that nothing interferes with the gratifying of his instinctual urge, self-preservation and its more abstracted form, self-fulfillment. The Taurean will not interfere with you if you don't interfere with him in these essentials, but will fight like a bear at bay for his rights to these things. He is the easiest person to live with, if you are willing to live *with* him and not *against* him. Anyone who is going to get along with a Taurean must understand that to him or her cooperation doesn't mean doing things together: it means doing things peacefully, in a friendly manner, even if the things are done separately. This kind of cooperation annoys people who are less self-sufficient until they learn that the heart of the Taurean comes home to roost only if you don't try to coerce it, and will break itself against bars of any kind, even if the bars are put up by love itself. The Taurean is so sure of his need for security that he resents any implication that he needs watching or holding; his instinct is to hold himself to what he needs and wants—and he can't by any force in the world be held to anything else. On the other hand, once he has polarized his instinct on an essential, he will cling to it with hands, teeth and toenails, and no one can tell him that it is unworthy, or wrong, or useless, or low. Once it is his, in that it satisfies his deepest needs, it is his forever, whether it be home, a man, a woman, ambition, love, money or anything. When the Taurean has determined in his deep and sometimes dark subconscious that his emotional or material security lies *there,* he goes there and stays there forever.

3. SUN IN GEMINI

"I celebrate myself and sing myself."
Walt Whitman, born in Gemini, May 31, 1819.

"Whoso would be a man must be a non-conformist."
            Ralph Waldo Emerson, born in Gemini,
                    May 25, 1803.

"Democracy wishes to elevate mankind, to teach it to think, to set it free."
Thomas Mann, born in Gemini, June 6, 1875.

Into strange paths leads the Gemini's desire to *be himself,* to think for himself, to do for himself, and, ultimately and in its highest form, to become his best self. It takes him a long time to learn that he can't possibly be anything except himself. The self he wants to be is at first not well defined, except that it has to be different from what his father, or his mother, or his brother, is. If the urge remains in the naive *be different* form, Gemini stays a bad child all his life, breaking rules, rebelling against authority, dashing hither and yon over the geographical, social and emotional world in order to make sure that he doesn't yield his individuality to one place or one wife (or husband). Education or other discipline must come to Gemini through his own volition, and when it does is his salvation; for then the passion to be different turns into creative originality in business or the arts, and Gemini forges ahead. He will generally be found in the camp of liberalism, because it is against the status quo if for no other reason. Sometimes Gemini rebels against the status quo of his own life, and thus the sign has a reputation for supporting Reno. But if his life gives him sufficient scope to be himself, Gemini stays settled. The more his concept of what it means to be himself diverges from the early, rebellious, sensational, adventurous urges toward intellectual excellence and a sense of social responsibility, the higher Gemini gets in the world, for his sense of what constitutes his best self is not limited. It often starts with free love, breaking school rules and talking back to cops. But here, with any luck at all, the Gemini versatility breaks in; also the Gemini practical good sense. He discovers that his self might just as well be something more stable, sets his self-development along another line, and gratifies his desire to be himself in progress rather than in destruction. Everything depends on his subjective reaction to himself; and it therefore becomes his moral obligation to develop to the point where he is innerly satisfied by what is constructive. He will never do anything because someone, or a convention, tells him to; but he may, and often does, grow up to the point where his behavior satisfies himself best when it is going somewhere in a straight line, instead of nowhere in a circle.

4. SUN IN CANCER

"We the people of the United States, in order to form a more perfect *union,* establish justice, insure *domestic tranquility,* provide for the common *defense, promote* the general *welfare,* and *secure* the blessings of liberty for *ourselves* and our *posterity,* do ordain and establish this Constitution for the United States of America."
Preamble to the Constitution of the United States, which as a nation was born in Cancer, July 4, 1776.

The defensive, protective instincts dominate Cancer, whose life aims primarily at security, material and domestic. Capable of great self-sufficiency, or of being a clinging vine (male or female), the Cancer branch will take the turn as indicated by the roots, which must always be in secure soil. If independence serves security, Cancer will be independent; if security depends on another, Cancer will cling. If security requires taking a chance, Cancer will take a chance—generally, if possible, with someone else's money; and once he has put his capital or someone's else's into a venture, he watches it like a hawk. His sense of responsibility toward another's money, security, etc., is as deep as if they were his own; he pays his debts and expects others to do the same. It was Coolidge, Cancer

President, whose solution to the war debts was of naive simplicity: "They hired the money, didn't they?" It is this simple, direct possessiveness toward what rightfully belongs to him that makes Cancer outstandingly successful in business, where he makes his fortune buying and selling, rather than in Wall Street. Cancer will gamble when he has a nest egg, not before, and then as a game rather than as a means of livelihood. With livelihood (security), Cancer takes no chances, either in getting it or keeping it. It is therefore tops as a home-making sign; the maternal-paternal instinct is powerful; and the Cancer, male or female, will go to great lengths to protect, defend and improve his home, mate and children. If Cancer remains unmarried, it is because protectiveness has turned somehow into fear or selfishness; or because he feels that in some way his security is best served alone. Cancer protects himself, as well as his possessions, and may protect himself from the chances of emotional hurt by withdrawing into himself and making his security there, alone. This is a pitiable sight, because Cancer really needs a home and should have children, and few persons give the effect of incompleteness more than the introverted Cancerian who has no one to lavish his protectiveness on but himself. For in its complete development, the Cancer protectiveness becomes encompassing love that fills all its world, and warms and comforts those who are lucky enough to live in the sphere of its radiations.

5. SUN IN LEO

" 'We are Earth's best, that learnt her lesson here.
Life is our cry. We have kept the faith!' we said;
'We shall go down with unreluctant tread,
Rose-crowned into the darkness!' . . . Proud we were,
And laughed, that had such brave true things to say.
—And then you suddenly cried, and turned away."
  Rupert Brooke, born in Leo, August 3, 1887.

The mainspring of Leo's great energy, vitality and charm is his instinctive desire for both public acclaim and self-approval. Of all the signs, Leo is perhaps the most aware of himself; in a sense he is always before the looking glass, seeing what effect he is making. In shallow types this makes for mere vanity, pompousness, pride and show. Add profundity, and all this is changed. Your best Leo type is earnest, sincere, eager to please himself and the world around him and willing, in order to do so, to take on infinite work and go to infinite trouble. He is not genuinely introspective; he has little capacity to discover his inner faults; but he is very sensitive to the effect he makes on others, and studies therefore what to do to make a better effect. There is a difference here from self-analysis to improve character from the inside, but the difference is in method rather than in result. For Leo, in the process of appearing something desirable, actually becomes something desirable. He knows instinctively the wisdom of the advice Hamlet gave his mother: "Assume a virtue if you have it not": by assuming the appearance of a virtue for the sake of winning approval, he actually acquires the virtue itself, for he is the soul of truth and cannot behave as he doesn't feel. He thus removes the curse from his playacting, for his sense of the dramatic is strong, and the roles he assumes are noble. This would be unbearable if in the process Leo did not actually become noble —but he does; some of the greatest spirits who have ever walked the earth are these very Leos who chose for themselves a high role in which to merit the world's approval, lived up to the role, and actually became what they wanted to be admired for. "Such a price do the gods exact for a song, to become what we sing." Whether he is found in business, on the stage (and he often is), or in a love affair (where also he often is), Leo is acutely aware of himself, always standing off and appraising the effect he is making. He will usually be found, if not conventional, at least discreet. Self-approval replaces conscience; he'll do anything if he thinks it is right, and will brave public opinion if his self-approval is sufficiently important to outweigh the loss of public approval. However he behaves, you can rest assured that he is always acutely aware of what people are thinking of him and that he is striving to make them think as well as possible.

6. SUN IN VIRGO

"Three things are to be looked to in a building: that it stand on the right spot, that it be securely founded, that it be successfully executed."
Johann Wolfgang von Goethe,
born in Virgo, August 18, 1749.

"The happiness of man consists in life. And life is in labor. . . . The vocation of every man and woman is to serve other people."
Count Tolstoy, born in Virgo, August 28, 1828.

To discover the motivating drive in the life of any Virgoan, it is necessary to look at the work he is doing; for so deep is Virgo's utilitarian sense that he identifies himself with his work and is quite willing to lose himself in it. His personality and character development depend, to a peculiar extent, on the nature of the work he has set himself, for he will be as big or as small as his job or mission. He is capable of becoming single-tracked, absorbed and narrow over whatever he happens to fall into. He is capable of making work his god, and thus going high and far in a chosen direction. He is capable of expanding his spirit by selecting a career somehow related to service. He is capable of the extremes of self-denial if he thinks his work calls him to that. And he is also capable of feeling that his work requires self-immolation, self-limitation and self-sacrifice to an inordinate degree. However you figure it, the puzzle of his nature will be solved if you find his attitude toward the hub of his universe, his work. So true is this that when you run across an unemployed Virgoan you have the most woe-begone and incomplete personality in the world. In losing his work, Virgo loses his whole reason for being. In its best forms, this makes for efficiency and brilliance in the performance of duty, and it may take the sense of duty into very humane realms of selflessness. In its worst form, it makes for narrowness of outlook, great inability to talk anything but shop, lack of interest in anything not related to work. So engrossed does Virgo become in his job (task, mission, message or whatever he calls it) that he sometimes seems intent on destroying all the rest of the personality that doesn't belong to his work. He loses interest in extracurricular activities, so that his life is one long routine of keeping the nose to the grindstone, and he is unhappy when for some reason or other the grindstone stops or his nose gets away from it. To fix the aim high, to select a job that requires diverse talents and wide knowledge, is Virgo's best bet for a well-rounded life. If he has the misfortune to be able to find progress and security in a rut, he is likely to see only the progress and not realize it is a rut. He needs activities, companions, fun, diversions, hobbies to broaden his life, and should seek these along constructive lines lest his overtaxed body and brain force him to seek them in undesirable forms of escapism, brooding and introversion.

7. SUN IN LIBRA

"He prayeth best who loveth best
All things both great and small."
*Samuel Taylor Coleridge,
born in Libra, October 21, 1772.*

Libra's aim is to identify himself with as much of the rest of the world as suits the demands of his very eclectic and elegant taste. Despite a gentle and firm sort of independence, he does not put much stock in "being himself," for he values other people a great deal and, if no principle is involved, will please others before thinking of what he wants. In a deep sense, what he wants is what makes others happy. In some this makes weakness. The girl who "made love only to her friends and didn't have an enemy in the world" was very likely a Libran. But so also is the girl whose charm is so great and whose interest so eager that she holds a man's attention without yielding to his carnal passions. And many who have tried to force the apparently yielding Libran along a path counter to his principles have felt the iron hand in the velvet glove. Libra's willingness to lose his identity in others —in society, in marriage—makes Librans ideal companions, or mates, for those who understand the curious need they have for independence that accompanies their selflessness. They merge with others, but they retain their identity, and will withdraw completely if their identity is attacked or endangered. They are democratic in spirit, but since they identify themselves with elegance, will not allow themselves to be forced into contact with things or people that offend their very strong sense of good taste. Thus they are often thought aristocrats or snobs, when in reality they have the deepest kind of respect, sympathy and understanding for all sorts and conditions of men. They also have a great deal of respect, sympathy and understanding for themselves, and see no reason why they should ever give this up. They are the living embodiment of the co-operative spirit; they will work *with* you till they drop, but rarely *for* you. By the same token, if they are executives (and they often are) they treat their subordinates as partners, not as servants. Much is expected of the man who works for a Libra boss, who in return pays him well and treats him as an equal. The girl who does housework for a Libra mistress must keep the place spotless, but is treated with respect, as a fellow mortal whose human dignity must never be violated or imposed on. Libra finds deepest satisfaction in harmonious union with those around him, and with the whole world, which is not too much to be taken in by his warm and tolerant spirit.

8. SUN IN SCORPIO

"I wish to preach not the doctrine of ignoble ease, but the doctrine of the strenuous life. . . . Far better it is to dare mighty things, to win glorious triumphs, even though checkered by failure, than to take rank with those poor spirits who neither enjoy much nor suffer much, because they live in the gray twilight that knows not victory or defeat."

Theodore Roosevelt,
born in Scorpio, October 27, 1858.

The dualism of Scorpio makes it a baffling sign, for the Scorpion combines materialism with spirituality. He is "the world, the flesh and the devil" and also the spirit that renounces them. He is full of the zest of life, which however is meaningful only after he has added a unique, almost mystic, significance. The search for inner values, for the key to the riddle of self, of world, of life itself, is Scorpio's basic motivation, and his search, whether it takes him to spiritual heights or into the darkest of subconscious depths, is always intense. To him, "Life is real, life is earnest, and the grave is not its goal." Scorpio takes himself, his work, his ideals, his love seriously and insists that others do the same; yet at the same time he is aware of the fleetingness of it, the futility of it, the smallness of it. Not usually religious in any orthodox sense, he has his own personal religion, which is more mystic than philosophic, and which is part of the depths of his profound nature. Scorpio is the only sign that never produces a shallow person. The best of the rest slip into nonentities from time to time, but a Scorpion is always consequential. You must reckon with him even if you dislike or despise him. He can sink to the lowest level of them all if the sense of futility turns his great energies inward instead of outward; but to whatever level he may sink, he carries with him an essential dignity, as if to represent the greatness of Lucifer in fall as well as in glory. At its best, Scorpio is a mechanical, spiritual or legal genius, though rarely an executive. Luxurious and extravagant in his tastes, he lacks interest in making money because, when he calls on his maximum powers, they lead him to noncommercial fields. So great is his magnetism that he will generally be found in a position where he can get all he wants without giving his all, which is reserved for private, perhaps secret, pursuits. He is careful of appearances, generally a conformist in all that meets the eye, and would not willingly let you into the private details of his life, thoughts and philosophies. Yet these are very clear to him and provide him with an unexpressed viewpoint that gives him great poise. He looks at the world with aware, perhaps accusing, eyes; he does not betray the secret he has with himself, which gives him reserve and self-assurance and an uncanny knack of making the other fellow feel that he knows more than he is expressing. Part of the secret of Scorpio (no one can tell you all of the secret except the individual Scorpion himself, and he won't) is the simplicity with which he accepts the merger of the material and the spiritual. He relates all problems of life to a standard of intangibles that is unknown to other men, achieves a practical answer in terms of his secret, perhaps unconscious, doctrine of the worlds, and thus adds to his personality the sort of magic one would have who consulted with an invisible, but ever-present, guardian angel.

9. SUN IN SAGITTARIUS

"If there were no God, it would be necessary to invent him."
Voltaire, born in Sagittarius, November 21, 1694.

"There is no cure for birth and death save to enjoy the interval."
George Santayana,
born in Sagittarius, December 16, 1863.

"The miracles of the Church seem to me to rest not so much upon faces or voices or healing power, coming suddenly near to us from afar, but upon our perceptions being made finer, so that for a moment our eyes can see and our ears hear what is there about us always."
Willa Cather, born in Sagittarius,
December 7, 1876.

The expansion of the ego to the uttermost bounds of human thought, experience and knowledge motivates the Sagittarian, who rushes out eagerly to greet life, equipped with a radiant nature, abundant vitality and a keen, alert mind eager for the fellowship of earth and willing to extend his knowledge to last limits of heaven. The approach to life is straightforward, for the aim is not subtle: it is to experience, to know, to try, to adventure. As a result, the Sagittarian goes far, literally and figuratively. He travels, either geographically or in thought, or both; and however he travels he likes to go fast. If he finishes things at all, it is because he is quick, not patient; life is too short for him to bother with details, and he feels that he will learn more, see more, know more if he goes more. He can thus be superficial, but is rarely shallow, for his sincerity goes right down into his marrow, and a platitude on his lips can become a great truth because of the wholeheartedness with which he believes it. The creative urge is strong; thus does the ego expand and perpetuate itself in its expanded state. Idealism is powerfully marked, as are religious and philosophic tendencies. Sagittarians take naturally to serious thought and, even if uneducated in the formal sense, are at home with abstract ideas, principles, beliefs. They have little use for dogma, and are not conventional in thought, though they are so straightforward that their actions are generally unimpeachable. A low-type Sagittarian is a rara avis. The worst the sign usually gets is mediocre and bromidic. Abundant energy and natural good spirits preserve them from the worst that life throws up. The better types, eagerly questing in the geographical and spiritual world, lead the abundant life up to the hilt. They leave the world better than they found it by the happiness they bring to others, if not indeed by some special contribution to philosophy, religion or science, in which they are especially likely to shine.

10. SUN IN CAPRICORN

"Let's look at the record."
Al Smith, born in Capricorn,
December 30, 1873.

"Early to bed and early to rise
Makes a man healthy, wealthy, and wise."
Benjamin Franklin,
born in Capricorn, January 17, 1706.

"National debt, if it is not excessive, will be to us a national blessing."
Alexander Hamilton,
born in Capricorn, January 11, 1757.

Self-preservation aggressively carried into ambition and aspiration is the key to Capricorn activity. Not content with keeping body and soul together, Capricorn must amount to something, must have some accomplishment to point to, some property to take care of, some obligation to fulfill. His mind is subtly balanced between defense and attack; he will rarely risk either, but will pyramid his life by stepping from one to the other. Since he will never voluntarily step backward, he first shoves his security a little above his ambition, and then his ambition a little ahead of his security, till finally he is top of the heap and has taken no risks at all. He is worldly and careful; selfish, but capable of great devotion if he thinks it is merited; a stickler for the proprieties. He drives a hard bargain, but not an unjust one, and he asks no mercy from anyone. He has plenty of suspicion, and figures that anyone who can "put one over" on him has earned what he gets. Not the most ardent of signs in personal relations, Capricorn's love is still a much-to-be-desired thing, stable and steady, able to put up with a good deal for the sake of loyalty if not indeed for affection. He will rarely marry beneath his station, and frequently marries above it. He understands "Thee shouldst marry for love, but thou canst just as well love where there is money." He is an excellent executive and will not long remain subordinate. He rules by instinct and sometimes makes those he rules quite angry. He has little interest in seeing their point of view or answering their questions, and believes that "orders is orders": he took 'em once, and now it's someone else's turn. When the main chance requires it, Capricorn can be mild and meek as a lamb, but he'll snap off the foreman's job if he gets a chance. Once arrived, however, he can be lavishly charitable. He loves the sense of importance it gives him, the feeling that he has made the world give to him, and now he can afford to give something back to it. Underlying all his virtues and faults is the primary instinct to vindicate himself with power, to preserve himself materially in the highest structure he can build; and if some affliction in the Vitasphere doesn't undermine his judgment (which it often does) and cause him to overplay his hand at some critical point, he generally emerges with the world or some considerable portion of it at his feet.

11. SUN IN AQUARIUS

"God must have loved the common people; he made so many of them."

"With malice toward none, with charity for all, with firmness in the right as God give us to see the right."

*Abraham Lincoln,
born in Aquarius, February 12, 1809.*

"We face the arduous days that lie ahead in the warm courage of national unity; with the clear consciousness of seeking old and precious moral values; with the keen satisfaction that comes from the stern performance of duty by young and old alike. We aim at the assurance of a rounded and permanent national life. We do not distrust the future of essential Democracy."

*Franklin D. Roosevelt,
born in Aquarius, January 30, 1882.*

The motivating force behind Aquarius is some form of the gregarious, or herd, instinct. He likes folks. He is sociable. In a higher manifestation, he is social. In a lower manifestation, he thinks that the world— the folks—owe him a living. Any way you look at the Aquarian, and whatever Aquarian you look at, you will find folks at the center of his attitude. Either he depends on them or they depend on him. The sign can go either way. Whether he is a social reformer, or a hobo, people will be around him; he will be holding them up, or they will be holding him up. He thinks himself a great individualist, and he may be, but you'll rarely find him alone. Rich or poor, great or small, deep or shallow, he is the life of the party. He may put his mind on the woes of humanity, solve their problems, give his life for theirs in a figurative or literal sense. Or he may fritter away his time in pool halls. But he will always be where there are people, in the flesh or in theory. His best expression comes when he has hitched his wagon to a star of social work or one of the social professions: invention, medicine, law, politics, architecture, literature, science, music or art, with some social application. His worst expression is going places and doing things to no purpose. Some prime examples of wasted talents come in this sign—as well as some of the greatest martyrs and benefactors of the human race. Aquarius is generally misunderstood even when he has achieved greatness—and always thinks he is misunderstood when he is wasting himself. In love, Aquarius is noble but not necessarily conventional; loyal, if not faithful; affectionate, if independent, and resentful of intrusion on his private studies, which may irk the spouse because they never seem to produce anything except big electric-light bills. Aquarius the social or sociable can be anything or nothing, but the one thing he will almost never be is lonesome. He may think his spirit yearns for understanding, but he will never be far from someone to listen while he attempts to explain himself.

12. SUN IN PISCES

"Labor to keep alive in your breast that little spark of celestial fire, conscience."

*George Washington,
born in Pisces, February 22, 1732.*

"The humblest citizen of all the land, when clad in the armor of a righteous cause, is stronger than all the hosts of error."

*William Jennings Bryan,
born in Pisces, March 19, 1860.*

Pisces seeks salvation within himself, striving always for self-sufficiency, self-knowledge and effacement of self. His aim is deep and worthy, and if he does not succeed, it is because of the difficulty of the goal rather than because he does not try. His early aim appears material, because he knows instinctively that the search for self goes on most successfully if physical wants are not a source of worry. But he is not always equipped by nature for the give-and-take of commerce, and often feels himself a failure when he should not.

His "failure" is more often than not that of a square peg in a round hole. When he finds his noncommercial place of service, love, understanding, he goes far toward the deep kind of satisfaction that is his personal, and therefore his true, success. Because his aim is different, he tries ill-advisedly to accommodate himself to what he thinks he ought to be instead of following what his heart and instinct tell him. And because he wishes deeply to do the right thing, he becomes confused about his true aims and gets bewildered and lost in the business of living. It all comes about because he has forgotten the still, small voice—because he has allowed himself to be distracted from his true desires—and because in following an uncongenial and unfamiliar path his feet stumble. He thinks he is misunderstood—but this is true only because he misunderstood himself, tried to palm himself off for something that he wasn't, and found he didn't have the heart to go through with it. When he is being his truest, deepest self he is crystal clear—unselfish, sweet, lovable, devoted, demanding little, giving much, eager always to sacrifice himself for others. It is only in the presence of the material world, when he tries to submerge the sweetness which he may come to be ashamed of, that he is unhappy. It is then that he becomes demanding, jealous, unreliable, self-deceived and perhaps even deceptive—because he is trying to force his meditative spirit into a harness where it must try to be something it isn't. Let Pisces follow his heart, his conscience, his inner desire for service, self-realization and self-knowledge, and the world be damned, and he is the happiest, most useful of mortals, living comfortably with deep spiritual truths that give him an almost mystic grip on other people and on the reins of his own life.

				YEARS BEFORE 1900				1900	YEARS AFTER 1900				
SUN IS IN THE SIGN	**Read Para.**			**1**	**2**	**3**	**0**		**1**	**2**	**3**	**0**	**TO GET DEGREE OF SUN IN YOUR SIGN**
Capricorn	10	Jan.	1-19	X	X	X		X					Add 10 to birth date
Capricorn	10	Jan.	1-20		X	X		X	X				Add 9 to birth date
Aquarius	11	Jan.	20-31		X	X			X			X	Subtract 20 from "
Aquarius	11	Jan.	21-31	X			X	X	X	X	X		Subtract 21 from "
Aquarius	11	Feb.	1-17	X									Add 12 to birth date
Aquarius	11	Feb.	1-18		X	X		X		X			Add 11 to birth date
Aquarius	11	Feb.	1-19	X				X	X	X		X	Add 10 to birth date
Pisces	12	Feb.	18-28	X	X	X							Subtract 18 from "
Pisces	12	Feb.	19-29		X	X				X		X	Subtract 19 from "
Pisces	12	Feb.	20-29		X	X		X	X	X	X	X	Subtract 20 from "
Pisces	12	Mar.	1-19	X	X	X		X					Add 10 to birth date
Pisces	12	Mar.	1-20		X	X		X	X				Add 9 to birth date
Pisces	12	Mar.	1-21				X	X	X	X		X	Add 8 to birth date
Aries	1	Mar.	20-31		X	X			X			X	Subtract 20 from "
Aries	1	Mar.	21-31	X				X	X	X	X		Subtract 21 from "
Aries	1	Mar.	22-31		X	X				X		X	Subtract 22 from "
Aries	1	Apr.	1-19	X	X	X		X				X	Add 10 to birth date
Aries	1	Apr.	1-20		X	X		X	X				Add 9 to birth date
Taurus	2	Apr.	20-30	X			X		X			X	Subtract 20 from "
Taurus	2	Apr.	21-30		X	X		X	X	X			Subtract 21 from "

J A N

F E B

M A R C H

A P R

		Sign	Month	Dates	Instruction
M A Y	2	Taurus	May	1-20	Add 9 to birth date
	2	Taurus	May	1-21	Add 8 to birth date
	3	Gemini	May	21-31	Subtract 21 from "
	3	Gemini	May	22-31	Subtract 22 from "
J U N E	4	Cancer	June	1-20	Add 9 to birth date
	3	Gemini	June	1-21	Add 8 to birth date
	3	Gemini	June	1-22	Add 7 to birth date
	4	Cancer	June	21-30	Subtract 21 from "
	4	Cancer	June	22-30	Subtract 22 from "
	3	Gemini	June	23-30	Subtract 23 from "
J U L Y	4	Cancer	July	1-21	Add 8 to birth date
	4	Cancer	July	1-22	Add 7 to birth date
	4	Cancer	July	1-23	Add 6 to birth date
	5	Leo	July	22-31	Subtract 22 from "
	5	Leo	July	23-31	Subtract 23 from "
	5	Leo	July	24-31	Subtract 24 from "
A U G	5	Leo	Aug.	1-22	Add 7 to birth date
	5	Leo	Aug.	1-23	Add 6 to birth date
	6	Virgo	Aug.	23-31	Subtract 23 from "
	6	Virgo	Aug.	24-31	Subtract 24 from "
S E P T	6	Virgo	Sept.	1-22	Add 7 to birth date
	6	Virgo	Sept.	1-23	Add 6 to birth date
	7	Libra	Sept.	23-30	Subtract 23 from "
	7	Libra	Sept.	24-30	Subtract 24 from "

SUN IS IN THE SIGN	Read Para.			YEARS BEFORE 1900				1900	YEARS AFTER 1900					TO GET DEGREE OF SUN IN YOUR SIGN
				1	2	3	0		0	1	2	3	0	
Libra	7	Oct.	1-22	X	X		X	X		X	X	X		Add 7 to birth date
Libra	7	Oct.	1-23	X	X	X		X		X	X	X	X	Add 6 to birth date
Scorpio	8	Oct.	23-31	X	X	X	X	X	X	X	X	X	X	Subtract 23 from "
Scorpio	8	Oct.	24-31	X	X	X	X	X	X	X	X	X	X	Subtract 24 from "
Scorpio	8	Nov.	1-21	X	X		X	X		X	X	X		Add 8 to birth date
Scorpio	8	Nov.	1-22	X	X	X		X		X	X	X	X	Add 7 to birth date
Sagittarius	9	Nov.	22-30	X	X	X	X	X	X	X	X	X	X	Subtract 22 from "
Sagittarius	9	Nov.	23-30	X	X	X	X	X	X	X	X	X	X	Subtract 23 from "
Sagittarius	9	Dec.	1-20	X	X		X	X		X	X	X		Add 9 to birth date
Sagittarius	9	Dec.	1-21	X	X	X		X		X	X	X	X	Add 8 to birth date
Sagittarius	9	Dec.	1-22	X	X		X	X		X	X	X		Add 7 to birth date
Capricorn	10	Dec.	21-31	X	X	X		X		X	X	X	X	Subtract 21 from "
Capricorn	10	Dec.	22-31	X	X	X	X	X	X	X	X	X	X	Subtract 22 from "
Capricorn	10	Dec.	23-31	X	X	X	X	X	X	X	X	X	X	Subtract 23 from "

THE MOON

While the Sun's position by sign determines what motives and urges dominate your life as it meets the naked eye, the sign position of the Moon tells the desire of your heart which may or may not be expressed or realized in your life. When you "know what you mean but you can't say it," it is your Moon that knows it and your Sun that can't say it. "Thoughts that do often lie too deep for tears" are the thoughts of your Moon's nature. The wordless ecstasy, the mute sorrow, the secret dream, the esoteric picture of yourself that you can't get across to the world, or which the world doesn't comprehend or value—these are the products of the Moon in your Vitasphere. When you are misunderstood, it is your Moon nature, expressed imperfectly through the Sun sign, that you feel is betrayed. When you know what you ought to do, but can't find the right way to do it, it is your Moon that knows and your Sun that refuses to react in harmony. Also, when you "don't know why I said that," it was your Moon expressing despite your Sun (if you are innerly satisfied with the involuntary speech), or the Sun expressing against the will of the Moon (if you are displeased with what has slipped out). Things you know without thought—intuitions, hunches, instincts —are the products of the Moon. Modes of expression that you feel are truly your deepest self belong to the Moon: art, letters, creative work of any kind; sometimes love; sometimes business. Whatever you feel is most deeply yourself, whether or not you are able to do anything about it in the outer world, is the product of your Moon and of the sign your Moon occupies at birth.

How to Find Your Moon's Place

This is the simplest and briefest table that has ever been devised for getting the Moon's place over a great number of years, and if you follow carefully the simple directions starting on page 151, you will have a part of your Vitasphere that is usually reserved for those who pay ten dollars to an astrologer for an individual horoscope.

		1870	1871	1872	1873	1874	1875	1876	1877	1878	1879
Jan.	1	275	48	162	312	85	211	333	124	256	21
	8	3	126	258	50	173	297	69	221	342	108
	15	89	220	1	135	259	33	171	306	69	206
	22	187	321	87	220	359	132	257	31	171	302
	29	284	49	172	321	95	219	343	132	266	29
Feb.	5	11	135	266	59	181	306	78	230	351	116
	12	96	231	9	144	266	44	179	314	77	216
	19	197	329	95	229	9	140	265	40	179	311
	26	293	57	181	329	104	227	352	140	276	37
Mar.	5	19	143	291	69	189	314	103	239	359	124
	12	104	242	29	153	275	55	200	323	86	227
	19	206	338	115	239	17	149	285	51	188	321
	26	303	65	204	337	114	235	15	149	285	45
Apr.	2	28	151	301	75	198	322	114	247	8	132
	9	113	252	38	161	284	64	208	331	96	236
	16	214	348	123	249	25	159	293	61	196	330
	23	312	73	213	347	123	243	23	159	293	54
	30	37	159	312	84	207	330	125	255	17	141
May	7	123	262	47	170	294	73	217	339	106	244
	14	223	357	131	259	34	169	301	70	205	339
	21	321	82	221	257	131	252	31	170	301	63
	28	46	168	323	93	216	340	135	263	25	151
June	4	133	271	56	177	304	81	226	347	116	253
	11	232	7	139	268	43	178	310	79	215	348
	18	329	91	229	8	139	261	40	180	309	72
	25	54	178	333	101	224	350	144	271	33	161
July	2	143	279	65	185	315	90	235	355	126	261
	9	241	16	148	277	53	186	319	88	225	356
	16	338	100	239	19	148	269	49	191	318	80
	23	62	188	342	110	232	359	153	281	41	172
	30	153	287	74	194	324	99	244	4	135	271
Aug.	6	252	24	157	285	64	194	328	96	236	4
	13	346	108	247	29	156	278	59	200	326	88
	20	70	196	351	119	239	10	161	290	50	182
	27	162	297	83	203	334	109	253	13	144	281
Sept.	3	263	32	166	293	74	202	337	105	246	12
	10	354	116	257	38	165	286	69	209	335	96
	17	78	209	359	128	248	20	169	299	58	191
	24	171	307	91	212	341	119	261	22	152	291
Oct.	1	273	40	175	303	85	210	345	114	256	20
	8	3	125	268	47	174	294	80	217	344	104
	15	87	218	7	137	257	29	179	307	68	200
	22	178	318	99	221	349	131	259	31	160	302
	29	283	49	183	313	94	219	353	125	265	29
Nov.	5	12	132	278	54	183	302	91	225	353	113
	12	95	227	17	145	266	37	188	315	77	208
	19	187	328	107	230	358	140	277	40	170	311
	26	291	57	191	323	102	228	1	136	272	38
Dec.	3	21	141	288	63	191	311	100	234	1	122
	10	104	235	27	153	275	45	198	323	86	216
	17	196	338	115	238	8	149	285	48	180	320
	24	299	66	199	334	110	237	9	146	280	47
	31	29	159	297	72	199	321	109	243	9	131

		1880	1881	1882	1883	1884	1885	1886	1887	1888	1889
Jan.	1	144	294	67	190	315	105	238	359	127	276
	8	240	32	152	278	52	202	323	89	224	12
	15	341	116	239	18	151	286	49	190	321	96
	22	67	202	342	113	236	13	153	284	46	185
	29	154	302	77	198	325	113	248	8	136	285
Feb.	5	250	41	161	286	63	211	331	97	235	20
	12	349	124	248	29	159	295	58	200	329	104
	19	75	212	351	122	244	24	161	293	59	196
	26	163	311	86	207	334	122	257	16	144	294
Mar.	5	275	49	170	294	88	218	340	105	260	28
	12	10	133	257	38	180	303	69	209	350	112
	19	94	222	359	132	264	34	169	302	74	205
	26	185	320	95	215	356	133	265	25	166	305
Apr.	2	286	57	179	303	98	226	349	114	270	36
	9	18	141	267	47	189	311	79	217	359	120
	16	102	232	7	141	272	43	178	311	83	214
	23	194	331	103	224	4	143	273	34	175	315
	30	297	65	187	312	108	235	357	124	279	45
May	7	28	149	278	54	198	319	89	225	8	128
	14	111	241	17	149	281	52	188	319	92	223
	21	202	342	111	233	13	154	281	43	184	325
	28	306	73	195	323	117	243	5	135	288	54
June	4	37	157	288	63	207	327	99	234	17	137
	11	119	250	27	158	291	60	199	327	101	231
	18	211	352	119	241	22	164	289	52	194	335
	25	315	82	203	333	126	252	13	145	296	63
July	2	46	165	297	72	216	336	108	244	26	146
	9	129	258	37	166	299	69	209	335	110	240
	16	220	2	127	250	32	173	298	59	204	343
	23	323	91	211	344	134	261	21	155	304	72
	30	54	174	306	82	224	345	117	254	34	156
Aug.	6	138	267	48	174	309	78	219	343	119	250
	13	231	11	136	258	43	181	307	68	215	352
	20	331	100	220	354	142	270	30	165	313	80
	27	63	184	314	93	232	355	125	265	42	165
Sept.	3	147	276	58	182	317	88	228	352	127	260
	10	242	19	145	266	54	190	316	76	226	359
	17	340	109	229	3	152	278	40	173	323	88
	24	70	193	323	103	239	4	134	275	50	174
Oct.	1	155	286	67	191	325	99	237	1	135	271
	8	252	27	154	274	64	198	324	85	236	8
	15	350	117	238	11	161	286	49	181	332	96
	22	78	202	332	113	248	12	144	284	58	182
	29	163	297	75	200	333	110	245	10	143	282
Nov.	5	262	36	163	283	74	207	332	94	245	18
	12	359	124	248	19	171	294	59	190	342	104
	19	87	210	342	122	257	20	154	292	67	190
	26	171	308	83	208	341	120	253	18	152	292
Dec.	3	271	45	171	293	82	216	340	104	253	27
	10	10	132	257	28	181	302	87	199	351	112
	17	95	218	353	130	265	28	165	300	76	198
	24	179	318	91	217	351	130	262	26	162	301
	31	279	55	179	302	89	226	348	113	261	37

		1890	1891	1892	1893	1894	1895	1896	1897	1898	1899
Jan.	1	49	170	298	87	220	340	109	258	30	149
	8	132	259	37	183	303	69	209	352	114	240
	15	221	2	131	266	32	174	301	76	203	335
	22	323	94	215	357	135	265	25	169	305	76
	29	58	178	307	96	229	348	117	268	39	157
Feb.	5	141	267	47	190	312	78	219	359	122	249
	12	230	12	140	274	42	182	310	84	214	353
	19	332	103	223	7	143	274	34	179	314	84
	26	67	187	315	106	236	357	125	278	46	168
Mar.	5	150	276	72	198	321	87	243	8	130	259
	12	241	20	161	282	52	190	331	92	225	1
	19	340	113	244	17	152	283	55	188	323	93
	26	75	196	337	117	244	6	148	289	54	177
Apr.	2	159	285	81	206	329	97	252	17	138	269
	9	251	28	170	290	63	198	340	100	235	9
	16	350	121	253	25	162	291	64	196	333	101
	23	83	204	346	127	252	15	157	299	62	185
	30	167	295	89	215	337	108	261	25	146	280
May	7	261	36	179	299	73	207	349	109	244	19
	14	0	129	262	33	172	299	73	204	344	108
	21	91	213	355	137	261	23	167	308	71	193
	28	174	307	98	224	345	119	269	34	155	291
June	4	271	46	188	308	81	217	357	119	253	29
	11	11	137	272	42	182	307	82	213	354	117
	18	99	221	6	146	269	31	178	316	80	201
	25	183	317	106	233	353	129	277	43	164	300
July	2	278	56	195	317	89	227	5	128	261	39
	9	21	145	281	51	192	315	91	223	3	125
	16	108	229	17	154	278	39	189	324	89	209
	23	192	327	115	241	2	138	286	51	173	309
	30	287	66	203	327	99	237	13	138	269	49
Aug.	6	31	153	289	62	201	324	99	234	11	134
	13	117	237	28	162	287	48	200	332	97	219
	20	201	336	124	250	12	147	296	59	183	317
	27	295	76	211	336	108	247	21	146	279	58
Sept.	3	39	162	297	72	209	333	107	245	19	143
	10	125	246	38	171	296	57	209	341	105	228
	17	211	344	134	257	22	155	305	67	193	326
	24	305	86	220	345	118	256	29	155	290	67
Oct.	1	47	171	305	83	217	341	116	256	27	151
	8	134	256	47	179	304	67	218	350	113	238
	15	220	352	144	265	31	164	315	75	202	335
	22	315	94	228	352	128	264	39	162	301	75
	29	55	179	314	94	225	350	125	266	36	160
Nov.	5	142	265	56	189	312	77	226	359	121	248
	12	229	2	153	274	40	173	324	84	210	346
	19	327	102	237	0	139	272	47	171	311	82
	26	64	188	323	103	234	358	135	275	45	167
Dec.	3	149	275	63	198	320	86	235	9	129	257
	10	237	12	162	282	47	184	332	93	218	356
	17	338	110	246	9	149	280	56	179	321	91
	24	72	196	333	112	243	5	145	282	54	175
	31	158	284	72	208	328	95	244	18	138	265

		1900	1901	1902	1903	1904	1905	1906	1907	1908	1909
Jan.	1	280	55	188	308	76	227	358	119	246	39
	8	21	149	272	37	179	320	82	208	350	129
	15	112	234	2	141	270	43	174	311	81	213
	22	195	327	101	234	353	138	273	44	164	309
	29	288	66	196	317	83	238	6	128	255	50
Feb.	5	31	158	280	46	188	328	89	219	359	138
	12	121	241	12	149	279	51	184	319	89	221
	19	204	335	111	242	2	146	283	52	173	317
	26	296	76	204	326	92	248	13	136	264	59
Mar.	5	40	166	288	57	211	334	98	229	21	147
	12	130	249	22	157	300	59	194	328	110	230
	19	213	344	121	250	24	154	293	59	195	325
	26	305	86	212	334	116	258	22	144	288	69
Apr.	2	49	175	296	68	219	345	106	240	29	156
	9	138	258	31	157	309	69	202	338	118	239
	16	222	352	132	258	33	163	304	68	204	334
	23	315	96	220	342	127	267	31	152	299	77
	30	57	184	304	78	227	354	114	250	38	164
May	7	177	268	40	177	316	78	210	348	126	249
	14	231	1	142	266	42	172	313	76	212	344
	21	325	104	229	350	138	275	40	160	310	85
	28	65	193	313	87	236	3	124	259	47	172
June	4	155	277	48	187	324	88	219	358	134	259
	11	239	11	151	275	50	182	322	85	220	355
	18	336	112	238	359	149	283	48	169	320	93
	25	74	201	322	96	245	11	133	267	57	180
July	2	163	286	57	197	333	97	228	8	142	267
	9	248	21	160	283	58	193	330	94	228	6
	16	347	121	247	7	159	291	57	178	330	102
	23	84	209	332	105	255	19	143	276	66	188
	30	171	295	66	206	341	105	239	17	151	275
Aug.	6	256	32	168	292	66	204	338	103	237	17
	13	357	130	255	17	168	301	65	188	339	111
	20	94	217	341	113	265	27	152	285	76	196
	27	179	303	77	215	350	113	250	25	160	283
Sept.	3	264	43	176	301	75	215	346	111	246	27
	10	6	229	263	27	176	310	73	198	347	121
	17	103	225	350	123	274	35	161	294	85	205
	24	188	311	88	223	358	122	261	33	169	292
Oct.	1	273	53	185	309	85	224	355	119	256	36
	8	14	149	271	36	185	320	81	207	356	130
	15	113	233	359	133	283	44	169	305	93	214
	22	197	319	99	231	7	130	271	42	177	301
	29	283	62	194	317	95	233	5	127	266	44
Nov.	5	22	158	279	45	193	329	89	216	5	139
	12	121	242	6	144	291	53	177	316	101	223
	19	206	328	109	239	15	140	281	50	185	311
	26	293	70	203	325	105	241	14	135	276	52
Dec.	3	31	167	288	54	203	338	98	224	15	147
	10	129	251	14	155	299	61	185	327	109	231
	17	214	338	118	248	23	149	289	59	193	322
	24	303	78	213	333	115	249	23	143	286	61
	31	41	176	296	61	213	346	107	232	26	155

139

		1910	1911	1912	1913	1914	1915	1916	1917	1918	1919
Jan.	1	168	289	57	211	337	100	228	23	147	270
	8	252	20	162	299	61	192	332	110	231	5
	15	346	122	251	23	158	293	61	193	329	103
	22	84	214	334	119	256	23	145	290	68	193
	29	175	298	65	221	345	108	237	32	155	278
Feb.	5	259	31	170	308	69	203	340	118	249	16
	12	356	130	260	32	167	302	70	203	338	113
	19	94	222	344	128	266	31	154	298	78	201
	26	184	306	75	231	353	116	248	41	164	286
Mar.	5	267	42	192	317	77	214	2	127	248	26
	12	5	140	280	41	176	311	89	212	346	123
	19	105	230	5	136	276	39	176	308	87	209
	26	192	314	100	239	2	124	273	49	173	294
Apr.	2	276	52	200	326	86	223	10	135	257	35
	9	13	149	288	51	184	321	97	232	355	133
	16	155	238	14	146	286	48	184	318	96	218
	23	201	322	111	247	11	132	284	57	181	303
	30	285	61	208	334	96	232	19	143	267	43
May	7	21	160	296	60	192	331	105	231	4	142
	14	124	246	22	157	294	56	192	329	104	227
	21	209	331	122	255	20	141	294	66	190	312
	28	294	69	218	342	106	240	29	151	277	51
June	4	30	170	304	69	202	341	114	249	14	151
	11	132	255	30	167	302	65	200	340	112	235
	18	218	340	132	264	28	151	304	74	198	322
	25	304	78	228	350	115	249	39	159	286	60
July	2	40	179	312	78	212	349	122	248	25	159
	9	140	264	38	178	310	74	209	350	120	244
	16	226	349	141	273	36	161	312	84	206	332
	23	314	87	237	358	125	258	48	168	295	70
	30	51	187	321	86	223	357	131	256	36	167
Aug.	6	148	272	48	188	319	82	219	359	129	252
	13	234	359	149	282	44	170	320	93	214	342
	20	323	96	246	6	133	268	57	177	303	81
	27	62	195	330	94	234	5	140	265	46	175
Sept.	3	157	281	57	198	328	90	229	8	138	260
	10	242	9	158	292	52	180	329	102	222	351
	17	331	107	255	15	141	279	65	186	312	91
	24	73	204	339	103	244	13	149	274	56	184
Oct.	1	166	289	68	206	337	98	239	17	148	268
	8	250	18	167	301	61	189	338	111	231	359
	15	339	118	263	24	149	290	73	195	320	102
	22	83	212	347	113	254	22	157	284	65	193
	29	176	296	78	214	346	106	250	25	157	276
Nov.	5	259	27	177	309	70	197	348	119	240	7
	12	347	129	270	33	158	300	81	203	329	112
	19	91	221	355	123	262	31	164	295	73	202
	26	185	305	88	223	355	115	259	34	165	285
Dec.	3	268	34	187	317	79	205	359	127	249	16
	10	356	138	279	41	168	310	89	211	340	120
	17	99	230	3	134	270	40	172	305	81	211
	24	194	313	97	232	4	124	267	44	173	294
	31	277	42	198	325	87	214	9	135	257	25

		1920	1921	1922	1923	1924	1925	1926	1927	1928	1929
Jan.	1	39	194	317	80	211	5	127	250	23	176
	8	143	278	41	177	313	90	211	349	93	260
	15	231	4	141	274	41	175	312	86	211	346
	22	316	101	239	3	127	292	51	172	297	83
	29	49	203	325	88	222	13	135	258	34	184
Feb.	5	150	289	49	187	321	99	220	359	131	269
	12	239	13	149	284	49	185	320	95	219	356
	19	325	109	249	11	135	281	60	181	305	95
	26	60	211	334	96	233	21	144	266	45	191
Mar.	5	172	297	58	197	343	107	230	8	153	276
	12	259	23	157	294	69	194	328	105	238	6
	19	346	119	258	19	157	292	68	189	327	104
	26	85	219	343	104	258	29	153	275	70	199
Apr.	2	181	305	68	205	352	115	240	16	263	284
	9	267	33	166	303	77	204	337	114	247	14
	16	355	130	266	28	164	303	76	198	335	114
	23	96	227	351	113	268	38	161	285	79	208
	30	190	313	78	213	1	123	350	25	172	292
May	7	275	31	176	313	85	212	348	123	256	23
	14	3	141	274	37	173	314	84	207	343	125
	21	105	236	359	123	277	47	169	294	88	217
	28	200	321	88	222	11	132	259	34	181	301
June	4	284	50	186	321	94	220	358	131	264	31
	11	11	152	292	45	182	324	93	215	354	135
	18	114	245	7	134	285	56	177	305	96	226
	25	209	329	97	232	20	139	268	44	190	310
July	2	293	58	197	329	103	229	9	139	273	40
	9	21	162	291	54	192	333	101	223	4	144
	16	123	254	15	144	294	65	185	315	104	236
	23	218	338	106	242	28	148	276	54	198	319
	30	302	67	208	337	112	238	20	147	282	49
Aug.	6	31	171	300	62	202	341	110	231	15	152
	13	131	264	24	153	302	74	182	324	114	244
	20	226	347	114	253	36	157	284	65	206	328
	27	310	76	218	345	120	248	29	156	290	59
Sept.	3	41	179	297	70	213	350	119	239	25	161
	10	140	273	32	162	312	83	203	332	123	252
	17	234	356	122	264	44	166	293	75	214	337
	24	319	86	227	354	128	258	38	165	298	70
Oct.	1	51	188	318	78	223	358	128	248	35	169
	8	151	281	41	170	322	91	212	340	134	260
	15	242	5	132	274	52	175	303	85	222	345
	22	326	97	235	3	136	269	46	174	306	83
	29	61	196	327	87	233	7	137	257	44	179
Nov.	5	161	289	50	178	332	99	221	349	144	268
	12	250	13	142	283	61	183	313	93	231	353
	19	334	107	243	12	144	279	54	183	315	91
	26	70	206	335	96	241	17	145	266	52	189
Dec.	3	171	297	59	187	343	107	229	358	154	276
	10	259	21	152	291	70	191	324	101	240	1
	17	343	117	252	21	153	289	63	191	324	99
	24	78	216	355	105	249	28	152	275	60	199
	31	181	305	67	197	352	115	237	9	163	285

		1930	1931	1932	1933	1934	1935	1936	1937	1938	1939
Jan.	1	297	60	195	346	107	221	8	156	278	41
	8	22	161	294	70	192	318	104	240	4	144
	15	123	257	20	158	294	68	190	328	104	239
	22	221	342	107	255	32	152	277	67	202	322
	29	306	68	206	353	116	238	18	163	286	49
Feb.	5	31	171	302	78	203	341	113	247	15	152
	12	131	266	28	167	302	77	198	338	112	248
	19	230	351	115	265	40	161	286	78	210	332
	26	314	76	217	1	144	248	29	171	294	59
Mar.	5	41	179	324	86	183	350	134	257	25	160
	12	140	276	48	176	311	86	219	347	123	256
	19	238	359	137	276	48	170	308	89	218	340
	26	323	86	241	9	132	258	52	180	302	70
Apr.	2	51	187	333	94	222	358	144	264	34	169
	9	149	284	57	184	321	95	227	355	133	264
	16	246	8	145	284	56	178	317	99	226	348
	23	331	96	250	18	140	268	60	189	310	80
	30	61	196	343	102	232	7	153	272	43	179
May	7	160	293	66	193	332	102	236	3	144	272
	14	254	17	155	297	64	187	326	108	234	356
	21	339	107	258	28	148	279	69	198	318	89
	28	70	205	351	111	240	18	161	283	51	189
June	4	171	300	75	201	343	110	245	13	154	280
	11	263	25	165	306	73	194	337	116	243	4
	18	347	117	266	37	156	288	77	207	328	99
	25	78	215	359	120	249	28	169	291	59	206
July	2	181	309	83	211	353	119	254	22	164	289
	9	272	33	176	314	82	202	348	125	253	13
	16	355	126	275	46	166	297	87	215	336	108
	23	87	226	7	130	258	38	177	300	68	210
	30	191	317	92	221	2	127	262	33	173	298
Aug.	6	281	41	187	323	91	211	359	133	261	21
	13	4	135	285	54	174	305	97	224	346	115
	20	95	237	15	138	266	48	185	308	78	219
	27	200	336	100	232	10	136	270	44	181	307
Sept.	3	290	49	196	331	100	220	8	142	269	31
	10	13	143	295	62	184	314	107	231	355	125
	17	105	246	23	147	277	58	194	317	89	228
	24	208	335	108	242	18	145	278	55	189	316
Oct.	1	298	58	206	341	108	229	17	152	279	40
	8	23	151	306	70	192	322	117	239	3	134
	15	115	255	32	155	288	66	203	324	100	236
	22	216	344	116	252	27	154	287	65	197	324
	29	307	68	214	350	116	239	25	162	286	50
Nov.	5	31	160	315	78	202	332	127	248	12	144
	12	126	264	41	162	298	74	211	333	110	243
	19	225	352	125	262	37	162	296	73	207	332
	26	314	77	222	1	124	248	33	172	293	58
Dec.	3	39	171	324	87	209	343	135	256	19	157
	10	137	272	50	170	308	82	220	342	119	252
	17	234	1	135	271	45	170	308	80	217	340
	24	322	86	229	10	132	257	42	181	302	67
	31	47	181	332	95	217	354	142	266	27	166

		1940	1941	1942	1943	1944	1945	1946	1947	1948	1949
Jan.	1	181	325	87	210	352	135	258	23	164	305
	8	277	49	175	315	85	219	348	126	256	29
	15	359	140	275	49	169	312	86	220	340	123
	22	88	239	12	133	258	51	182	306	69	223
	29	191	333	96	220	2	143	266	31	174	313
Feb.	5	284	57	186	322	94	227	358	134	265	37
	12	7	150	284	58	178	320	97	228	348	131
	19	97	250	19	141	266	62	189	312	78	233
	26	200	342	104	231	10	152	273	43	182	323
Mar.	5	305	65	196	330	116	235	8	142	286	46
	12	29	158	295	66	199	328	107	236	10	139
	19	119	260	27	150	290	72	198	320	102	243
	26	222	350	111	241	33	161	281	53	204	331
Apr.	2	314	74	205	340	124	244	16	152	294	55
	9	38	166	305	74	208	337	118	243	19	148
	16	128	270	36	158	300	81	206	328	112	252
	23	31	359	119	252	41	170	290	63	212	340
	30	323	83	213	350	132	254	25	162	302	64
May	7	46	174	315	82	216	346	127	252	27	158
	14	139	279	45	166	311	89	216	336	123	260
	21	239	9	128	261	50	179	298	82	221	349
	28	331	92	222	2	140	262	32	173	310	73
June	5	55	184	325	90	225	356	136	261	36	168
	11	149	287	54	174	311	98	224	344	134	268
	18	248	17	137	270	59	187	308	81	231	257
	25	339	101	230	11	148	272	42	183	318	82
July	2	63	194	334	99	233	7	145	259	43	179
	9	160	295	61	182	332	106	233	353	144	277
	16	258	25	147	279	70	196	318	89	241	4
	23	347	110	240	20	156	281	52	192	327	91
	30	72	205	343	108	241	18	153	278	52	190
Aug.	6	170	304	72	192	342	115	241	2	153	286
	13	268	33	156	287	80	203	327	98	251	12
	20	355	118	250	30	165	288	62	200	336	99
	27	80	216	351	118	250	28	161	287	61	200
Sept.	3	179	313	80	201	350	125	249	13	160	296
	10	278	41	165	296	89	211	337	108	260	21
	17	6	126	261	38	174	297	73	208	344	108
	24	88	226	359	126	259	38	170	295	69	209
Oct.	1	188	323	88	211	358	134	258	21	169	306
	8	288	49	174	306	98	220	344	118	268	29
	15	13	135	272	46	183	305	84	216	353	116
	22	110	235	8	134	269	47	179	303	80	207
	29	196	333	96	220	7	144	265	31	178	315
Nov.	5	297	58	182	317	107	229	351	129	277	39
	12	22	142	282	54	192	314	93	225	1	126
	19	108	244	19	141	279	55	189	311	91	225
	26	205	342	104	229	16	153	274	39	188	323
Dec.	3	305	67	189	328	114	237	0	140	284	47
	10	29	152	292	63	199	323	103	234	9	136
	17	118	250	28	149	289	63	199	319	100	234
	24	214	352	112	236	27	162	282	46	199	331
	31	313	75	198	338	122	246	10	150	292	55

		1950	1951	1952	1953	1954	1955	1956	1957	1958	1959
Jan.	1	67	194	336	115	238	6	147	285	47	178
	8	160	297	67	199	331	107	237	9	143	278
	15	258	29	150	294	70	200	320	104	242	9
	22	351	114	240	35	161	284	51	207	331	94
	29	75	204	344	124	245	17	155	294	55	189
Feb.	5	170	305	76	201	341	116	246	18	152	287
	12	269	38	159	302	80	208	330	112	252	17
	19	359	122	249	45	169	292	61	216	340	102
	26	83	214	351	133	253	27	165	303	63	199
Mar.	5	179	314	96	216	350	125	266	27	160	297
	12	279	46	180	310	91	216	351	121	262	25
	19	8	160	274	51	178	300	86	224	349	110
	26	91	225	14	142	262	37	185	312	72	208
Apr.	2	188	324	104	226	357	135	274	37	169	307
	9	289	54	189	319	70	224	359	131	271	34
	16	17	138	285	62	187	308	97	232	357	118
	23	100	235	23	150	271	46	195	320	82	216
	30	195	334	112	235	7	145	282	46	178	317
May	7	299	32	197	330	109	232	8	142	279	42
	14	26	146	296	70	196	316	107	240	6	127
	21	110	243	31	158	280	54	201	238	91	225
	28	204	343	120	244	15	155	290	54	187	326
June	4	307	71	204	340	117	241	16	153	287	51
	11	36	155	306	79	204	325	117	249	14	137
	18	119	252	42	166	290	63	214	336	101	234
	25	213	354	129	253	26	164	298	63	198	335
July	2	316	80	214	351	125	250	24	164	296	60
	9	42	164	315	88	213	335	126	259	22	147
	16	129	260	52	174	299	72	223	344	110	243
	23	225	3	137	261	37	172	308	71	209	343
	30	324	89	222	2	134	258	33	171	304	68
Aug.	6	51	174	324	97	221	345	134	268	30	156
	13	138	269	61	182	308	82	232	353	118	254
	20	235	11	146	269	48	181	316	79	220	351
	27	332	98	232	11	173	267	43	183	314	76
Sept.	3	58	183	332	107	228	8	143	278	38	165
	10	146	280	70	191	316	92	241	2	127	265
	17	246	18	155	277	58	189	325	89	230	359
	24	341	105	242	20	152	274	54	191	323	84
Oct.	1	67	193	341	116	236	4	152	287	47	174
	8	154	291	79	200	321	103	248	10	135	276
	15	256	27	163	287	68	198	333	98	239	8
	22	351	113	252	28	162	282	64	199	332	92
	29	75	201	350	125	245	12	162	295	56	182
Nov.	5	162	302	87	209	333	113	256	19	144	286
	12	265	36	171	297	75	207	341	109	247	17
	19	0	121	262	36	171	291	73	208	341	101
	26	84	209	1	133	254	20	173	303	64	190
Dec.	3	171	312	95	217	342	124	265	27	154	295
	10	273	45	179	307	84	216	348	119	255	27
	17	10	129	257	46	179	299	82	218	350	110
	24	93	217	11	141	263	28	183	311	73	199
	31	180	321	104	225	352	132	273	35	164	303

		1960	1961	1962	1963	1964	1965	1966	1967	1968	1969
Jan.	1	317	96	217	350	127	266	27	163	298	76
	8	47	167	314	89	218	350	126	260	27	161
	15	131	275	53	179	302	86	225	349	112	257
	22	223	18	141	264	35	190	311	74	207	359
	29	325	105	225	0	135	275	36	172	306	85
Feb.	5	56	188	323	98	225	359	134	270	35	171
	12	140	284	64	187	310	94	235	357	121	267
	19	233	26	150	272	46	197	320	82	218	7
	26	333	113	234	10	144	283	45	182	315	93
Mar.	5	75	198	331	109	245	9	143	280	54	180
	12	161	293	73	195	331	105	244	5	142	277
	19	259	34	159	280	71	204	329	90	243	15
	26	356	122	243	19	167	291	54	190	338	101
Apr.	2	83	208	340	119	253	18	151	290	62	189
	9	169	303	81	204	339	116	252	14	150	288
	16	269	43	167	289	81	213	337	100	252	23
	23	5	130	253	27	176	299	64	198	347	109
	30	91	216	349	128	261	27	161	298	71	197
May	7	178	314	89	213	348	127	259	23	159	299
	14	279	51	176	298	91	222	345	109	262	32
	21	15	137	263	36	186	307	73	207	357	117
	28	100	225	359	136	270	35	172	307	80	205
June	4	186	325	98	222	356	137	268	31	168	309
	11	288	30	184	308	99	231	353	119	270	42
	18	25	146	272	45	195	315	82	217	6	126
	25	109	233	10	145	279	43	183	315	89	214
July	2	195	336	106	240	6	146	277	40	178	318
	9	297	70	192	318	108	240	1	129	278	51
	16	34	154	280	46	204	324	90	227	14	135
	23	118	241	21	153	288	52	193	323	98	223
	30	204	345	115	238	16	156	286	47	188	327
Aug.	6	305	79	200	327	115	250	10	138	288	60
	13	42	163	289	66	212	333	99	238	22	144
	20	126	250	32	161	296	61	203	332	106	233
	27	215	353	124	246	27	164	295	55	199	335
Sept.	3	314	88	208	336	126	258	19	147	297	68
	10	50	172	297	77	220	342	108	249	30	152
	17	135	260	41	170	304	72	212	340	114	244
	24	225	1	134	254	37	173	304	64	208	344
Oct.	1	324	97	217	344	136	267	28	155	308	76
	8	58	180	306	88	228	1	117	259	38	161
	15	143	270	50	145	312	82	220	350	122	254
	22	235	10	143	230	47	180	313	73	217	353
	29	334	105	226	316	146	274	37	163	318	84
Nov.	5	66	189	315	97	236	359	127	264	47	169
	12	150	281	58	188	320	93	228	359	130	264
	19	244	19	151	272	55	192	321	82	225	3
	26	345	113	235	1	157	282	45	173	328	92
Dec.	3	75	197	325	106	245	7	138	276	45	176
	10	158	291	66	197	328	102	237	7	139	274
	17	252	30	159	280	62	202	329	91	233	13
	24	355	122	243	11	166	291	53	183	337	101
	31	84	204	336	113	254	14	149	284	64	185

		1970	1971	1972	1973	1974	1975	1976	1977	1978	1979
Jan.	1	197	335	109	246	8	146	279	56	179	318
	8	297	72	197	332	109	243	6	144	278	54
	15	36	158	283	69	207	329	93	240	18	139
	22	122	244	20	169	292	54	192	339	102	224
	29	206	344	107	255	17	156	288	64	189	327
Feb.	5	305	81	204	342	116	253	14	153	287	63
	12	45	167	291	79	215	337	101	251	26	147
	19	130	252	30	177	330	62	202	347	110	234
	26	216	353	126	263	27	164	297	72	209	334
Mar.	5	313	91	224	337	124	262	34	162	297	72
	12	54	176	312	90	224	346	122	262	34	156
	19	139	261	85	184	339	72	226	357	118	244
	26	226	1	149	270	37	172	320	80	208	343
Apr.	2	323	100	233	360	134	270	43	170	307	81
	9	62	184	320	101	232	353	131	273	41	164
	16	147	271	64	194	317	82	235	5	126	254
	23	235	9	158	278	47	181	329	88	217	352
	30	333	109	242	8	145	278	52	178	318	88
May	7	70	193	329	111	240	3	141	282	50	166
	14	155	281	73	203	324	92	243	14	134	264
	21	245	19	167	287	55	201	337	97	226	3
	28	344	117	251	16	156	286	61	187	329	96
June	4	78	201	339	120	249	11	151	291	59	180
	11	163	291	81	213	333	102	251	23	143	273
	18	253	29	176	296	64	201	346	106	234	13
	25	355	125	259	25	167	295	69	196	338	105
July	2	87	209	349	129	258	19	162	300	68	188
	9	171	293	90	229	341	211	261	32	151	282
	16	261	40	184	335	72	212	354	115	242	24
	23	5	133	268	35	176	303	78	207	347	113
	30	96	217	360	137	267	27	172	308	77	197
Aug.	6	180	309	99	230	350	120	271	40	161	290
	13	270	51	192	343	81	222	2	124	252	47
	20	14	142	276	45	185	312	86	217	356	123
	27	106	225	10	146	276	36	182	317	86	200
Sept.	3	189	317	109	238	360	128	281	48	170	299
	10	279	61	200	322	90	232	10	132	262	43
	17	23	151	284	56	193	321	94	228	4	133
	24	115	234	20	154	284	45	191	326	94	215
Oct.	1	198	325	120	246	9	136	291	56	179	308
	8	289	70	208	330	101	241	19	140	273	51
	15	31	160	292	66	201	330	102	238	12	140
	22	123	243	28	164	292	54	199	336	102	225
	29	207	334	130	254	17	146	301	64	187	318
Nov.	5	299	79	217	338	111	249	27	148	283	59
	12	39	169	300	76	210	339	111	247	21	148
	19	131	253	36	175	300	63	207	347	110	234
	26	215	343	139	262	25	153	310	73	195	329
Dec.	3	310	87	226	346	122	256	36	157	294	67
	10	48	177	310	85	219	347	121	255	31	156
	17	139	262	45	185	308	72	216	356	118	242
	24	223	355	148	271	33	167	318	81	203	340
	31	320	95	235	355	132	265	44	166	303	77

		1980	1981	1982	1983	1984	1985	1986	1987	1988	1989
Jan.	1	90	226	350	129	260	36	162	300	71	205
	8	176	315	89	225	346	126	260	35	156	297
	15	263	52	188	309	73	225	358	119	244	37
	22	4	148	272	35	176	319	82	206	348	129
	29	99	234	360	137	270	43	172	308	81	213
Feb.	5	184	324	98	234	354	135	270	44	164	306
	12	271	64	196	317	81	236	6	128	252	48
	19	14	157	280	45	185	328	90	217	356	138
	26	109	242	10	145	279	51	182	316	90	221
Mar.	5	204	332	108	242	15	143	281	52	185	313
	12	293	74	203	326	104	246	14	136	276	57
	19	37	166	288	55	208	337	98	227	18	147
	26	130	248	20	154	300	60	191	326	111	230
Apr.	2	213	340	119	250	24	151	291	60	194	322
	9	302	84	212	334	114	255	22	144	286	66
	16	46	175	296	66	216	346	106	237	27	156
	23	139	259	28	164	309	69	199	336	119	240
	30	222	349	130	258	33	160	302	68	203	331
May	7	312	93	221	342	124	264	31	152	297	74
	14	54	184	304	75	225	355	114	246	36	165
	21	147	268	36	175	317	78	207	347	127	249
	28	231	358	140	266	41	170	311	76	211	341
June	4	323	102	230	350	135	272	40	160	307	83
	11	63	193	313	84	234	3	123	255	45	173
	18	153	277	45	185	325	87	216	357	135	258
	25	239	8	149	275	49	180	320	85	219	352
July	2	334	110	239	359	145	280	49	169	317	92
	9	72	202	322	93	244	11	133	263	55	181
	16	163	286	54	196	333	96	225	7	143	266
	23	247	19	158	284	57	191	328	94	227	3
	30	344	119	248	7	155	289	57	178	327	101
Aug.	6	82	210	331	101	254	19	142	272	66	189
	13	171	294	64	205	341	104	236	16	152	274
	20	255	30	166	293	66	202	336	103	236	13
	27	353	128	256	17	164	299	65	187	335	111
Sept.	3	93	217	340	110	264	27	151	281	75	197
	10	180	302	75	214	350	112	247	24	160	282
	17	264	40	174	302	74	212	345	112	245	23
	24	1	138	264	26	173	309	73	197	343	112
Oct.	1	103	226	349	119	274	36	159	292	84	206
	8	189	310	85	222	359	120	258	32	169	291
	15	273	50	183	310	84	221	354	120	255	313
	22	10	148	272	35	181	319	81	206	352	130
	29	112	234	357	130	282	44	167	303	92	215
Nov.	5	198	318	96	230	8	129	268	40	178	300
	12	282	58	193	318	93	229	4	128	265	39
	19	18	158	280	44	190	328	90	214	2	139
	26	120	243	5	141	290	53	175	314	100	223
Dec.	3	206	327	106	238	16	139	277	49	185	310
	10	292	66	203	326	103	237	14	135	274	48
	17	28	167	288	52	200	337	98	222	12	154
	24	128	252	13	152	298	62	184	324	108	232
	31	214	337	114	248	24	149	285	59	193	320

		1990	1991	1992	1993	1994	1995	1996	1997	1998	1999
Jan.	1	333	110	242	15	145	281	53	185	317	92
	8	72	206	326	108	244	16	136	271	56	186
	15	167	289	54	210	337	99	225	21	147	270
	22	252	18	158	299	61	190	329	110	231	1
	29	343	119	251	23	155	290	62	193	326	101
Feb.	5	82	214	335	116	254	24	145	287	66	193
	12	175	298	63	220	345	108	235	31	155	278
	19	260	29	166	308	69	201	337	119	239	12
	26	353	128	260	32	163	299	70	202	335	117
Mar.	5	93	222	356	124	265	32	166	295	76	201
	12	183	306	87	229	354	116	259	39	164	285
	19	267	39	189	329	77	211	360	128	248	22
	26	1	138	280	41	172	310	90	212	343	121
Apr.	2	103	230	5	133	275	40	175	305	86	210
	9	192	314	98	237	3	124	270	47	173	294
	16	276	49	198	326	86	220	9	136	257	31
	23	9	147	288	50	180	320	- 98	221	351	132
	30	113	238	13	143	284	48	183	315	95	218
May	7	201	319	109	245	12	123	281	55	182	302
	14	285	58	207	335	95	228	18	144	267	39
	21	18	158	296	59	189	330	106	230	1	141
	28	122	247	21	154	292	57	191	326	103	227
June	4	210	330	119	253	21	141	291	64	190	312
	11	294	66	217	343	105	236	28	152	276	48
	18	27	168	304	68	199	339	114	238	11	150
	25	130	256	29	165	300	66	199	337	111	236
July	2	219	339	129	262	29	150	300	73	198	321
	9	304	74	227	350	114	245	38	160	285	57
	16	37	177	313	76	210	348	123	246	22	158
	23	133	265	38	175	309	75	208	347	120	245
	30	227	349	152	272	37	160	308	83	206	331
Aug.	6	310	83	237	359	123	255	48	169	294	67
	13	48	186	322	84	221	356	132	254	33	166
	20	147	273	47	185	318	83	218	356	129	253
	27	235	358	146	282	45	169	317	93	214	340
Sept.	3	321	93	246	7	131	265	56	177	302	78
	10	59	194	331	92	231	4	141	263	43	174
	17	156	281	56	194	327	91	228	5	138	260
	24	243	8	154	291	53	178	326	102	223	349
Oct.	1	329	104	254	16	139	276	64	186	310	89
	8	70	202	339	101	241	13	149	273	53	183
	15	165	289	66	202	337	99	238	13	148	269
	22	251	16	164	301	61	187	336	111	231	357
	29	337	115	262	25	148	287	72	195	318	99
Nov.	5	79	211	347	111	250	22	157	283	61	193
	12	175	297	76	211	346	107	247	22	157	277
	19	260	24	174	309	70	194	346	119	240	5
	26	345	126	270	33	157	297	80	203	328	109
Dec.	3	88	220	355	121	258	31	165	293	69	202
	10	185	305	85	220	355	115	256	31	165	286
	17	269	32	185	317	79	203	357	127	249	13
	24	355	135	278	54	166	292	89	211	338	117
	31	96	217	3	131	266	41	173	303	78	211

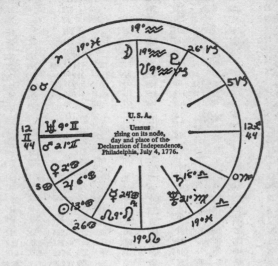

U.S.A.

Uranus
rising on its node,
day and place of the
Declaration of Independence,
Philadelphia, July 4, 1776.

This is the traditional Gemini-rising chart for the birth of the United States, showing on the ascendant the exact degree occupied by Uranus' North Node at that time, with the planet Uranus just above the ascendant, and thus almost exactly on his own node. Uranus contacts his own north node only once in about 85 years; the association of Uranus with Democracy as it was initiated on July 4, 1776, is signified in this chart, giving ascendant-prominence to the nodal position of Uranus at the time of the birth of the American Democracy. Note the exact mundane square of the Moon to the node of Uranus. See also the nodal charts on pages 183 (U.S.S.R.) and 201 (NAZI).

Table of Base Numbers

	Aries	Taurus	Gemini	Cancer	Leo	Virgo	Libra	Scorpio	Sagittarius	Capricorn	Pisces	Aquarius
0 deg.	0	30	60	90	120	150	180	210	240	270	300	330
1 deg.	1	31	61	91	121	151	181	211	241	271	301	331
2 deg.	2	32	62	92	122	152	182	212	242	272	302	332
3 deg.	3	33	63	93	123	153	183	213	243	273	303	332
4 deg.	4	34	64	94	124	154	184	214	244	274	304	334
5 deg.	5	35	65	95	125	155	185	215	245	275	305	335
6 deg.	6	36	66	96	126	156	186	216	246	276	306	336
7 deg.	7	37	67	97	127	157	187	217	247	277	307	337
8 deg.	8	38	68	98	128	158	188	218	248	278	308	338
9 deg.	9	39	69	99	129	159	189	219	249	279	309	339
10 deg.	10	40	70	100	130	160	190	220	250	280	310	340
11 deg.	11	41	71	101	131	161	191	221	251	281	311	341
12 deg.	12	42	72	102	132	162	192	222	252	282	312	342
13 deg.	13	43	73	103	133	163	193	223	253	283	313	343
14 deg.	14	44	74	104	134	164	194	224	254	284	314	344
15 deg.	15	45	75	105	135	165	195	225	255	285	315	345
16 deg.	16	46	76	106	136	166	196	226	256	286	316	346
17 deg.	17	47	77	107	137	167	197	227	257	287	317	347
18 deg.	18	48	78	108	138	168	198	228	258	288	318	348
19 deg.	19	49	79	109	139	169	199	229	259	289	319	349
20 deg.	20	50	80	110	140	170	200	230	260	290	320	350
21 deg.	21	51	81	111	141	171	201	231	261	291	321	351
22 deg.	22	52	82	112	142	172	202	232	262	292	322	352
23 deg.	23	53	83	113	143	173	203	233	263	293	323	353
24 deg.	24	54	84	114	144	174	204	234	264	294	324	354
25 deg.	25	55	85	115	145	175	205	235	265	295	325	355
26 deg.	26	56	86	116	146	176	206	236	266	296	326	356
27 deg.	27	57	87	117	147	177	207	237	267	297	327	357
28 deg.	28	58	88	118	148	178	208	238	268	298	328	358
29 deg.	29	59	89	119	149	179	209	239	269	299	329	359

Directions

1. Find your birth year in the tables (pages 136-148.

2. Run down the left-hand column and see if your date is there.

3. IF YOUR DATE IS IN THE LEFT-HAND COLUMN, run over this line till you come to the column under your birth year. Here you will find a number. This is your BASE NUMBER. Write it down, and go directly to the part of the directions below under the head-

ing, "What to Do with Your Base Number" on page 152.

4. IF YOUR BIRTH DATE IS NOT IN THE LEFT-HAND COLUMN, get a pencil and paper. Your birth date falls between two numbers in the left-hand column. Look at the date closest *after* your birth date, run over this line to your birth year. Write down the number you find there, and label it TOP NUMBER. Having done this, write directly beneath it on your piece of paper the number printed just above it in the table. Label this BOTTOM NUMBER.

SUBTRACT the bottom number from the top number. If the TOP NUMBER is smaller, add 360 to it and then subtract. The result is your DIFFERENCE.

5. Go back to the left-hand column and find the date next *before* your birth date. Determine the number of days between this date and your birth date by subtracting or counting on your fingers. Write this down and label it INTERVENING DAYS.

6. In the Table of Difference below, note which group your DIFFERENCE (found at 4 above) falls in.

Difference	Daily Motion
80-87	12 degrees
88-94	13 degrees
95-101	14 degrees
102-106	15 degrees

Note: if you were born in leap year *and* use the difference between February 26 and March 5, use the special table following:

Difference	Daily Motion
94-99	12 degrees
100-108	13 degrees
109-115	14 degrees
116-122	15 degrees

Write down the DAILY MOTION corresponding to your place in the proper Table of Difference above.

7. Multiply this daily motion by the number labeled INTERVENING DAYS (found at 5, above).

8. Add the result of 7 to your BOTTOM NUMBER (under 4). The result of this is your BASE NUMBER. If it is more than 360, subtract 360 from it and call the result your BASE NUMBER.

What to Do with Your Base Number

Turn to the Table of Base NUMBERS (page 150) and locate your Base Number in it. At the top of the column you will find the SIGN your Moon WAS IN. At the left you will find the DEGREE your Moon occupied at—

7 A.M. of your birth date if you were born under Eastern Standard Time

6 A.M. of your birth date if you were born under Central Standard Time

5 A.M. of your birth date if you were born under Mountain Standard Time

4 A.M. of your birth date if you were born under Pacific Standard Time

If you don't know the hour of your birth, accept this as your Moon's sign and degree.

IF YOU DO KNOW THE HOUR OF YOUR BIRTH, get the exact degree as follows:

If you were born *after* 7 A.M., Eastern Standard Time (6 A.M. Central Standard Time, etc.), determine the number of hours after this time that you were born. Divide this by two. *Add* this to your BASE NUMBER, and the result in the table will be the exact degree and sign of the Moon on the year, month, date, and hour of your birth.

If you were born *before* 7 A.M., E.S.T. (6 A.M. C.S.T., etc.), determine the number of hours before that time that you were born. Divide this by two. *Subtract* this from your base number, and the result in the table will be the exact degree and sign of the Moon on the year, month, date and hour of your birth.

RECORD THIS IN ITS PROPER PLACE ON YOUR RECORD CHART. THE NUMBER AT THE TOP OF THE COLUMN, WITH THE SIGN'S NAME, TELLS YOU THE PARAGRAPH TO READ FOR AN INTERPRETATION OF THE MOON'S INFLUENCE ON YOU.

13. MOON IN ARIES

You are best satisfied by a picture of yourself as an independent thinker, a mental force, a person of intellectual or physical daring and courage. The truth is important to you—the truth, that is, as you see it individualistically, which may or may not bear a relation to proved facts. Your message to yourself is: *Be strong, be forceful, be independent, be brave;* and so powerful is this lunar position that you are likely to become these things in some degree even if your Sun sign tries to make you a Caspar Milquetoast. The meek and mild gentleman with the bar of steel inside him very likely has Moon in Aries; likewise the sweet lady who looks as if butter wouldn't melt in her mouth and nevertheless rules her husband ruthlessly. This is one of the positions in which the Moon can be strong enough to take the dominance of the nature away from the Sun and cause you actually to become in the outer world what you imagine yourself to be. You may do this slowly, with quiet firmness, or swiftly, with bluster and braggadocio. You think well of yourself, and any trend to inferiority-feeling indicated elsewhere in the Vitasphere is more than likely to meet its match here. This is a weak position only if the Sun is in Libra, in which case the dictates of the Sun must be followed and the lunar instincts ignored. In any case, the studious development of mental powers, through formal education and a willingness to use your mind power to rule yourself rather than to rule others, is essential to your success and happiness.

14. MOON IN TAURUS

Your image of yourself is flattering not because of any special quality you select so much as because you just think well of yourself. This can make for smugness, conceit and laziness; and it always warns you not to take too seriously what you tell yourself, but to keep your eye on what other people think of you. Follow your Sun-nature energetically or you will be lost in relaxation and uselessness. You have such a good time being pleased with life! You need to stimulate yourself consciously, for you are not a self-starter. You're likely to be popular because, demanding little of yourself, you also demand little of others and are the most agreeable of companions. You are not likely to be ardent in human relations; you take what comes, especially if it isn't too much trouble. Your assumption that you have the good things of life coming to you generally is carried out in the facts; you seem to make your picture of yourself as a luxurious creature come true in material affairs. When you have learned to follow aggressively your solar urges, when you are determined to be before the world the best that your Sun-sign has to offer, you go far. You then turn self-satisfaction into active self-confidence, and you can have the world at your feet. The danger is that, sensing this, you won't ever do anything about it, will remain content in knowing you could if you would, and thus never be anything but a gracious, affable and charming person. And, of course, that's not to be sneezed at.

15. MOON IN GEMINI

Nothing ever loses any fat in the telling when you tell it, and the tales of your own prowess and ability that you tell yourself are tall indeed. The picture of yourself that pleases you best is that you are a great intellect to which the world listens gratefully. To be as intellectual as you would like to be is a big order and may take more application than you are willing to put in on it. Cleverness pleases you better than profundity. You would rather be funny than fair, exciting than stable, provocative than learned. Said George Bernard Shaw, with Moon in Gemini, "My method is to take the utmost trouble to find the right thing to say, and then to say it with the utmost levity." The great wit told the truth in the latter half of this statement, but it is much to be doubted if anyone with the Moon in Gemini ever took "the utmost trouble" over anything. You don't have to. What you want doesn't take trouble: if it did, you wouldn't want it, and you would find excellent, clever, sophistical reasons why it would be silly to want it. You are a master of chop-logic, of making the worse appear the better cause, and of making yourself appear the best cause in the world. Being articulate, loving to have your words applauded, you go to the limit of your capacity and will not stop going till you have extracted the maximum from life according to your tastes and your abilities. By spreading yourself thin, you cover a prodigious amount of ground, collect hosts of "friends" (whom another might think of as mere acquaintances), please yourself mightily and appear more dashing, popular and successful than many an honest soul who, with deep integrity, has dug consistently in one spot to strike more valuable, if less flashy, ore.

16. MOON IN CANCER

You take yourself very seriously, as a person to be reckoned with. You feel that you understand others and that you deserve to be understood yourself; yet you frequently feel misunderstood. Things are very clear to you; your intuitions are powerful, and whether right or wrong, they convince you utterly and are likely to control your actions. Sometimes your hunches are away off the track, especially if emotions are involved. You regard your inner nature as something precious, to be guarded from the "slings and arrows of outrageous fortune," and are all too likely to think the slings and arrows are aimed at you when no one else in the world is thinking about you. You exude a desire to be understood, to be loved—also, to understand, and to love, if you have objectified your approach, which you must do if you are to be happy or successful. Your tendency is to withdraw, to meditate, and meditation often turns to brooding, brooding to depression. Activate your sympathies by becoming interested in others. Deserve their understanding by acting so that they can understand with approval. Forget yourself, your emotions, your reactions; harness your instincts to other people's problems or to creative work in business, science or the arts. To *use,* to *become,* to *prove,* to *love* must replace in your nature the deep tendency to be content with to *have,* to *be,* to *know,* to *expect.* No doors are closed to you when you have turned your understanding outward to the world—and no doors are open to you when you turn it exclusively inward. Know your self first, through pain and struggle if necessary, and once you know it, don't brood about it; get to know something else.

17. MOON IN LEO

The portrait you paint of yourself is heroic and towers above the world you inhabit. To live up to the level of your inner picture is a lifetime job requiring energy, courage and considerable sense of the drama of existence. Private satisfactions are not very important to you; you are less introspective than most. You want to see the tangible evidence of success, and like it best if the rest of the world can see it, too. You are a bit of a show-off, but since you are utterly honest with yourself, you can laugh at your own vanities, even when they remain important. You want valuable possessions, well-groomed children, good clothes, accomplishments and evidences of accomplishment that others can applaud. Your desires are basically simple, and your methods of getting them direct; you know what you want and are willing to make sacrifices for them. You won't sacrifice personal integrity, however, or honor, which are the intangibles that do matter to you. Education, culture, art, music, however, matter less. You can take 'em or leave 'em alone; and ten to one, if you do take 'em, it isn't because they really feed your soul, but because you think evidence of such a soul will in some way add to your prestige. Throughout your life you will strive to fulfill an image of yourself which is less a portrait than a statue dominating the landscape of your life by its size, its beauty, the dramatic quality of its setting and the colorful beauty of its trappings. And in becoming this statue you are likely to become a lot of other more spiritual things which you don't even desire and which are added to you because of the honest workmanship that goes into your self-sculpture.

18. MOON IN VIRGO

You look upon yourself as an intelligent and useful person, and pretty generally turn out to be that, if not also a great deal more. You have no desire to rule the world or other people or even to make a great splash before them. In fact, you prefer not to be in the limelight, and if you find yourself in it, it is by accident, because you have earned it by the integrity of your private labors. Your wish is *to serve,* and in whatever sphere you may be you will find the chance to do it. Your personality, while strong and stable, does not obtrude itself on others; you don't make loud noises or ask personal questions, yet people feel your presence, value your reserve, and are likely to make you their confidant. You have an acute sense of your own worth which you base in a sense of your intelligence. Yet you can value other people who are far from intelligent. You are an intellectual snob only so far as you are concerned, and here you apply the theory of *noblesse oblige* to realms of the mind, demanding of yourself that you belong to the aristocracy of the intellect so that you may better understand all things, and serve those who can't. In fulfilling this quiet and modest picture, you are likely to run into some pleasant surprises. You don't really expect other people to take you very seriously, and are therefore delighted and amazed when they do, and you see your dreams of yourself coming true in the sight of the whole world.

19. MOON IN LIBRA

This is a Cinderella position, for no matter what humble hearth you may slave over, the vision of yourself as you see it is one of elegance, grace and refinement. So strong is this vision, so eager are you to make it a reality, and so genuine is the aristocracy of your spirit that more likely than not the fairy godmother (who is no more than the angel of your own graces) actually appears to carry you to the heights you dream of. You are one of nature's gentlefolk, and the privileged picture of yourself that you carry in your heart finds its expression in courtesy, graciousness and kindness to everyone. You should never forget your best dream of yourself, or allow the true kindliness and gentleness of your nature to be balked by a blustering exterior. *Dare to be true* should be your motto. Your courage should be the courage of sympathy and understanding, which you have in such great abundance. Be no more and no less than your heart tells you to be: your instincts are sound, especially in the realm of human relations, and since your special genius lies in this realm, you should follow your instincts unfalteringly. This position gives a peculiar elusive sweetness to the nature, a curious charm to the speech and manner, and allows the best of the inner self to shine before the world, which is brightened and made happier by it. It strengthens the chart of a woman by giving elegance to the expression of the feminine graces; and, in a man, adds depth, strength and character to his masculinity if he is not ashamed to admit to the gentler qualities he possesses.

20. MOON IN SCORPIO

You take yourself seriously, conjuring up the image of a profound, wise and consequential person. To live up to this private picture in reality is a lifetime task, for you are your own accusing angel; your spirit stands aloof from the antics of your body, criticizing often, approving sometimes, always holding before the eyes of your soul a standard of profundity and depth which the poor flesh does not always achieve. Your standards are moral only in the highest and most general sense, with the morality of heaven and hell rather than of the confining flesh. You may be, or may become, angelic; but in the process you may first be the devil's child, following your instincts even to the brink of The Pit, strong in the consciousness that "if I am the devil's child, I must do as the devil bids." A mystic strength enshrouds you even in weakness; you are supported by inner, perhaps unexpressed, convictions; you know what you're doing, even when no one else in the world does, when your physical body acts strangely, and when your brain and your speech refuse to explain, even to yourself. There is a good deal of martyr in you; if you get the idea that your special genius requires a destructive course, you will follow it with whole-souled intensity, to the despair of your rational nature and all your friends. By the same token, if you get the idea that your genius requires self-betterment, self-sacrifice, even to monasticism, you will follow that, often to great heights. Your will is powerful; it will always work over-time on the side of the image you conjure of yourself. To conjure a high image which requires controlled ac-tions for its realization is your way to control of self and others and to the high successes of which you are capable.

21. MOON IN SAGITTARIUS

Whatever mundane tasks your life may be occu-pied with, your spirit will range the earth and the uni-verse, adventuring in the high hills and among the stars themselves. And to whatever task you bring your tal-ents, you will touch it with a universality of approach; for the effort of your soul is to identify itself with large and broad concepts, and you will do it from whatever base your feet of clay must rest in. You are acutely aware of the limitations of the flesh, of the height of your desires, and of the "wide gulf that exists be-tween intention and performance." In its worst form you will dedicate your life to making the paving bricks of hell: good intentions; and get no further. You always "mean well," and when you don't succeed, it is because your goal has been too lofty. "Not failure, but low aim is crime": no one understands this better than you. When you also understand that setting an unattainable goal is one of the means of escaping responsibility, you will be on the highroad to self-knowledge and therefore success. You must make your goal high, but possible of achievement; and you must learn to gear your methods to the tools that you can lay your hands on. Your soar-ing spirit is all too likely to ignore realities, to consider itself above good and evil, above the dust of earthly competition, secure in the mansions of the blessed to which you don't have to earn the key. Or you can go to the other extreme, envision high things, and so despair of achievement. You must take your picture of yourself as a broad and deep person, and paint it in earthly oils on a practical canvas. When you have learned the technique of life-as-it-is, you will be able to make your image of yourself stand forth in the light and color of success for all to see as clearly as you see it yourself.

22. MOON IN CAPRICORN

You conceive yourself as a practical, hardheaded individual who can compete successfully with the world on its own terms and who finds therein his deepest satisfaction and greatest success. The game itself, rather than the stakes, interests you; you aren't likely to be grasping of money, but you will fasten onto all the power in sight. The security of your soul lies in authority. As a result your chances of success are great, because you don't have to do any play-acting in looking for it: the contest is the very breath of your spirit. Some of the greatest leaders of the world have Moon in Capricorn, and owe their success to the image of success that always plays on their mind. Sad are the cases of Moon in Capricorn who get the image inverted: whose great inner need is no less for success, but who feel themselves frustrated and incapable ever of achieving it, and who in consequence become bitter and hard in failure. The free flow of your intuitions, if you don't try too hard, will carry you where you want to go. Your instinct may not be for kindness, charity, fellowship, love, but in your depths you won't miss these when you command authority and respect. Dare to be yourself, to seek what you want by the means that are required, even if being true to yourself means being false to softer things required by softer people. You are cast for a certain role and must play in character if you are to get yourself over the footlights. You can't sway the audience by acting another part: they spot phoniness quickly. But they will recognize the power of your true role when you play it truly. And, as you must never forget, to win recognition as an important and powerful person is the deep desire of your heart.

23. MOON IN AQUARIUS

You'd like to be a force for social good, and will strive in whatever sphere you move to live up to this ideal of yourself. Whatever errors you make are likely to be forgiven because people know you mean well. They may tire after a while of good intentions gone wrong; but you'll be given another chance where less whole-souled mortals are condemned or laughed off. You are a poet of life, rather than a philosopher: you feel instinctively the needs of human beings and that they must be satisfied. You may be a social theorist, but more likely you are just a social worker, as a humane avocation and hobby, if not as a profession. In helping others, you satisfy your deepest inner needs; and thus you don't even care if you are imposed on: that money has been misused is less important to you than that your heart was in the right place. In fulfilling this image of yourself as "friend of all the world" you can become a great force for good, and in whatever circle you move you will be sure to make your influence felt in behalf of a humane understanding of human needs and human relations. Outside of charity itself, your understanding extends to social life, to make you charming, gracious, lively. To make the world a better and happier place is your path to satisfying your picture of yourself—and a pleasant path it is, as anyone knows who shares it with you.

24. MOON IN PISCES

To achieve wisdom, to dwell in the high secluded valley of Shangri-la, to know yourself and your relation to the universe, to be in tune with the infinite, and to be recognized as a person of understanding: these are the constant aims of your life, in the fulfillment of which you satisfy most truly your esoteric picture of yourself. If you want material things, it is so that your study and contemplation may be comfortable, untroubled by worry over security; and if material things are hard to get, you are capable of achieving a philosophy that makes them unnecessary to your contentment and self-development, which is always the kernel of your nut of life. On the other hand, if material things come easily, if circumstances and your total personality conspire to start you on an upward spiral toward success, your inner nature will tell you that success and luxury are, for some deep spiritual reason, your due; and the comfort they bring your spirit may lend you power in getting more and more of them. In no case, however, are material concerns of first import to your deepest and truest self, whose search is always for self-knowledge, self-understanding and self-fulfillment in the intangible sense that depends on nothing outside of you. You are unhappy only when you violate, in action, thought, word, some truth that is essential to you, or when you realize you have acted counter to the dictates of your own self-taught wisdom. Too continuous violation of your own code causes brooding and deep unhappiness, and thus your only sure path to contentment, which is your success, is to make sure that you adhere always to the wisdom already acquired, and build stone by stone toward that high pyramid of wisdom in the completion of which is your success.

THE PLANETS

The planets are the antennae and arms of the Vitasphere, of which the body and soul are the Sun and Moon. No planet will ever cause you to act counter to the testimony of the Sun and Moon in their combined influence on you. Remember this when you proceed with the following readings. All planetary vibration must be considered in light of the basic solar-lunar readings, for these are your character, your basic nature, which the planets will help or hinder but cannot materially change.

According to the sign position of your Sun, one planet will be more important than the others and should probably be read first.

If your Sun is in—	*Your dominant planet will be*
Aries	Mars
Taurus	Venus
Gemini	Mercury
Cancer	The Moon
Leo	The Sun
	(also Mars and Jupiter)
Virgo	Mercury
Libra	Venus
Scorpio	Mars
Sagittarius	Jupiter
Capricorn	Saturn
Aquarius	Saturn
	(and Uranus)
Pisces	Jupiter
	(and Neptune)

Not only the action of this ruling planet will be very important in your life, but also the attribute over which it rules. Thus Gemini, ruled by Mercury, lives a great deal in the senses; Libra, ruled by Venus, responds most readily to emotional stimuli; and so on. Study your ruler carefully, whether you read it now or come up to it in normal order.

Remember in all planetary readings that they work within the pattern of your solar-lunar nature; never against it. The synthesis of your Vitasphere from a series of paragraphs to a working unit depends on your keeping this in mind, which will enable you to weld all the readings into a unified and significant whole.

MERCURY

Mercury is the sense-impression antennae of your Vitasphere. His position by sign indicates your reactions to sights, sounds, odors, tastes and touch impressions, affording a key to the attitude you have toward the physical world around you. Mercury is the messenger through which your physical body and brain (the Sun) and your inner nature (the Moon) are kept in contact with the outer world, which will appear to you according to the index of Mercury's position by sign in the Vitasphere.

Get Mercury's sign position from the tables on

pages 172–183, record the sign in your birth record, and read the indicated paragraph.

(Please note that just as the planets appear, occasionally, to retrace their path through the constellations (i.e., to *retrogress*), the table occasionally retraces its steps. For example, if you were born in 1925 between March 13 and March 30, Mercury was in Aries, moving on to Taurus between April 1 and April 15. Then Mercury returned to Aries (April 16 to May 16) and Taurus (May 17 to June 6), before proceeding through Gemini, Cancer, and the rest.)

25. MERCURY IN ARIES

Your reaction to sense impressions is keen and alert. You detect smells, sounds, sights and tastes acutely and are very much alive to what you do or don't like in the world of sense impressions. Your sense of touch is not as alert as the others, though you are capable of training this sense if one of the others is served by it. Thus you can develop the sensitive fingers of a musician (violinist or pianist), making your touch serve hearing; or the robust hands of a sculptor, to make touch serve sight. Your reaction to sense impressions is personal; you interpret what you sense in the light of your ego, and are a scientific observer only if your total ego development is along these lines. Generally you will be impressed by, and remember, what serves your purposes, let the chips fall where they may. Sound is very important to you and you should strive to live only amid harmonious and agreeable sounds. Cultivate the habit of listening to music, for sound penetrates directly to your ego centers, and if it is harmonious, serves to harmonize your whole nature.

26. MERCURY IN TAURUS

You are eye-minded; that is, you get your maximum sense contact with the world through sight rather than through sound. You get more from reading a book than from hearing a lecture. Silent movies are almost as good for you as talkies. Since what you see is important, you will always strive to make your surroundings as attractive as possible, and for this reason your home, or your office, will have some beauty about it even when it gets disorderly. Touch is well developed, and you visualize through your fingers—get an image in the dark of something touched, know how a fabric will look by feeling it—and conversely, how it will feel by looking at it. Taste and smell are fairly well marked, and hearing worst of all. You can shut out sound from your life and live calmly through a hurricane or the squawking of children that would drive others to distraction. You don't hear the sound of your voice accurately, and sometimes sound like you don't feel for this reason. Study elocution, and learn to pay attention to what meets your ears.

27. MERCURY IN GEMINI

All the senses are keen and alert. The ability to react to shades of difference of light, color and sound makes you sensitive to beauty and needful of gratifying your senses with art (visual) and music (auditory). Too great awareness of everything that goes on around you tires your nerves, and you need solitude and dim lights once in a while to give your senses a vacation. You frequently give the impression of a hound snuffing the air to catch some scent in it—of having all your "feelers" out for whatever is going on. Your sense reactions are impersonal, detached and critical; you have likes and dislikes, but they don't elate or depress you. To you it is joyous to live in a world that continuously gives exercise to your senses; you know that a sight, sound or smell that you don't like isn't going to plague you forever—another that you like better will replace it; and even this, too will go its way and should not be mourned, because something else is tripping over its heels to get into the limelight.

28. MERCURY IN CANCER

What you hear, smell, taste, feel and see are of intimate and close concern to you. You are sensitive to every breath of air; you take it to your heart and cherish your reaction to it. The smell of the garbage truck is a personal affront to your nostrils, while the rose was created exclusively to delight the same. Loud noises persecute you, and you tend to think they were made for that purpose; while music is art's personal gift to you alone. You adopt the beauty of the landscape as if no one ever looked on it with true worship before. This personalizing of sense impressions can make you an awful fuss-budget, and also a bore if you insist on telling everyone how much you love, or hate, everything. On the other hand, the sensitiveness of your reactions and the intimacy with which you regard them make you capable of creative power, for art is only the personalized sense impressions of the artist, absorbed into the total personality and given forth in form. Add a point of view to your tendency to gush, develop a philosophy of beauty to give weight to your natural appreciation; learn to make sense impressions your own, and then release them into a significance larger than personal, and you have all the ingredients to make you a master in one of the arts.

29. MERCURY IN LEO

Your reaction to sense impressions from the outer world is less important than the way you react to the sound of your own voice, the figure you are cutting in the world. You see yourself in everything you see. You're hard to impress, for though you are detached enough in some ways, you haven't got your antennae tuned outward and just don't take in a lot that goes on. Your viewpoint is pretty fixed, and what comes to the senses is related to it. For this reason you aren't a very good observer. The outer world of sight, hearing, taste, smell and touch has to fight its way through a sort of steel plate before it reaches the brain centers and causes a reaction. Your reactions are slow, not because you are stupid, but because you aren't interested. You must cultivate attention, become consciously aware of the world around you, and develop your faculties, which are sound enough but need more exercise than you give them.

30. MERCURY IN VIRGO

Sense impressions never reach you till they have been interpreted. What you see, hear, smell, taste and feel is swiftly given significance before it arrives at the reacting center of the brain. You never see just a chair; you see a beautiful chair, an old chair, a charming chair, a chair that looks comfortable or uncomfortable. You never hear just a noise; before you have heard it, it has been labeled pleasant or raucous or sweet or whatever. Your senses take the impression, hold it for ransom, and say to the brain, "Name it and you can have it." Thus you tend to card-index and catalogue every sense experience that comes to you. This leads to boredom, because pretty soon everything drops into its own niche and there is nothing new under the sun. Your pleasure in the physical world thus tends to diminish as life wears on, and through too much intellectualizing you can lose the zest for life. To get it back, try to regard things for their own sake. Remember that "a rose by any other name would smell as sweet" and that you get more fun out of a kiss if you don't think of it as a deception of Nature to encourage reproduction. Exorcise the demon of words from the temple of nature, and in the name of simple animal enjoyment, throw away the dictionary!

31. MERCURY IN LIBRA

Sense impressions reach you through a strict moral and aesthetic censor. You see, hear, taste, smell and feel with the proprieties of art and society in mind, and have few sensory reactions that do not have to submit to this type of judgment. A color is not just red to you; it is a warm red, or a cold red, or a beautiful or ugly red. Further, in addition to the artistic standard, you apply the standard of good taste, and what you see or hear will revolt you if it doesn't conform with your idea of what is "out of the top drawer." You are a kind of sensation snob, and the simple meaning of sense experience is likely to be lost on you if it in any way offends the standards of nicety you set up for yourself. Needless to say, you are very sensitive to odors and all kinds of physical surroundings. Your house must be spick-and-span (so that your sight will not be offended); noises if any must be subdued and quiet (not to affront

your ears); the odors of cookery must not penetrate to
the living room (for your nose's sake); what you eat
must be seasoned just so (or your tongue and maybe
your stomach by attraction will revolt); and last, but not
least, your wife's face and hands must be smooth
(even if she has to do the cooking and the laundry), so
that your reaction will be pleasant when you touch her.
All these niceties can make you fussy, but, if turned to
their best use, make you gentle, considerate of others,
and gifted in one or more of the arts where your great
sensitivity is translated to creations that reflect it in
beauty.

32. MERCURY IN SCORPIO

You see, hear, experience with the legalistic attitude of a judge. Anything that stands before the bar
of your senses isn't likely to get off easily, for you
interpret critically what passes before your eyes, and
not always kindly. As a result, when you give expression to your judgment, you may earn the reputation
for having a sharp tongue. Your powers of observation
are acute; you have the eye of an eagle, and a kind of
permanent awareness of what is going on around you
makes it impossible for anyone to put anything over on
you. You have eyes in the back of your head, and a
sixth sense tells you things that the other five miss.
Criticism is part of your process of taking in the world,
and you never take in much of it without passing judgment in the process. You observe accurately but not
always charitably; the nerve channels through which
impressions reach the brain are apparently filled with
acid which eats away the superficialities that impress
others and leaves only the stark realities to be recorded
on your cerebellum. You are therefore a first-class cri-
tic and debunker, seeing through phoniness, sham and
pretension and, since your eyes and ears rarely deceive
you, pretty generally getting to the truth of what goes
on.

33. MERCURY IN SAGITTARIUS

You tend to overlook what is right before your
eyes, to neglect what is shouting right in your ear, be-

cause your attention is on bigger, or anyway farther-off, things. You don't see details. Sometimes you don't hear little squibs of conversation and thus miss the whole point. Your senses were wool-gathering or else fixed your attention on something else. They are keen enough, but tend to scatter; they do not need to be sharpened so much as they need to be directed. Your feet may stumble because your eyes missed the rock in the path; you get bumped by a trolley car because you didn't hear the bell. No doubt you were listening to or looking at something more important. To fix your attention, to gain dominion over the direction in which your senses are pointed, is to achieve success, for your senses are sharp enough and require only more care in the use of them.

34. MERCURY IN CAPRICORN

You never miss a trick. You can hear the grass grow, see out of the back of your head, smell garlic three blocks off, taste the faintest suggestion of flavoring, and feel the difference in the diameter of two hairs. Your sense impressions are right down to earth: you see, etc., things for what they are, without any ifs, buts or ands. You don't intrude any judgment, any moral or aesthetic or social code, between yourself and reality. Morals and judgment may exist in your life, but they have no bearing, in your mind, on things. A sofa is a sofa. A bed is a bed. The moral aspect of these pieces of useful furniture will not occur to you till someone else thinks of it. Your practical reaction to sense impressions makes your viewpoint the realest and sanest in the world, and you can often help others to get down to cases by calling them back from irrelevant details to a contemplation of the real thing under discussion.

35. MERCURY IN AQUARIUS

All your senses are keen, alert, strong and sensitive. There is a robustness about your contemplation of the real world that is not injured by a very keen sense of beauty. Your great ability is to see beauty in things without finding it necessary to deny their reality. Conversely, you make all useful things as beautiful as possible; and thus believe in the utility of art and the art of utility. Nothing real is likely to be offensive to you if it has a use; you will smell the odors of a pigsty less than others because you are thinking of bacon rather than of filth. But on the other hand, the beauty of an army will leave you cold because you will shudder at the slaughter. Your sense reactions are conditioned by a rugged and realistic approach to experience that causes you to regard everything you see, hear and touch in the light of your appraisal of its utilitarian and artistic merits, and little reaches you through the senses without passing through this nicely balanced court of values.

36. MERCURY IN PISCES

Your sensitiveness to impressions from the outer world is conditioned by the use they can be to you personally. You see, hear, feel and taste what you want to. If you want to like a pie (because someone you love made it for you), it will actually taste to you like the best pie in the world. If you want to dislike a drawing (because someone you dislike drew it), it will look hideous to you. Your approach to things is far from scientific; you have to struggle to exercise an objective judgment—to see anything for its own sake, without the intrusion of some personal irrelevancy that alters your vision and therefore your judgment. If your best friend has the voice of a screech owl, you'll think it music; and if your worst enemy were a Caruso, you'd actually believe he was singing off key. Depersonalization of the approach to life is what you need to study, if you are to see the world as it is and not see always in it a reflection of yourself. You probably think you are the fairest-minded person in the world, and may be as far as abstract justice is concerned. But in what reaches you through your senses, beware of the intrusion of personal biases. Let a spade be a spade. Even if it is digging your own grave, you can't make it into a screwdriver by wishing you didn't have to die!

	ARIES 25	TAURUS 26	GEMINI 27	CANCER 28	LEO 29	VIRGO 30
1870	4/2-4/16	4/17-5/1	5/2-7/9	7/10-7/24	7/25-8/9	8/10-8/28
1871	3/25-4/8	4/9-6/13	6/14-7/2	7/3-7/16	7/17-8/1	8/2-8/26 9/12-10/9
1872	3/16-3/31 5/4-5/12	4/1-5/3 5/13-6/7	6/8-6/22	6/23-7/7	7/8-7/26	7/27-10/1
1873	3/8-5/14	5/15-5/31	6/1-6/14	6/15-6/30	7/1-9/7	9/8-9/23
1874	3/3-3/16 4/18-5/7	5/8-5/22	5/23-6/5	6/6-6/25 7/30-8/10	6/26-7/29 8/11-8/30	8/31-9/15
1875	4/14-4/30	5/1-5/14	5/15-5/30	5/31-8/7	8/8-8/22	8/23-9/8
1876	4/6-4/20	4/21-5/5	5/6-7/12	7/13-7/29	7/30-8/13	8/14-8/31
1877	3/29-4/12	4/13-4/29	4/30-7/6	7/7-7/20	7/21-8/5	8/6-8/26 10/1-10/10
1878	3/21-4/4	4/5-6/12	6/13-6/28	6/29-7/12	7/13-7/29	7/30-10/5
1879	3/13-4/1 4/13-5/16	4/2-4/12 5/17-6/5	6/6-6/19	6/20-7/4	7/5-7/25 8/25-9/10	7/26-8/24 9/11-9/28
1880	3/5-5/11	5/12-5/27	5/28-6/10	6/11-6/27	6/28-9/3	9/4-9/19
1881	4/16-5/4	5/5-5/18	5/19-6/2	6/3-6/28 7/10-8/10	6/29-7/9 8/11-8/26	8/27-9/11
1882	4/10-4/26	4/27-5/10	5/11-5/28	5/29-8/3	8/4-8/18	8/19-9/4
1883	4/3-4/17	4/18-5/2	5/3-7/10	7/11-7/26	7/27-8/10	8/11-8/29
1884	3/25-4/8	4/9-4/30 5/13-6/13	5/1-5/12 6/14-7/2	7/3-7/16	7/17-8/2	8/3-8/25
1885	3/17-4/1	4/2-6/9	6/10-6/24	6/25-7/8	7/9-7/27	7/28-10/2
1886	3/9-5/15	5/16-6/1	6/2-6/15	6/16-7/1	7/2-7/28 8/7-9/8	7/29-8/6 9/9-9/24
1887	3/3-3/22 4/18-5/9	5/10-5/24	5/25-6/7	6/8-6/26	6/27-9/1	9/2-9/17
1888	4/14-4/30	5/1-5/14	5/15-5/30	5/31-8/7	8/8-8/22	8/23-9/8
1389	4/7-4/22	4/23-5/6	5/7-5/28 6/16-7/12	5/29-6/15 7/13-7/30	7/31-8/14	8/15-9/1
1890	3/31-4/13	4/14-4/30	5/1-7/7	7/8-7/22	7/23-8/6	8/7-8/26
1891	3/22-4/5	4/6-6/13	6/14-6/29	6/30-7/13	7/14-7/30	7/31-10/7
1892	3/13-3/30 4/20-5/15	3/31-4/19 5/16-6/5	6/6-6/20	6/21-7/4	7/5-7/25 8/30-9/9	7/26-8/29 9/10-9/29

	LIBRA 31	SCORPIO 32	SAGITTARIUS 33	CAPRICORN 34	AQUARIUS 35	PISCES 36
1870	8/29-11/3	11/4-11/22	11/23-12/11	1/1-1/5 12/12-12/31	1/6-3/14	3/15-4/1
1871	8/27-9/11 10/10-10/27	10/28-11/14	11/15-12/4	1/16-2/14 12/5-12/31	1/1-1/15 2/15-3/7	3/8-3/24
1872	10/2-10/18	10/19-11/6	11/7-11/30 12/12-12/31	1/1-2/9 12/1-12/11	2/10-2/28	2/29-3/15
1873	9/24-10/11	10/12-10/31	1/1-1/11 11/1-11/31	1/12-2/1	2/2-2/19	2/20-3/7
1874	9/16-10/4	10/5-10/30 11/8-12/10	1/1-1/5 10/31-11/7 12/11-12/30	1/6-1/25 12/31	1/26-2/11	2/12-3/2 3/17-4/17
1875	9/9-9/28 11/6-11/10	9/29-11/5 11/11-12/3	12/4-12/23	1/1-1/17 12/24-12/31	1/18-2/4	2/5-4/13
1876	9/1-11/6	11/7-11/25	11/26-12/14	1/1-1/10 12/15-12/31	1/11-2/2 2/6-3/16	2/3-2/6 3/17-4/5
1877	8/27-9/30 10/11-10/31	11/1-11/18	11/19-12/7	1/1-1/2 2/3-2/13 12/8-12/31	1/3-2/2 2/14-3/11	3/12-3/28
1878	10/6-10/23	10/24-11/11	11/12-12/2 12/30-12/31	1/1-2/12 12/3-12/29	2/13-3/3	3/4-3/20
1879	9/29-10/16	10/17-11/4	1/1-1/13 11/5-12/31	1/14-2/6	2/7-2/24	2/25-3/12
1880	9/20-10/7	10/8-10/29 11/25-12/12	1/1-1/10 10/30-11/24 12/13-12/31	1/11-1/30	1/31-2/16	2/17-3/4
1881	9/12-10/1	10/2-12/7	1/1-1/3 12/8-12/26	1/4-1/21 12/27-12/31	1/22-2/8	2/9-4/15
1882	9/5-9/27 10/23-11/10	9/28-10/22 11/11-11/30	12/1-12/19	1/1-1/14 12/20-12/31	1/15-2/1 2/26-3/17	2/2-2/25 3/18-4/9
1883	8/30-11/4	11/5-11/23	11/24-12/12	1/1-1/7 12/13-12/31	1/8-3/15	3/16-4/2
1884	8/26-9/16 10/10-10/27	9/17-10/9 10/28-11/15	11/16-12/4	1/1 1/21-2/14 12/5-12/31	1/2-1/20 2/15-3/7	3/8-3/24
1885	10/3-10/19	10/20-11/8	11/9-11/30 12/17-12/31	1/1-2/9 12/1-12/16	2/10-2/28	3/1-3/16
1886	9/25-10/12	10/13-11/1	1/1-1/12 11/2-12/31	1/13-2/3	2/4-2/20	2/21-3/8
1887	9/18-10/5 11/14-12/11	10/6-10/29	1/1-1/7 10/30-11/13 12/12-12/31	1/8-1/26	1/27-2/13	2/14-3/2 3/23-4/17
1888	9/9-9/28	9/29-12/4	12/5-12/23	1/1-1/19 12/24-12/31	1/20-2/5	2/6-4/13
1889	9/2-9/27 10/9-11/8	9/28-10/8 11/9-11/27	11/28-12/16	1/1-1/10 12/17-12/31	1/11-1/30 2/12-3/17	1/31-2/11 3/18-4/6
1890	8/27-11/1	11/2-11/19	11/20-12/9	1/1-1/4 12/10-12/31	1/5-3/12	3/13-3/30
1891	10/8-10/24	10/25-11/12	11/13-12/2	1/1 1/7-2/13 12/3-12/31	1/2-1/6 2/14-3/5	3/6-3/21
1892	9/30-10/16	10/17-11/4	1/3-1/13 11/5-12/31	1/1-1/2 1/14-2/7	2/8-2/25	2/26-3/12

	ARIES 25	TAURUS 26	GEMINI 27	CANCER 28	LEO 29	VIRGO 30
1893	3/6-5/12	5/13-5/28	5/29-6/11	6/12-6/28	6/29-9/5	9/6-9/21
1894	4/17-5/5	5/6-5/20	5/21-6/3	6/4-6/26 7/18-8/10	6/27-7/17 8/11-8/28	8/29-9/13
1895	4/12-4/27	4/28-5/11	5/12-5/28	5/29-8/5	8/6-8/20	8/21-9/5
1896	4/4-4/18	4/19-5/3	5/4-7/10	7/11-7/26	7/27-8/10	8/11-8/29
1897	3/27-4/9	4/10-4/29 5/22-6/12	4/30-5/21 6/13-7/4	7/5-7/18	7/19-8/3	8/4-8/25 9/22-10/10
1898	3/19-4/2	4/3-6/10	6/11-6/25	6/26-7/10	7/11-7/27	7/28-10/4
1899	3/11-5/15	5/16-6/3	6/4-6/17	6/18-7/2	7/3-7/26	7/27-8/14 9/10-9/26
1900	3/4-3/29	3/30-4/16	4/17-5/10 6/26-7/12	6/9-6/26 7/13-8/2	6/27-9/2	9/3-9/18
1901	4/16-5/3	5/4-5/17	5/18-6/1	6/2-8/9	8/10-8/25	8/26-9/10
1902	4/9-4/24	4/25-5/9	5/10-5/28 6/26-7/12	5/29-6/25 7/13-8/2	8/3-8/17	8/18-9/3
1903	4/2-4/16	4/17-5/2	5/3-7/10	7/11-7/25	7/26-8/9	8/10-8/29
1904	3/24-4/7	4/8-6/13	6/14-7/1	7/2-7/15	7/16-8/1	8/2-8/27 9/8-10/8
1905	3/16-4/1 4/29-5/15	4/2-4/28 5/16-6/8	6/9-6/22	6/23-7/7	7/8-7/26	7/27-10/1
1906	3/8-5/14	5/15-5/31	6/1-6/14	6/15-6/30	7/1-9/7	9/8-9/23
1907	3/4-3/13 4/18-5/8	5/9-5/22	5/23-6/6	6/7-6/26 7/27-8/12	6/27-7/26 8/13-8/30	8/31-9/15
1908	4/13-4/29	4/30-5/13	5/14-5/29	5/30-8/6	8/7-8/21	8/22-9/7
1909	4/6-4/20	4/21-5/5	5/6-7/12	7/13-7/29	7/30-8/13	8/14-8/31
1910	3/29-4/12	4/13-4/30 6/2-6/11	5/1-6/1 6/12-7/6	7/7-7/21	7/22-8/5	8/6-8/26 9/29-10/11
1911	3/21-4/4	4/5-6/12	6/13-6/28	6/29-7/12	7/13-7/30	7/31-10/6
1912	3/12-5/16	5/17-6/4	6/5-6/18	6/19-7/3	7/4-7/25 8/21-9/10	7/26-8/20 9/11-9/27
1913	3/5-4/7 4/14-5/11	5/12-5/27	5/28-6/10	6/11-6/27	6/28-9/3	9/4-9/19
1914	4/17-5/4	5/5-5/18	5/19-6/2	6/3-8/10	8/11-8/26	8/27-9/12

	LIBRA 31	SCORPIO 32	SAGITTARIUS 33	CAPRICORN 34	AQUARIUS 35	PISCES 36
1893	9/22-10/9	10/10-10/30 11/30-12/12	1/1-1/10 10/31-11/29 12/13-12/31	1/11-1/30	1/31-2/17	2/18-3/5
1894	9/14-10/2	10/3-12/8	1/1-1/4 12/9-12/28	1/5-1/23 12/29-12/31	1/24-2/9	2/10-4/16
1895	9/6-9/27	9/28-10/27 11/12-12/1	10/28-11/11 12/2-12/21	1/1-1/15 12/22-12/31	1/16-2/2 3/4-3/16	2/3-3/3 3/17-4/11
1896	8/30-11/4	11/5-11/23	11/24-12/12	1/1-1/8 12/13-12/31	1/9-3/15	3/16-4/3
1897	8/26-9/21 10/11-10/28	10/29-11/16	11/17-12/6	1/1 1/25-2/14 12/7-12/31	1/2-1/24 2/15-3/9	3/10-3/26
1898	10/5-10/21	10/22-11/9	11/10-11/30 12/22-12/31	1/1-2/10 12/1-12/21	2/11-3/1	3/2-3/18
1899	8/15-9/9 9/27-10/13	10/14-11/2	1/1-1/13 11/3-12/31	1/14-2/4	2/5-2/22	2/23-3/10
1900	9/19-10/6	10/7-10/29 11/19-12/12	1/1-1/8 10/30-11/18 12/13-12/31	1/9-1/28	1/29-2/14	2/15-3/3
1901	9/11-9/30	10/1-12/6	1/1-1/2 12/7-12/25	1/3-1/20 12/26-12/31	1/21-2/6	2/7-4/15
1902	9/4-9/27 10/16-11/10	9/28-10/15 11/11-11/29	11/30-12/18	1/1-1/13 12/19-12/31	1/14-2/1 2/19-3/18	2/2-2/18 3/19-4/8
1903	8/30-11/3	11/4-11/22	11/23-12/11	1/1-1/6 12/12-12/31	1/7-3/14	3/15-4/1
1904	8/28-9/7 10/9-10/26	10/27-11/14	11/15-12/4	1/1 1/14-2/14 12/5-12/31	1/2-1/13 2/15-3/6	3/7-3/23
1905	10/2-10/18	10/19-11/7	11/8-12/1 12/10-12/31	11/1-2/8 12/2-12/9	2/9-2/27	2/28-3/15
1906	9/24-10/11	10/12-11/1 12/7-12/12	1/1-1/12 11/2-12/6 12/13-12/31	1/13-2/1	2/2-2/19	2/20-3/7
1907	9/16-10/4	10/5-12/10	1/1-1/6 12/11-12/30	1/7-1/25 12/31	1/26-2/11	2/12-3/3 3/14-4/17
1908	9/8-9/28 11/2-11/11	9/29-11/1 11/12-12/3	12/4-12/22	1/1-1/18 12/23-12/31	1/29-2/4	2/5-4/12
1909	9/1-11/7	11/8-11/26	11/27-12/15	1/1-1/9 12/16-12/31	1/10-3/16	3/17-4/5
1910	8/27-9/28 10/12-10/31	11/1-11/18	11/19-12/8	1/1-1/3 1/31-2/15 12/9-12/31	1/4-1/30 2/16-3/11	3/12-3/28
1911	10/7-10/23	10/24-11/11	11/12-12/2 12/28-12/31	1/1-2/12 12/3-12/27	2/13-3/4	3/5-3/20
1912	9/28-10/15	10/16-11/4	1/1-1/14 11/5-12/31	1/15-2/6	2/7-2/24	2/25-3/11
1913	9/20-10/8	10/9-10/30 11/24-12/12	1/1-1/9 10/31-11/23 12/13-12/31	1/10-1/29	1/30-2/15	2/16-3/4 4/8-4/13
1914	9/13-10/1	10/2-12/7	1/1-1/3 12/8-12/27	1/4-1/22 12/28-12/31	1/23-2/8	2/9-4/4

	ARIES 25	TAURUS 26	GEMINI 27	CANCER 28	LEO 29	VIRGO 30
1915	4/11-4/26	4/27-5/10	5/11-5/28	5/29-8/3	8/4-8/18	8/19-9/4
1916	4/2-4/16	4/17-5/2	5/3-7/10	7/11-7/25	7/26-8/9	8/10-8/28
1917	3/25-4/8	4/9-6/14	6/15-7/2	7/3-7/17	7/18-8/2	8/3-8/26 9/15-10/9
1918	3/17-4/2	4/3-6/9	6/10-6/24	6/25-7/8	7/9-7/27	7/28-10/2
1919	3/9-5/15	5/16-6/1	6/2-6/15	6/16-7/1	7/2-9/8	9/9-9/25
1920	3/3-3/19 4/18-5/8	5/9-5/23	5/24-6/6	6/7-6/26 8/3-8/9	6/27-8/2 8/10-8/31	9/1-9/16
1921	4/14-4/30	5/1-5/14	5/15-5/30	5/31-8/7	8/8-8/23	8/24-9/8
1922	4/7-4/22	4/23-5/6	5/7-5/31 6/11-7/13	6/1-6/10 7/14-7/31	8/1-8/14	8/15-9/1
1923	3/31-4/13	4/14-4/30	5/1-7/8	7/9-7/22	7/23-8/6	8/7-8/27 10/5-10/11
1924	3/22-4/5	4/6-6/12	6/13-6/28	6/29-7/12	7/13-7/29	7/30-10/6
1925	3/13-3/31 4/16-5/16	4/1-4/15 5/17-6/6	6/7-6/20	6/21-7/4	7/5-7/25 8/27-9/10	7/26-8/26 9/11-9/29
1926	3/6-5/12	5/13-5/28	5/29-6/11	6/12-6/28	6/29-9/5	9/6-9/21
1927	4/17-5/5	5/6-5/20	5/21-6/3	6/4-6/27 7/14-8/11	6/28-7/13 8/12-8/28	8/29-9/13
1928	4/11-4/26	4/27-5/10	5/11-5/28	5/29-8/4	8/5-8/18	8/19-9/4
1929	4/4-4/18	4/19-5/2	5/3-7/11	7/12-7/26	7/27-8/10	8/11-8/29
1930	3/27-4/9	4/10-4/30 5/17-6/13	5/1-5/16 6/14-7/4	7/5-7/18	7/19-8/3	8/4-8/25 9/20-10/10
1931	3/19-4/2	4/3-6/10	6/11-6/25	6/26-7/10	7/11-7/28	7/29-10/3
1932	3/9-5/15	5/16-6/2	6/3-6/16	6/17-7/1	7/2-7/27 8/11-9/8	7/28-8/10 9/9-9/25
1933	3/3-3/25 4/18-5/9	5/10-5/24	5/25-6/7	6/8-6/26	6/27-9/1	9/2-9/17
1934	4/15-5/1	5/2-5/16	5/17-5/31	6/1-8/8	8/9-8/24	8/25-9/9
1935	4/8-4/24	4/25-5/7	5/8-5/29 6/21-7/13	5/30-6/20 7/14-8/1	8/2-8/15	8/16-9/2
1936	3/31-4/14	4/15-4/30	5/1-7/8	7/9-7/22	7/23-8/7	8/8-8/28
1937	3/24-4/6	4/7-6/13	6/14-6/30	7/1-7/14	7/15-7/31	8/1-10/7

	LIBRA 31	SCORPIO 32	SAGITTARIUS 33	CAPRICORN 34	AQUARIUS 35	PISCES 36
1915	9/5-9/27 10/21-11/11	9/28-10/20 11/12-11/30	12/1-12/19	1/1-1/14 12/20-12/31	1/15-2/1 2/24-3/19	2/2-2/23 3/20-4/10
1916	8/29-11/4	11/5-11/22	11/23-12/11	1/1-1/7 12/12-12/31	1/8-3/14	3/15-4/1
1917	8/27-9/14 10/10-10/27	10/28-11/15	11/16-12/5	1/1 1/18-2/14 12/6-12/31	1/2-1/17 2/15-3/8	3/9-3/24
1918	10/3-10/20	10/21-11/8	11/9-12/1 12/16-12/31	1/1-1/2/9 12/2-12/15	2/10-2/28	3/1-3/16
1919	9/26-10/12	10/13-11/2	1/1-1/13 11/3-12/31	1/14-2/3	2/4-2/21	2/22-3/8
1920	9/17-10/4	10/5-10/30 11/11-12/10	1/1-1/7 10/31-11/10 12/11-12/30	1/8-1/27 12/31	1/28-2/13	2/14-3/2 3/20-4/17
1921	9/9-9/29	9/30-12/4	12/5-12/23	1/1-1/18 12/24-12/31	1/19-2/4	2/5-4/13
1922	9/2-9/30 10/5-11/8	10/1-10/4 11/9-11/27	11/28-12/16	1/1-1/10 12/17-12/31	1/11-1/31 2/9-3/17	2/1-2/8 3/18-4/6
1923	8/28-10/4 10/12-11/1	11/2-11/20	11/21-12/9	1/1-1/4 2/7-2/13 12/10-12/31	1/5-2/6 2/14-3/12	3/13-3/30
1924	10/7-10/23	10/24-11/11	11/12-12/2	1/1-1/2/13 12/3-12/31	2/14-3/4	3/5-3/12
1925	9/30-10/16	10/17-11/5	1/1-1/13 11/6-12/31	1/14-2/6	2/7-2/24	2/25-3/21
1926	9/22-10/9	10/10-10/30 11/28-12/13	1/1-1/10 10/31-11/27 12/14-12/31	1/11-1/30	1/31-2/17	2/18-3/5
1927	9/14-10/2	10/3-12/8	1/1-1/4 12/9-12/28	1/5-1/23 12/29-12/31	1/24-2/9	2/10-4/16
1928	9/5-9/26 10/25-11/10	9/27-10/24 11/11-11/30	12/1-12/20	1/1-1/6 12/21-12/31	1/7-2/2 2/29-3/17	2/3-2/28 3/18-4/10
1929	8/30-11/4	11/5-11/23	11/24-12/13	1/1-1/7 12/14-12/31	1/8-3/15	3/16-4/3
1930	8/26-9/19 10/11-10/28	10/29-11/16	11/17-12/5	1/1 1/23-2/14 12/6-12/31	1/2-1/22 2/15-3/8	3/9-3/26
1931	10/4-10/21	10/22-11/9	11/10-12/1 12/21-12/31	1/1-1/2/10 12/2-12/20	2/11-3/1	3/2-3/18
1932	9/26-10/12	10/13-11/1	11/1-1/13 11/2-12/31	1/14-2/4	2/5-2/22	2/23-3/8
1933	9/18-10/5	10/6-10/29 11/16-12/11	11/1-1/7 10/30-11/15 12/12-12/31	1/8-1/28	1/29-2/13	2/14-3/2 3/26-4/17
1934	9/10-9/29	9/30-12/5	12/6-12/24	1/1-1/19 12/25-12/31	1/20-2/5	2/6-4/14
1935	9/3-9/27 10/13-11/9	9/28-10/12 11/10-11/28	11/29-12/17	1/1-1/12 12/18-12/31	1/13-1/31 2/15-3/17	2/1-2/14 3/18-4/7
1936	8/29-11/1	11/2-11/20	11/21-12/9	1/1-1/5 12/10-12/31	1/6-3/12	3/13-3/30
1937	10/8-10/25	10/26-11/13	11/14-12/3	1/10-2/13 12/4-12/31	1/1-1/9 2/14-3/5	3/6-3/23

	ARIES 25	TAURUS 26	GEMINI 27	CANCER 28	LEO 29	VIRGO 30
1938	3/15-3/31 4/24-5/16	4/1-4/23 5/17-6/7	6/8-6/21	6/22-7/6	7/7-7/26 9/3-9/10	7/27-9/2 9/11-9/30
1939	3/7-5/13	5/14-5/30	5/31-6/13	6/14-6/29	6/30-9/6	9/7-9/22
1940	3/3-3/8 4/7-5/6	5/7-5/20	5/21-6/4	6/5-6/25 7/21-8/11	6/26-7/20 8/12-8/28	8/29-9/13
1941	4/12-4/28	4/29-5/12	5/13-5/28	5/29-8/5	8/6-8/20	8/21-9/6
1942	4/5-4/20	4/21-5/4	5/5-7/11	7/12-7/28	7/29-8/12	8/13-8/30
1943	3/28-4/11	4/12-4/29 5/26-6/13	4/30-5/25 6/14-7/5	7/6-7/19	7/20-8/4	8/5-8/26 9/25-10/11
1944	3/19-4/2	4/3-6/10	6/11-6/26	6/27-7/10	7/11-7/27	7/28-10/4
1945	3/11-5/15	5/16-6/3	6/4-6/17	6/18-7/2	7/3-7/25 8/17-9/9	7/26-8/16 9/10-9/26
1946	3/4-3/31 4/16-5/10	5/11-5/26	5/27-6/9	6/10-6/26	6/27-9/2	9/3-9/18
1947	4/16-5/3	5/4-5/17	5/18-6/1	6/2-8/9	8/10-8/25	8/26-9/10
1948	4/9-4/24	4/25-5/8	5/9-5/27 6/28-7/10	5/28-6/27 7/11-8/1	8/2-8/16	8/17-9/2
1949	4/1-4/15	4/16-5/1	5/2-7/9	7/10-7/24	7/25-8/8	8/9-8/27
1950	3/24-4/8	4/9-6/13	6/14-7/1	7/2-7/15	7/16-8/1	8/2-8/26
1951	3/16-4/2 5/2-5/15	4/3-5/1 5/16-6/9	6/10-6/24	6/25-7/8	7/9-7/27	7/28-10/2
1952	3/8-5/14	5/15-5/31	6/1-6/14	6/15-6/30	7/1-9/7	9/8-9/23
1953	3/3-3/15 4/18-5/8	5/9-5/23	5/24-6/6	6/7-6/26 7/29-8/11	6/27-7/28 8/12-8/30	8/31-9/15
1954	4/14-4/30	5/1-5/14	5/15-5/30	5/31-8/7	8/8-8/22	8/23-9/8
1955	4/7-4/21	4/22-5/6	5/7-7/13	7/14-7/30	7/31-8/14	8/15-9/1
1956	3/29-4/12	4/13-4/29	4/30-7/6	7/7-7/20	7/21-8/5	8/6-8/25 9/30-10/10
1957	3/21-4/4	4/5-6/12	6/13-6/28	6/29-7/12	7/13-7/29	7/30-10/6
1958	3/13-4/1 4/11-5/16	4/2-4/10 5/17-6/5	6/6-6/19	6/20-7/4	7/5-7/25 8/24-9/10	7/26-8/23 9/11-9/28
1959	3/6-5/12	5/13-5/28	5/29-6/11	6/12-6/28	6/29-9/4	9/5-9/20
1960	4/16-5/4	5/5-5/18	5/19-6/2	6/3-6/30 7/7-8/10	7/1-7/6 8/11-8/26	8/27-9/12

	LIBRA 31	SCORPIO 32	SAGITTARIUS 33	CAPRICORN 34	AQUARIUS 35	PISCES 36
1938	10/1-10/17	10/18-11/6	1/7-1/12 11/7-12/31	1/1-1/6 1/13-2/7	2/8-2/26	2/27-3/14
1939	9/23-10/10	10/11-10/31 12/3-12/13	1/1-1/11 11/1-11/2 12/14-12/31	1/12-1/31	2/1-2/18	2/19-3/6
1940	9/14-10/2	10/3-12/8	1/1-1/5 12/9-12/28	1/6-1/24 12/29-12/31	1/25-2/10	2/11-3/2 3/9-4/7
1941	9/7-9/27 10/30-11/11	9/28-10/29 11/12-12/2	12/3-12/21	1/1-1/16 12/22-12/31	1/17-2/2 3/7-3/16	2/3-3/6 3/17-4/11
1942	8/31-11/6	11/7-11/24	11/25-12/14	1/1-1/8 12/15-12/31	1/9-3/16	3/17-4/4
1943	8/27-9/24 10/12-10/30	10/31-11/17	11/18-12/7	1/1-1/2 1/28-2/14 12/8-12/31	1/3-1/27 2/15-3/10	3/11-3/27
1944	10/5-10/21	10/22-11/9	11/10-11/30 12/24-12/31	1/1-2/11 12/1-12/23	2/12-3/7	3/3-3/18
1945	9/27-10/14	10/15-11/3	1/1-1/13 11/4-12/31	1/14-2/4	2/5-2/22	2/23-3/10
1946	9/19-10/7	10/8-10/29 11/20-12/12	1/1-1/8 10/30-11/19 12/13-12/31	1/9-1/28	1/29-2/14	2/15-3/3 4/1-4/15
1947	9/11-9/30	10/1-12/6	1/1-1/2 12/7-12/25	1/3-1/20 12/26-12/31	1/21-2/7	2/8-4/15
1948	9/3-9/26 10/17-11/9	9/27-10/16 11/10-11/28	11/29-12/17	1/1-1/14 12/18-12/31	1/15-2/1 2/20-3/17	2/2-2/19 3/18-4/8
1949	8/28-11/2	11/3-11/21	11/22-12/10	1/1-1/5 12/11-12/31	1/6-3/13	3/14-3/31
1950	8/27-9/9 10/9-10/26	10/27-11/14	11/15-12/4	1/15-2/13 12/5-12/31	1/1-1/14 2/14-3/7	3/8-3/23
1951	10/3-10/19	10/20-11/8	11/9-12/1 12/13-12/31	1/1-2/9 12/2-12/12	2/10-2/28	3/1-3/15
1952	9/24-10/11	10/12-11/1	1/1-1/13 11/2-12/31	1/14-2/3	2/4-2/20	2/21-3/7
1953	9/16-10/4	10/5-10/31 11/7-12/10	1/1-1/6 11/1-11/6 12/11-12/31	1/7-1/25	1/26-2/11	2/12-3/2 3/16-4/11
1954	9/9-9/29 11/5-11/11	9/30-11/4 11/12-12/4	12/5-12/23	1/1-1/18 12/24-12/31	1/19-2/4	2/5-4/13
1955	9/2-11/7	11/8-11/26	11/27-12/15	1/1-1/10 12/16-12/31	1/11-3/17	3/18-4/6
1956	8/26-9/29 10/11-10/31	11/1-11/18	11/19-12/7	1/1-1/3 2/3-2/14 12/8-12/31	1/4-2/2 2/15-3/10	3/11-3/28
1957	10/7-10/23	10/24-11/11	11/12-12/1 12/29-12/31	1/1-2/11 12/2-12/28	2/12-3/3	3/4-3/20
1958	9/29-10/15	10/16-11/4	1/1-1/13 11/5-12/31	1/14-2/6	2/7-2/24	2/25-3/12
1959	9/21-10/8	10/9-10/30 11/26-12/13	1/1-1/10 10/31-11/25 12/14-12/31	1/11-1/30	1/31-2/16	2/17-3/5
1960	9/13-10/1	10/2-12/7	1/1-1/4 12/8-12/27	1/5-1/23 12/28-12/31	1/24-2/9	2/10-4/15

	ARIES 25	TAURUS 26	GEMINI 27	CANCER 28	LEO 29	VIRGO 30
1961	4/11-4/26	4/27-5/10	5/11-5/28	5/29-8/3	8/4-8/18	8/19-9/4
1962	4/3-4/18	4/19-5/3	5/4-7/11	7/12-7/26	7/27-8/10	8/11-8/29
1963	3/26-4/9	4/10-5/2 5/11-6/14	5/3-5/10 6/15-7/3	7/4-7/18	7/19-8/3	8/4-8/26 9/17-10/10
1964	3/17-4/1	4/2-6/8	6/9-6/24	6/25-7/8	7/9-7/27	7/28-10/2
1965	3/10-5/15	5/16-6/2	6/3-6/15	6/16-7/1	7/2-7/30 8/4-9/8	7/31-8/3 9/9-9/25
1966	3/3-3/22 4/18-5/9	5/10-5/24	5/25-6/6	6/7-6/26	6/27-9/1	9/2-9/17
1967	4/15-5/1	5/2-5/16	5/17-5/31	6/1-8/8	8/9-8/24	8/25-9/9
1968	4/7-4/22	4/23-5/6	5/7-5/29 6/14-7/12	5/30-6/13 7/13-7/31	8/1-8/14	8/15-9/1
1969	3/31-4/14	4/15-4/30	5/1-7/7	7/8-7/22	7/23-8/6	8/7-8/27 10/8-10/9
1970	3/23-4/6	4/7-6/13	6/14-6/30	7/1-7/12	7/13-7/31	8/1-10/7
1971	3/15-4/1 4/19-5/17	4/2-4/18 5/18-6/7	6/8-6/21	6/22-7/6	7/7-7/26 8/30-9/11	7/27-8/29 9/12-9/30
1972	3/6-5/12	5/13-5/29	5/30-6/12	6/13-6/28	6/29-9/5	9/6-9/21
1973	4/17-5/6	5/7-5/20	5/21-6/4 7/17-8/11	6/5-6/27	6/28-7/16 8/12-8/28	8/29-9/13
1974	4/12-4/28	4/29-5/12	5/13-5/29	5/30-8/5	8/6-8/20	8/21-9/6
1975	4/5-4/19	4/20-5/4	5/5-7/12	7/13-7/29	7/30-8/12	8/13-8/30
1976	3/27-4/10	4/11-4/29 5/20-6/13	4/30-5/19 6/14-7/4	7/5-7/18	7/19-8/3	8/4-8/25 9/22-10/10
1977	3/19-4/3	4/4-6/10	6/11-6/26	6/27-7/10	7/11-7/28	7/29-10/4
1978	3/11-5/16	5/17-6/3	6/4-6/17	6/18-7/2	7/3-7/27 8/14-9/9	7/28-8/13 9/10-9/26
1979	3/4-3/28 4/18-5/10	5/11-5/26	5/27-6/9	6/10-6/27	6/28-9/2	9/3-9/18
1980	4/15-5/2	5/3-5/16	5/17-5/30	5/31-8/9	8/10-8/24	8/25-9/10
1981	4/9-4/24	4/25-5/8	5/9-5/28 6/23-7/12	5/29-6/22 7/13-8/1	8/2-8/16	8/17-9/2
1982	4/1-4/15	4/16-5/1	5/2-7/9	7/10-7/24	7/25-8/8	8/9-8/28
1983	3/24-4/7	4/8-6/14	6/15-7/1	7/2-7/15	7/16-8/1	8/2-8/29 9/7-10/8

	LIBRA 31	SCORPIO 32	SAGITTARIUS 33	CAPRICORN 34	AQUARIUS 35	PISCES 36
1961	9/5-9/27 10/23-11/10	9/28-10/22 11/11-11/30	12/1-12/19	1/1-1/4 12/20-12/31	1/5-2/1 2/25-3/18	2/2-2/24 3/19-4/10
1962	8/30-11/4	11/5-11/23	11/24-12/12	1/1-1/7 12/13-12/31	1/8-3/15	3/16-4/2
1963	8/27-9/16 10/11-10/28	10/29-11/16	11/17-12/5	1/1-1/2 1/21-2/15 12/6-12/31	1/3-1/20 2/16-3/9	3/10-3/25
1964	10/3-10/20	10/21-11/8	11/9-11/30 12/17-12/31	1/1-2/10 12/1-12/16	2/11-2/29	3/1-3/16
1965	9/26-10/12	10/13-11/2	1/1-1/12 11/3-12/31	1/13-2/3	2/4-2/21	2/22-3/9
1966	9/18-10/5	10/6-10/29 11/14-12/11	1/1-1/7 10/30-11/13 12/12-12/31	1/8-1/26	1/27-2/13	2/14-3/2 3/23-4/17
1967	9/10-9/29	9/30-12/5	12/6-12/24	1/1-1/19 12/25-12/31	1/20-2/5	2/6-4/14
1968	9/2-9/27 10/8-11/8	9/28-10/7 11/9-11/27	11/28-12/16	1/1-1/12 12/17-12/31	1/13-2/1 2/12-3/17	2/2-2/11 3/18-4/6
1969	8/28-10/7 10/10-11/1	11/2-11/20	11/21-12/9	1/1-1/4 12/10-12/31	1/5-3/12	3/13-3/30
1970	10/8-10/25	10/26-11/12	11/13-12/3	1/1-2/13 12/4-12/31	2/14-3/5	3/6-3/22
1971	10/1-10/17	10/18-11/6	1/2-1/14 11/7-12/31	1/1 1/15-2/7	2/8-2/26	2/27-3/14
1972	9/22-10/10	10/11-10/30 11/30-12/12	1/1-1/11 10/31-11/29 12/13-12/31	1/12-1/31	2/1-2/18	2/19-3/5
1973	9/14-10/2	10/3-12/8	1/1-1/4 12/9-12/28	1/5-1/23 12/29-12/31	1/24-2/9	2/10-4/16
1974	9/7-9/28 10/27-11/11	9/29-10/26 11/12-12/2	12/3-12/21	1/1-1/16 12/22-12/31	1/17-2/2	2/3-4/11
1975	8/31-11/6	11/7-11/25	11/26-12/14	1/1-1/8 12/15-12/31	1/9-3/16	3/17-4/4
1976	8/26-9/21 10/11-10/29	10/30-11/16	11/17-12/6	1/1-1/2 1/27-2/15 12/7-12/31	1/3-1/26 2/16-3/9	3/10-3/26
1977	10/5-10/21	10/22-11/9	11/10-12/1 12/22-12/31	1/1-2/10 12/2-12/21	2/11-3/2	3/3-3/18
1978	9/27-10/14	10/15-11/3	1/1-1/13 11/4-12/31	1/14-2/4	2/5-2/22	2/23-3/10
1979	9/19-10/7	10/8-10/30 11/19-12/12	1/1-1/8 10/31-11/18 12/13-12/31	1/9-1/28	1/29-2/14	2/15-3/3 3/29-4/17
1980	9/11-9/30	10/1-12/5	1/1-1/2 12/6-12/25	1/3-1/21 12/26-12/31	1/22-2/7	2/8-4/14
1981	9/3-9/27 10/15-11/10	9/28-10/14 11/11-11/28	11/29-12/17	1/1-1/12 12/18-12/31	1/13-1/31 2/17-3/18	2/1-2/16 3/19-4/8
1982	8/29-11/3	11/4-11/21	11/22-12/12	1/1-1/5 12/13-12/31	1/6-3/13	3/14-3/31
1983	8/30-9/6 10/9-10/26	10/27-11/14	11/15-12/4	1/1 1/13-2/14 12/5-12/31	1/2-1/12 2/15-3/7	3/8-3/23

	ARIES 25	TAURUS 26	GEMINI 27	CANCER 28	LEO 29	VIRGO 30
1984	3/15-3/31 4/26-5/15	4/1-4/25 5/16-6/7	6/8-6/22	6/23-7/6	7/7-7/26	7/27-9/30
1985	3/7-5/14	5/15-5/30	5/31-6/13	6/14-6/29	6/30-9/6	9/7-9/22
1986	3/4-3/11 4/18-5/7	5/8-5/22	5/23-6/5	6/6-6/26	6/27-7/23	7/24-8/11
1987	4/13-4/29	4/30-5/13	5/14-5/30	5/31-8/6	8/7-8/21	8/22-9/7
1988	4/15-4/20	4/21-5/4	5/5-7/12	7/13-7/28	7/29-8/12	8/13-8/30
1989	3/29-4/11	4/12-4/29 5/29-6/12	4/30-5/28 6/13-7/6	7/7-7/20	7/21-8/6	8/7-8/26 9/27-10/11
1990	3/20-4/4	4/5-6/12	6/13-6/27	6/28-7/11	7/12-7/29	7/30-10/5
1991	3/12-5/16	5/17-6/5	6/6-6/19	6/20-7/4	7/5-7/26 8/20-9/10	7/27-8/19 9/11-9/28
1992	3/4-4/3 4/15-5/11	5/12-5/26	5/27-6/9	6/10-6/27	6/28-9/3	9/4-9/19
1993	4/16-5/3	5/4-5/18	5/19-6/2	6/3-8/10	8/11-8/26	8/27-9/11
1994	4/10-4/25	4/26-5/9	5/10-5/28 7/3-7/10	5/29-7/2 7/11-8/3	8/4-8/18	8/19-9/4
1995	4/3-4/17	4/18-5/3	5/4-7/10	7/11-7/25	7/26-8/10	8/11-8/29
1996	3/25-4/8	4/9-6/13	6/14-7/2	7/3-7/16	7/17-8/1	8/2-8/26
1997	3/17-4/1 5/6-5/12	4/2-5/5 5/13-6/8	6/9-6/23	6/24-7/8	7/9-7/27	7/28-10/2
1998	3/9-5/15	5/16-6/1	6/2-6/15	6/16-6/30	7/1-9/8	9/9-9/24
1999	3/3-3/18 4/18-5/8	5/9-5/23	5/24-6/7	6/8-6/26 8/1-8/11	6/27-7/31 8/12-8/31	9/1-9/16

	LIBRA 31	SCORPIO 32	SAGITTARIUS 33	CAPRICORN 34	AQUARIUS 35	PISCES 36
1984	10/1-10/18	10/19-11/6 12/18-12/31	11/7-12/1	1/1-2/10 12/2-12/7	2/11-2/27	2/28-3/14
1985	9/23-10/10	10/11-10/31 12/5-12/12	1/1-1/11 11/1-12/4 12/13-12/31	1/12-2/1	2/2-2/18	2/19-3/6
1986	8/12-8/30 9/16-10/4	8/31-9/15 10/5-12/10	1/1-1/5 12/11-12/29	1/6-1/25 12/30-12/31	1/26-2/11	2/12-3/3 3/12-4/17
1987	9/8-9/28 11/2-11/11	9/29-11/1 11/12-12/3	12/4-12/22	1/1-1/17 12/23-12/31	1/18-2/4 3/12-3/13	2/5-3/11 3/14-4/12
1988	8/31-11/6	11/7-11/25	11/26-12/14	1/1-1/10 12/15-12/31	1/11-3/16	3/17-4/14
1989	8/27-9/26 10/12-10/30	10/31-11/18	11/19-12/7	1/1-1/2 1/30-2/14 12/8-12/31	1/3-1/29 2/15-3/10	3/11-3/28
1990	10/6-10/23	10/24-11/18	11/19-12/2 12/26-12/31	1/1-2/12 12/3-12/25	2/13-3/3	3/4-3/19
1991	9/29-10/15	10/16-11/5	1/1-1/14 11/5-12/31	1/15-2/5	2/6-2/24	2/25-3/11
1992	9/20-10/7	10/8-10/29 11/22-12/12	1/1-1/10 10/30-11/21 12/13-12/31	1/11-1/29	1/30-2/16	2/17-3/3 4/4-4/14
1993	9/12-10/1	10/2-12/7	1/1-1/2 12/8-12/26	1/3-1/21 12/27-12/31	1/22-2/7	2/8-4/15
1994	9/5-9/27 10/20-11/10	9/28-10/19 11/11-11/30	12/1-12/19	1/1-1/14 12/20-12/31	1/15-2/1 2/22-3/18	2/2-2/21 3/19-4/9
1995	8/30-11/4	11/5-11/22	11/23-12/12	1/1-1/6 12/13-12/31	1/7-3/14	3/15-4/2
1996	8/27-9/12 10/10-10/27	9/13-10/9 10/28-11/14	11/15-12/4	1/1 1/18-2/15 12/5-12/31	1/2-1/17 2/16-3/7	3/8-3/24
1997	10/3-10/19	10/20-11/7	11/8-11/30 12/14-12/31	1/1-2/9 12/1-12/13	2/10-2/28	3/1-3/16
1998	9/25-10/12	10/13-11/1	1/1-1/12 11/2-12/31	1/13-2/2	2/3-2/20	2/21-3/8
1999	9/17-10/5	10/6-10/30 11/10-12/11	1/1-1/7 10/31-11/9 12/12-12/31	1/8-1/26	1/27-2/12	2/13-3/2 3/19-4/17

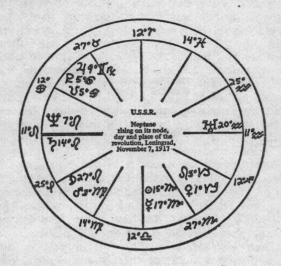

U.S.S.R.
Neptune
rising on its node,
day and place of the
revolution, Leningrad,
November 7, 1917

*After the American Revolution (see page 149)
the next of the three outer, or social-movement,
planets (Uranus, Neptune, Pluto) to contact its
own node was Neptune, which touched its north
node near a conjunction to Saturn, Aug. 1, 1917.
The above chart is erected for the moment Neptune's Node rose on the Ascendant, with Neptune near its node, on the date of the Russian
Revolution, Nov. 7, 1917. Note the power of the
chart, with the Moon in Leo, rising, and high-
lighting the nodal position of Neptune, with
Saturn close by. See now the chart of the Nazi
revolution, page 201.*

VENUS

Venus is the emotional antenna of your Vita-sphere. Through Venus, impressions come to you from the outer world because of which you feel and react emotionally. The position of Venus by sign at the time of your birth gives the key to your attitude toward these emotional experiences. As Mercury is the messenger linking sense impressions (sight, smell, etc.) to the basic nature of your Sun and Moon, so Venus is the messenger linking emotional impressions. *If Venus is found in the same sign with the Sun,* emotions gain importance in your life, having a direct bearing on your actions and generally causing you to put your best foot forward. *If Venus is in the same sign with the Moon,* emotions also gain importance, bearing directly on your inner nature, adding to self-confidence, making you sensitive to emotion impressions, and frequently indicating that you have more love in your heart than you are able to express. *If Venus is in the same sign with Mercury,* emotion impressions and sense impressions work together; you tend to idealize the world of the senses and to sensualize the world of the emotions; to interpret emotionally what you see and hear; and perhaps through this to become proficient in one of the arts.

Get Venus' sign position from the tables on pages 191–200. Note the sign in your birth record, and read the indicated paragraph.

37. VENUS IN ARIES

Your reaction to emotional stimuli is highly personal. You will do anything for someone you love, and little for anyone or any group that has not won your personal affection. Love, sympathy, human kindness are all related to yourself; you are therefore not a great humanitarian, nor especially interested in group social problems. But you may be much interested in society—that is, social gatherings, social position, social graces. You are warm and even ardent when you feel you are loved, but can also be touchy with friends and easily offended. This is a somewhat narrowing position for Venus, and with it you should make a conscious effort to find sympathy and understanding for people whom you don't love and who never will love you. By universalizing the Venusian vibrations you broaden your whole nature, widen your interests and give greater scope to your abundant emotional vitality, which benefits you in direct proportion to the number of individuals whose problems you are able to take to your heart.

38. VENUS IN TAURUS

You have a robust, physical, sensuous (or sensual) response to emotional vibrations. You are demonstrative, affectionate as well as passionate. You love to touch, to hold and be held by, the loved one. You are both sensational and passional; to know the difference, and to let the true instinct replace the false one is to achieve mastery of yourself and of others. Plenty of love addicts have this position, to whom love means physical enjoyment and little more. Raised to its best, this position of Venus enables you to elevate physical earthly love to a high spiritual plane and to understand the beauty of true union in a union of true beauty. You understand love deeply; accept it with your whole being, are content to express it wordlessly, value love's silences more than its speeches. You know both ecstasy and despair of love; and you cling to a love once given and received with unbelievable tenacity, even in the face of great obstacles. You believe in love, in its earthly as well as its spiritual form, and will not be content till you have found both in one individual. Your emotional responses color your whole life; all sense reactions are intensified by this position, and your love of color, art, music and beauty in any form relates directly to the creative impulse which draws on, and interprets to you, all the experiences that earth has to offer.

39. VENUS IN GEMINI

You are emotionally aware, very susceptible to emotional stimuli, sensitive in that you react to them swiftly. But in the other sense you are not sensitive or touchy. Your emotions color your life and your reactions in a very lively manner; they are like a constant sheet of clear warm water that bathes you always, without necessarily penetrating very far beneath the surface. The alertness with which you relate sense experience to your emotional nature, and the glibness with which you can tell how you feel about everything, can make you a clever writer or artist. To express your emotions is almost as important to you as to feel them. You may learn to understand a whole lot about love and the world of the senses in theory, because you cover so much of it so swiftly. You are a gay companion, sophisticated, knowing all the answers. You may go on to another love, another experience, but you will retain a comradely interest in everyone you have ever known. You don't usually quarrel with people. You ought to probe yourself to see if you are getting the most out of life, or if you are only skimming the surface. "The world is so full of a number of things"—what one thing is *your* heart set on?

40. VENUS IN CANCER

Your emotional responses are related to a simple and direct standard, your need for security and a home. Since this is a basic life urge, your love is loyal and devoted, and deep with the depth of self-preservation, which does not, however, make you selfish. Your whole nature hides in a protective shell till you have taken the emotional step that means your security; then it unfolds graciously, like a flower in the warm sun, and beautifies your whole world. The fear of being hurt by love—of being thus innerly insecure—is very strong. You may seem sensitive and touchy, not to the superficial niceties but to the bigger things that could shake your world. You can harness your emotions to making your own security, and so can be successful in business, to which you bring the primitive maternal, or paternal, forces. This, however, is the only way in which you are materialistic. You like sentimental gestures only if you think they spring from sincerity. The forced kiss, the dutiful embrace, mean nothing to you. Your emotional polarity is not primarily physical, and though you can respond to ardor you can take it or leave it alone.

41. VENUS IN LEO

You dramatize emotional experience to the hilt. Your emotional responses are both honest and calculated, if you understand that. They aren't spontaneous, but they aren't hypocritical. They are geared to serve your total personality and to insure that they will make the right effect. You know how you look when you're kissing or being kissed; and you're clever enough to avoid the appearance of posing. You are something of an introvert; love is yours to give or withhold, according to your wishes. If your desires are strong, it is due to some other position in the Vitasphere, because Venus in Leo, considered as a unit, enables you to shut desire on or off at will. When on, it can be a wow; when off, cold as ice and unapproachable. No one with Venus in Leo ever was talked into anything. In emotions, you do all the talking, and the only plea you hear is your own. This position is wonderful if you're on the stage and tends to make a stage of your life even if the theater isn't your profession.

42. VENUS IN VIRGO

You relate emotional experience to a well-organized code of conduct. You have strong family feeling and generally have genuine affection for your relatives. Your belief in the proprieties is so strong that you just don't have emotions that would involve their violation. Your impulses are usually strictly proper; if you stray from the beaten track, it is because you have convinced yourself that it is all right: you satisfy your conscience before the transgression, and rarely after. You substitute self-justification for remorse. Small niceties are emotionally important to you, and if you're not careful, you will substitute the sentimentalities of love for love itself. The proprieties as you conceive them stand guard over your emotional reactions; your sense of good taste is your emotional censor, and will

keep you from many unconventionalities of those less
sure of the right thing. This need not detract from the
warmth of your nature, provided you don't let the tail
wag the dog. Remember that the proprieties were made
to serve a purpose, and that before there can be an
emotional code there must be emotions. To have proprieties for their own sake is like having a general and
no army.

43. VENUS IN LIBRA

Your emotions are simple, direct, crystal clear.
You are one of the young and pure in heart. The difficulties of life don't destroy your faith in the beauty
of love, and since this is the sort of faith that vindi-
cates itself, you are likely to find more genuine happiness in life than most. You are easily hurt, but you
aren't touchy about it; you can't hold a grudge, or
even condemn those who hurt you. You have a knack
for thinking the best of people who repay you by
thinking the best of you. The directness of your response to social relations, the genuineness of your af-
fections, which you express with a combination of sincerity and impersonality—these endear you to many,
make you a sought-after companion and guest and a
charming host or hostess. You can safely allow emotional experience to be the breath of your life because
when it is filtered through your clarifying responses it
is a pure, sweet and exhilarating air.

44. VENUS IN SCORPIO

You have passionate, profound and controlled
emotional responses, and a deep need for love, which
must be satisfied according to very high standards. The
directness and obvious sincerity of your reactions to
social contacts earn respect, while your willingness to
"give all for love" frequently brings you love without
requiring your all in return. Sex may be important in
your life, but you elevate it to a glorious plane, and
will have none of it otherwise. You are deeply aware
of your environment, atmospheres, odors, colors; your
love, which is your life, must be beautifully surrounded. Thus you love luxury, and sometimes have a

garish taste in color and dress. But you can get away with it. Your personality is made vivid by your emotional power. You wear the capacity to love as a shining armor that catches the sun of life and reflects it with much of your spiritual strength added.

45. VENUS IN SAGITTARIUS

You react to emotional stimuli eagerly. Your heart is unafraid of love; you dare to feel, and to follow your instincts to the last outpost of experience. You are not an experimenter in love; you don't trifle with your emotions; but others may, because your eagerness may be mistaken for lightness. You see no reason why emotions aren't made to be followed, and are among the most impulsive of the children of Venus. Because of your sincerity you can get into trouble, until you learn that all the world isn't as direct and earnest as you are. But though you may give yourself to unworthy takers and be hurt (for you are very sensitive), you will never lose your high standards nor your emotional courage, and will go on from disappointments undefeated to trust your emotions again, matured but unafraid.

46. VENUS IN CAPRICORN

You are wise beyond your years where emotions are concerned, accept naturally the dictates of society, and will rarely be found in a compromising position. Emotional response will genuinely be along the lines of the conventions, sometimes even of the main chance; you won't marry beneath you, and understand "Thee shouldst marry for love, but it is just as easy to love where there is money." Since your emotions are geared to your defense and ambition responses, you will rarely find yourself struggling between love and duty, desire and ambition; they automatically work together. Your emotions are not so much controlled as they are natural adjuncts to practical wishes; you instinctively do the right thing, make the tactful response, refuse to be hurt, and easily refrain from doing things that hurt others. Emotional response is self-repressed and may even become selfish. If you have a lot of trouble with your emotions, it is from something else in your Vitasphere, and not from Venus in Capricorn.

47. VENUS IN AQUARIUS

Your emotional responses are frank and heart-felt, even when they are directed toward generalizations and groups, as they often are, or toward art in some form. Your emotions serve your aesthetic sense; you are capable of a detached and spiritual form of personal love which you relate to beauty rather than to passion. You worship beauty concretely and in the abstract; and can want nothing more than to look up-on the beautiful face of your beloved (who must have a beautiful face) or on her beautiful body, which she can let you do without fear of being betrayed or thought immodest. You are sensuous, but not sensual; your emotions feed on the stimuli of eye, ear and the olfactory senses; less on touch. You belong to the perpetually pure of heart, and because of this your emotional responses to individuals are high-minded and beautiful in the extreme, and can be transmuted into the pure gold of universalized love by the alchemy of your spiritual strength.

48. VENUS IN PISCES

Your response to emotional stimuli is a good deal deeper than you are able to get across to those you love. What you feel is difficult for you to express, and frequently you are misunderstood and imposed on because of this. Your muscles react to emotional stimuli —your impulse is to do something for the loved one, to run errands, give presents; and you get genuine joy from the giving. Your judgment of people isn't too good; this is because your deepest interest is in your emotions for their own sake, and secondarily in the person on whom they are fixed. As a result they frequently fix on someone not especially interested in you, and you may lavish a lot of emotion and attention before you find out that your love is not reciprocated. Your own responses are true and fine; you expect the same of others—and must learn to estimate others better in order to get back from the world some fair return for all the devotion you give to it.

	ARIES 37	TAURUS 38	GEMINI 39	CANCER 40	LEO 41	VIRGO 42
1870	5/7-6/3	6/4-6/30	7/1-7/26	7/27-8/20	8/21-9/13	9/14-10/8
1871	3/1-3/25	3/26-4/18	4/19-5/14	5/15-6/9	6/10-7/6	7/7-8/9 10/1-11/3
1872	4/14-5/8	5/9-6/1	6/2-6/26	6/27-7/20	7/21-8/13	8/14-9/7
1873	2/3-3/3	3/4-7/7	7/8-8/6	8/7-9/2	9/3-9/27	9/28-10/22
1874	3/16-4/8	4/9-5/2	5/3-5/27	5/28-6/21	6/22-7/16	7/17-8/11
1875	4/28-5/23	5/24-6/17	6/18-7/11	7/12-8/5	8/6-8/29	8/30-9/22
1876	2/15-3/10	3/11-4/5	4/6-5/4	5/5-6/17	6/18-6/27 9/7-10/7	6/28-9/6 10/8-11/3
1877	3/30-4/23	4/24-5/17	5/18-6/10	6/11-7/5	7/6-7/29	7/30-8/23
1878	5/7-6/3	6/4-6/30	7/1-7/25	7/26-8/19	8/20-9/13	9/14-10/7
1879	3/1-3/24	3/25-4/18	4/19-5/13	5/14-6/8	6/9-7/6	7/7-8/10 9/25-11/4
1880	4/14-5/7	5/8-6/1	6/2-6/25	6/26-7/20	7/21-8/13	8/14-9/6
1881	2/3-3/3	3/4-7/7	7/8-8/5	8/6-9/1	9/2-9/27	9/28-10/21
1882	3/15-4/7	4/8-5/2	5/3-5/26	5/27-6/20	6/21-7/15	7/16-8/10
1883	4/28-5/22	5/23-6/16	6/17-7/11	7/12-8/4	8/5-8/29	8/30-9/22
1884	2/15-3/10	3/11-4/5	4/6-5/4	5/5-9/7	9/8-10/7	10/8-11/3
1885	3/30-4/22	4/23-5/16	5/17-6/10	6/11-7/4	7/5-7/29	7/30-8/23
1886	5/7-6/3	6/4-6/29	6/30-7/25	7/26-8/19	8/20-9/12	9/13-10/7
1887	2/28-3/24	3/25-4/17	4/18-5/13	5/14-6/8	6/9-7/6	7/7-8/11 9/19-11/5
1888	4/13-5/7	5/8-5/31	6/1-6/25	6/26-7/19	7/20-8/12	8/13-9/6
1889	2/3-3/4	3/5-7/7	7/8-8/5	8/6-9/1	9/2-9/26	9/27-10/21
1890	3/15-4/7	4/8-5/1	5/2-5/26	5/27-6/20	6/21-7/15	7/16-8/10
1891	4/27-5/22	5/23-6/16	6/17-7/10	7/11-8/4	8/5-8/28	8/29-9/21
1892	2/14-3/9	3/10-4/4	4/5-5/4	5/5-9/7	9/8-10/7	10/8-11/2
1893	3/29-4/22	4/23-5/16	5/17-6/9	6/10-7/4	7/5-7/28	7/29-8/22
1894	5/5-6/2	6/3-6/29	6/30-7/24	7/25-8/18	8/19-9/12	9/13-10/6
1895	2/28-3/23	3/24-4/17	4/18-5/12	5/13-6/7	6/8-7/6	7/7-8/13 9/13-11/6
1896	4/13-5/6	5/7-5/31	6/1-6/24	6/25-7/19	7/20-8/12	8/13-9/5
1897	2/2-3/4	3/5-7/7	7/8-8/5	8/6-8/31	9/1-9/26	9/27-10/20
1898	3/14-4/6	4/7-5/1	5/2-5/25	5/26-6/19	6/20-7/14	7/15-8/10
1899	4/27-5/21	5/22-6/15	6/16-7/10	7/11-8/3	8/4-8/28	8/29-9/21

	LIBRA 43	SCORPIO 44	SAGITTARIUS 45	CAPRICORN 46	AQUARIUS 47	PISCES 48
1870	10/9-11/1	11/2-11/25	11/26-12/18	12/19-12/31	1/1-1/4 3/4-3/28	1/5-3/3 3/29-5/6
1871	8/10-9/30 11/4-12/8	12/9-12/31		1/1-1/11	1/12-2/4	2/5-2/28
1872	9/8-10/1	1/1-1/5 10/2-10/25	1/6-1/30 10/26-11/19	1/31-2/24 11/20-12/13	2/25-3/20 12/14-12/31	3/21-4/13
1873	10/23-11/15	11/16-12/9	12/10-12/31		1/1-1/7	1/8-2/2
1874	8/12-9/7	9/8-10/6	1/1-1/2 10/7-12/31	1/3-1/26	1/27-2/19	2/20-3/15
1875	9/23-10/16	10/17-11/9	1/1-2/4 11/10-12/3	2/5-3/6 12/4-12/27	3/7-4/2 12/28-12/31	4/3-4/27
1876	11/4-11/28	11/29-12/23	12/24-12/31		1/1-1/21	1/22-2/14
1877	8/24-9/17	9/18-10/12	1/1-1/16 10/13-11/7	1/17-2/9 11/8-12/4	2/10-3/5 12/5-12/31	3/6-3/29
1878	10/8-10/31	11/1-11/24	11/25-12/18	12/19-12/31	1/1-1/5 2/25-3/30	1/6-2/24 3/31-5/6
1879	8/11-9/24 11/5-12/8	12/9-12/31		1/1-1/11	1/12-2/4	2/5-2/28
1880	9/7-9/30	1/1-1/4 10/1-10/25	1/5-1/30 10/26-11/19	1/31-2/24 11/19-12/13	2/25-3/19 12/14-12/31	3/20-4/13
1881	10/22-11/14	11/15-12/8	12/9-12/31		1/1-1/7	1/8-2/2
1882	8/11-9/6	9/7-10/6	1/1 10/7-12/31	1/2-1/25	1/26-2/18	2/19-3/14
1883	9/23-10/16	10/17-11/9	1/1-2/4 11/10-12/3	2/5-3/6 12/4-12/27	3/7-4/1 12/28-12/31	4/2-4/27
1884	11/4-11/28	11/29-12/22	12/23-12/31		1/1-1/20	1/21-2/14
1885	8/24-9/16	9/17-10/12	1/1-1/16 10/13-11/6	1/17-2/9 11/7-12/4	2/10-3/5 12/5-12/31	3/6-3/29
1886	10/8-10/31	11/1-11/23	11/24-12/17	12/18-12/31	1/1-1/6 2/19-4/1	1/7-2/18 4/2-5/6
1887	8/12-9/18 11/6-12/8	12/9-12/31		1/1-1/10	1/11-2/3	2/4-2/27
1888	9/7-9/30	1/1-1/4 10/1-10/24	1/5-1/29 10/25-11/18	1/30-2/23 11/19-12/12	2/24-3/19 12/13-12/31	3/20-4/12
1889	10/22-11/14	11/15-12/8	12/9-12/31		1/1-1/6	1/7-2/2
1890	8/11-9/6	9/7-10/7	1/1 10/8-12/31	1/2-1/25	1/26-2/18	2/19-3/14
1891	9/22-10/15	10/16-11/8	1/1-2/5 11/9-12/2	2/6-3/5 12/3-12/26	3/6-4/1 12/27-12/31	4/2-4/26
1892	11/3-11/27	11/28-12/22	12/23-12/31		1/1-1/20	1/21-2/13
1893	8/23-9/16	9/17-10/11	1/1-1/15 10/12-11/6	1/16-2/8 11/7-12/4	2/9-3/4 12/5-12/31	3/5-3/28
1894	10/7-10/30	10/31-11/23	11/24-12/17	12/18-12/31	1/1-1/8 2/13-4/2	1/9-2/12 4/3-5/4
1895	8/14-9/12 11/7-12/8	12/9-12/31		1/1-1/10	1/11-2/3	2/4-2/27
1896	9/6-9/29	1/1-1/3 9/30-10/24	1/4-1/29 10/25-11/17	1/30-2/23 11/18-12/12	2/24-3/18 12/13-12/31	3/19-4/12
1897	10/21-11/13	11/14-12/7	12/8-12/31		1/1-1/6	1/7-2/1
1898	8/11-9/6	9/7-10/7	10/8-12/31	1/1-1/24	1/25-2/17	2/18-3/13
1899	9/22-10/15	10/16-11/8	1/1-2/5 11/9-12/2	2/6-3/5 12/3-12/26	3/6-3/31 12/27-12/31	4/1-4/26

	ARIES 37	TAURUS 38	GEMINI 39	CANCER 40	LEO 41	VIRGO 42
1900	2/14-3/10	3/11-4/5	4/6-5/5	5/6-9/8	9/9-10/8	10/9-11/3
1901	3/30-4/22	4/23-5/16	5/17-6/10	6/11-7/4	7/5-7/29	7/30-8/23
1902	5/7-6/3	6/4-6/29	6/30-7/25	7/26-8/19	8/20-9/12	9/13-10/7
1903	2/28-3/23	3/24-4/17	4/18-5/13	5/14-6/8	6/9-7/7	7/8-8/17 9/7-11/8
1904	4/13-5/7	5/8-5/31	6/1-6/25	6/26-7/19	7/20-8/12	8/13-9/6
1905	2/3-3/5 5/9-5/27	3/6-5/8 5/28-7/7	7/8-8/5	8/6-9/1	9/2-9/26	9/27-10/21
1906	3/15-4/7	4/8-5/1	5/2-5/26	5/27-6/20	6/21-7/15	7/16-8/10
1907	4/28-5/22	5/23-6/16	6/17-7/10	7/11-8/3	8/4-8/28	8/29-9/21
1908	2/14-3/9	3/10-4/5	4/6-5/5	5/6-9/8	9/9-10/7	10/8-11/2
1909	3/29-4/21	4/22-5/16	5/17-6/9	6/10-7/4	7/5-7/28	7/29-8/22
1910	5/7-6/3	6/4-6/29	6/30-7/24	7/25-8/18	8/19-9/12	9/13-10/6
1911	2/28-3/23	3/24-4/17	4/18-5/12	5/13-6/8	6/9-7/7	7/8-11/8
1912	4/13-5/6	5/7-5/31	6/1-6/24	6/25-7/18	7/19-8/12	8/13-9/5
1913	2/3-3/6 5/2-5/30	3/7-5/1 5/31-7/7	7/8-8/5	8/6-8/31	9/1-9/26	9/27-10/20
1914	3/14-4/6	4/7-5/1	5/2-5/25	5/26-6/19	6/20-7/15	7/16-8/10
1915	4/27-5/21	5/22-6/15	6/16-7/10	7/11-8/3	8/4-8/28	8/29-9/21
1916	2/14-3/9	3/10-4/5	4/6-5/5	5/6-9/8	9/9-10/7	10/8-11/2
1917	3/29-4/21	4/22-5/15	5/16-6/9	6/10-7/3	7/4-7/28	7/29-8/21
1918	5/7-6/2	6/3-6/28	6/29-7/24	7/25-8/18	8/19-9/11	9/12-10/5
1919	2/27-3/22	3/23-4/16	4/17-5/12	5/13-6/7	6/8-7/7	7/8-11/8
1920	4/12-5/6	5/7-5/30	5/31-6/23	6/24-7/18	7/19-8/11	8/12-9/4
1921	2/3-3/6 4/26-6/1	3/7-4/25 6/2-7/7	7/8-8/5	8/6-8/31	9/1-9/25	9/26-10/20
1922	3/13-4/6	4/7-4/30	5/1-5/25	5/26-6/19	6/20-7/14	7/15-8/9
1923	4/27-5/21	5/22-6/14	6/15-7/9	7/10-8/3	8/4-8/27	8/28-9/20
1924	2/13-3/8	3/9-4/4	4/5-5/5	5/6-9/8	9/9-10/7	10/8-11/2
1925	3/28-4/20	4/21-5/15	5/16-6/8	6/9-7/3	7/4-7/27	7/28-8/21
1926	5/7-6/2	6/3-6/28	6/29-7/23	7/24-8/17	8/18-9/11	9/12-10/5
1927	2/27-3/22	3/23-4/16	4/17-5/11	5/12-6/7	6/8-7/7	7/8-11/9
1928	4/12-5/5	5/6-5/29	5/30-6/23	6/24-7/17	7/18-8/11	8/12-9/4
1929	2/3-3/7 4/20-6/2	3/8-4/19 6/3-7/7	7/8-8/4	8/5-8/30	8/31-9/25	9/26-10/19
1930	3/13-4/5	4/6-4/30	5/1-5/24	5/25-6/18	6/19-7/14	7/15-8/9

	LIBRA 43	SCORPIO 44	SAGITTARIUS 45	CAPRICORN 46	AQUARIUS 47	PISCES 48
1900	11/4-11/28	11/29-12/22	12/23-12/31		1/1-1/19	1/20-2/13
1901	8/24-9/16	9/17-10/12	1/1-1/15	1/16-2/9	2/10-3/5	3/6-3/29
			10/13-11/7	11/8-12/5	12/6-12/31	
1902	10/8-10/30	10/31-11/23	11/24-12/17	12/18-12/31	1/1-1/11	1/12-2/6
					2/7-4/4	4/5-5/6
1903	8/18-9/6	12/10-12/31		1/1-1/10	1/11-2/3	2/4-2/27
	11/9-12/9					
1904	9/7-9/30	1/1-1/4	1/5-1/29	1/30-2/23	2/24-3/19	3/20-4/12
		10/1-10/24	10/25-11/18	11/19-12/12	12/13-12/31	
1905	10/22-11/14	11/15-12/8	12/9-12/31		1/1-1/7	1/8-2/2
1906	8/11-9/7	9/8-10/8	1/1	1/2-1/25	1/26-2/18	2/19-3/14
		12/16-12/25	10/9-12/15			
			12/26-12/31			
1907	9/22-10/15	10/16-11/8	1/1-2/6	2/7-3/6	3/7-4/1	4/2-4/27
			11/9-12/2	12/3-12/26	12/27-12/31	
1908	11/3-11/27	11/28-12/22	12/23-12/31		1/1-1/20	1/21-2/13
1909	8/23-9/16	9/17-10/11	1/1-1/15	1/16-2/8	2/9-3/3	3/4-3/28
			10/12-11/6	11/7-12/5	12/6-12/31	
1910	10/7-10/30	10/31-11/23	11/24-12/17	12/18-12/31	1/1-1/15	1/16-1/28
					1/29-4/4	4/5-5/6
1911	11/9-12/8	12/9-12/31		1/1-1/10	1/11-2/2	2/3-2/27
1912	9/6-9/30	1/1-1/4	1/5-1/29	1/30-2/23	2/24-3/18	3/19-4/12
		10/1-10/24	10/25-11/17	11/18-12/12	12/13-12/31	
1913	10/21-11/13	11/14-12/7	12/8-12/31		1/1-1/6	1/7-2/2
1914	8/11-9/6	9/7-10/9	10/10-12/5	1/1-1/24	1/25-2/17	2/18-3/13
		12/6-12/30	12/31			
1915	9/22-10/15	10/16-11/8	1/1-2/6	2/7-3/6	3/7-4/1	4/2-4/26
			11/9-12/2	12/3-12/26	12/27-12/31	
1916	11/3-11/27	11/28-12/21	12/22-12/31		1/1-1/19	1/20-2/13
1917	8/22-9/16	9/17-10/11	1/1-1/14	1/15-2/7	2/8-3/4	3/5-3/28
			10/12-11/6	11/7-12/5	12/6-12/31	
1918	10/6-10/29	10/30-11/22	11/23-12/16	12/17-12/31	1/1-4/5	4/6-5/6
1919	11/9-12/8	12/9-12/31		1/1-1/9	1/10-2/2	2/3-2/26
1920	9/5-9/30	1/1-1/3	1/4-1/28	1/29-2/22	2/23-3/18	3/19-4/11
		9/31-10/23	10/24-11/17	11/18-12/11	12/12-12/31	
1921	10/21-11/13	11/14-12/7	12/8-12/31		1/1-1/6	1/7-2/2
1922	8/10-9/6	9/7-10/10	10/11-11/28	1/1-1/24	1/25-2/16	2/17-3/12
		11/29-12/31				
1923	9/21-10/14	1/1	1/2-2/6	2/7-3/5	3/6-3/31	4/1-4/26
		10/15-11/7	11/8-12/1	12/2-12/25	12/26-12/31	
1924	11/3-11/26	11/27-12/21	12/22-12/31		1/1-1/19	1/20-2/12
1925	8/22-9/15	9/16-10/11	1/1-1/14	1/15-2/7	2/8-3/3	3/4-3/27
			10/12-11/6	11/7-12/5	12/6-12/31	
1926	10/6-10/29	10/30-11/22	11/23-12/16	12/17-12/31	1/1-4/5	4/6-5/6
1927	11/10-12/8	12/9-12/31	1/1-1/7	1/8	1/9-2/1	2/2-2/26
1928	9/5-9/28	1/1-1/3	1/4-1/28	1/29-2/22	2/23-3/17	3/18-4/11
		9/29-10/23	10/24-11/16	11/17-12/11	12/12-12/31	
1929	10/20-11/12	11/13-12/6	12/7-12/30	12/31	1/1-1/5	1/6-2/2
1930	8/10-9/6	9/7-10/11	10/12-11/21	1/1-1/23	1/24-2/16	2/17-3/12
		11/22-12/31				

	ARIES 37	TAURUS 38	GEMINI 39	CANCER 40	LEO 41	VIRGO 42
1931	4/26-5/20	5/21-6/13	6/14-7/8	7/9-8/2	8/3-8/26	8/27-9/19
1932	2/12-3/8	3/9-4/3	4/4-5/5 7/13-7/27	5/6-7/12 7/28-9/8	9/9-10/6	10/7-11/1
1933	3/27-4/19	4/20-5/28	5/29-6/8	6/9-7/2	7/3-7/26	7/27-8/20
1934	5/6-6/1	6/2-6/27	6/28-7/22	7/23-8/16	8/17-9/10	9/11-10/4
1935	2/26-3/21	3/22-4/15	4/16-5/10	5/11-6/6	6/7-7/6	7/7-11/8
1936	4/11-5/4	5/5-5/28	5/29-6/22	6/23-7/16	7/17-8/10	8/11-9/4
1937	2/2-3/8 4/14-6/3	3/9-4/13 6/4-7/6	7/7-8/3	8/4-8/29	8/30-9/24	9/25-10/18
1938	3/12-4/4	4/5-4/28	4/29-5/23	5/24-6/18	6/19-7/13	7/14-8/8
1939	4/25-5/19	5/20-6/13	6/14-7/8	7/9-8/1	8/2-8/25	8/26-9/19
1940	2/12-3/7	3/8-4/3	4/4-5/5 7/5-7/31	5/6-7/4 8/1-9/8	9/9-10/5	10/6-10/31
1941	3/27-4/19	4/20-5/13	5/14-6/6	6/7-7/1	7/2-7/26	7/27-8/20
1942	5/6-6/1	6/2-6/26	6/27-7/22	7/23-8/16	8/17-9/9	9/10-10/3
1943	2/25-3/20	3/21-4/14	4/15-5/10	5/11-6/6	6/7-7/6	7/7-11/8
1944	4/10-5/3	5/4-5/28	5/29-6/21	6/22-7/16	7/17-8/9	8/10-9/2
1945	2/2-3/10 4/7-6/3	3/11-4/6 6/4-7/6	7/7-8/3	8/4-8/29	8/30-9/23	9/24-10/18
1946	3/11-4/4	4/5-4/28	4/29-5/23	5/24-6/17	6/18-7/12	7/13-8/8
1947	4/25-5/19	5/20-6/12	6/13-7/7	7/8-8/1	8/2-8/25	8/26-9/18
1948	2/11-3/7	3/8-4/3	4/4-5/6 6/29-8/2	5/7-6/28 8/3-9/7	9/8-10/5	10/6-10/31
1949	3/26-4/19	4/20-5/13	5/14-6/6	6/7-6/30	7/1-7/25	7/26-8/19
1950	5/5-5/31	6/1-6/26	6/27-7/21	7/22-8/15	8/16-9/9	9/10-10/3
1951	2/25-3/21	3/22-4/15	4/16-5/10	5/11-6/6	6/7-7/7	7/8-11/9
1952	4/10-5/4	5/5-5/28	5/29-6/21	6/22-7/16	7/17-8/9	8/10-9/3
1953	2/2-3/13 4/1-6/5	3/14-3/31 6/6-7/7	7/8-8/3	8/4-8/29	8/30-9/24	9/25-10/18
1954	3/12-4/4	4/5-4/28	4/29-5/23	5/24-6/17	6/18-7/13	7/14-8/8
1955	4/25-5/19	5/20-6/13	6/14-7/7	7/8-8/1	8/2-8/25	8/26-9/18
1956	2/12-3/7	3/8-4/4	4/5-5/7 6/24-8/4	5/8-6/23 8/5-9/8	9/9-10/5	10/6-10/31
1957	3/26-4/19	4/20-5/13	5/14-6/6	6/7-7/1	7/2-7/26	7/27-8/19
1958	5/6-5/31	6/1-6/26	6/27-7/22	7/23-8/15	8/16-9/9	9/10-10/3
1959	2/25-3/20	3/21-4/14	4/15-5/10	5/11-6/6	6/7-7/8 9/21-9/24	7/9-9/20 9/25-11/9

	LIBRA 43	SCORPIO 44	SAGITTARIUS 45	CAPRICORN 46	AQUARIUS 47	PISCES 48
1931	9/20-10/13	1/1-1/3	1/4-2/6	2/7-3/4	3/5-3/31	4/1-4/25
		10/14-11/6	11/7-11/30	12/1-12/24	12/25-12/31	
1932	11/2-11/25	11/26-12/20	12/21-12/31		1/1-1/18	1/19-2/11
1933	8/21-9/14	9/15-10/10	1/1-1/13	1/14-2/6	2/7-3/2	3/3-3/26
			10/11-11/5	11/6-12/4	12/5-12/31	
1934	10/5-10/28	10/29-11/21	11/22-12/15	12/16-12/31	1/1-4/5	4/6-5/5
1935	11/9-12/7	12/8-12/31		1/1-1/7	1/8-1/31	2/1-2/25
1936	9/5-9/27	1/1-1/2	1/3-1/27	1/28-2/21	2/22-3/16	3/17-4/10
		9/28-10/22	10/23-11/15	11/16-12/10	12/11-12/31	
1937	10/19-11/11	11/12-12/5	12/6-12/29	12/30-12/31	1/1-1/5	1/6-2/1
1938	8/9-9/6	9/7-10/13	10/14-11/14	1/1-1/22	1/23-2/15	2/16-3/11
		11/15-12/31				
1939	9/20-10/13	1/1-1/3	1/4-2/5	2/6-3/4	3/5-3/30	3/31-4/24
		10/14-11/6	11/7-11/30	12/1-12/24	12/25-12/31	
1940	11/1-11/25	11/26-12/19	12/20-12/31		1/1-1/18	1/19-2/11
1941	8/21-9/14	9/15-10/9	1/1-1/5	1/13-2/5	2/6-3/1	3/2-3/26
			10/10-11/5	11/6-12/4	12/5-12/31	
1942	10/4-10/27	10/28-11/20	11/21-12/14	12/15-12/31	1/1-4/4	4/6-5/5
1943	11/9-12/7	12/8-12/31		1/1-1/7	1/8-1/31	2/1-2/24
1944	9/3-9/27	1/1-1/2	1/3-1/27	1/28-2/20	2/21-3/16	3/17-4/9
		9/28-10/21	10/22-11/15	11/16-12/10	12/11-12/31	
1945	10/19-11/11	11/12-12/5	12/6-12/29	12/30-12/31	1/1-1/4	1/5-2/1
1946	8/9-9/6	9/7-10/15	10/16-11/7	1/1-1/21	1/22-2/14	2/15-3/10
		11/8-12/31				
1947	9/19-10/12	1/1-1/4	1/5-2/5	2/6-3/4	3/5-3/29	3/30-4/23
		10/13-11/5	11/6-11/29	11/30-12/23	12/24-12/31	
1948	11/1-11/25	11/26-12/19	12/20-12/31		1/1-1/17	1/18-2/10
1949	8/20-9/14	9/15-10/9	1/1-1/12	1/13-2/5	2/6-3/1	3/2-3/25
			10/10-11/5	11/6-12/5	12/6-12/31	
1950	10/4-10/27	10/28-11/20	11/21-12/13	12/14-12/31	1/1-4/5	4/6-5/4
1951	11/10-12/7	12/8-12/31		1/1-1/7	1/8-1/31	2/1-2/24
1952	9/4-9/27	1/1-1/2	1/3-1/27	1/28-2/20	2/21-3/16	3/17-4/9
		9/28-10/21	10/22-11/15	11/16-12/10	12/11-12/31	
1953	10/19-11/11	11/12-12/5	12/6-12/29	12/30-12/31	1/1-1/5	1/6-2/1
1954	8/9-9/6	9/7-10/22	10/23-10/27	1/1-1/22	1/23-2/15	2/16-3/11
		10/28-12/31				
1955	9/19-10/13	1/1-1/6	1/7-2/5	2/6-3/4	3/5-3/30	3/31-4/24
		10/14-11/5	11/6-11/30	12/1-12/24	12/25-12/31	
1956	11/1-11/25	11/26-12/19	12/20-12/31		1/1-1/17	1/18-2/11
1957	8/20-9/14	9/15-10/9	1/1-1/12	1/13-2/5	2/6-3/1	3/2-3/25
			10/10-11/5	11/6-12/6	12/7-12/31	
1958	10/4-10/27	10/28-11/20	11/21-12/14	12/15-12/31	1/1-4/6	4/7-5/5
1959	11/10-12/7	12/8-12/31		1/1-1/7	1/8-1/31	2/1-2/24

	ARIES 37	TAURUS 38	GEMINI 39	CANCER 40	LEO 41	VIRGO 42
1960	4/10-5/3	5/4-5/28	5/29-6/21	6/22-7/15	7/16-8/9	8/10-9/2
1961	2/3-6/5	6/6-7/7	7/8-8/3	8/4-8/29	8/30-9/23	9/24-10/17
1962	3/11-4/3	4/4-4/28	4/29-5/22	5/23-6/17	6/18-7/12	7/13-8/8
1963	4/24-5/18	5/19-6/12	6/13-7/7	7/8-7/31	8/1-8/25	8/26-9/18
1964	2/11-3/7	3/8-4/4	4/5-5/9 6/18-8/5	5/10-6/17 8/6-9/8	9/9-10/5	10/6-10/31
1965	3/26-4/18	4/19-5/12	5/13-6/6	6/7-6/30	7/1-7/25	7/26-8/19
1966	5/6-5/31	6/1-6/26	6/27-7/21	7/22-8/15	8/16-9/8	9/9-10/2
1967	2/24-3/20	3/21-4/14	4/15-5/10	5/11-6/6	6/7-7/8 9/10-10/1	7/9-9/9 10/2-11/9
1968	4/9-5/3	5/4-5/27	5/28-6/20	6/21-7/15	7/16-8/8	8/9-9/2
1969	2/3-6/6	6/7-7/6	7/7-8/3	8/4-8/28	8/29-9/22	9/23-10/17
1970	3/11-4/3	4/4-4/27	4/28-5/22	5/23-6/16	6/17-7/12	7/13-8/8
1971	4/24-5/17	5/18-6/12	6/13-7/6	7/7-7/31	8/1-8/24	8/25-9/17
1972	2/11-3/7	3/8-4/3	4/4-5/10 6/12-8/6	5/11-6/11 8/7-9/7	9/8-10/4	10/5-10/30
1973	3/25-4/18	4/19-5/12	5/13-6/5	6/6-6/30	7/1-7/25	7/26-8/19
1974	5/5-5/31	6/1-6/25	6/26-7/21	7/22-8/14	8/15-9/8	9/9-10/2
1975	2/24-3/19	3/20-4/13	4/14-5/9	5/10-6/6	6/7-7/9 9/3-10/4	7/10-9/2 10/5-11/9
1976	4/9-5/2	5/3-5/27	5/28-6/20	6/21-7/14	7/15-8/8	8/9-9/1
1977	2/3-6/6	6/7-7/6	7/7-8/2	8/3-8/28	8/29-9/22	9/23-10/17
1978	3/10-4/2	4/3-4/27	4/28-5/22	5/23-6/16	6/17-7/12	7/13-8/8
1979	4/24-5/18	5/19-6/11	6/12-7/6	7/7-7/30	7/31-8/24	8/25-9/17
1980	2/10-3/6	3/7-4/3	4/4-5/12 6/6-8/6	5/13-6/5 8/7-9/7	9/8-10/4	10/5-10/30
1981	3/25-4/17	4/18-5/12	5/13-6/5	6/6-6/29	6/30-7/24	7/25-8/18
1982	5/5-5/30	5/31-6/25	6/26-7/20	7/21-8/14	8/15-9/7	9/8-10/2
1983	2/23-3/19	3/20-4/13	4/14-5/9	5/10-6/6	6/7-7/10 8/28-10/5	7/11-8/27 10/6-11/9
1984	4/8-5/2	5/3-5/26	5/27-6/20	6/21-7/14	7/15-8/7	8/8-9/1
1985	2/3-6/6	6/7-7/6	7/7-8/2	8/3-8/28	8/29-9/22	9/23-10/16
1986	3/10-4/2	4/3-4/26	4/27-5/21	5/22-6/15	6/16-7/11	7/12-8/7
1987	4/23-5/17	5/18-6/11	6/12-7/5	7/6-7/30	7/31-8/23	8/24-9/16
1988	2/10-3/6	3/7-4/3	4/4-5/17 5/28-8/6	5/18-5/27 8/7-9/7	9/8-10/4	10/5-10/29
1989	3/24-4/16	4/17-5/11	5/12-6/4	6/5-6/29	6/30-7/24	7/25-8/8
1990	5/5-5/30	5/31-6/25	6/26-7/20	7/21-8/13	8/14-9/7	9/8-10/1
1991	2/23-3/18	3/19-4/13	4/14-5/9	5/10-6/6	6/7-7/11 8/22-10/6	7/12-8/21 10/7-11/9

	LIBRA 43	SCORPIO 44	SAGITTARIUS 45	CAPRICORN 46	AQUARIUS 47	PISCES 48
1960	9/3-9/26	1/1-1/2 9/27-10/21	1/3-1/27 10/22-11/15	1/28-2/20 11/16-12/10	2/21-3/15 12/11-12/31	3/16-4/9
1961	10/18-11/11	11/12-12/4	12/5-12/28	12/29-12/31	1/1-1/5	1/6-2/2
1962	8/9-9/6	9/7-12/31		1/1-1/21	1/22-2/14	2/15-3/10
1963	9/19-10/12	1/1-1/6 10/13-11/5	1/7-2/5 11/6-11/29	2/6-3/4 11/30-12/23	3/5-3/29 12/24-12/31	3/30-4/23
1964	11/1-11/24	11/25-12/19	12/20-12/31		1/1-1/16	1/17-2/10
1965	8/20-9/13	9/14-10/9	1/1-1/12 10/10-11/5	1/13-2/5 11/6-12/7	2/6-3/1 12/8-12/31	3/2-3/25
1966	10/3-10/26	10/27-11/19	11/20-12/13	2/7-2/25 12/14-12/31	1/1-1/26 2/26-4/6	4/7-5/5
1967	11/10-12/7	12/8-12/31		1/1-1/6	1/7-1/30	1/31-2/23
1968	9/3-9/26	1/1 9/27-10/21	1/2-1/26 10/22-11/14	1/27-2/20 11/15-12/9	2/21-3/15 12/10-12/31	3/16-4/8
1969	10/18-11/10	11/11-12/4	12/5-12/28	12/29-12/31	1/1-1/4	1/5-2/2
1970	8/9-9/7	9/8-12/31		1/1-1/21	1/22-2/14	2/15-3/10
1971	9/18-10/17	1/1-1/7 10/18-11/5	1/8-2/5 11/6-11/29	2/6-3/4 11/30-12/23	3/5-3/29 12/24-12/31	3/30-4/23
1972	10/31-11/24	11/25-12/18	12/19-12/31		1/1-1/16	1/17-2/10
1973	8/20-9/13	9/14-10/9	1/1-1/11 10/10-11/5	1/12-2/4 11/6-12/7	2/5-2/28 12/8-12/31	3/1-3/24
1974	10/3-10/26	10/27-11/19	11/20-12/13	1/30-2/28 12/14-12/31	1/1-1/29 3/1-4/6	4/7-5/4
1975	11/10-12/7	12/8-12/31		1/1-1/6	1/7-1/30	1/31-2/23
1976	9/2-9/26	1/1 9/27-10/20	1/2-1/26 10/21-11/14	1/27-2/19 11/15-12/9	2/20-3/15 12/10-12/31	3/16-4/8
1977	10/18-11/10	11/11-12/4	12/5-12/27	12/28-12/31	1/1-1/4	1/5-2/2
1978	8/9-9/7	9/8-12/31		1/1-1/20	1/21-2/13	2/14-3/9
1979	9/18-10/11	1/1-1/7 10/12-11/4	1/8-2/5 11/5-11/28	2/6-3/3 11/29-12/22	3/4-3/29 12/23-12/31	3/30-4/23
1980	10/31-11/24	11/25-12/18	12/19-12/31		1/1-1/16	1/17-2/9
1981	8/19-9/12	9/13-10/8	1/1-1/11 10/9-11/5	1/12-2/4 11/6-12/8	2/5-2/28 12/9-12/31	3/1-3/24
1982	10/3-10/26	10/27-11/18	11/19-12/12	1/24-3/2 12/13-12/31	1/1-1/23 3/3-4/6	4/7-5/4
1983	11/10-12/6	12/7-12/31		1/1-1/5	1/6-1/29	1/30-2/22
1984	9/2-9/25	1/1 9/26-10/20	1/2-1/25 10/21-11/13	1/26-2/19 11/14-12/9	2/20-3/14 12/10-12/31	3/15-4/7
1985	10/17-11/9	11/10-12/3	12/4-12/27	12/28-12/31	1/1-1/4	1/5-2/2
1986	8/8-9/7	9/8-12/31		1/1-1/20	1/21-2/13	2/14-3/9
1987	9/17-10/10	1/1-1/7 10/11-11/3	1/8-2/5 11/4-11/28	2/6-3/3 11/29-12/22	3/4-3/28 12/23-12/31	3/29-4/22
1988	10/30-11/23	11/24-12/17	12/18-12/31		1/1-1/15	1/16-2/9
1989	8/9-9/12	9/13-10/8	1/1-1/10 10/9-11/5	1/11-2/3 11/6-12/10	2/4-2/27 12/11-12/31	2/28-3/23
1990	10/2-10/25	10/26-11/18	11/19-12/12	1/17-3/3 12/13-12/31	1/1-1/16 3/4-4/6	4/7-5/4
1991	11/10-12/6	12/7-12/31		1/1-1/5	1/6-1/29	1/30-2/22

	ARIES 37	TAURUS 38	GEMINI 39	CANCER 40	LEO 41	VIRGO 42
1992	4/8-5/1	5/2-5/26	5/27-6/19	6/20-7/13	7/14-8/7	8/8-8/31
1993	2/3-6/6	6/7-7/6	7/7-8/1	8/2-8/27	8/28-9/21	9/22-10/16
1994	3/9-4/1	4/2-4/26	4/27-5/21	5/22-6/15	6/16-7/11	7/12-8/7
1995	4/23-5/16	5/17-6/10	6/11-7/5	7/6-7/29	7/30-8/23	8/24-9/16
1996	2/10-3/6	3/7-4/3	4/4-8/7	8/8-9/7	9/8-10/4	10/5-10/29
1997	3/24-4/16	4/17-5/10	5/11-6/4	6/5-6/28	6/29-7/23	7/24-8/17
1998	5/4-5/29	5/30-6/24	6/25-7/19	7/20-8/13	8/14-9/6	9/7-9/30
1999	2/22-3/18	3/19-4/12	4/13-5/8	5/9-6/5	6/6-7/12 8/16-10/7	7/13-8/15 10/8-11/9

	LIBRA 43	SCORPIO 44	SAGITTARIUS 45	CAPRICORN 46	AQUARIUS 47	PISCES 48
1992	9/1-9/25	9/26-10/19	1/1-1/25 10/20-11/13	1/26-2/18 11/14-12/8	2/19-3/13 12/9-12/31	3/14-4/7
1993	10/17-11/9	11/10-12/2	12/3-12/26	12/27-12/31		1/4-2/2
1994	8/8-9/7	9/8-12/31		1/1-1/19	1/20-2/12	2/13-3/8
1995	9/17-10/10	1/1-1/7 10/11-11/3	1/8-2/4 11/4-11/27	2/5-3/2 11/28-12/21	3/3-3/28 12/22-12/31	3/29-4/22
1996	10/30-11/23	11/24-12/17		12/18-12/31	1/1-1/15	1/16-2/9
1997	8/18-9/12	9/13-10/8	1/1-1/10 10/9-11/5	1/11-2/3 11/6-12/12	2/4-2/27 12/13-12/31	2/28-3/23
1998	10/1-10/24	10/25-11/17	11/18-12/11	1/10-3/4 12/12-12/31	1/1-1/9 3/5-4/6	4/7-5/3
1999	11/10-12/5	12/6-12/31		1/1-1/4	1/5-1/28	1/29-2/21

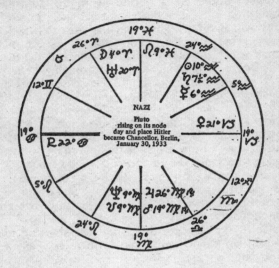

When Pluto, the third of the social-movement planets, came to his north node in Cancer, the Nazi revolution brought Hitler to power in Germany. The above chart is set for the rising of Pluto on its own node, on the date Hitler became Chancellor, January 30, 1933. Note the exact mundane square of the retrograde Mars to Pluto's rising node, with Pluto himself in zodiacal square to the 10th House Uranus. See also pages 149 (U.S. chart) and 183 (U.S.S.R. chart). These charts, with their interlockings and developments according to planetary movement, tell much of the history of our times, and will well repay study.

MARS

Mars is the energy principle in the Vitasphere. His position by sign indicates the channels into which energy will naturally flow, and the uses to which energy will most easily be directed. It is the planet through which the activities of the Sun and the desires of the Moon express in action—through which your body and your mind react to the sense impressions of Mercury and the emotional impressions of Venus. *In the same sign with the Sun,* Mars gives abundant energy, sometimes misdirected in temper, temperament and quarrels. *In the same sign with the Moon,* great capacity to make use of the innermost aims, and to make the inner desires articulate and practical. *In the same sign with Venus,* quickens emotional reactions and causes you to act on them; makes for ardor and passion in love, and a general earthly awareness of emotional realities.

Get Mars' sign position from the tables on pages 211–218. Note the sign in your birth record, and read the indicated paragraph.

49. MARS IN ARIES

Your usually abundant energies are directed primarily along lines of ego assertion. You feel best, act best when you are not limited or restricted by elders, superiors, authority of any kind. You are swift to anger at any intrusion on your personal rights; you are quick on the trigger—the adrenal gland, controlling fight and/or flight is sensitive, reacting sharply and generally on the aggressive side. You are a formidable adversary, for all your vitality is brought at once to bear on anyone who challenges your pre-eminence. Even in the chart of an otherwise timid soul, this will lend scrappiness to the nature. If your life aim is more detached, if you are ambitious for worldly success, popularity, or any of the things that require self-control, your Mars will periodically trip you by directing your energies toward self-assertion at times when you ought to be thinking of something else. The abrupt, aggressive speech, the sharp retort when your independence is assailed (or when you imagine it to be), can stand between you and the rewards of self-control. To serve the deeper ends of life that frequently require forgetfulness of self, you must continuously stand guard over the tendency of your energies to flow through the millrace of the ego into strife and disharmony.

50. MARS IN TAURUS

You work most naturally along lines related to security, and are your best self only when this is assured. Worry over money throws you off balance: you need to be able to take for granted at least the essential comforts of life, and can get to demand a good deal more on the luxury side. You may get, have, spend and lose much property in your lifetime; conservatism in finances is not well marked, and you have to learn it by main strength and ignorance. In a deep sense you relate security to emotional as well as financial matters, are ardent and stable in love, require (and generally get) plenty of sex satisfaction. Yet in this, as in money, your energies can run away into prodigality and excesses. You are "sot in your ways," know how you want to do things, and generally manage to do them that way. You are not exactly aggressive in your search for independence; you don't make a big fuss about it, but you get what you want. Your motto is, "I don't want to fight; just let's do it my way," and with or without the consent of the governed, you generally prevail. You are a master of the art of passive aggression and passive resistance; whether your habits are right or wrong, good or bad, constructive or destructive, you keep plowing along in the same furrow, and those who would oppose you generally stand to one side or get mowed down. Love and finances alike can fall before you, and your constant aim in life should be to stand aside from your own desires, your own intuition, and the things you take for granted, in order that you may judge objectively the value of your fixation and your effort.

51. MARS IN GEMINI

Your energies flow naturally into adventurous paths. Movement, physical and mental, is essential to you, and you express best when working, playing, living actively, preferably at high speed. You are rarely bored or boring, but you can wear others, and yourself, out by the ferocity of your attack on life. You are extraordinarily aware of the world around you; sense perceptions are acute, swift, probably accurate; and you are voluble in expressing what you take in. Energy flows naturally to the tongue; you are a better talker than a listener; and are generally glib, discursive, extensive in your remarks written or spoken. With any concentrative force, this position gains value, without it, you scatter your energies. You are something of a sensualist and like the physical expressions of love; you probably think sex is more important to you than it really is, and by thinking make it so. Energy flows into mind force as well as into physical activity; this is peculiarly a position in which, to have a sound mind, you must also have a sound body. You must beware of neglecting your physical well-being through letting your energies dam up in the pools of the mind; also of being blocked by sensational thoughts which from time to time will tend to dominate you. The negative reactions of the sex urge, such as envy, jealousy, hatred, can frustrate you if you let them get hold. Mind control and bodily vigor are the two things for which you should constantly strive.

52. MARS IN CANCER

You are at a disadvantage, for the aggressive energetic urges work here through the defensive sectors of the Vitasphere, and the result can more often than not be an undermining of the very security you think you are working for. In its best manifestation, this makes you a gentle and peaceful soul, content to give yourself to the establishing of a home and the rearing of children. But this best manifestation is rare. You will in any case *think* this is what you would want out of life if—alas!—so many things did not demand attention first! Women with this position have a curious way of ruling the roost, at the same time that they think they want a strong brave man to shield them from the world. Men with this position frequently are ruled by their women or by the psychological biases rooted in the mother inheritance. You must constantly strive to direct your energies, your passions, your intuitions, and prevent them from directing you. You tend to try too hard, and thus to lose the benefits of the free flow of instinct. And through trying too hard, or demanding too much, you run the risk of endangering the very security without which you never will express your best self. Your fears are all too likely to get the upper hand and to cause you to exaggerate little troubles. You make mountains out of molehills, and the mountains bring forth an avalanche on your head. You take yourself and your private life too seriously; and must beware of destructively directing into them the energies that should be flowing out to the world of business or society.

53. MARS IN LEO

Energy flows normally in self-centered channels, serving the main bent of your nature by insuring that you will always, as if by instinct, put your best foot forward. You have abundant animal magnetism and charm, and can "get away with murder": people take things from you that they'd be angry at another about, and you like to "make 'em take it and like it." You are probably easy to look at, and make the most of your natural graces. Your energies are the willing servant of your ego, enabling you to dramatize whatever life task you set yourself. Energy may or may not be abundant, but in any case you make the most of what you have: this is the position of someone who "dies with his boots on" and can always be counted on to do his duty, provided the duty is one that he can relate to his deep ego centers. This is not a genuinely unselfish position for Mars, though if the total personality requires unselfishness, the energies will work toward this end as readily as toward another. This position of Mars in itself tells little about the character or personality, except that whatever the ego demands, Mars will serve with stability and a good deal of self-dramatization.

54. MARS IN VIRGO

Your energies are directed to system, or, in the negative manifestation, to no-system. "When it's good it's very very good, and when it's bad, it's horrid." One way or another, your effort is related to the order of your life. You will be the most systematic, logical, orderly, precise person in the world. Or else you will live from hand to mouth, your rooms in disorder, in constant rebellion against putting things where they belong. To get anywhere with this position of Mars you must learn how to accept the details of life, to take them for granted, so as to release your excellent mental energies into progressive channels. Until you have put your house in order, there is no place for you in the outer world. Once you have achieved order, you must progress to the point where you take it for granted; because to spend all your time dusting and straightening up is as wasteful as to spend all your time looking for things. Master detail, forget it, and then let your cleverness—of which you have plenty! —go to work on more essential things. The danger of this position is narrowness of effort through inability to see the forest for the trees; its great virtue can be mastery of detail, and the ability to bring large ventures into being from small, sound beginnings.

55. MARS IN LIBRA

Your social urges are powerful—sometimes too powerful for your own good. You are emotionally impressionable—your energies flow out to others and carom back to you with the added magnetism of other people, good or bad. You are sensitive to what you call love, and one way or another will have a lot of it in your life. You seem to sense instinctively that you are too impressionable, and in an effort to seem more independent than you are, will quarrel unnecessarily with those who impress you most forcibly—it is your defense against succumbing to them utterly. You must strive for true co-operativeness of spirit, instead of being alternately as meek as a lamb and as mad as a hornet. Your energies and your emotions are always working together or against each other: your emotions express energetically and physically, and your energies run wild through emotional channels. You require detachment of spirit, objectivity of approach to other people, and moderation in the social and love instincts which tend to run away with you, upset your life and destroy your peace. Learn to accept other people more easily, to achieve true union with others and to fight down all extremes of human relations. Enmity and anger disturb the ego centers in you more than in most people; to be your best self requires harmony, and to achieve true harmony, you must learn that living with others is a two-way business and is not helped either by complete self-surrender or complete self-assertion.

56. MARS IN SCORPIO

The most impressive position of Mars in the Vitasphere. It can be the best or the worst of all possible things to find in the chart. In its best form the energies flow into channels that make for deep personal security, through business and love. Magnetism is powerful; the vital forces serve the ego forcefully, to draw others and hold them, and to extract from the world the maximum of material and spiritual benefits. In its worst form, the same security urges turn to fear that the ends of the ego will not be achieved, and the native seeks escape in a variety of undesirable forms. He becomes timid, vacillating, quarrelsome, self-indulgent and apparently weak. Some of the good and some of the bad are likely to show forth in your life as a result of this position. Your constant aim must be self-control—to direct your energies and your habits away from yourself into objective action; to draw other people to you, and to hold them, with love rather than fear; to avoid the negative, destructive instincts of jealousy, fear, suspicion; and to achieve faith in yourself, your world and the people who inhabit it with you. Your energies are an almost tangible force emanating from you in a sort of aura; you make yourself felt wherever you are; and can genuinely build up or tear down another person by what you think about him. This is because your instincts are so powerful that you show in movement, action and tone what you innerly are believing, and you are nearly as effective in silence as in speech. You should cultivate mind power, reserve, self-discipline in order to lead your magnetism into channels where it will help and not hinder you.

57. MARS IN SAGITTARIUS

You lead your energies into physical channels. Exercise is important to you; vigorous activity helps both body and brain. Any tendency to become studious or bookish will have an admirable balance here, for this is one of the most vital positions of Mars, leading to proficiency in sports and a love for games and contests of all kinds. You're a gracious winner, a cheerful loser: the excitement of the game itself is as important to you as winning. This detachment of spirit carries over from the realm of sports into the realm of learning, and you are capable of high scholastic achievement, more likely in *belles-lettres* than in science. You love to generalize, and may be irked by the details of life: a love of order is not usual with this position of Mars, and must be studiously cultivated. A kind of haphazard, slapdash way of going at things should also be overcome—you try to move faster than possible sometimes, and trip over things or over your own feet. For this reason you have to be careful of accidents. Also, you have to beware that, by keeping your eyes fixed on high and far-off things, you don't miss the essentials of life. All well enough to have your head in the clouds, if your feet don't stumble on the path. Many things are forgiven you because of the loftiness of your aims; but you should never forgive yourself for failure because your aim is high. Remember that the hill of dreams has its base in the earth, and that any-

one who would reach the top must first fight his way
through the brambles on the lower pathways.

58. MARS IN CAPRICORN

You have practical control over your energies,
which normally express themselves in a way that pro-
motes your highest and most worldly aspirations.
Controlled actions and speech come naturally to you;
your vitality works well in the harness of the world as
it is, and you can master details as well as the executive functions. You are tactful in a proud sort of way:
you say the right thing without yielding your dignity
or compromising with the truth as you see it. You are
a born leader, having the first requisites of leadership:
control of yourself and ability to take orders. This is
one of the most favorable positions of Mars for worldly success, for you will rarely do anything that interferes with your security, or with security's broader
manifestation, desire for power; and in one way or
another, authority will accumulate in your hands if
you don't block the free flow of your vitality with too
much self-confidence. You can afford to "sit loose in
the saddle of fate" in the assurance that your mount
will carry you where you want to go, and you should
respect the steed by sparing whip and spur.

59. MARS IN AQUARIUS

Your energies flow into social channels which
may be quite idealistic or quite personal. The more
idealistic you can make them, the more you can prevent the social urges from becoming centered in yourself, the greater will be your success and happiness.
There is a constant struggle within you between self
and others; you are a pretty high-strung person. To
translate your energies away from nerves and into
channels of material and social progress is to achieve
the best that this position has to offer. You have constantly to fight a curious trend toward introversion, for
as indicated by all the positions of Mars in the fixed
signs, you may become set in your ways and your de-

sires, and must therefore see to it that your desires reside primarily outside yourself, in the world of material affairs. If you run into difficulties with the world—and you often do, one way or another—you will tend to feel sorry for yourself, and perhaps to console yourself in ways that block your progress. Genuine humanitarianism is your best role; whether you are in business, a profession or the arts, gear your energies to thoughts of others, and rest assured that the benefits of your efforts will thus come back to you, like bread cast on the waters.

60. MARS IN PISCES

Mars tends to disappear in Pisces, and your vitality is likely to be low and jumpy. You tire easily, and thus withdraw a good deal into yourself. Energy can waste itself in brooding, introspection, and fears, if you aren't constantly on guard against these. You should select for yourself activities that don't tax the physical body too much, and learn to follow the ebb and flow of your strength. You can in this way, by being on the *qui vive* for the tides of your life, go a long way, for when you are not working, you are storing up ideas and vitality in the conscious and subconscious that express later. But when you try to keep going all the time, you lose energy, magnetism and ideas. You shouldn't try for too much physical expression of love, for your energies don't work here any more constantly than in other physical matters. When you're tired, you aren't worth much and tend to think badly of yourself. Master yourself by allowing plenty of time for rest and by being willing to go at a slower pace. Your mind works best in repose and solitude, and you should learn to lapse into both of these gracefully, without allowing them to become brooding and depression of spirits.

	ARIES 49	TAURUS 50	GEMINI 51	CANCER 52	LEO 53	VIRGO 54
1870	3/23-4/30	5/1-6/10	6/11-7/24	7/25-9/8	9/9-10/28	10/29-12/30
1871						3/18-6/15
1872	3/2-4/10	4/11-5/21	5/22-7/3	7/4-8/18	8/19-10/5	10/6-11/24
1873						
1874	2/9-3/21	3/22-5/2	5/3-6/15	6/16-7/30	7/31-9/15	9/16-11/2
1875						
1876	1/17-2/27	2/28-4/10	4/11-5/25	5/26-7/11	7/12-8/27	8/28-10/13
1877	12/10-12/31					
1878	1/1-1/30	1/31-3/19	3/20-5/5	5/6-6/22	6/23-8/9	8/10-9/25
1879	6/9-7/23	7/24-12/31				
1880		1/1-2/13	2/14-4/11	4/12-6/1	6/2-7/20	7/21-9/5
1881	5/13-6/21	6/22-8/3	8/4-9/23	9/24-12/31		
1882			1/12-2/25	1/1-1/11 2/26-5/7	5/8-6/30	7/1-8/18
1883	4/21-5/29	5/30-7/10	7/11-8/23	8/24-10/14	10/15-12/31	
1884					1/1-6/4	6/5-7/27
1885	3/31-5/8	5/9-6/18	6/19-7/31	8/1-9/16	9/17-11/8	11/9-12/31
1886						1/1-7/1
1887	3/11-4/18	4/19-5/29	5/30-7/11	7/12-8/26	8/27-10/13	10/14-12/5
1888						
1889	2/17-3/28	3/29-5/9	5/10-6/22	6/23-8/6	8/7-9/22	9/23-11/10
1890						
1891	1/26-3/7	3/8-4/19	4/20-6/3	6/4-7/19	7/20-9/4	9/5-10/21
1892	12/28					
1893	1/1-2/10	2/11-3/28	3/29-5/13	5/14-6/29	6/30-8/15	8/16-10/1
1894	6/23-8/18 10/13-12/30	8/19-10/12 12/31				
1895		1/1-3/1	3/2-4/21	4/22-6/10	6/11-7/28	7/29-9/13
1896	5/22-7/1	7/2-8/15	8/16-12/31			
1897			1/1-3/21	3/22-5/17	5/18-7/8	7/9-8/25
1898	4/29-6/6	6/7-7/18	7/19-9/2	9/3-10/30	10/31-12/31	
1899				1/16-4/14	1/1-1/15 4/15-6/15	6/16-8/5
1900	4/8-5/16	5/17-6/26	6/27-8/9	8/10-9/26	9/27-11/22	11/23-12/31
1901					3/2-5/10	1/1-3/1 5/11-7/13
1902	3/19-4/26	4/27-6/6	6/7-7/20	7/21-9/4	9/5-10/23	10/24-12/19
1903						4/20-5/30
1904	2/27-4/6	4/7-5/17	5/18-6/30	7/1-8/14	8/15-10/1	10/2-11/19
1905						
1906	2/5-3/16	3/17-4/28	4/29-6/11	6/12-7/27	7/28-9/12	9/13-10/29
1907						
1908	1/11-2/22	2/23-4/6	4/7-5/22	5/23-7/7	7/8-8/23	8/24-10/9
1909	7/21-9/26 11/21-12/31	9/27-11/20				
1910	1/1-1/22	1/23-3/13	3/14-5/1	5/2-6/18	6/19-8/5	8/6-9/21

	LIBRA 55	SCORPIO 56	SAGITTARIUS 57	CAPRICORN 58	AQUARIUS 59	PISCES 60
1870	12/31			1/1-1/5	1/6-2/12	2/13-3/22
1871	1/1-3/17 6/16-8/12	8/13-9/26	9/27-11/6	11/7-12/5	12/16-12/31	
1872	11/24-12/31				1/1-1/23	1/24-3/1
1873	1/1-1/22 5/20-6/24	1/23-5/19 6/25-8/29	8/30-10/13	10/14-11/22	11/23-12/31	
1874	11/3-12/12	12/22-12/31				1/1-2/8
1875		1/1-2/11	2/12-4/19 6/16-8/31	4/20-6/15 9/1-10/23	10/24-12/5	12/6-12/31
1876	11/14-11/29	11/30-12/31				1/1-1/16
1877		1/1-1/14	1/15-3/1	3/2-4/16	4/17-6/6	6/7-12/9
1878	9/26-11/9	11/12-12/23	12/24-12/31			
1879			1/1-2/4	2/5-3/18	3/19-4/28	4/29-6/8
1880	9/6-10/21	10/22-12/3	12/4-12/31			
1881			1/1-1/13	1/14-2/22	2/23-4/2	4/3-5/12
1882	8/19-10/2	10/3-11/14	11/15-12/25	12/26-12/31		
1883				1/1-2/2	2/3-3/12	3/13-4/20
1884	7/28-9/12	9/13-10/25	10/26-12/5	12/6-12/31		
1885				1/1-1/12	1/13-2/19	2/20-3/30
1886	7/2-8/21	8/22-10/5	10/6-11/14	11/15-12/23	12/24-12/31	
1887	12/6-12/31				1/1-1/30	1/31-3/10
1888	1/1-2/26 3/10-7/21	2/27-3/9 7/22-9/10	9/11-10/22	10/23-12/1	12/2-12/31	
1889	11/11-12/31				1/1-1/9	1/10-2/16
1890		1/1-2/28 6/17-7/21	3/1-6/16 7/22-9/23	9/24-11/5	11/6-12/16	12/17-12/31
1891	10/22-12/7	12/8-12/31				1/1-1/25
1892	1/1-1/24	1/24	1/25-3/13	5/7-11/8	11/9-12/27	12/28
1893	10/2-11/16	11/17-12/31				
1894			1/1-2/13	2/14-3/27	3/29-5/9	5/10-6/22
1895	9/14-10/29	10/30-12/11	12/12-12/31			
1896			1/1-1/22	1/23-3/2	3/3-4/11	4/12-5/21
1897	8/26-10/9	10/10-11/21	11/12-12/31			
1898			1/1	1/2-2/10	2/11-3/20	3/21-4/28
1899	8/6-9/20	9/21-11/2	11/3-12/13	12/14-12/31		
1900				1/1-1/21	1/22-2/28	3/1-4/7
1901	7/14-8/31	9/1-10/14	10/15-11/23	11/24-12/31		
1902	12/20-12/31			1/1	1/2-2/8	2/9-3/18
1903	1/1-4/19 5/31-8/6	8/7-9/22	9/23-11/2	11/3-12/11	12/12-12/31	
1904	11/20-12/31				1/1-1/19	1/20-2/26
1905	1/1-1/13		8/22-10/7	10/8-11/17	11/18-12/27	12/28-12/31
1906	10/30-12/16	12/17-12/31				1/1-2/4
1907		1/1-2/4	2/5-4/1	4/2-10/13	10/14-11/28	11/29-12/31
1908	10/10-11/25	11/26-12/31				1/1-1/10
1909		1/1-1/9	1/10-2/23	2/24-4/9	4/10-5/25	5/26-7/20
1910	9/22-11/6	11/7-12/19	12/20-12/31			

	ARIES 49	TAURUS 50	GEMINI 51	CANCER 52	LEO 53	VIRGO 54
1911	6/3-7/15	7/16-9/5 11/30-12/31	9/6-11/29			
1912		1/1-1/30	1/31-4/4	4/5-5/27	5/28-7/16	7/17-9/2
1913	5/8-6/16	6/17-7/28	7/29-9/15	9/16-12/31		
1914				1/1-5/1	5/2-6/26	6/26-8/14
1915	4/17-5/25	5/26-7/5	7/6-8/18	8/19-10/7	10/8-12/31	
1916					1/1-5/28	5/29-7/22
1917	3/27-5/4	5/5-6/14	6/15-7/27	7/28-9/11	9/12-11/1	11/2-12/31
1918						1/1-1/10 2/26-6/23
1919	3/7-4/14	4/15-5/25	5/26-7/8	7/9-8/22	8/23-10/9	10/10-11/29
1920						
1921	2/13-3/24	3/25-5/5	5/6-6/18	6/19-8/2	8/3-9/18	9/19-11/6
1922						
1923	1/21-3/3	3/4-4/15	4/16-5/30	5/31-7/15	7/16-8/31	9/1-10/17
1924	12/19-12/31					
1925	1/1-2/4	2/5-3/23	3/24-5/9	5/10-6/25	6/26-8/12	8/13-9/28
1926	6/15-7/31	8/1-12/31				
1927		1/1-2/21	2/22-4/16	4/17-6/5	6/6-7/24	7/25-9/10
1928	5/17-6/25	6/26-8/8	8/9-10/2 12/20-12/31	10/3-12/19		
1929			1/1-3/10	3/11-5/12	5/13-7/3 3/30-6/10	7/4-8/21
1930	4/25-6/2	6/3-7/14	7/15-8/27	8/28-10/20	10/21-12/31	
1931				2/17-3/29	1/1-2/16 3/30-6/10	6/11-8/1
1932	4/3-5/11	5/12-6/21	6/22-8/4	8/5-9/30	10/1-11/13	11/14-12/31
1933						1/1-7/6
1934	3/14-4/22	4/23-6/2	6/3-7/15	7/16-8/30	8/31-10/17	10/18-12/10
1935						
1936	2/23-4/2	4/3-5/13	5/14-6/26	6/27-8/10	8/11-9/27	9/28-11/15
1937						
1938	2/1-3/13	3/14-4/24	4/25-6/8	6/9-7/23	7/24-9/8	9/9-10/26
1939						
1940	1/5-2/18	2/19-4/2	4/3-5/18	5/19-7/4	7/5-8/20	8/21-10/6
1941	7/4-12/31					
1942	1/1-1/12	1/13-3/8	3/9-4/27	4/28-6/15	6/16-8/2	8/3-9/18
1943	5/29-7/8	7/9-8/24	8/25-12/31			
1944			1/1-3/29	3/30-5/23	5/24-7/13	7/14-8/30
1945	5/4-6/12	6/13-7/24	7/25-9/8	9/9-11/12 12/28-12/31	11/13-12/27	
1946				1/1-4/23	4/24-6/21	6/22-8/10
1947	4/13-5/22	5/23-6/30	7/1-8/14	8/15-10/2	10/3-12/2	12/3-12/31
1948					2/14-5/19	1/1-2/13 5/20-7/18
1949	3/23-5/1	5/2-6/11	6/12-7/24	7/25-9/8	9/9-10/28	10/29-12/27
1950						3/30-6/12
1951	3/2-4/9	4/10-5/20	5/21-7/3	7/4-8/17	8/18-10/4	10/5-11/23
1952						

	LIBRA 55	SCORPIO 56	SAGITTARIUS 57	CAPRICORN 58	AQUARIUS 59	PISCES 60
1911			1/1-1/31	2/1-3/13	3/14-4/22	4/23-6/2
1912	9/3-10/17	10/18-11/29	11/30-12/31			
1913			1/1-1/10	1/11-2/18	2/19-3/29	3/30-5/7
1914	8/15-9/28	9/29-11/10	11/11-12/21	12/22-12/31		
1915				1/1-1/29	1/30-3/9	3/10-4/16
1916	7/23-9/8	9/9-10/21	10/22-12/1	12/2-12/31		
1917				1/1-1/9	1/10-2/16	2/17-3/26
1918	1/11-2/25					
	6/24-8/16	8/17-9/30	10/1-11/10	11/11-12/19	12/20-12/31	
1919	11/30-12/31				1/1-1/26	1/27-3/6
1920	1/1-1/31	2/1-4/23				
	4/24-7/10	7/11-9/4	9/5-10/18	10/19-11/27	11/28-12/31	
1921	11/7-12/25	12/26-12/31		-	1/1-1/4	1/5-2/12
1922		1/1-2/18	2/19-9/13	9/14-10/30	10/31-12/11	12/12-12/31
1923	10/18-12/3	12/4-12/31				1/1-1/20
1924		1/1-1/19	1/20-3/6	3/7-4/24	4/25-6/24	6/25-8/24
					8/25-10/19	10/20-12/18
1925	9/29-11/13	11/14-12/27	12/28-12/31			
1926			1/1-2/8	2/9-3/22	3/23-5/3	5/4-6/12
1927	9/11-10/25	10/26-12/7	12/8-12/31			
1928			1/1-1/18	1/19-2/27	2/28-4/7	4/8-5/16
1929	8/22-10/5	10/6-11/18	11/19-12/28	12/29-12/31		
1930				1/1-2/6	2/7-3/16	3/17-4/24
1931	8/2-9/16	9/17-10/30	10/31-12/9	12/10-12/31		
1932				1/1-1/17	1/18-2/24	2/25-4/2
1933	7/7-8/25	8/26-10/8	10/9-11/18	11/19-12/27	12/28-12/31	
1934	12/11-12/31				1/1-2/3	2/4-3/13
1935	1/1-7/29	7/30-9/16	9/17-10/29	10/30-12/7	12/8-12/31	-
1936	11/16-12/31				1/1-1/15	1/16-2/22
1937	1/1-1/6	1/7-3/13	3/14-5/15	10/1-11/12	11/13-12/22	12/23-12/31
		5/16-8/9	8/10-9/30			
1938	10/27-12/12	12/13-12/31				1/1-1/31
1939		1/1-1/30	1/31-3/22	3/23-5/25	5/26-7/22	7/23-9/25
				7/23-9/25	9/26-11/20	11/21-12/31
1940	10/7-11/21	11/22-12/31				1/1-1/4
1941		1/1-1/5	1/6-2/18	2/19-4/3	4/4-5/17	5/18-7/3
1942	9/19-11/2	11/3-12/16	12/17-12/31			
1943			1/1-1/27	1/28-3/9	3/10-4/18	4/19-5/28
1944	8/31-10/14	10/15-11/26	11/27-12/31			
1945			1/1-1/6	1/7-2/15	2/16-3/26	3/27-5/3
1946	8/11-9/25	9/26-11/7	11/8-12/18	12/19-12/31		
1947				1/1-1/26	1/27-3/5	3/6-4/12
1948	7/19-9/4	9/5-10/18	10/19-11/27	11/28-12/31		
1949	12/28-12/31			1/1-1/5	1/6-2/12	2/13-3/22
1950	1/1-3/29	8/12-9/26	9/27-11/7	11/8-12/16	12/17-12/31	
	6/13-8/11					
1951	11/24-12/31				1/1-1/22	1/23-3/1
1952	1/1-1/19	1/20-8/26	8/27-10/11	10/12-11/21	11/22-12/30	12/31

	ARIES 49	TAURUS 50	GEMINI 51	CANCER 52	LEO 53	VIRGO 54
1953	2/8-3/19	3/20-4/30	5/1-6/13	6/14-7/28	7/29-9/14	9/15-11/1
1954						
1955	1/15-2/25	2/26-4/10	4/11-5/25	5/26-7/10	7/11-8/26	8/27-10/12
1956	12/7-12/31					
1957	1/1-1/28	1/29-3/17	3/18-5/4	5/5-6/20	6/21-8/7	8/8-9/23
1958	6/7-7/20	7/21-9/20 10/30-12/31	9/21-10/29			
1959		1/1-2/10	2/11-4/10	4/11-5/31	6/1-7/19	7/20-9/5
1960	5/11-6/19	6/20-8/1,	8/2-9/20	9/21-12/31		
1961				1/1-5/5	5/6-6/28	
1962	4/20-5/28	5/29-7/8	7/9-8/21	8/22-10/11	10/12-12/31	6/29-8/16
1963					1/1-6/2	6/3-7/26
1964	3/29-5/6	5/7-6/16	6/17-7/30	7/31-9/14	9/15-11/5	11/6-12/31
1965						1/1-6/28
1966	3/9-4/17	4/18-5/28	5/29-7/10	7/11-8/25	8/26-10/12	10/13-12/3
1967						
1968	2/17-3/27	3/28-5/8	5/9-6/20	6/21-8/4	8/5-9/21	9/22-11/8
1969						
1970	1/25-3/6	3/7-4/18	4/19-6/1	6/2-7/17	7/18-9/2	9/3-10/19
1971	12/27-12/31					
1972	1/1-2/10	2/11-3/27	3/28-5/12	5/13-6/28	6/29-8/15	8/16-9/30
1973	6/21-8/12 10/30-12/24	8/13-10/29 12/25-12/31				
1974		1/1-2/27	2/28-4/20	4/21-6/8	6/9-7/27	7/28-9/12
1975	5/22-7/1	7/2-8/14	8/15-10/16 11/26-12/31	10/17-11/25		
1976			1/1-3/18	3/19-5/16	5/17-7/6	7/7-8/24
1977	4/28-6/5	6/6-7/17	7/18-8/31	9/1-10/26	10/27-12/31	
1978				1/27-4/10	1/1-1/26 4/11-6/13	6/14-8/4
1979	4/7-5/15	5/16-6/25	6/26-8/8	8/9-9/24	9/25-11/19	11/20-12/31
1980					3/12-5/3	1/3-3/11 5/4-7/10
1981	3/18-4/25	4/26-6/5	6/6-7/18	7/19-9/2	9/3-10/21	10/22-12/16
1982						
1983	2/25-4/5	4/6-5/16	5/17-6/29	6/30-8/13	8/14-9/29	9/30-11/18
1984						
1985	2/3-3/15	3/16-4/26	4/27-6/10	6/11-7/25	7/26-9/10	9/11-10/27
1986						
1987	1/9-2/20	2/21-4/5	4/6-5/21	5/22-7/6	7/7-8/22	8/23-10/8
1988	7/14-10/23 11/2-12/31					
1989	1/1-1/19	1/20-3/11	3/12-4/29	4/30-6/16	6/17-8/3	8/4-9/19
1990	6/1-7/12	7/13-8/31 12/15-12/31	9/1-12/14			
1991		1/1-1/21	1/22-4/3	4/4-5/26	5/27-7/15	7/16-9/1
1992	5/6-6/14	5/15-7/26	7/27-9/12	9/13-12/31		
1993				1/1-4/27	4/28-6/23	6/24-8/12
1994	4/15-5/23	5/24-7/3	7/4-8/16	8/17-10/4	10/5-12/12	12/12-12/31
1995					1/23-5/25	1/1-1/22 5/26-7/21

	LIBRA 55	SCORPIO 56	SAGITTARIUS 57	CAPRICORN 58	AQUARIUS 59	PISCES 60
1953	11/2-12/20	12/21-12/31				1/1-2/7
1954		1/1-2/9	2/10-4/12	4/13-7/3	10/22-12/3	12/4-12/31
			7/4-8/24	8/25-10/21		
1955	10/13-11/28	11/29-12/31				1/1-1/14
1956		1/1-1/13	1/14-2/28	2/29-4/14	4/15-6/2	6/3-12/6
1957	9/24-11/8	11/9-12/22	12/23-12/31			
1958			1/1-2/3	2/4-3/16	3/17-4/26	4/27-6/6
1959	9/6-10/20	10/21-12/3	12/4-12/31			
1960			1/1-1/13	1/14-2/22	2/23-4/1	4/2-5/10
1961	8/17-10/1	10/2-11/13	11/14-12/24	12/25-12/31		
1962				1/1-2/1	2/3-3/11	3/12-4/19
1963	7/27-9/11	9/12-10/25	10/26-12/4	12/5-12/31		
1964				1/1-1/12	1/13-2/19	2/20-3/28
1965	6/29-8/20	8/21-10/3	10/4-11/13	11/14-12/22	12/23-12/31	
1966	12/4-12/31				1/1-1/29	1/30-3/8
1967	1/1-2/12	2/13-3/31	9/10-10/22	10/23-12/1	12/2-12/31	
	4/1-7/19	7/20-9/9				
1968	11/9-12/29	12/30-12/31			1/1-1/8	1/9-2/16
1969		1/1-2/24	2/25-9/20	9/21-11/4	11/5-12/15	12/16-12/31
1970	10/20-12/6	12/7-12/31				1/1-1/24
1971		1/1-1/23	1/24-3/12	3/13-5/3	5/4-11/6	11/7-12/12
1972	10/1-11/15	11/16-12/30	12/31			
1973			1/1-2/12	2/13-3/26	3/27-5/8	5/9-6/20
1974	9/13-10/28	10/29-12/10	12/11-12/31			
1975			1/1-1/21	1/22-3/3	3/4-4/11	4/12-5/21
1976	8/25-10/8	10/9-11/20	11/21-12/31			
1977				1/1-2/9	2/10-3/19	3/20-4/27
1978	8/5-9/19	9/20-11/1	11/2-12/12	12/13-12/31		
1979				1/1-1/20	1/21-2/27	2/28-4/6
1980	7/11-8/28	8/29-10/12	10/13-11/21	11/22-12/30	12/31	
1981	12/17-12/31				1/1-2/6	2/7-3/17
1982	1/1-8/3	8/4-9/20	9/21-10/31	11/1-12/10	12/11-12/31	
1983	11/19-12/31				1/1-1/17	1/18-2/24
1984	1/1-1/11	1/12-8/17	8/18-10/5	10/6-11/15	11/16-12/25	12/26-12/31
1985	10/28-12/14	12/15-12/31				1/1-2/2
1986		1/1-2/2	2/3-3/29	3/29-10/9	10/10-11/26	11/27-12/31
1987	10/9-11/24	11/25-12/31				1/1-1/8
1988		1/1-1/8	1/9-2/22	2/23-4/6	4/7-5/22	5/23-7/13
						10/24-11/1
1989	9/20-11/4	11/15-12/18	12/19-12/31			
1990			1/1-1/29	1/30-3/11	3/12-4/20	4/21-5/31
1991	9/2-10/16	10/17-11/29	11/30-12/31			
1992			1/1-1/9	1/10-2/18	2/19-3/28	3/29-5/5
1993	8/13-9/27	9/28-11/9	11/10-12/20	12/21-12/31		
1994				1/1-1/28	1/29-3/7	3/8-4/14
1995	7/22-9/7	9/8-10/20	10/21-11/30	12/1-12/31		

	ARIES 49	TAURUS 50	GEMINI 51	CANCER 52	LEO 53	VIRGO 54
1996	3/25-5/2	5/3-6/12	6/13-7/25	7/26-9/9	9/10-10/30	10/31-12/31
1997						1/1-1/3 3/9-6/19
1998	3/5-4/13	4/14-5/24	5/25-7/6	7/7-8/20	8/21-10/7	10/8-11/27
1999						

	LIBRA 55	SCORPIO 56	SAGITTARIUS 57	CAPRICORN 58	AQUARIUS 59	PISCES 60
1996				1/1-1/8	1/9-2/15	2/16-3/24
1997	1/4-3/8					
	6/20-8/14	8/15-9/28	9/29-11/9	11/10-12/18	12/19-12/31	
1998	11/28-12/31				1/1-1/25	1/26-3/4
1999	1/1-1/26	1/27-5/5	9/3-10/17	10/18-11/26	11/27-12/31	
	5/6-7/5	7/6-9/2				

JUPITER

Jupiter is the feeler you have out in the world for opportunity. Through it the chances of a lifetime are passed along for consideration according to the basic nature of Sun and Moon. Jupiter's sign position indicates the places in which you will look for opportunity, the uses to which you wish to put it, and the capacity you have to react to and profit by it. Jupiter is ordinarily, and erroneously, called the Planet of Luck. It is "luck" in so far as it is the index of opportunity; but your luck depends less on what comes to you (Jupiter) than on what you do with it (the total personality). Opportunity appeals to you along lines laid down by your Jupiter, and you should study carefully the paragraph in this section relating to you. *In the same sign with Sun or Moon,* Jupiter gives a direct and generally effective response to opportunity and is likely to show forth at its "luckiest." *If Jupiter is in the same sign with Mercury,* sense impressions are interpreted opportunistically—what you see and hear is grist to your mill; this also makes for considerable stubbornness and hard-headedness. *If Jupiter is in the same sign with Venus,* you interpret emotions in such a way as to turn them to your advantage; your feelings work harmoniously with the chances for progress that the world has to offer, and you won't often be found torn between love and a career. *If Jupiter is in the same sign with Mars,* you follow opportunity with energy, dash, enthusiasm and courage, take long chances and play your cards wide open.

In the table for finding Jupiter's place, find your birth year, and period that includes your birth date. Above this is the sign occupied by Jupiter, and the number of the paragraph that interprets it in your Vitasphere.

61. JUPITER IN ARIES

Opportunity appeals to you along lines related directly to ego justification. This can take the aggressive "I-can-do-anything" form or the passive, timid "Am-I-fitted-for-that—am-I-capable-of-doing-that?" Opportunity isn't primarily a chance to make money, to achieve glory, or to serve, but is something more, and personal. Depending on the biases of your ego, this will be a broad or a narrow influence. It tends to add fire to an already self-assured nature and to give some self-assurance to the timid soul. One of two dangers besets you: (1) overoptimism about your own talents, and a consequent eagerness to try anything once, resulting from the feeling that nothing is too big for you; (2) limitation of opportunity to a narrow ego demand, the result of a limitation in self-confidence, and a resultant refusal to step outside the confining areas you have set up for yourself. In any case, you're likely to be happy in your work, because you naturally gravitate to a work that satisfies you, and you cannot see opportunity along any other line. You must stand aside from yourself, examine your inner career motives carefully, and discover whether, by following your deepest desires, you are not limiting unnecessarily your field.

62. JUPITER IN TAURUS

Opportunity and security are one in your mind. You will not see those openings that require taking a chance. This frequently accompanies a sheltered life which has always had security, doesn't have to exert itself much for material necessities, and consequently doesn't react much at all to material opportunity. In a life less sheltered, it still limits the capacity for material success by limiting daring, but at the same time it tends to insure against want and privation. You have no flair for gambling or following new money-making ideas. Having inherited or having achieved security, you seek things that are not material and can let your energies flow freely in personal and cultural channels where you are likely to find your main interests. You're likely to seem the least materialistic of mortals because you take material comforts for granted, secure them, and then are able to forget them.

63. JUPITER IN GEMINI

You have an adventurous attitude toward opportunity. The far-off, dangerous, exciting venture is where your chance lies, and you will be found following the light that never was on land or sea. Tends to make you impractical and charming; you're willing to try anything once, for opportunity to you means, not a chance to make money or acquire fame, but to see life, do things, go places. You can be a wanderer of the wastelands, a hobo, a traveler, an adventurer of the spirit or of the flesh. You may also acquire some, even much, of the world's goods—but this will be more the result of good luck than of good management, for the almighty dollar is not your beacon, and if there is a pot of gold at the end of your rainbow you will stumble over it by accident rather than come upon it by design.

64. JUPITER IN CANCER

This position causes you to see opportunity along lines that promote security and luxury, and is therefore an excellent business, money-making position. You aren't grasping, but you are careful, because your wants are comparatively great, and you strive in every way you can to satisfy them. The final end of opportunity is to you a pleasantly furnished home with all the trimmings of luxury, and one way or another you will generally have it. You will not see opportunity along lines that jeopardize this, and play your hand close to your chest, even when you may appear to be daring. You have just as much regard for the security and comfort of others as you have for your own, and thus are generous, charitable and openhanded with what you possess. Home, children, friends are important, and in gratifying this side of your ego, you are likely to become a substantial and respectable pillar of the society whose niceties you value and want for your own.

65. JUPITER IN LEO

Opportunity appeals to you most when it includes a chance to exhibit your special virtues and abilities. No obscure job for you, no matter how much money there is in it. You'll pass it up in favor of the worse-paid job that gives more publicity. You can be a prodigious worker for little pay if you think you're appreciated—

and you'll sulk and loaf if you aren't. The stage lures you; if you don't actually become a professional actor, you'll make a stage of your life and act upon it to win approval for the traits that are most important to you. Financial matters come second, unless you happen to relate self-justification to money, in which case you become a prodigious earner and spender. When you save money at all, it is to spend it later along ego-satisfying lines. You will always see the main chance on a road to a high hill on which you can stand triumphant for all to see, and will exert yourself best when you are best satisfied with the effect you are making on others.

66. JUPITER IN VIRGO

This position enables you to find opportunity in small beginnings, to take infinite pains with the little things that underlie success, and to plug along at a hopeless cause until—lo and behold!—it amounts to something. The effect you give is of care, caution, and routine perfection of details; and because of this, you are often able to win support from financial interests who value these traits and consider them good credit reference. You will generally be able to get backing for your business; you believe in putting all your eggs in one basket and watching the basket, with the result that you frequently hatch quite a brood. Spectacular or risky ventures don't appeal to you. If this position limits the imagination somewhat, it is also likely to get you farther in the long run than the dashing fellow who has been through several fortunes, or jobs, while you have studiously been cultivating your own garden and raising a fine crop of security and possessions.

67. JUPITER IN LIBRA

This is a curious position, capable of seeing opportunity almost everywhere. There is a certain perversity about it, because you seem willing to do anything except what your nature is best fitted for. The opportunity that will appeal most to you is very likely to be the last thing in the world you ought to do. You are all too likely to follow what someone else says you ought to do, or what chance throws in your way. You need to cultivate firmness of purpose, and to concentrate on one line in which you want to excel. Your need for appearing successful in the eyes of others, rather than in your eyes, causes you to see too much with the eyes of others, so that you lack the drive of those who work outward from their wells of ego into the world. You are all too likely to try to fit your ego into the demands of other people, and thus to founder because your anchor is not within your own heart.

68. JUPITER IN SCORPIO

You relate opportunity to deep personal needs, and are generally successful because there is no inharmony between the inner nature and what the outer world makes important. The lens of the spirit eliminates what would make unhappiness and follows instinctively what satisfies. This is a good position for acquiring and spending money; you give a sort of magical effect of being the right man (or woman) for the job that is open, if the job happens to appeal to you; and you proceed to make it your own in a curiously effective way. All the primary instincts merge in your approach to work and give you a high degree of efficiency. When you're where you want to be, you work easily, authoritatively, gaining the respect of superiors and subordinates. Opportunity flows to you naturally; and an inherent wisdom enables you to select your right niche. You're not likely to be a square peg in a round hole; and you are very likely to be successful in whatever you put your mind on.

69. JUPITER IN SAGITTARIUS

Opportunity appeals to you only if closely related to ideals. Work of its own sake means little, for to you the prime opportunity of life is not labor, but knowledge, philosophy, adventure. If, however, work gets related to a philosophic ideal (such as duty, security, making the best of things, or whatever), then you can throw yourself into it—but only for so long as the ideal sustains you; if this fails, you gravitate to your nature, which is to seek opportunity along non-material lines. To relate the necessities of life to some philosophic or religious code of your own is your way to success and happiness, for without some such union of the ideal and the material, you are likely to drift with the alluring currents of your imagination.

70. JUPITER IN CAPRICORN

This position presents opportunity to you through very practical glasses. Anything will appeal which helps present you as an authoritative and consequential person, and you will follow most readily those beacons that lead to the mountain tops of public acclaim. You combine daring and caution in a nice mixture. Money is not important in itself, though it may be as a means to power or as a symptom of success. You will risk money to get fame or power; but you'll never risk fame or power to get money. Because you see only such opportunities as tend to advance you in the eyes of the world, irrelevant bypaths and blind alleys don't distract you, and you plug mercilessly along the only path you see, leading upward and onward to the High Place.

71. JUPITER IN AQUARIUS

This position causes you to see opportunity in very broad social, artistic, political matters. If your aim gets broader than your capacities—and it may!—you can be a drifter with high principles and little to show for them. If your abilities are up to your aims, you go far, for then you will see opportunity in all manner of big public things, and the free flow of your energies in these directions will lead effortlessly to success. Nothing is too big for you to envision, and even if it's too big for you to tackle or master, you dare to think about it. Air castles can be your downfall; you have to strive continuously to find the practical if rough methods by which they may be constructed into houses of earth. You are capable of passing up financial chances if they interfere with your larger aims. You have to learn the value of security because this position doesn't give it to you. Your tendency is to see life through the wrong end of the opera glasses; realities recede in favor of other things, and a liberal dose of the earth is necessary somewhere else in the chart if this position is to contribute to success.

72. JUPITER IN PISCES

Opportunity will appeal to you directly as it relates to your own private dream of self-justification. You can pass by material gain if there's something undesirable connected with it. You can neglect doing for others if you don't happen to want to. You may seem capricious or whimsical in your selections, but there is nothing whimsical about them to you: every choice is related to a fixed code which no one may know about but yourself, but which is crystal clear to you. If this code is big and unselfish, your whole life will be a miracle of service and selflessness. If it is little and narrow, your life will also be a miracle of service—to yourself. To be satisfied with that which also satisfies others is your key to success and happiness, for thus you overcome the tendency of this position to introversion, and allow the genial Jupiterean qualities to shine forth through the sign, which, in its best manifestation, gives you the power to lose yourself in large, humane ideals.

	ARIES 61	TAURUS 62	GEMINI 63	CANCER 64	LEO 65	VIRGO 66
1870		1/1-5/9	5/10-12/31			
1871			1/1-5/23	5/24-12/31		
1872				1/1-6/11	6/12-11/15	11/16-12/31
1873					1/17-7/7	1/1-1/16 7/8-12/12
1874						2/19-8/6
1875						
1876						
1877						
1878						
1879						
1880	4/3-12/21					
1881	1/1-4/11	4/12-12/31				
1882		1/1-4/21	4/22-9/19 11/18-12/31	9/20-11/17		
1883			1/1-5/4	5/5-9/26	9/27-12/31	
1884				1/17-5/21	1/1-1/16 5/22-10/17	10/18-12/31
1885					2/26-6/14	1/1-2/25 6/15-11/15
1886						3/30-7/15
1887						
1888						
1889						
1890						
1891						
1892	3/17-12/31					
1893	1/1-3/24	3/25-8/20 10/20-12/31	8/21-10/19			
1894		1/1-4/1	4/2-8/13	8/14-12/31		
1895			1/1-4/10	4/11-9/4	9/5-12/31	

	LIBRA 67	SCORPIO 68	SAGITTARIUS 69	CAPRICORN 70	AQUARIUS 71	PISCES 72
1870						
1871						
1872						
1873	12/13-12/31					
1874	1/1-2/18 8/7-12/31					
1875	1/1-1/12 3/21-9/6	1/13-3/20 9/7-12/31				
1876		1/2-2/9 4/24-10/3	2/10-4/23 10/4-12/31			
1877			1/1-2/28 6/10-10/25	3/1-6/9 10/26-12/31		
1878				1/1-3/14 8/12-11/3	3/15-8/11 11/4-12/31	
1879					1/1-3/25	3/26-12/31
1880						1/1-4/2
1881						
1882						
1883						
1884						
1885	11/16-12/31					
1886	1/1-3/29 7/16-12/16	12/17-12/31				
1887	4/29-8/15	1/1-4/28 8/16-12/31				
1888		1/1-1/14 6/3-9/10	1/15-6/2 9/11-12/31			
1889			1/1-2/5 7/24-9/25	2/6-7/23 9/26-12/31		
1890				1/1-2/22	2/23-12/31	
1891					1/1-3/7	3/8-12/31
1892						1/1-3/16
1893						
1894						
1895						

	ARIES 61	TAURUS 62	GEMINI 63	CANCER 64	LEO 65	VIRGO 66
1896				3/1-4/17	1/1-2/29 4/18-9/27	9/28-12/31
1897						1/1-10/27
1898						
1899						
1900						
1901						
1902						
1903						
1904	3/1-8/8 9/1-12/31	8/9-8/31				
1905	1/1-3/7	3/8-7/20 12/5-12/31	7/21-12/4			
1906		1/1-3/9	3/10-7/30	7/31-12/31		
1907				1/1-8/18	8/19-12/31	
1908					1/1-9/11	9/12-12/31
1909						1/1-10/11
1910						
1911						
1912						
1913						
1914						
1915						
1916	2/12-6/25 10/27-12/31	6/26-10/26				
1917	1/1-2/12	2/13-6/29	6/30-12/31			
1918			1/1-6/12	6/13-12/31		
1919				1/1-8/1	8/2-12/31	
1920					1/1-8/26	8/27-12/31
1921						1/1-9/25
1922						
1923						
1924						

	LIBRA 67	SCORPIO 68	SAGITTARIUS 69	CAPRICORN 70	AQUARIUS 71	PISCES 72
1896						
1897	10/28-12/31					
1898	1/1-11/26	11/27-12/31				
1899		1/1-12/25	12/26-12/31			
1900			All Year			
1901			1/1-1/18	1/19-12/31		
1902				1/1-2/6	2/7-12/31	
1903					1/1-2/19	2/20-12/31
1904						1/1-2/29
1905						
1906						
1907						
1908						
1909	10/12-12/31					
1910	1/1-11/11	11/12-12/31				
1911		1/1-12/9	12/10-12/31			
1912			All Year			
1913			1/1 & 2	1/3-12/31		
1914				1/1-1/21	1/22-12/31	
1915					1/1-2/3	2/4-12/31
1916						1/1-2/11
1917						
1918						
1919						
1920						
1921	9/26-12/31					
1922	1/1-10/26	10/27-12/31				
1923		1/1-11/24	11/25-12/31			
1924			1/1-12/17	12/18-12/31		

	ARIES 61	TAURUS 62	GEMINI 63	CANCER 64	LEO 65	VIRGO 66
1925						
1926						
1927	6/6-9/10					
1928	1/23-6/3	6/4-12/31				
1929		1/1-6/11	6/12-12/31			
1930			1/1-6/26	6/27-12/31		
1931				1/1-7/16	7/17-12/31	
1932					1/1-8/10	8/11-12/31
1933						1/1-9/9
1934						
1935						
1936						
1937						
1938						
1939	5/13-10/30 12/21-12/31					
1940	1/1-5/17	5/18-12/31				
1941		1/1-5/27	5/28-12/31			
1942			1/1-6/11	6/12-12/31		
1943				1/1-6/30	7/1-12/31	
1944					1/1-7/27	7/28-12/31
1945						1/1-8/26
1946						
1947						
1948						
1949						
1950						
1951	4/21-12/31					

	LIBRA 67	SCORPIO 68	SAGITTARIUS 69	CAPRICORN 70	AQUARIUS 71	PISCES 72
1925				All Year		
1926				1/1-1/5	1/6-12/31	
1927					1/1-1/17	1/18-6/5 9/11-12/31
1928						1/1-1/22
1929						
1930						
1931						
1932						
1933	9/10-12/31					
1934	1/1-10/10	10/11-12/31				
1935		1/1-11/8	11/9-12/31			
1936			1/1-12/2	12/3-12/31		
1937				1/1-12/20	12/21-12/31	
1938					1/1-5/15 7/31-12/30	5/16-7/30 12/31
1939						1/1-5/12 10/31-12/20
1940						
1941						
1942						
1943						
1944						
1945	8/27-12/31					
1946	1/1-9/26	9/27-12/31				
1947		1/1-10/25	10/26-12/31			
1948			1/1-11/16	11/17-12/31		
1949				1/1-4/12 6/29-11/30	4/13-6/28 12/1-12/31	
1950					1/1-4/16 9/17-12/3	4/17-9/16 12/4-12/31
1951						1/1-4/20

	ARIES 61	TAURUS 62	GEMINI 63	CANCER 64	LEO 65	VIRGO 66
1952	1/1-4/26	4/27-12/31				
1953		1/1-5/10	5/11-12/31			
1954			1/1-5/21	5/22-12/31		
1955				1/1-6/10	6/11-11/20	11/21-12/31
1956						1/1-1/10
					1/11-7/5	7/6-12/15
1957						2/16-8/5
1958						
1959						
1960						
1961						
1962						
1963	4/5-12/31					
1964	1/1-4/9	4/10-12/31				
1965		1/1-4/20	4/21-9/20 11/15-12/31	9/21-11/15		
1966			1/1-5/5	5/6-9/27	9/28-12/31	
1967				1/17-5/23	1/1-1/16 5/24-10/19	10/20-12/31
1968					2/28-6/15	1/1-2/27 6/16-11/15
1969						3/31-7/15
1970						
1971						
1972						
1973						
1974						
1975	3/19-12/31					
1976	1/1-3/26	3/27-8/23 10/17-12/31	8/24-10/16			
1977		1/1-4/3	4/4-8/20	8/21-12/31		

	LIBRA 67	SCORPIO 68	SAGITTARIUS 69	CAPRICORN 70	AQUARIUS 71	PISCES 72
1952						
1953						
1954						
1955						
1956	12/16-12/31					
1957	1/1-2/15 8/6-12/31					
1958	1/1-1/14 3/16-9/5	1/15-3/15 9/6-12/31				
1959		1/1-2/9 4/21-10/5	2/10-4/20 10/6-12/31			
1960			1/1-2/29 6/8-10/21	3/1-6/7 10/22-12/31		
1961				1/1-3/16 8/12-10/31	3/17-8/11 11/1-12/31	
1962					1/1-3/25	3/26-12/31
1963						1/1-4/4
1964						
1965						
1966						
1967						
1968	11/16-12/31					
1969	1/1-3/30 7/16-12/16	12/15-12/31				
1970	5/1-8/15	1/1-4/30 8/16-12/31				
1971		1/1-1/14 6/6-9/11	1/15-6/5 9/12-12/31			
1972			1/1-2/6 7/25-9/25	2/7-7/24 9/26-12/31		
1973				1/1-2/23	2/24-12/31	
1974					1/1-3/8	3/9-12/31
1975						1/1-3/18
1976						
1977						

	ARIES 61	TAURUS 62	GEMINI 63	CANCER 64	LEO 65	VIRGO 66
1978			1/1-4/11	4/12-9/5	9/6-12/31	
1979				3/2-4/20	1/1-3/1 4/21-9/29	9/30-12/31
1980						1/1-10/27
1981						
1982						
1983						
1984						
1985						
1986						
1987	3/3-12/31					
1988	1/1-3/8	3/9-7/21 12/1-12/31	7/22-11/30			
1989		1/1-3/11	3/12-7/30	7/31-12/31		
1990				1/1-8/18	8/19-12/31	
1991					1/1-9/12	9/13-12/31
1992						1/1-10/10
1993						
1994						
1995						
1996						
1997						
1998						
1999	2/14-6/28 10/24-12/31	6/29-10/23				

	LIBRA 67	SCORPIO 68	SAGITTARIUS 69	CAPRICORN 70	AQUARIUS 71	PISCES 72
1978						
1979						
1980	10/28-12/31					
1981	1/1-11/27	11/28-12/31				
1982		1/1-12/26	12/27-12/31			
1983			All Year			
1984			1/1-1/19	1/20-12/31		
1985				1/1-2/6	2/7-12/31	
1986					1/1-2/20	2/21-12/31
1987						1/1-3/2
1988						
1989						
1990						
1991						
1992	10/11-12/31					
1993	1/1-11/10	11/11-12/31				
1994		1/1-12/9	12/10-12/31			
1995			All Year			
1996			1/1-1/3	1/4-12/31		
1997				1/1-1/21	1/22-12/31	
1998					1/1-2/4	2/5-12/31
1999						1/1-2/13

SATURN

Saturn indicates the direction that will be taken in life by the self-preservative principle which, in its highest manifestation, ceases to be purely defensive and becomes ambitious and aspirational. Your defense, or attack, against the world is shown by the sign position of Saturn in the Vitasphere of birth. *If Saturn is in the same sign with Sun or Moon,* defense predominates, and there is danger of introversion. The further Saturn is from Sun, Moon and Ascendant, the better for objectivity and extroversion. *If Saturn is in the same sign with Mercury,* profound and serious reaction to sense impressions; generally accompanies a deep and efficient mind. *If Saturn is in the same sign with Venus,* defensive attitude toward emotional experience makes for apparent coolness in love, and difficulty through the emotions and human relations; conservative in finance, and generally a "lucky-in-cards-unlucky-in-love" position. *If Saturn is in the same sign with Mars,* confusion between defensive and aggressive urges can make an indecisive person—or, if Sun and Moon are strong, and total personality well developed, a balanced, peaceful and calm individual of sober judgment and moderate actions. *If Saturn is in the same sign with Jupiter,* reaction to opportunity is sober and balanced.

In the table for finding Saturn's place find your birth year, and the period in it which includes your birth date. Beside this period is the sign Saturn occupies and the number indicating the paragraph that applies to you.

73. SATURN IN ARIES

Your defense mechanism is directed toward *self*-defense and *self*-justification. The problems of living constitute to you a direct frontal attack of the world on your own personality, and the vindication of this steals the show from concerns of material progress and security. In its worst form this makes for narrowness, self-centeredness, touchiness, up to and including delusions of persecution. All the forces of your nature unite to defend the ego, which imagines itself badly used and needful of the maximum protection. From this can arise an almost unbelievable capacity to misunderstand others and a sort of chip-on-the-shoulder attitude which defies others to understand you. Carried upward and onward and broadened into spheres of usefulness, this makes you deeply desirous of self-betterment, capable of long, arduous mental work by which you succeed in making yourself the sort of person who will not require defending, but whose genuine traits will be the best defense against the world's attack. Not usually accompanied by introspection in any marked degree, this position, developed on its best side, makes you an aware, alert, profound personality. You eliminate the need for defending yourself by becoming an effective person when you have learned what every good general knows: that the best defense is an attack—and when you have marshaled your forces to attack life, instead of following your natural inclination to draw them around in a bristling ring of defiance.

74. SATURN IN TAURUS

This position presents the simplest and most direct manifestation of the instinct of self-preservation, which you satisfy by material comfort and security. If you have these, life cannot attack you in any way that matters deeply. The need to defend yourself in emotional, intellectual matters is not deep, and you are therefore an easy person to live with because your deep ego centers don't bristle and writhe at imagined affronts or offenses. You are secure if your body is secure; and are able to bring a great deal of idealism to bear on all of life's other problems in which you, unlike many others, can be detached and gracious. When you're materially secure, you have to look out for smugness and self-satisfaction and for a tendency to identify yourself and your work too closely with your possessions and your material status. You are deeply a conservative in finance and can be a penny pincher. You will rarely gamble, and/or lose property because of your own actions, unless through taking security too much for granted, you feel it can't possibly be lost.

Self-satisfaction then becomes overconfidence and is, of course, dangerous. The tendency to take things too much for granted can also lead you to trust some less careful person with your security and to lose it through the bad judgment of others on whom you have, because of oversureness, not exercised the proper control. Losing security throws you entirely off balance, and you cannot be yourself till you get it back again. You can be secure on little, for stretching money is your long suit, but what little there is must be established as firmly as the Rock of Gibraltar. Needless to say, you are a pillar of society, a believer in life insurance, and a sure-fire customer for gilt-edged government bonds.

75. SATURN IN GEMINI

You attack the world vigorously, finding your natural defense in a swift flanking movement in which, by speed and profundity, you justify your existence. This is one of the best positions for Saturn, sharpening and deepening your reaction to experience and giving you mastery of mind and therefore of life. You justify yourself actively and articulately, and work outward into the world in intellectual or physical endeavor. You are shrewd in business dealings and can be slick. You are likely to range far in your battle with life, which is a sort of intellectual guessing game that you are determined to win by force of superior intellect. You are rarely stalemated even by the most complicated of situations that you get yourself into, for you always have an "out" which is likely to be an "up" as well. Adaptability is your great strength; your notion of how to justify yourself is not limited, and you have few vocational inhibitions. This is also a weakness: you're willing to try anything once. But you concentrate readily and can master many things in one lifetime. In its best manifestation, this is Goethe's "universal man" to whom no doors were closed, or the ideal of Francis Bacon, who took all knowledge for his province. In its worst form it is a dilettante—but you generally will emerge even from this adventurous extreme with something to show for life.

76. SATURN IN CANCER

This is a powerful if complicated position and generally indicates a parent fixation. The need for self-justification is the deepest driving force of the life, welded into the psychological background by circumstances of the early environment, and causes you to take one of two directions. (1) You became an introvert: you despair of being able to justify yourself and withdraw into yourself defeated. This of course is a destructive development, and should be fought off in favor of: (2) You require the maximum of self-justification to overcome a deep sense of inferiority and go out to battle the world aggressively to compensate for your (real or imagined) shortcomings. Psychologically, this is a "little man" position: your opinion of yourself is low, and you make up for it by assuming it to be high and living up to the assumption. This leads to success through considerable tension and stress. Material matters are important to you; security is one of your requisites, and you may acquire, and lose, much property before you die. Acquisition may be closely linked to your need for self-justification and thus make you grasping. You may come from a poor family and feel the need for overcoming the initial handicap. Or the power urge may be related to possessions. Though a home is important to you, you are not a warm-natured person. You may delude yourself into thinking you need love and sympathy which you don't get, but close examination will prove that what you really want is respect—which you will get. You can utilize this position of Saturn as the hub of your life, and from it make the spokes extend far in almost any direction.

77. SATURN IN LEO

This position directs your personality to defend itself against life as dramatically as possible. If the total personality is aggressive, you will find self-justification in the public eye. Nothing will justify you in your own eyes if you aren't attracting attention. Not for you the obscure job with the big pay: you'd rather lead the parade for nothing, and may even pay for the privilege. People who are eager to subscribe to books that print their name very likely have Saturn in Leo. The need for approval and the public gaze is linked to the ego-protective centers, and the limelight becomes the Sun of Life. If the total personality is passive rather than active, the need for attention is no less present, but you may get it in a variety of ways. Invalidism is a favorite; some variety of physical ailment with a neurotic background is frequent in this sign, and if you think there's anything the matter with you, it's worth analyzing yourself, or being analyzed, to see if it isn't a means of stealing the show of your private life. If the dramatic urge leads into constructive channels, you will go far and high; but the danger is that, loving drama, acclaim and glory for their own sake, you will seek them regardless of aim and motive. Be careful of hurting others in your attack on life; be careful also that you don't hurt yourself. Too much limelight blisters the skin, and it is possible with this position to be too smart for your own good.

78. SATURN IN VIRGO

This position in its best form finds justification in work or service, is a bear for detail, and a tough drillmaster but no executive. You're a stickler for rules and methods, and can fail to see the forest for the trees. This is a narrowing position and should not be taken as the hub of the life, though your tendency is to feel pretty well pleased with yourself if you are doing efficiently and accurately what is expected of you. You will work overtime to do what you have to do thoroughly, or to do added work that is in the direct line of duty. But you probably won't work overtime on something that could broaden your scope unless some other indication in the chart is very impelling and very broad in effect. In its worst form, you complain about work, and may refuse to work at all; this occurs if your whole personality is shown to be passive or resentful, when Saturn in Virgo seems to make all the burdens of the world light on your shoulder for you to complain about. To do what's expected of you carefully and gracefully, without allowing duty and detail to limit your viewpoint, is the way to justify yourself without hampering progress.

79. SATURN IN LIBRA

You appear to have little need to defend yourself, because your justification comes directly through others. You are capable of being one of the best adjusted of mortals, living easily with your associates, in getting along with whom your deepest ego is vindicated. This position of Saturn is bound to take you out of yourself and turn a major portion of your attention to the outer world and the people in it. If you're a naturally aggressive and extroverted person, this gives you great tact and charm, because of which you get what you want with a minimum of struggle. You don't have to fight your way along because your deepest intuitions tell you how to win friends and influence people graciously. If your nature is passive or tends to be introverted, you devote your life wholeheartedly to service of others and satisfy your tendency to inwardness by self-fulfillment through sacrifice. In any case, and along whatever lines the total personality leads, this position of Saturn is one of the best insurances of usefulness, and will tend to strengthen and lend significance to an otherwise undistinguished chart.

80. SATURN IN SCORPIO

This position is an index of a complex personality. Your defense mechanism works deep below the level of consciousness on the primal instincts and urges; your battle with life goes on within yourself continuously, even when you are unaware of it. Your thoughts, words, acts are almost automatically determined for you. You have to train yourself to know your own motives and to bring into the light of reason the urges behind what you do. The reproductive urge is directly linked with the self-preservation instinct, and you will seek for security in sex fulfillment and therefore marriage. But your defenses are up against yielding yourself to anyone else, and this stands in the way of sex and married harmony, and perhaps causes you to replace the love instinct with something more sensational that gratifies superficially without demanding as much of the whole personality. Because self-justification joins with these deep primal instincts, you are very suspicious and wary about almost everything and can be, among other things, a demon of jealousy. Your constant struggle is wearing, because you want the maximum of self-justification with the minimum of self-yielding. If true success demands too much, you are capable of giving up the struggle entirely, of denying the urge for self-preservation and self-justification utterly, rather than yield your inner self to get it. You must strive not to take yourself so seriously, to compete with life on its own terms, and to realize that before you can vindicate the self that is so important to you, you must both know yourself and permit yourself to be known by others. They can't applaud you if you hide your light under a bushel, nor can they feel your strength when it is all working inside.

81. SATURN IN SAGITTARIUS

You seek self-justification in command of abstractions, and try to master life by mastering the philosophy of it. Power, wealth, social position will not convince you that you have justified your existence, nor will fame, unless it be achieved in intellectual or spiritual accomplishment. Your fields of thought and activity are not limited; you go forth to life eagerly with an open mind, in the filling of which is your deepest satisfaction. You are unlikely to be hampered by complexes because of this position, for little sense of inferiority is indicated by it. In fact, a superiority complex in its pure direct form is suggested by this placing of Saturn, which gives you a whole-souled respect for your ability and little doubt that you are as able, mentally and physically, as the next fellow. You don't feel that the world holds you back, nor are you driven from within by any psychological necessities. Life is your cry—especially the life of the mind—and you will range the seven seas of the world and of the intellect if you get half a chance. You will earn your success by intelligence and true worth, and without necessarily being conceited you will have a wholesome feeling within yourself that you have it coming to you. Whatever your job may be, you'll find your self-justification in mental and spiritual excellence and, holding up for yourself a very high personal standard, are likely to find yourself saddled with the responsibilities of leadership in whatever sphere you may move.

82. SATURN IN CAPRICORN

This position requires success in the materialistic, financial or fame sense of the word, and will not long be satisfied with unrecognized worth. Some subtlety attaches to your mentality; you may work long and hard for little pay and little acclaim, but your aim is to get more, and you never forget it. In this way, you are hardheaded, if not hardhearted, and can very well be both. Your deep ego urge is to defend yourself against the world by conquering it and by forcing it to recognize you; and since this urge is deeply ingrained in the subconscious and demands recognition, you are never likely to lose sight of it. This leads to heights of success or to embittered failure if it operates in its simple form. Your aim should be to become less materialistic, to discover wells of power within yourself. You can have no control over the world till you have control over yourself; and in gaining this essential to your success, you should discover also that "your mind to you a kingdom is" in which it is as gratifying to rule as in any temporal empire. It is possible for you to learn that there are all kinds of power over the world, and that wealth and fame are not the only ways of achieving it. There is the sense of power you get from giving, from serving, from helping. To transmute the power urge from its primitive, materialistic, strong-arm form to its more esoteric and refined uses is to insure that your powerful subconscious drive to success shall be vindicated along the most civilized lines, which are in the end most gratifying.

83. SATURN IN AQUARIUS

You seek self-justification and acclaim and material success very much as Saturn in Capricorn (Paragraph 82, which you should read), but aren't likely to be so hard-boiled about it. Saturn in Aquarius wants fame, recognition and power, but is more concerned with keeping the good opinion of other people in getting it and will rarely if ever hurt them. This position adds gentleness and strength to any chart: the ego requires the approval of society for its own justification —requires the good opinion of men more than their obedience, and is willing to trade respect for love. The social urge in this way is strong, and Saturn in Aquarius will spend a lot of time justifying its transgressions (which may be numerous) and making explanations and excuses for shortcomings. Since society is important to you, you tend to assume that you are important to society, and if your whole chart is very passive, you may come to think that it owes you a living and that your existence is best justified when you are collecting unearned increment. This is an inversion of the urge to serve society which is the best Saturn-in-Aquarius type of self-vindication. If this goes into reverse, you're vindicated when you enable society to demonstrate its goodness with you as the recipient. To cultivate the social urges on their positive side, to seek the approval of men for progressive and constructive works, to accept responsibility to society as your true means of self-justification, is to live up to the best of this idealistic position of Saturn.

84. SATURN IN PISCES

This position causes you to seek vindication within yourself. Your struggle with the world is the inner struggle between the good and the bad within you; and you are capable of being content with self-approval when you have mastered yourself. If from this point introspection goes deeper, you realize that self-approval is not enough, and require that self-approval shall be further served by the approval of others. Your defense against the hardships of life (and life does seem hard to you) lies not in open struggle with it, but in struggle within yourself to make life seem less difficult. This in its worst form results in introversion, withdrawal, brooding, giving up the struggle, and holing up alone to feel sorry for yourself. In its middle form, you fight off the lethargy and the withdrawal and find the key to your problem within yourself. In its advanced and best form, you improve your doleful outlook, redirect your energies outward, discover your virtues and your abilities, and make complete self-approval wait till you have won some objective testimony of your worth. This is a difficult position, but being flexible, gives great inner strength. You are moody and tend to fluctuate from heights of being pleased with yourself and the world to depths in which you and everything else is at sixes and sevens. Your reaction to experience is almost wholly subjective: sunshine is shadow if you're feeling bad; and clouds are harbingers of joy if you're feeling good. You are one of the people who thinks a rainstorm was sent solely to destroy your outing, and who rebels personally against the weather. In acute form this leads on to delusions of persecution or some minor neurosis. But your capacity for knowing yourself is great, and once you have learned the trick of self-analysis, you can lead your temperament into creative and constructive channels to become one of the most useful members of society.

Year	Dates	Sign	Para.	Year	Dates	Sign	Para.
1870	1/1-12/14	Sagittarius	81	1896	All Year	Scorpio	80
	12/15-12/31	Capricorn	82	1897	1/1-2/6	Scorpio	80
1871	All Year	Capricorn	82		2/7-4/9	Sagittarius	81
1872	All Year	Capricorn	82		4/10-10/26	Scorpio	80
1873	1/1-3/13	Capricorn	82		10/27-12/31	Sagittarius	81
	3/14-7/13	Aquarius	83	1898	All Year	Sagittarius	81
	7/14-12/10	Capricorn	82	1899	All Year	Sagittarius	81
	12/11-12/31	Aquarius	83	1900	1/1-1/20	Sagittarius	81
1874	All Year	Aquarius	83		1/21-7/18	Capricorn	82
1875	All Year	Aquarius	83		7/19-10/16	Sagittarius	81
1876	1/1-2/29	Aquarius	83		10/17-12/31	Capricorn	82
	3/1-12/31	Pisces	84	1901	All Year	Capricorn	82
1877	All Year	Pisces	84	1902	All Year	Capricorn	82
1878	1/1-5/14	Pisces	84	1903	1/1-1/19	Capricorn	82
	5/15-9/15	Aries	73		1/20-12/31	Aquarius	83
	9/16-12/31	Pisces	84	1904	All Year	Aquarius	83
1879	1/1-2/5	Pisces	84	1905	1/1-4/12	Aquarius	83
	2/6-12/31	Aries	73		4/13-8/16	Pisces	84
1880	All Year	Aries	73		8/17-12/31	Aquarius	83
1881	1/1-4/5	Aries	73	1906	1/1-1/7	Aquarius	83
	4/6-12/31	Taurus	74		1/8-12/31	Pisces	84
1882	All Year	Taurus	74	1907	All Year	Pisces	84
1883	1/1-5/23	Taurus	74	1908	1/1-3/18	Pisces	84
	5/24-12/31	Gemini	75		3/19-12/31	Aries	73
1884	All Year	Gemini	75	1909	All Year	Aries	73
1885	1/1-7/5	Gemini	75	1910	1/1-5/16	Aries	73
	7/6-12/31	Cancer	76		5/17-12/14	Taurus	74
1886	All Year	Cancer	76		12/15-12/31	Aries	73
1887	1/1-8/18	Cancer	76	1911	1/1-1/19	Aries	73
	8/19-12/31	Leo	77		1/20-12/31	Taurus	74
1888	1/1-3/9	Leo	77	1912	1/1-7/16	Taurus	74
	3/10-4/20	Cancer	76		7/17-11/30	Gemini	75
	4/21-12/31	Leo	77		12/1-12/31	Taurus	74
1889	1/1-10/6	Leo	77	1913	1/1-3/25	Taurus	74
	10/7-12/31	Virgo	78		3/26-12/31	Gemini	75
1890	1/1-2/24	Virgo	78	1914	1/1-8/24	Gemini	75
	2/25-6/27	Leo	77		8/25-12/6	Cancer	76
	6/28-12/31	Virgo	78		12/7-12/31	Gemini	75
1891	1/1-12/26	Virgo	78	1915	1/1-5/11	Gemini	75
	12/27-12/31	Libra	79		5/12-12/31	Cancer	76
1892	1/1-1/22	Libra	79	1916	1/1-10/16	Cancer	76
	1/23-8/29	Virgo	78		10/17-12/7	Leo	77
	8/20-12/31	Libra	79		12/8-12/31	Cancer	76
1893	All Year	Libra	79	1917	1/1-7/23	Cancer	76
1894	1/1-11/6	Libra	79		7/24-12/31	Leo	77
	11/7-12/31	Scorpio	80	1918	All Year	Leo	77
1895	All Year	Scorpio	80	1919	1/1-8/11	Leo	77
					8/12-12/31	Virgo	78

Year	Dates	Sign	Para.	Year	Dates	Sign	Para.
1920	All Year	Virgo	78	1946	1/1-8/3	Cancer	76
1921	1/1-10/7	Virgo	78		8/4-12/31	Leo	77
	10/8-12/31	Libra	79	1947	All Year	Leo	77
1922	All Year	Libra	79	1948	1/1-9/20	Leo	77
1923	1/1-12/19	Libra	79		9/21-12/31	Virgo	78
	12/20-12/31	Scorpio	80	1949	1/1-4/4	Virgo	78
1924	1/1-4/5	Scorpio	80		4/5-5/30	Leo	77
	4/6-9/13	Libra	79		5/31-12/31	Virgo	78
	9/14-12/31	Scorpio	80	1950	1/1-11/21	Virgo	78
1925	All Year	Scorpio	80		11/22-12/31	Libra	79
1926	1/1-12/2	Scorpio	80	1951	1/1-3/7	Libra	79
	12/3-12/31	Sagittarius	81		3/8-8/13	Virgo	78
1927	All Year	Sagittarius	81		8/14-12/31	Libra	79
1928	All Year	Sagittarius	81	1952	All Year	Libra	79
1929	1/1-3/14	Sagittarius	81	1953	1/1-10/20	Libra	79
	3/15-5/4	Capricorn	82		10/21-12/31	Scorpio	80
	5/5-11/29	Sagittarius	81	1954	All Year	Scorpio	80
	11/30-12/31	Capricorn	82	1955	All Year	Scorpio	80
1930	All Year	Capricorn	82	1956	1/1-1/10	Scorpio	80
1931	All Year	Capricorn	82		1/11-5/20	Sagittarius	81
1932	1/1-2/23	Capricorn	82		5/21-10/10	Scorpio	80
	2/24-8/13	Aquarius	83		10/11-12/31	Sagittarius	81
	8/14-11/19	Capricorn	82	1957	All Year	Sagittarius	81
	11/20-12/31	Aquarius	83	1958	All Year	Sagittarius	81
1933	All Year	Aquarius	83	1959	All Year	Capricorn	82
1934	All Year	Aquarius	83	1960	All Year	Capricorn	82
1935	1/1-2/13	Aquarius	83	1961	1/1-4/30	Capricorn	82
	2/14-12/31	Pisces	84		5/1-5/31	Aquarius	83
1936	All Year	Pisces	84		6/1-12/31	Capricorn	82
1937	1/1-4/25	Pisces	84	1962	All Year	Aquarius	83
	4/26-10/18	Aries	73	1963	All Year	Aquarius	83
	10/19-12/31	Pisces	84	1964	1/1-3/24	Aquarius	83
1938	1/1-1/15	Pisces	84		3/25-9/15	Pisces	84
	1/16-12/31	Aries	73		9/16-12/15	Aquarius	83
1939	1/1-7/7	Aries	73		12/16-12/31	Pisces	84
	7/8-9/23	Taurus	74	1965	All Year	Pisces	84
	9/24-12/31	Aries	73	1966	All Year	Pisces	84
1940	1/1-1/20	Aries	73	1967	1/1-3/3	Pisces	84
	1/21-12/31	Taurus	74		3/4-12/31	Aries	73
1941	All Year	Taurus	74	1968	All Year	Aries	73
1942	1/1-5/9	Taurus	74	1969	1/1-4/29	Aries	73
	5/10-12/31	Gemini	75		4/30-12/31	Taurus	74
1943	All Year	Gemini	75	1970	All Year	Taurus	74
1944	1/1-6/21	Gemini	75	1971	1/1-6/18	Taurus	74
	6/22-12/31	Cancer	76		6/19-12/31	Gemini	75
1945	All Year	Cancer	76				

Year	Dates	Sign	Para.	Year	Dates	Sign	Para.
1972	1/1-1/10	Gemini	75	1985	1/1-11/17	Scorpio	80
	1/11-2/21	Taurus	74		11/18-12/31	Sagittarius	81
	2/22-12/31	Gemini	75	1986	All Year	Sagittarius	81
1973	1/1-8/1	Gemini	75	1987	All Year	Sagittarius	81
	8/2-12/31	Cancer	76	1988	1/1-2/13	Sagittarius	81
1974	1/1-1/7	Cancer	76		2/14-6/10	Capricorn	82
	1/8-4/18	Gemini	75		6/11-11/12	Sagittarius	81
	4/19-12/31	Cancer	76		11/13-12/31	Capricorn	82
1975	1/1-9/17	Cancer	76	1989	All Year	Capricorn	82
	9/18-12/31	Leo	77	1990	All Year	Capricorn	82
1976	1/1-1/14	Leo	77	1991	1/1-2/6	Capricorn	82
	1/15-6/5	Cancer	76		2/7-12/31	Aquarius	83
	6/6-12/31	Leo	77	1992	All Year	Aquarius	83
1977	1/1-11/16	Leo	77	1993	1/1-5/21	Aquarius	83
	11/17-12/31	Virgo	78		5/22-6/30	Pisces	84
1978	1/1-1/5	Virgo	78		7/1-12/31	Aquarius	83
	1/6-7/26	Leo	77	1994	1/1-1/28	Aquarius	83
	7/27-12/31	Virgo	78		1/29-12/31	Pisces	84
1979	All Year	Virgo	78	1995	All Year	Pisces	84
1980	1/1-9/21	Virgo	78	1996	1/1-4/7	Pisces	84
	9/22-12/31	Libra	79		4/8-12/31	Aries	73
1981	All Year	Libra	79	1997	All Year	Aries	73
1982	1/1-11/29	Libra	79	1998	1/1-6/9	Aries	73
	11/30-12/31	Scorpio	80		6/10-10/25	Taurus	74
1983	1/1-5/6	Scorpio	80		10/26-12/31	Aries	73
	5/7-8/24	Libra	79	1999	1/1-3/1	Aries	73
	8/25-12/31	Scorpio	80		3/2-12/31	Taurus	74
1984	All Year	Scorpio	80				

URANUS, NEPTUNE AND PLUTO

These planets remain in one sign so long—Uranus seven years; Neptune fourteen years, Pluto, twelve to thirty years—that their influence conditions whole generations at a time. Their significance by sign, therefore, must be regarded in a very general nature when you read it in your Vitasphere. They are the planets of genius—and obviously everyone born in a seven or fourteen year period is not a genius. To know this, the relation of Uranus or Neptune to the Ascendant, the Midheaven, the Sun, Moon and the planets must be determined, and this complete picture is beyond the scope of this book. When you find the four essential house cusps (Chapter XI), you may discover that Uranus is in the sign on the Ascendant (1st sector) or in the 10th sector (the Midheaven). If you do have one of these positions in your Vitaphere, you may belong in the genius (or eccentric!) class. Also, Uranus in the same sign with Sun, Moon, Mercury, or Jupiter elevates you. Neptune in the same sign with Sun or Moon has similar effect, but is more dangerous because Neptune relates to the deepest subconscious, and its near-conjunction to Sun or Moon sometimes injures the sense of reality and causes the native to live in a dream world of his own. Pluto's effects are more subtle, but its influence is strengthened when it is in the same sign as the Sun, Moon or Mars, or when it is found near the Ascendant or Midheaven.

URANUS in a general way relates to the neuro-mentality, the creative originality or individuality, and his position by sign in the Vitaphere tells the direction along which you will seek to express your most characteristic self in creative and original effort. *In the same sign with the Sun,* great nervous activity, high-strung nature, original, creative or eccentric. *In the same sign with Mercury or the Moon,* acute awareness, quick reaction to sense impressions and experience; a hair-trigger mind. *In the same sign with Venus,* unusual reaction to emotional experience, highly idealistic though sensual, original ideas of love and human relations. *In the same sign with Mars,* high speed activity, love of swift motion and perhaps of danger. *In the same sign with Jupiter,* makes opportunity, creates wealth and the means of getting it, inventive, daring, executive. *In the same sign with Saturn,* good sense lending expedience to original ideas; can be a practical-creative position, but more often than not sets up a destroying conflict between practicality and originality that can result in a stalemate.

NEPTUNE relates to the deepest wells of the subconscious, inherited mentality and spirituality, indicating what you take deeply for granted in life. *Neptune in the same sign with Sun or Moon* indicates that intuitions and hunches—or delusions—dominate; a need for rigidly holding to reality. *In the same sign with Mercury,* sharp sense perceptions, a sensitive mind, perhaps creative, a quivering intensity of reaction to sense experience. *In the same sign with Venus,* idealistic and romantic (or sentimental) reaction to emotional experience, danger of sensationalism and love of strange pleasures. *In the same sign with Mars,* energy and intuition that work together to make mastery of life—one of the signs of having angels (or devils) on your side. *In the same sign with Jupiter,* intuitive response to opportunity generally along practical and money-making lines; one of the signs of security if not indeed of wealth. *In the same sign with Saturn,* intuitive defense and attack on the world generally successful unless Saturn polarizes on the negative side; then danger of delusions and unhappiness.

PLUTO was discovered in 1930, so not enough about it was known at the time of the writing of this book in 1940 for it to be included. However, today there is general agreement among astrologers that Pluto rules Scorpio. Pluto relates to the ability to let go of things, to get rid of irrelevant prejudices and outdated habit patterns. It relates to subconscious feelings, inner urges and repressed emotions. A strong Pluto gives the ability to see the hidden side of life, and thus bestows power on the native—power which can be used for good or ill. *In the same sign as the Sun,* Pluto gives a love of power and an ambitious, ruthless nature. *In the same sign as the Moon,* it gives a deep psychological awareness and the ability to perceive others' hidden motives. It also shows moodiness and a sensitive nature. *In the same sign as Mercury,* it signifies an investigative, penetrative mind and the power to persuade others. *In the same sign as Venus,* Pluto gives a strong love nature, with a tendency to be possessive and self-indulgent. *In the same sign as Mars,* it increases the independence and ego strength, and gives power over others. Courage and cruelty can both be present. *In the same sign as Jupiter,* it produces an inquisitive nature with a desire to understand the hidden side of life. *In the same sign as Saturn,* it points to a serious nature given to self-denial and self-discipline.

In the table for finding Uranus' place, find your birth year and the period which includes your birthdate. Uranus' sign at your birth is given and the paragraph which relates to you.

85. URANUS IN ARIES*

If your Jupiter is also in Aries, read that paragraph carefully and link it with this one. Uranus in Aries causes you to express your genius directly and openly to the world. You have around you a cheerful forthrightness that can make for great honesty, simplicity, and charm. You are protected from sensitiveness by having a good solid sense of your own worth and a willingness to believe that other people accept you for what you are. You can be blunt and tactless, and you have to look out that independence of spirit does not make you a lone wolf. Mentally, you are quick, apt, facile, able to grap mechanical details readily and to apply them practically. You are aggressive to some extent at least and are rarely afraid to think your own thoughts or to express them. You care a great deal about "being understood" and will go out of your way to explain yourself if you think you are being misinterpreted. You love action, both physical and mental, and are rarely found idle. Laziness is not for you; your mind at least is always working, no matter what your

---

*Courtesy of Dell's *Horoscope* magazine.

body may be doing. Concentration is the thing you have to learn in order to put your pioneering intellect to best use.

86. URANUS IN TAURUS*

This transit brought the Age of Dictators, and the genius (Uranus) of this period was directed toward revolutionizing (Uranus) ideas of geographic boundaries (Taurus) and property rights (Taurus). Children born will come to maturity with quite different ideas of wealth, however, than those current when they were born, for this generation may well begin to show the reaction against the socializing of the world that was going on at their birth. This is a "property" position, and favors wealth if other things in the reading don't upset the promise. Since all these children have Neptune in Virgo as their basic intuitive influence, that paragraph should be heeded carefully. Uranus in Taurus tends toward individualism in property matters, and must be prevented from undermining the broader, more social requirements of Neptune in Virgo. At worst this makes a selfish and self-seeking person; at best a socially-conscious and highly effective crusader for security (Taurus) for all (Uranus). This position adds glamor to the nature; a steady fire burns within, drawing from the world and from individuals the love which is so important when the warm-hearted Taurus is illumined by the brilliance of Uranus.

87. URANUS IN GEMINI*

This position of Gemini represents the genius of America in all its phases. It was in force when the Declaration of Independence was signed, and again during the Civil War it brought the Emancipation Proclamation. It stands for freedom, liberty, independence of action and of conscience. It makes you mentally alert and is one of the indexes of genius. It gives quickness of perception, and an exalted mental approach to all problems, whether personal or social. You think things through quickly and logically, appearing

---

*Courtesy of Dell's *Horoscope* magazine.

because of this to have "intuition" which is probably in your case a super-rapid working of logical processes. You love freedom, and one way or another will have it. At the same time you respect the rights of others, and will fight for abstract principles even more effectively than for your own individual rights. Mental training is what you need to rise to the best of this very important position. Without training and a conscious effort to concentrate, your great mental energies are likely to scatter. You can be a dilettante, covering many fields swiftly; or a creator of importance if you stress one and stick to it.

88. URANUS IN CANCER

The world in which you grew up was expanding rapidly, and the symptoms of growth impressed you deeply. The genius of your generation was exerted along lines of material expansion. Inventions increased the comforts of living, and the wonder of new things suddenly becoming familiar influenced you greatly. Your originality finds its most characteristic expression in seeking security in change and improvement; you are restless, a pioneer eager to move your home (literally or figuratively) onward to new frontiers, never so happy as when you are applying your individualism to an upheaval of some sort, as a result of which you see living conditions bettered. Plenty of unsettlement has accompanied your life as a result of this urge to go upward and onward. However, the adventurous spirit has been yours, and even if your impatient genius has upset your world, you wouldn't live your life any other way.

89. URANUS IN LEO

This position represents a generation in which the creative instinct manifests itself, when at all, through an extraordinary confidence in the dramatization of the total personality. This was the era of imperial expansion in England and America—the time when "men grew tall" and there were "giants in the earth." Born in this era, you saw around you in the great world of your childhood examples of daring which succeeded dramatically. You were, because of Uranus' position in the self-conscious and dramatic Leo, impressionable to the prowess of these Great Men. A kind of hero worship is natural to you; and the individualistic creative expression which will suit you best is the sort which will allow you to stand in the limelight and hear applause for your originality, your daring, your cleverness, your genius. The aim of your mental, creative originality is recognition, acclaim, applause, and you exert your deepest originality in its most characteristic form and to its best advantage when this goal is in sight.

90. URANUS IN VIRGO

Your originality is most likely to assert itself along lines of organization, routine, or social welfare. If you ever work along your most characteristic lines, it will be to make some contribution to social or business systems. You can be an efficiency expert in the service of capitalist industry and make your genius valuable along that line. Or your desire to serve may take a broader and more humanitarian form, and you may become a leader of social thought, applying your systematic genius to large problems of labor and social welfare. Your most characteristic expression will be found in connection with work, its methods and its efficiency; or in connection with social service and progress in the large. You are more likely than not to be on the side of social change aiming at division of labor and the general good of society, and probably feel at home with the changes that are now going on in the turbulent world around you.

91. URANUS IN LIBRA

Yours is a peculiar hidden genius, for you tend to identify yourself with large groups and interests and to "lose yourself in order to find yourself." You can be a great leader (if your expression of originality works outward to the rest of the world) or a dreadful eccentric (if it works inward). If you identify yourself *with* others on the positive and aggressive side, you make definite contributions to your group or to society as a whole, having an uncanny knack for unifying divergent groups and factions into a cooperative whole. If you identify yourself *against* others (the negative expression of the characteristic urge to cooperation), you may think the hand of the world is against you and become a lone wolf, antisocial and quarrelsome. Your best and truest expression of originality will come in connection with cooperative ventures, for when you learn to work with others, there is no end to the organizational genius which you can bring to bear on your progress and the general welfare of others.

92. URANUS IN SCORPIO

If Saturn is also in Scorpio in your Vitasphere, read that paragraph carefully and link it with this one. Uranus in Scorpio causes your genius to work through deep wells of the subconscious and makes for tremendous power for good or bad. You are angel or devil— or, at different times, both. Your personal magnetism is powerful, and you seek for your originality personal tribute from the world or from individuals. You can be content with the worship (or fear) of a small circle and can, because of this, be capable of limiting the scope of your great powers. Love, or sex, is important to you; you rule others if you control yourself, and if you don't, you are the slave to others, or to your own instincts, which are very powerful. You are capable of gratifying your need for power by identifying yourself with machinery, and are often successful in mechanical or engineering fields, where you are able to feel your own strength in the strength of the machine you make or operate. You love speed and feel at home when moving swiftly. If self-controlled, you are a powerful executive requiring absolute military obedience. Your deep need for self-control is manifest in your worship of method, system, efficiency and obedience. You should learn the law of obedience in the abstract, allow your great magnetism to express itself freely without mastering you, and thus have the world at your feet.

93. URANUS IN SAGITTARIUS

Your originality requires scope and proceeds from vision. You generalize readily, feeling yourself most at home, and in the sphere of your greatest mental efficiency, when dealing in large terms, ideas, symbols. This can make you a great artist or thinker or philosopher or preacher—or it can make you just a fuzzy thinker, never getting down to cases. You should learn the worship of facts, and you need never worry about getting stodgy, for facts will always be to you the stones to build generalizations from and will never make you a groundling. You have a kind of fear and contempt for the earthbound, feeling that your true genius takes you out of the class of mere bookworms and grubbers into a higher atmosphere of the spirit. No idea is too lofty for you to grasp—or so you think. And by being willing to grasp facts first and build the ideas from them, you can be really as high and profound as you imagine yourself to be. When you learn the value of knowledge (as insurance for your ideas), you can be a real intellectual force, and it is in this role that you find your truest expression.

94. URANUS IN CAPRICORN

This period produced a generation whose most impressionable years (six to fourteen) were shaken by war. They never knew a stable world and have not yet known one. Throughout this period Uranus in Capricorn was opposed by Neptune in Cancer, so it is impossible to estimate the force Uranus in Capricorn alone would have in the contemporary world. It is therefore necessary to consider this position in connection with Neptune's opposition from Cancer. All the deep primal instincts of Neptune in Cancer (for a home, for security, for personal identification with these self-preservative factors) were shaken by Uranus' opposition from Capricorn (worldly circumstance and necessities). Capricorn is the so-called World sign and it is natural that the genius Uranus therein should produce a generation that would upset old traditions. And indeed this was the generation that passed through a nightmare of war and postwar, when the old ideals (Naptune in Cancer) tottered before individualistic expression (Uranus) brought on by rebellion (Uranus) against a world condition (Capricorn). With this position, you are likely to feel that you are giving expression to your truest genius in rebellion against things as they are, or as they were, for you still remember the revolt against conventions that occupied your youth, when to be part of the general iconoclasm of the day was considered personally daring. Mass individualism was the product of Uranus in Capricorn. To progress from the conventional unconventionality to truly finding yourself and your individual expression has been quite a task. When you find it you will discover that your great contribution must be along lines of social progress, probably quite conservative in aim, even if unusual in method. You seek not to destroy the law and the prophets, but to fulfill them with all the vigor and individualism of the New Dispensation.

95. URANUS IN AQUARIUS

By the time you started remembering, the first World War was over and the world was being reborn. The individualism for which those born with Uranus in Capricorn rebelled and fought, you take for granted. Their legacy to you was a world from which by the sweat of their hearts they had stripped old pruderies, old taboos, old conventions. The freedom to be themselves for which they struggled came naturally to you, and because of this, you take for granted the dignity of the individual that was questioned in the generation before you. In your hands in the fighting of the next war, whether it be fought on battlefields in the old bloody manner or in legislative halls for social changes. You know instinctively that your individual genius requires a mass expression, that there is no personal freedom for anyone till everyone is free, and that no individual can be happier than the sum total of his society is happy. You are the lamplighters of the new birth of freedom in the hour of the world's darkness. In the depths of your spirits you know that there is no individualism, no personal genius, no true expression possible to any one human being till all of mankind has found the level at which it can live securely together. This is the great message of the Aquarian age of which you and those of your generation are the acolytes.

96. URANUS IN PISCES

Survivors of the second World War have fallen heir to the legacy of a new social order, and you will be able to go on to the true expression of individual genius in avenues of self-fulfillment and self-discovery. Your genius is for inner truth and self-sufficiency. Rugged individualism in the economic sense will not appeal to you, but in the security of a new social order you will achieve a new individualism, based on self-knowledge and self-respect. You will take for granted the new world in which your maturity will be spent, a world of greater social equality. And in this world you will not drop to the mediocre level that is prophesied by the reactionary prophets of doom: you will, on the contrary, develop a new genius: the genius of personal developmment for its own sake, quite apart from the necessity of earning a living. You will know yourself better than your fathers and mothers and your older brothers and sisters knew themselves: you will make demands on yourself and drive yourself to new heights of personal accomplishment. Your genius is for the adventure of self-discovery and self-development, and in this adventure you will range new fields of unprecedented profundity.

Year	Dates	Sign	Para.	Year	Dates	Sign	Para.
1870	All Year	Cancer	88	1904	1/1-12/19	Sagittarius	93
1871	1/1-9/13	Cancer	88		12/20-12/31	Capricorn	94
	9/14-12/31	Leo	89	1905	All Year	Capricorn	94
1872	1/1-6/27	Cancer	88	1906	All Year	Capricorn	94
	6/28-12/31	Leo	89	1907	All Year	Capricorn	94
1873	All Year	Leo	89	1908	All Year	Capricorn	94
1874	All Year	Leo	89	1909	All Year	Capricorn	94
1875	All Year	Leo	89	1910	All Year	Capricorn	94
1876	All Year	Leo	89	1911	All Year	Capricorn	94
1877	All Year	Leo	89	1912	1/1-1/30	Capricorn	94
1878	1/1-8/24	Leo	89		1/31-9/4	Aquarius	95
	8/25-12/31	Virgo	90		9/5-11/11	Capricorn	94
1879	All Year	Virgo	90		11/12-12/31	Aquarius	95
1880	All Year	Virgo	90	1913	All Year	Aquarius	95
1881	All Year	Virgo	90	1914	All Year	Aquarius	95
1882	All Year	Virgo	90	1915	All Year	Aquarius	95
1883	All Year	Virgo	90	1916	All Year	Aquarius	95
1884	1/1-10/13	Virgo	90	1917	All Year	Aquarius	95
	10/14-12/31	Libra	91	1918	All Year	Aquarius	95
1885	1/1-4/11	Libra	91	1919	1/1-3/31	Aquarius	95
	4/12-7/28	Virgo	90		4/1-8/16	Pisces	96
	7/29-12/31	Libra	91		8/17-12/31	Aquarius	95
1886	All Year	Libra	91	1920	1/1-1/21	Aquarius	95
1887	All Year	Libra	91		1/22-12/31	Pisces	96
1888	All Year	Libra	91	1921	All Year	Pisces	96
1889	All Year	Libra	91	1922	All Year	Pisces	96
1890	1/1-12/9	Libra	91	1923	All Year	Pisces	96
	12/10-12/31	Scorpio	92	1924	All Year	Pisces	96
1891	1/1-4/4	Scorpio	92	1925	All Year	Pisces	96
	4/5-9/25	Libra	91	1926	All Year	Pisces	96
	9/26-12/31	Scorpio	92	1927	1/1-3/30	Pisces	96
1892	All Year	Scorpio	92		3/31-11/4	Aries	85
1893	All Year	Scorpio	92		11/5-12/31	Pisces	96
1894	All Year	Scorpio	92	1928	1/1-1/12	Pisces	96
1895	All Year	Scorpio	92		1/13-12/31	Aries	85
1896	All Year	Scorpio	92	1929	All Year	Aries	85
1897	1/1-12/1	Scorpio	92	1930	All Year	Aries	85
	12/2-12/31	Sagittarius	93	1931	All Year	Aries	85
1898	1/1-7/3	Sagittarius	93	1932	All Year	Aries	85
	7/4-9/10	Scorpio	92	1933	All Year	Aries	85
	9/11-12/31	Sagittarius	93	1934	1/1-6/5	Aries	85
1899	All Year	Sagittarius	93		6/6-10/9	Taurus	86
1900	All Year	Sagittarius	93		10/10-12/31	Aries	85
1901	All Year	Sagittarius	93	1935	1/1-3/27	Aries	85
1902	All Year	Sagittarius	93		3/28-12/31	Taurus	86
1903	All Year	Sagittarius	93	1936	All Year	Taurus	86

Year	Dates	Sign	Para.	Year	Dates	Sign	Para.
1937	All Year	Taurus	86	1969	1/1-5/22	Libra	91
1938	All Year	Taurus	86		5/23-6/24	Virgo	90
1939	All Year	Taurus	86		6/25-12/31	Libra	91
1940	All Year	Taurus	86	1970	All Year	Libra	91
1941	1/1-8/8	Taurus	86	1971	All Year	Libra	91
	8/9-10/6	Gemini	87	1972	All Year	Libra	91
	10/7-12/31	Taurus	86	1973	All Year	Libra	91
1942	1/1-5/15	Taurus	86	1974	1/1-11/21	Libra	91
	5/16-12/31	Gemini	87		11/22-12/31	Scorpio	92
1943	All Year	Gemini	87	1975	1/1-5/1	Scorpio	92
1944	All Year	Gemini	87		5/2-9/8	Libra	91
1945	All Year	Gemini	87		9/9-12/31	Scorpio	92
1946	All Year	Gemini	87	1976	All Year	Scorpio	92
1947	All Year	Gemini	87	1977	All Year	Scorpio	92
1948	1/1-8/31	Gemini	87	1978	All Year	Scorpio	92
	9/1-11/13	Cancer	88	1979	All Year	Scorpio	92
	11/14-12/31	Gemini	87	1980	All Year	Scorpio	92
1949	1/1-6/11	Gemini	87	1981	1/1-2/17	Scorpio	92
	6/12-12/31	Cancer	88		2/18-3/20	Sagittarius	93
1950	All Year	Cancer	88		3/21-11/16	Scorpio	92
1951	All Year	Cancer	88		11/17-12/31	Sagittarius	93
1952	All Year	Cancer	88	1982	All Year	Sagittarius	93
1953	All Year	Cancer	88	1983	All Year	Sagittarius	93
1954	All Year	Cancer	88	1984	All Year	Sagittarius	93
1955	1/1-8/15	Cancer	88	1985	All Year	Sagittarius	93
	8/16-12/31	Leo	89	1986	All Year	Sagittarius	93
1956	1/1-2/3	Leo	89	1987	All Year	Sagittarius	93
	2/4-5/31	Cancer	88	1988	1/1-2/14	Sagittarius	93
	6/1-12/31	Leo	89		2/15-5/26	Capricorn	94
1957	All Year	Leo	89		5/27-12/2	Sagittarius	93
1958	All Year	Leo	89		12/3-12/31	Capricorn	94
1959	All Year	Leo	89	1989	All Year	Capricorn	94
1960	All Year	Leo	89	1990	All Year	Capricorn	94
1961	1/1-10/31	Leo	89	1991	All Year	Capricorn	94
	11/1-12/31	Virgo	90	1992	All Year	Capricorn	94
1962	1/1-1/15	Virgo	90	1993	All Year	Capricorn	94
	1/16-7/31	Leo	89	1994	All Year	Capricorn	94
	8/1-12/31	Virgo	90	1995	1/1-4/1	Capricorn	94
1963	All Year	Virgo	90		4/2-6/9	Aquarius	95
1964	All Year	Virgo	90		6/10-12/31	Capricorn	94
1965	All Year	Virgo	90	1996	1/1-1/12	Capricorn	94
1966	All Year	Virgo	90		1/13-12/31	Aquarius	95
1967	All Year	Virgo	90	1997	All Year	Aquarius	95
1968	1/1-9/28	Virgo	90	1998	All Year	Aquarius	95
	9/29-12/31	Libra	91	1999	All Year	Aquarius	95

In the table for finding Neptune's place, find your birth year and the period which includes your birthdate. Neptune's sign at your birth is given and the paragraph which relates to you.

97. NEPTUNE IN ARIES

This position makes you a great individualist and egoist, for the subconscious is always whispering to you of your own importance. This can be anything from a creative genius to a bumptious egotist. Mind power is great and must be carefully controlled. You can invent things for personal glory and mass benefit. You can dominate those around you to their ruin and your own. You can give up your life to service, or you can make others give up their lives serving you. Self-deception is especially dangerous, for your subconscious intrudes between you and reality, and you miss the facts of life by being too impressed with your interpretations of them, which can be far from right. You need to become detached and objective, and this requires deep awareness and hard mental work, for you tend to follow hunches and instincts and to rule out the reasonable things which might help you. You have a fine courageous spirit; your self-confidence makes you a rock of strength; and through proper control of inner, subconscious forces you are a big influence in whatever sphere you move.

98. NEPTUNE IN TAURUS

You were born in the Golden Age of economic expansion and took material conditions as you found them for granted. Your deepest subconscious springs proceed from the economic soil in which you grew. (1) If you were poor or economically insecure, your whole personality has been conditioned by your acceptance of, or rebellion against, this circumstance. Your intuitions come directly from this source; your instinctive reactions are related to poverty or the overcoming of it. (2) If you were rich or secure, you have taken this for granted, and you have your intuitions and instincts self-assured, though this doesn't mean that they have been correct. Whatever condition surrounded your birth and early life, you will discover that the wellsprings of your instinct are somehow rooted in concepts of property and security, and that deep below everything else the security motive, the property motive, is permanently fixed.

99. NEPTUNE IN GEMINI

The era of change and invention dominated your formative years, and consequently your subconscious is geared to ideas of change and development. You take naturally to innovations and novelties. This can make you (a) broad, tolerant, creative; or (b) flighty, irresponsible, jittery. Either development is possible, for both have their roots in flexibility, which because of the era in which you grew up was built into your nature deeply. This is a complex position for Neptune, for you probably appear to have no complexes—that is, no roots—at all. But the very absence of roots is your complex, and you need to find roots in the outside world to make up for the shifting sands on which your subconscious builds. You need to study the externals of life carefully and find your stability in things and ideas gained intellectually. When you have done this, your natural flexibility will help elevate you toward a high personal and cultural standard, and you will find yourself highly tolerant, understanding and creative in your approach to life.

100. NEPTUNE IN CANCER

If you also have Uranus in Capricorn, Paragraph 94 covers Neptune in Cancer for you also. If you have Uranus in Sagittarius or Aquarius, your Neptune in Cancer escapes the opposition to Uranus, and your inner psychic pattern will follow Neptune in Cancer considered in its own right. Your early home environment impressed you deeply and even more than most fixed your instinctive reactions to life and conditioned your intuitions. You may range far from the ideal of your subconscious, but this will forever remain fixed in a home of your own, and you will never feel yourself till you are settled in one. Since this demand of the ego is fairly easy of fulfillment, you stand a chance of escaping the worst complexes that beset human beings; and once you have established your own hearth and fireside, and rested your soul in it, your instinctual urges should work naturally toward the smooth fulfillment of the total personality. You are extremely sensitive to atmospheres and moods, of places as well as of people, and should allow your instinct to guide you in the selection of a location for your home. Congenial surroundings are necessary for your best development, and peace in the places where you live and work is essential to the best growth of the ego, which instinctively remembers the peace of infancy and the protective atmosphere of the mother and seeks to rediscover these in its physical and psychic environment. If the total personality is passive, weak rather than strong, this can make you a spoiled child all your life, causing you to expect your wife or husband or friends to stand *in loco parentis* and humor your whims. But in an aggressive strong nature it causes the personality to be based firmly in simple domestic security, from which it draws strength and the materials of success and progress.

101. NEPTUNE IN LEO

Your instinctual urges are for self-fulfillment or self-dramatization and, above all, for self-approval, to have which you must also have love, not as a protection or a haven, but as an index of your personal worth. This is a highly creative position, polarizing all the instincts toward expression in art or service of some kind. You were "born wise" and belong to a generation that takes a lot for granted without being smart-alecky or sophisticated in its effect. The intuitions are direct and warmhearted; the need for approval gratifies itself by seeking love rather than respect, and generally winds up with both. You must guard against soft-heartedness and sensational tendencies, for you are so sure of yourself that you are willing to try anything once and can get burned through romanticizing too far.

You can be imposed on and get into trouble by thinking everyone as magnanimous as you are.

102. NEPTUNE IN VIRGO*

This position of Neptune brought the depression and the beginnings of a new age. Those born under it will come to maturity with a new slant on social and political matters, a new assurance of the dignity of work, a new consecration to humanity and to service. Your deepest wells of consciousness understand these things, and throughout your life unselfishness will be the keynote of your best expression. To learn early that the ego is of only secondary importance is to give yourself your surest foundation for happiness and success. You work best, you play best, you love best when your mind isn't on yourself. Learn the value of work for its own sake and you give yourself the best key to contentment. If your Uranus is in Aries, make your individual genius work to promote some ideal of service. If your Uranus is in Taurus, individual and collective security can be made mutually to serve each other. In any case, awareness of big social, collective, political, economic forces, and identification of yourself with them, enables you to get the detached view of the world and yourself which will encourage you to draw on the deep and abiding strength within yourself and use it to gain the peace of mind and happiness you need.

103. NEPTUNE IN LIBRA*

This position of Neptune brought reaction from the depression and dictator years, launched the world on its new era. The children born under this position will have a broad and idealistic outlook on the world. They will take for granted a kind of cooperative enterprise that may be novel to their elders; and will express themselves naturally, in word and deed, in ways that may seem cloud-treading and too idealistic to the more earth-bound. A conviction that individuality is

---

*Courtesy of Dell's *Horoscope* magazine.

best served by self-respecting alignment with others pervades their thinking and governs their lives; and this conviction is more than something reasoned out logically, for it is drawn from the deep wells of instinct and intuition, below the level of consciousness. In the social world, Neptune in Libra gives grace, charm and *noblesse oblige:* the sense of obligation and responsibility attaching to nobility of spirit. It makes its natives gentle, affectionate, idealistic, artistic; it enhances any creative gifts; and makes one a lover of peace, harmony, and personal progress through cooperative as well as individual endeavor.

104. NEPTUNE IN SCORPIO*

The people and nations of the world become aware of the awesome, death-dealing possibilities of nuclear war. Atomic-powered submarines in the depths of the seas play their role in the struggle for power. Those born under this influence want to plumb the secrets of the universe. The mystery of life and death is theirs to fathom. They are enthralled by occult studies, chemistry, invention. Neptune in this position intensifies the emotional nature, causes the native to have deep feelings, to be secretive and mystical. If Neptune is well aspected, there is gain through inheritance and financial ties with others; also, through partnership, including marriage. There is a great possibility of possessing marked extra-sensory perception. When Neptune is afflicted, every caution must be exercised regarding drugs and strong beverages, and dabbling in spiritualism. The sex instincts must be channeled in the right direction since the craving for sensation is very strong. Recuperative power is shown; also, a desire for reforms.

105. NEPTUNE IN SAGITTARIUS

Sagittarius is symbolized by the Centaur—a mythical half horse/half man, and so we find Neptune in this sign characterized by conflict between the Higher

*Courtesy of Dell's *Horoscope* magazine.

and Lower Selves. There is much interest in religion and mythology. There is the desire to explore, travel, move about, try new ideas, experiment with new ways of seeing and feelings things.

But just as there is an emphasis on "Spiritual" things, so is there an emphasis on Sensuality. There may be considerable prophetic ability, and there are many inspirations and vivid dreams. The intuition is highly developed and generally dependable in the professions of journalism and teaching.

Neptune in Sagittarius is expansive and exuberant, even extravagant. The Spirit of Adventure is high, and there is deep interest in new areas—such as parapsychology, esoteric healing methods, mind-drugs, etc.

106. NEPTUNE IN CAPRICORN

There is intuition in business matters, and big business attracts. The native can either have a real genius in financial matters, if well aspected, or tend toward selfishness and miserliness if badly aspected.

Likewise, this position may bring an interest in political and economic reconstruction, but it is also likely to make one overly susceptible to suggestion, and thus could involve him in fuzzy-headed schemes. If well aspected, there is an attraction to public service; if badly aspected, there could be attraction to conspiracy and fraud.

107. NEPTUNE IN AQUARIUS

This brings a deep interest in humanitarian causes, but with a tendency toward a messianic feeling about social and economic reconstruction. There is an inclination toward rather dubious methods in accomplishing worthwhile goals—an "end justifies the means" way of thought.

This position will likely bring friends who are deceptive, and likewise may lead to the native's imposing on his friends. There is great originality in this position, although there may be some eccentricity in one's private life.

108. NEPTUNE IN PISCES

This is presumably the most favorable position for Neptune, and should increase natural psychic faculties. At the same time, it is not a wealth-producing or even wealth-keeping position—for idealism and self-sacrifice are very strong. It brings a tendency towards escapism, typified by thinking that one can solve problems by entering a monastery.

If well aspected, benefits are derived through psychic and imaginative faculties. If badly aspected, one suffers through trickery and deceit of others, making the native highly subject to oral and mental suggestion. Unless discipline is trained, unless the mind is trained, this is a position favoring fuzzy, wishy-washy thinking.

(We include this as a matter of general interest, although Neptune will not be in Pisces until well into the 21st Century.)

Year	Dates	Sign	Para.	Year	Dates	Sign	Para.
1870	All Year	Aries	97	1905	All Year	Cancer	100
1871	All Year	Aries	97	1906	All Year	Cancer	100
1872	All Year	Aries	97	1907	All Year	Cancer	100
1873	All Year	Aries	97	1908	All Year	Cancer	100
1874	1/1-6/6	Aries	97	1909	All Year	Cancer	100
	6/7-9/30	Taurus	98	1910	All Year	Cancer	100
	10/1-12/31	Aries	97	1911	All Year	Cancer	100
1875	1/1-4/6	Aries	97	1912	All Year	Cancer	100
	4/7-12/31	Taurus	98	1913	All Year	Cancer	100
1876	All Year	Taurus	98	1914	1/1-9/23	Cancer	100
1877	All Year	Taurus	98		9/22-12/14	Leo	101
1878	All Year	Taurus	98		12/15-12/31	Cancer	100
1879	All Year	Taurus	98	1915	1/1-7/18	Cancer	100
1880	All Year	Taurus	98		7/19-12/31	Leo	101
1881	All Year	Taurus	98	1916	1/1-3/19	Leo	101
1882	All Year	Taurus	98		3/20-5/1	Cancer	100
1883	All Year	Taurus	98		5/2-12/31	Leo	101
1884	All Year	Taurus	98	1917	All Year	Leo	101
1885	All Year	Taurus	98	1918	All Year	Leo	101
1886	All Year	Taurus	98	1919	All Year	Leo	101
1887	1/1-8/15	Taurus	98	1920	All Year	Leo	101
	8/16-9/21	Gemini	99	1921	All Year	Leo	101
	9/22-12/31	Taurus	98	1922	All Year	Leo	101
1888	1/1-5/25	Taurus	98	1923	All Year	Leo	101
	5/26-12/31	Gemini	99	1924	All Year	Leo	101
1889	1/1-3/20	Taurus	98	1925	All Year	Leo	101
	3/21-12/31	Gemini	99	1926	All Year	Leo	101
1890	All Year	Gemini	99	1927	All Year	Leo	101
1891	All Year	Gemini	99	1928	1/1-9/20	Leo	101
1892	All Year	Gemini	99		9/21-12/31	Virgo	102
1893	All Year	Gemini	99	1929	1/1-2/19	Virgo	102
1894	All Year	Gemini	99		2/20-7/23	Leo	101
1895	All Year	Gemini	99		7/24-12/31	Virgo	102
1896	All Year	Gemini	99	1930	All Year	Virgo	102
1897	All Year	Gemini	99	1931	All Year	Virgo	102
1898	All Year	Gemini	99	1932	All Year	Virgo	102
1899	All Year	Gemini	99	1933	All Year	Virgo	102
1900	All Year	Gemini	99	1934	All Year	Virgo	102
1901	1/1-7/19	Gemini	99	1935	All Year	Virgo	102
	7/20-12/25	Cancer	100	1936	All Year	Virgo	102
	12/26-12/31	Gemini	99	1937	All Year	Virgo	102
1902	1/1-5/20	Gemini	99	1938	All Year	Virgo	102
	5/21-12/31	Cancer	100	1939	All Year	Virgo	102
1903	All Year	Cancer	100	1940	All Year	Virgo	102
1904	All Year	Cancer	100				

Year	Dates	Sign	Para.	Year	Dates	Sign	Para.
1941	All Year	Virgo	102	1971	All Year	Sagittarius	105
1942	1/1-10/4	Virgo	102	1972	All Year	Sagittarius	105
	10/5-12/31	Libra	103	1973	All Year	Sagittarius	105
1943	1/1-4/19	Libra	103	1974	All Year	Sagittarius	105
	4/20-8/3	Virgo	102	1975	All Year	Sagittarius	105
	8/4-12/31	Libra	103	1976	All Year	Sagittarius	105
1944	All Year	Libra	103	1977	All Year	Sagittarius	105
1945	All Year	Libra	103	1978	All Year	Sagittarius	105
1946	All Year	Libra	103	1979	All Year	Sagittarius	105
1947	All Year	Libra	103	1980	All Year	Sagittarius	105
1948	All Year	Libra	103	1981	All Year	Sagittarius	105
1949	All Year	Libra	103	1982	All Year	Sagittarius	105
1950	All Year	Libra	103	1983	All Year	Sagittarius	105
1951	All Year	Libra	103	1984	1/1-1/18	Sagittarius	105
1952	All Year	Libra	103		1/19-6/22	Capricorn	106
1953	All Year	Libra	103		6/23-11/21	Sagittarius	105
1954	All Year	Libra	103		11/22-12/31	Capricorn	106
1955	All Year	Libra	103	1985	All Year	Capricorn	106
1956	1/1-4/30	Scorpio	104	1986	All Year	Capricorn	106
	5/1-10/15	Libra	103	1987	All Year	Capricorn	106
	10/16-12/31	Scorpio	104	1988	All Year	Capricorn	106
1957	All Year	Scorpio	104	1989	All Year	Capricorn	106
1958	All Year	Scorpio	104	1990	All Year	Capricorn	106
1959	All Year	Scorpio	104	1991	All Year	Capricorn	106
1960	All Year	Scorpio	104	1992	All Year	Capricorn	106
1961	All Year	Scorpio	104	1993	All Year	Capricorn	106
1962	All Year	Scorpio	104	1994	All Year	Capricorn	106
1963	All Year	Scorpio	104	1995	All Year	Capricorn	106
1964	All Year	Scorpio	104	1996	All Year	Capricorn	106
1965	All Year	Scorpio	104	1997	All Year	Capricorn	106
1966	All Year	Scorpio	104	1998	1/1-1/28	Capricorn	106
1967	All Year	Scorpio	104		1/29-8/23	Aquarius	107
1968	All Year	Scorpio	104		8/24-11/27	Capricorn	106
1969	All Year	Scorpio	104		11/28-12/31	Aquarius	107
1970	1/5-5/2	Sagittarius	105	1999	All Year	Aquarius	107
	5/3-11/6	Scorpio	104				
	11/7-12/31	Sagittarius	105				

In the table for finding Pluto's place, find your birth year and the period which includes your birthdate. Pluto's sign at your birth is given and the paragraph which relates to you.

109. PLUTO IN ARIES

Militant political movements and courageous pioneering. Revolutions in politics, social interactions, and economics tear down existing ideas and structures to replace them with more individualistic behavior patterns. Nothing is sacred.

110. PLUTO IN TAURUS

We find greed, speculation in real estate, strong procreational urge, jealousy in a sexual sense, love of art, oratorial and singing ability. Well aspected, a refined erotic sense. Badly aspected, sex crimes, vindictiveness, etc.

111. PLUTO IN GEMINI

Spiritual energy, adventurousness, inventiveness, good judgment, ability to see weakness in others. There is a tendency to take up several vocations, and others frequently find it difficult to pin Pluto in Gemini down. There is an intellectual vanity here.

112. PLUTO IN CANCER

Emphasis on family loyalty, fond of ceremonial cultism, interest in magic, extreme tenacity, an ability to transform tradition into new values. The emphasis on family loyalty often is carried to such extremes as to attempt to solve all of our social ills by a "return to the family unit" thinking. It also accepts "Special Privilege" as a part of politics.

113. PLUTO IN LEO

There is great faith in oneself, and a great sense of propriety over ideas and "spheres of influence." There is a tendency to "feel like a king." There is more respect for government, and experimentation with government as a solver of social ills. There is a demand for loyalty from one's friends.

114. PLUTO IN VIRGO

An interest in the perfection of society. While life is viewed rather critically, it is with the confidence that it can be improved. Nutrition is looked upon as an answer to all problems. There can be innovation in the means of food production.

115. PLUTO IN LIBRA

A greater individualism, a feeling that life's problems can be solved in terms of the arts. Life is an adventure and a game to be played well.

116. PLUTO IN SCORPIO

Psychic research and education allow more people to become aware of their inner natures. Psychic talents are developed among many more people as spiritual awareness, peak experiences and ego loss become more common.

117. PLUTO IN SAGITTARIUS

The world is united along lines of energy forces which are recognized and strengthened. Collective energy becomes more important than nationalism or individualism. The universality of all religions is recognized.

118. PLUTO IN CAPRICORN

Authoritarianism, political rigidity and fascism are torn apart as Pluto restructures the economic system. Power bases are changed and reformulated along patterns of psychic energy flow.

119. PLUTO IN AQUARIUS

Scientific thought is revolutionized. Man's inventiveness is turned outward toward the planets in a united effort to expand the collective unconscious.

120. PLUTO IN PISCES

Subtle changes in psychic and spiritual development occur. New energy sources are discovered, ushering in a non-scientific, more mystical approach to life.

Year	Dates	Sign	Para.	Year	Dates	Sign	Para.
1870-1881	All Year	Taurus	110	1940-1955	All Year	Leo	113
1882	1/1-7/29	Taurus	110	1956	1/1-10/19	Leo	113
	7/30-9/27	Gemini	111		10/20-12/31	Virgo	114
	9/28-12/31	Taurus	110	1957	1/1-1/16	Virgo	114
1883	1/1-6/24	Taurus	110		1/17-8/18	Leo	113
	6/25-11/27	Gemini	111		8/19-12/31	Virgo	114
	11/28-12/31	Taurus	110	1958-1970	All Year	Virgo	114
1884	1/1-4/23	Taurus	110	1971	1/1-10/4	Virgo	114
	4/24-12/31	Gemini	111		10/5-12/31	Libra	115
1885-1911	All Year	Gemini	111	1972	1/1-4/17	Libra	115
1912	1/1-9/24	Gemini	111		4/18-7/30	Virgo	114
	9/25-10/2	Cancer	112		7/31-12/31	Libra	115
	10/3-12/31	Gemini	111	1973-1982	All Year	Libra	115
1913	1/1-7/12	Gemini	111	1983	1/1-11/20	Libra	115
	7/13-12/24	Cancer	112		11/21-12/31	Scorpio	116
	12/25-12/31	Gemini	111	1984	1/1-5/20	Scorpio	116
1914	1/1-5/23	Gemini	111		5/21-7/29	Libra	115
	5/24-12/31	Cancer	112		7/30-12/31	Scorpio	116
1915-1936	All Year	Cancer	112	1985-1994	All Year	Scorpio	116
1937	1/1-10/8	Cancer	112	1995	1/1	Scorpio	116
	10/9-11/15	Leo	113		1/2-4/22	Sagittarius	117
	11/16-12/31	Cancer	112		4/23-11/18	Scorpio	116
1938	1/1-8/5	Cancer	112		11/19-12/31	Sagittarius	117
	8/6-12/31	Leo	113	1996-1999	All Year	Sagittarius	117
1939	1/1-2/7	Leo	113				
	2/8-6/15	Cancer	112				
	6/16-12/31	Leo	113				

XI

Planetary Influence in Your Life

Check-Up of the Past: Forecast for Ten Years

With the birth record complete, we now follow the transits of the planets through your life.

As the transiting planets go through certain signs, they make aspects to your natal planets, whose sign positions you now have in the birth record. These "transits" influence you during the years they are in force. We wish to know—

(1) In what sign a transiting planet must be to set up an influence on you. To answer the question WHERE?

(2) When it is in this sign. To answer the question WHEN?

(3) What the influence is in that period. How does it act? To answer the question HOW?

The answers to these questions are expressed in the birth record blank, when filled in, as follows:

A Birth Position		B Where?	C When?	D How?
My SUN	conj. falls in			158
is in the sign	opp. falls in			159
....	sq. u. falls in			160
Par. no.	sq. l. falls in			161

A is the position at birth.

Column B, when filled in, tells in what sign the transiting planet must be to exert its influence as conjunction, opposition, upper square or lower square.

Column C, when filled in, tells WHEN this influence will be in force.

Column D shows the paragraph reading that covers the period of life indicated in Column C and answers the question HOW DOES THE PLANET WORK AT THIS TIME?

The first thing to do is to fill in Column B.

My SUN	conj. falls in	Sign Gemini
is in the sign	opp. falls in	Sagittarius
Gemini	sq. u. falls in	Pisces
Par. 3	sq. l. falls in	Virgo

This small piece of a sample birth record is properly filled in from the table on page 276, which you should look at carefully. For any planet (Sun or Moon) in Gemini, the conjunction will fall in Gemini, the opposition in Sagittarius, the upper square in Pisces and the lower square in Virgo.

The table gives the position of aspects for any sign of the Zodiac. Fill in your blank for all the planets, the Sun, and the Moon, from it, using in each case *the sign occupied by the planet* (in the left column), and copying out the signs from which a transiting planet makes the indicated aspects.

(On your birth-record sheet, certain spaces have no corresponding numbers. Don't fill these in: the influences are unimportant, and no readings are given for them.)

Transits in Your Vitasphere

We now have this much information:

A Birth Position	B Where?	C When?	D How?
My SUN	conj. falls in Gemini	1912–14, '42–4	158
is in the sign	opp. falls in Sagittarius	1926–29	159
Gemini 16 deg.	sq. u. falls in Pisces	1935–38	160
Par. No. 3	sq. l. falls in Virgo	1919–20, '48–'50	161

We know that a planet (Sun, Moon) in Gemini—in this case, the Sun—will be influenced when a transiting planet is in Gemini, Sagittarius, Pisces or Virgo. We now wish to know when a planet—the planet Saturn, in our example—will be there.

To find this, we use the tables on pages 246–248 —Saturn's place from 1870 through 1999. (The birth date we are using in June 8, 1902, and we will naturally not record any transit before this year.)

On page 247 we find that Saturn was in Gemini (transiting in conjunction in this example) in 1912–15, so we write "1912–15" in the indicated space.

On page 247 we find that Saturn was in Virgo (lower square) in 1919–21, so we record this.

On page 247 we find that Saturn was in Sagittarius (opposition) from 1926 to 1929; and in Pisces (upper square) from 1935–38. Record these.

We also find that Saturn was again in Gemini (conjunction) in 1942–44—thirty years after the first time—and we must record this, too. And we find that in 1948–51, Saturn was again in Virgo, the lower square, which we also record.

We know now that the life represented by this Vitasphere passed through the influence indicated by Paragraphs—

158 in 1912–15
161 in 1919–21
159 in 1926–29
160 in 1935–38
158 in 1942–44
161 in 1948–61

Reading these paragraphs in order will give us a chronological life history as indicated by Saturn's transits to the Sun in the life of the person born June 8, 1902.

A transiting Planet will be in

If you have a planet in the sign	CONJUNCTION (Conj. ☌) when it is In the sign	OPPOSITION (Opp. ☍) when it is In the sign	Upper Square (Sq. U ◰) when it is In the sign	Lower Square (Sq. L ◳) when it is In the sign
Aries	Aries	Libra	Capricorn	Cancer
Taurus	Taurus	Scorpio	Aquarius	Leo
Gemini	Gemini	Sagittarius	Pisces	Virgo
Cancer	Cancer	Capricorn	Aries	Libra
Leo	Leo	Aquarius	Taurus	Scorpio
Virgo	Virgo	Pisces	Gemini	Sagittarius
Libra	Libra	Aries	Cancer	Capricorn
Scorpio	Scorpio	Taurus	Leo	Aquarius
Sagittarius	Sagittarius	Gemini	Virgo	Pisces
Capricorn	Capricorn	Cancer	Leo	Aries
Aquarius	Aquarius	Leo	Virgo	Taurus
Pisces	Pisces	Virgo	Sagittarius	Gemini

Go ahead and fill in the WHEN column in your birth record for Neptune, Uranus and Saturn, using—

Tables for Finding Planets' Places

Neptune	Pages 268–269
Uranus	Pages 259–260
Saturn	Pages 246–248

Remember: Don't fill in years before you were born!

In Saturn's column, the same influence repeats every thirty years, and must be recorded and read each time.

The paragraph numbers (printed on the birth-record blank) tell the influence in force at the time you fill in beside them.

You now have the time of the influences of Neptune, Uranus and Saturn fixed in your life.

If you don't know the hour of your birth, skip to page 279, subheading *Interpretation of Influences.*

If you know your hour of birth (within an hour—the more accurately you know it, the better) you will want to trace the motion of Saturn through the sectors of your Vitasphere, to see how you have reacted to this influence which, as we have seen in Chapters VI, VII, VIII and IX, has been responsible for the flux of success and failure in the lives of both great and small.

To do this, you must first fill in the lower part of the birth record by placing in the sign column the proper sign or signs for Ascendant, Obscure Period, etc.

1. Find your birth-date period in the left hand column of the small table at the top of pages 282–283, and take out the number under your birth month. (Example: Born May 26— of any year—your number is 28:30, which is read 28 hours, 30 minutes.)

2. *If born after noon* ADD to this number your hour of birth. (Example: Born 7:30 P.M., May 26, 28:30 + 7:30 = 35:60. This is 35 hours and 60 minutes, or 36 hours even.)

If born in the morning, SUBTRACT from this number the number of hours you were born before noon. (Example: 6:30 A.M. is five and a half hours before noon. Thus: 28:30 — 5:30 = 23:00.) If the result of either of these operations comes out greater than 24 (first example above) subtract 24 from it, and call this your SIDEREAL TIME AT BIRTH. Thus, above, the first example came out 36, so 12 is the SIDEREAL TIME AT BIRTH. The second example came out 23, which is the SIDEREAL TIME AT BIRTH.

3. When you have your SIDEREAL TIME AT BIRTH, locate it in the left-hand column of the big table. (Example: "23" falls on the lowest line, which covers all sidereal time between 22 h. 33 m. and 23 h. 59 m. In this group, "23" falls; "12" falls farther up, in the line covering "12 to 13:24.")

Taking the lowest line, we discover that the 1st sector, Ascendant, is in Cancer; that the obscure period is in Leo and Virgo; that the cusp of the 4th sector is in Virgo; that the first-rise period is in Libra, Scorpio and Sagittarius; that the cusp of the 7th (emergence) is in Capricorn; that the public-rise sector is in Aquarius and Pisces; that the 10th sector (climax) is in Pisces; that the consolidation-of-achievement period is in Aries, Taurus and Gemini.

Using your own birth date and hour, find the signs that occupy these positions in your Vitasphere of birth and fill them in in the proper places in your birth record.

Now fill in the WHEN column, by finding when Saturn and Uranus occupied these signs, from the tables on pages 246–248, and 259–260. You will find Saturn occupying one sign for about two and a half years; and one sector (as the obscure sector, first rise sector) for about seven to eight years. Fill in these periods in the WHEN column; they will indicate important life phases and periodic long-range developments as interpreted in paragraphs 121 (Saturn) and 122 (Uranus).

Interpretation of Influences

When you have filled in the WHEN column for Neptune, Uranus and Saturn (and the lower part of your chart if you know your birth hour), arrange the following paragraphs in chronological order and read them first.

121, 122 (known birth hour) should be read first and the rest related to them.
123, 124, 125, 126
139, 140, 141, 142
158, 159, 160, 161
127, 128, 129
143, 144, 145
162, 163, 164
173, 174

Not all of these will be filled in, but whichever are influential in your life are of primary import. Read them in the order of their appearance in your life up to the present, and on into the future, using the tables, to see what's ahead.

The other influences already recorded can be fitted in as you wish. Eventually read the whole set in chronological order for a complete picture of your life and for a complete index as to when and how the planets have influenced you in the past and will continue to do so in the future.

Jupiter and Mars

In the same way that you placed the "when" of the influence of the three planets above, you can place the "when" of Jupiter and Mars as they have affected your life.

Tables of Places
Jupiter   Pages 226–235
Mars   Pages 211–217

You will discover that Jupiter returns to the same place every twelve years, and Mars every two years,

and that it is impractical to fill them all in the birth record.

Use Jupiter and Mars influences to pin down to a
special year (Jupiter) or a special month (Mars) some
longer influence of Saturn, Uranus or Neptune.

Jupiter's influence, as indicated by paragraphs
178, 182, and 187, will be found especially important in identifying certain important years.

Mars's influence, as indicated by paragraphs 193,
197, 203 and 204, will fix important months in your
life.

Not every occurrence of these will be of striking
importance. But within a larger Saturn cycle or Uranus period of great importance, these briefer influences
will be found to act as the second or minute hand of
the clock of destiny, as Saturn the Indicator, or Uranus,
or both, act as the hour hand.

Special Events

You remember a best year, a worst year, a happiest summer. What planetary action accounted for it?
In each planet's table, discover where the planet was in
the period you want to check. Relate these back to your
own planets, to see what aspects were in force. Collect
the five paragraphs—one each for Neptune, Uranus,
Saturn, Jupiter and Mars—that describe that period in
your life. The check-up will give you food for thought!

Checking Planets' Places to Approximate Degrees

You will note in some of the paragraphs the words
"Calculate exactly." In order to pin these influences
down to the time when they worked in your life, you
must estimate the approximate position of the planet
within the sign. You have this for Sun, Moon, Uranus
and Neptune. You can estimate the others as follows:

Saturn stays in each sign about two and a half
years. Thus in the table (page 246–248) he
was in Pisces during part of 1905, part of
1906, all of 1907 and part of 1908. In the
earliest year, he is in the beginning of the

sign—around 5 degrees; in the next year or years, in the middle of the sign (around 15 degrees); and at the end, in the last part of the sign (around 25 degrees). Approximate the degree of Saturn in your Vitasphere by applying this rule, which will enable you to get more accurately the time at which transists to your Saturn influence you.

Jupiter stays in each sign about one year. Judge him to be at about 8 degrees in his first four months, 16 degrees his second four months, 26 degrees his last four months in each sign.

Mars stays in each sign about five weeks and moves at the rate of 2 degrees in three days. He enters at 0 degrees and emerges at 29 degrees, and you can approximate his position in the sign by determining for how long he has been moving into the sign, and adding 2 degrees for every three days he has been there.

Venus moves at about 1 degree per day; add 1 degree (to 0 degrees) for every day she has been in the sign prior to your birthday.

Mercury's motion is variable. Divide 30 degrees by the number of days he is in the sign; this gives the daily motion. Multiply the daily motion by the number of days he is in the sign and add this to 0 degrees for his approximate position in the sign.

Birthdate	JAN	FEB	MAR	APR	MAY	JUNE
1-5	18:50	20:45	22:30	24:45	26:45	28:45
6-10	19:00	21	23	25	27	29
11-15	19:30	21:30	24:30	25:45	27:45	29:15
16-20	19:45	21:45	23:15	25:30	28	29:45
21-25	20	22	23:45	26:30	28:30	30
26-31	20:30	22:15	24	26	27:15	30:30

HOW TO PLACE THE SECTORS IN YOUR VITASPHERE

Sidereal Time at Birth	End rise-begin Recession	Obscure Period		End, Failure, New Start		Rise Period
hr.min.-hr.min.	1st	2nd	3rd	4th	5th	6th
0:0 to 0:59	24	16	7	6	12	19
	Cancer	Leo	Virgo	Libra	Scorpio	Sagittarius
1:0 to 1:50	5	29	24	18	0	5
	Leo	Virgo	Virgo	Lib.-Vir.	Sagittarius	Capricorn
1:51 to 3:29	18	14	11	12	16	18
	Leo	Virgo	Libra	Scorpio	Sagittarius	Capricorn
3:30 to 5:59	0-29			0-29		
	Virgo	Libra	Scorpio	Sagittarius	Capricorn	Aquarius
6 to 8:07	0-25			0-29		
	Libra	Scorpio	Sagittarius	Capricorn	Aquarius	Pisces
8:08 to 8:30	27	24	28	4	7	5
	Libra	Scorpio	Sag.-Capr.	Aquarius	Pisces	Aries
8:31 to 10:07	0-17			6-29		
	Scorpio	Sagittarius	Capricorn	Aquarius	Pisces	Aries
10:08 to 10:59	17-29			0-13		
	Scorpio	Sagittarius	Capr.-Aquar.	Pisces	Aries	Taurus
11 to 11:59	0-12			14-29		
	Sagittarius	Capricorn	Aquarius	Pisces	Aries	Taurus
12 to 13:24	12-29			0-22		
	Sagittarius	Capricorn	Aquar.-Pisc.	Aries	Taurus	Gemini
13:25 to 13:50	3	10	19	28	25	13
	Capricorn	Aquarius	Pisces	Aries	Taurus	Gemini
13:51 to 15:17	3-29			0-22		
	Capricorn	Pisces	Aries	Taurus	Gemini	Cancer
15:18 to 15:50	6	22		27		
	Aquarius	Pisc.-Aries	Taurus	Taurus	Gemini	Cancer
15:51 to 16:45	6-29			0-12		
	Aquar.(Pisc.)	Aries	Taurus	Gemini	Cancer	Cancer
16:46 to 17:59	0-29			12-29		
	Pisces	Aries-Taur.	Gemini	Gemini	Cancer	Leo
18:00 to 19:10	0-29			0-16		
	Aries	Taurus	Gemini	Cancer	Leo	Virgo
19:11 to 11:17	1-19			17-29		
	Taurus	Gemini	Cancer	Cancer	Leo	Virgo-Libra
20:08 to 20:35	20-29			6	5	4
	Taurus	Gemini	Cancer	Leo	Virgo	Libra
20:36 to 22:07	0-22			7-29		
	Gemini	Cancer	Leo	Leo	Virgo	Libra-Scorpio
22:08 to 22:32	23-29			5	12	18
	Gemini	Cancer	Leo	Virgo	Libra	Scorpio
22:33 to 23:59	0-17			8-29		
	Cancer	Leo	Virgo	Virgo	Libra-Scorpio	Sagittarius

Birthdate	JULY	AUG	SEPT	OCT	NOV	DEC
1-5	30:45	32:45	34:45	12:45	14:45	16:45
6-10	31	33	35	13	15	17
11-15	31:30	33:30	35:30	13:30	15:30	17:30
16-20	31:45	33:45	35:45	13:45	15:45	17:45
21-25	32	34	12	14	16	18
26-30	32:30	34:30	12:30	14:30	16:30	18:30

HOW TO PLACE THE SECTORS IN YOUR VITASPHERE

Sidereal Time at Birth	Emergence	Public Rise		Climax	Consolidation of Achievement	
hr.min.-hr.min.	7th	8th	9th	10th	11th	12th
0:0 to 0:59	24	16	7	6	12	19
	Capricorn	Aquarius	Pisces	Aries	Taurus	Gemini
1:0 to 1:50	5	29	24	18	0	5
	Aquarius	Aquarius	Pisces	Aries-Tayr.	Gemini	Cancer
3:30 to 5:59	18	14	11	12	16	18
	Aquarius	Pisces	Aries	Taurus 0-29	Gemini	Cancer
1:51 to 3:29	0-29			0-29		
	Pisces	Aries	Taurus	Gemini	Cancer	Leo
6 to 8:07	0-25			0-29		
	Aries	Taurus	Gemini	Cancer	Leo	Virgo
8:08 to 8:30	27	24	28	4	7	5
	Aries	Taurus	Gemini-Cancer	Leo	Virgo	Libra
8:31 to 10:07	0-17			6-29		
	Taurus	Gemini	Cancer	Leo	Virgo	Libra
10:08 to 10:59	17-29			6-13		
	Taurus	Gemini	Cancer-Leo	Virgo	Libra	Scorpio
11 to 11:59	0-12			14-29		
	Gemini	Cancer	Leo	Virgo	Libra	Scorpio
12 to 13:24	12-29			0-22		
	Gemini	Cancer	Leo-Virgo	Libra	Scorpio	Sagittarius
13:25 to 13:50	3	10	19	28	25	13
	Cancer	Leo	Virgo	Libra	Scorpio	Sagittarius
13:51 to 15:17	3-29			0 22		
	Cancer	Leo-Virgo	Libra	Scorpio	Sagittarius	Capricorn
15:18 to 15:50	6			27		
	Leo	Virgo-Libra	Scorpio	Scorpio	Sagittarius	Capricorn
15:51 to 16:45	6-29			0-12		
	Leo-Pisces	Libra	Scorpio	Sagittarius	Capricorn	Capricorn
16:46 to 17:59	0-29			12-29		
	Virgo	Libra-Scorpio	Sagittarius	Sagittarius	Capricorn	Aquarius
18:00 to 19:10				0-16		
	Libra	Scorpio	Sagittarius	Capricorn	Aquarius	Pisces
19:11 to 20:07	1-19			17-29	Aquarius	
	Scorpio	Sagittarius	Capricorn	Capricorn	5	Pisces-Aries
20:08 to 20:35	20-29			6	Pisces	
	Scorpio	Sagittarius	Capricorn	Aquarius		Taurus
20:36 to 22:07	0-22			7-29	Pisces	Gemini
	Sagittarius	Capricorn	Aquarius	Aquarius	12	18
22:08 to 22:32	23-29			5	Aries	Aries-Taurus
	Sagittarius	Capricorn	Aquarius	Pisces		
22:33 to 23:59	0-17			8-29	Aries-Taurus	4
	Capricorn	Aquarius	Pisces	Pisces		Aries

Readings of the Influence of Transits

121. SATURN'S TRANSIT THROUGH THE SECTORS OF YOUR VITASPHERE

This has been dealt with extensively in Chapters VI, VII and VIII, in which Saturn's action has been traced through the lives of great and small. In a general way, *the transit of the 4th sector* represents the end of one phase and the beginning of another; *the period of first rise* represents progress and development toward *contact with the 7th* (emergence), when you get public development of what has been built into your life since the transit of the 4th. *From 7th to 10th* (second rise), the most public part of the career develops toward the 10th influence (climax). *From 10th to 1st* you consolidate the position held at 10th and try to build for security rather than further expansion, as Saturn contacts the cusp of 1st (Ascendant) and goes into the *obscure period*. This is the most difficult period, especially if you have come up to the Ascendant with all flags flying, for then the obscure period is almost sure to be a setback of some kind, lasting till Saturn hits the 4th cusp to give you a new start. Your aim should be (if Saturn goes into the obscure period in the near future) to make this a period of voluntary withdrawal and semi-retirement and to seek security in it rather than new advances. Go back over Chapter VIII and see how other individuals have reacted to these transits of Saturn and how the pattern of your life coincides with theirs when you consider it in the light of Saturn's indicator-influence.

122. URANUS' TRANSIT THROUGH THE SECTORS OF YOUR VITASPHERE

Unlike Saturn, Uranus will perhaps not ever transit all the sectors, since it takes him eighty-four years to get around (to Saturn's thirty) and few live out the whole cycle. The sectors he occupies during your "prime of life" will tell a lot about whether your life is public or private—whether you seek to get recognition (if he occupies the rise sectors in important periods) or whether your work is worthy and obscure (if he occupies mainly the obscure and first-rise sectors during your best years). He will bring, like Saturn, new starts in 4th, emergence in 7th, climax in 10th, consolidation from 10th to 1st, and retirement at 1st and in the obscure sector. Note especially where *Gemini* falls in your chart. Here, in 1942, Saturn and Uranus came together, and the sector in which this occurred will give you a clue to the general scope of your life thereafter for a long time. Uranus remains in each of the twelve sectors for seven years, setting up long-range vibrations of the same general nature as Saturn's. Note the long-range pace and direction of your life from Uranus' position at any given time (whether up, down, public, private) and look then to Saturn, to see how circumstances (Saturn) will aid and abet the important pattern of Uranus.

123. NEPTUNE TRANSITS CONJUNCTION YOUR SUN

Calculate exactly; and note also the years during which Neptune is in the same *sign* with your Sun. This is a long-range influence, setting up attitudes and vibrations that seem permanently a part of your nature and may become so if you let them. It brings set conditions —emotional, financial, physical—and inclines to fixed ideas, especially about yourself. Your task is to see that they are the kind you can make good use of. The danger is that they will be merely obsessions and that they will rule you. Among the "obsessions" (major and minor) which you should guard against are: *self-pity, inferiority, physical inferiority* (*hypochondria*), *moodiness, sensationalism* (giving way to emotions, feelings, sensations). You are likely to feel, "This is the way I am, and I can't do anything about it," which obviously is not a strong attitude. However, it is possible under this transit to get fixed ideas that will benefit you by giving drive to your abilities and ambitions. Among these plus obsessions are *self-confidence* (the fixed idea of personal worth and strength); *profundity* (the fixed idea that you are a weighty and reckonable person with important thoughts, ideas, etc.); *creativeness* (the fixed idea that you are able to do something); *compassion* (the fixed idea that you like to help others, listen to others' troubles, be a pillar of society, etc.); *sensitiveness* (the fixed idea that you understand and appreciate nice things, etc.). Any or all these latter fixed ideas, if they become part of your nature, will serve you well through life and eliminate the other set of fixed ideas, which are self-destructive because self-indulgent. Study yourself in relation to (a) the period of Neptune's transit of your whole Sun sign (about fourteen years) and (b) the specific period of Neptune's contact with your Sun (about two years), in order to discover the basis which you are creating within yourself for the whole structure of your life to rest on. And realize that, if the basis isn't what you like, you have made it yourself and can, at will, remake it.

124. NEPTUNE TRANSITS OPPOSITION YOUR SUN

Calculate exactly, influences most intense for two years before and after exact aspect, but noticeable during Neptune's transit of whole sign. Confusion is the key note of this condition. Human relations are bewildering; those around you are hard to understand and may find it hard to understand you. You feel that "all the world is mad save thee and me, and even thee is a little mad" and as a result can be difficult to live with. Your thoughts and emotions are complicated. You are oversubtle, prone to escape into a type of reasoning which makes you feel superior to others, and somewhat proud that they can't understand you. Danger of introversion through refusal to get the other fellow's point of view. This can result in a breakdown of activity, loss of position through self-centeredness, difficulty in getting and keeping jobs, friends, etc. You tend to turn against those who demand too much of you and to expect too much from others. Psychic disturbances due to refusal to face the facts; perhaps physical ailments which can be genuine, but which are no doubt heavily contributed to by your desire to force sympathy, understanding, support from others. Need for rigid self-analysis. *In its best form* (seldom achieved in full), gives you a vast number of friends, a rare kind of popularity, and surrounds you with an aura of unusual charm and magnetism. To achieve this requires the maximum of self-effacement, a true humility of spirit and a willingness to give to others out of all proportion to what you receive. Heightens creative powers in art, music or literature; or gives you the equivalent of creative power in human relationships and an effortless dominion over your world, which you earn through understanding and compassion.

125. NEPTUNE TRANSITS UPPER SQUARE YOUR SUN

Peculiar conditions related to work, employment, worldly position, which tend to become fixed at a given level and stay there. A long period of good or bad luck is likely to come under this, and the mold is very difficult to break, whichever way it goes. Many people don't "feel" this vibration at all, consciously, and for this reason it tends to set up a fatalistic attitude toward events and to cause a "what can I do about it?" attitude. What you can do about it is to examine carefully the difficult factors involved in your life, relate them to your deepest self, and try to bring the things within yourself and things outside yourself into an ordered and reasonable pattern. Frequently this is a period of aimless drifting; you tend to fall into a frame of mind of taking what comes, good or bad, as something you can't control anyway. Thus it is possible to neglect opportunity through sheer inertia. On the other hand, this relaxation can act in a different manner, especially if things are going well. You may "relax in the saddle of fate" and find yourself carried high, wide and handsome. Study carefully the other transits affecting you during this long period. You can make the best of them work for you by applying your energies properly along the lines of force indicated by the other planets. Or you can also encourage the worst of them, if you let self-centeredness down you. The illusion of "being fated" here is only an illusion; your will is never more powerful, for good or bad, then it is now. But you must

use will power on the positive side and not let it turn
into *won't* power.

126. NEPTUNE TRANSITS LOWER SQUARE YOUR SUN

Very similar to 125, which you should read. The
center of operations under this is in your home and
your private life, and factors there should receive intelligent attention. You need a stable base of operations
for maximum accomplishment and should work slowly and determinedly toward this end. A strong tendency
toward letting inspirations undermine practicality must
be fought down; you must learn how to let the idealistic
forces work along tangible lines. All that is said under
125 applies here, plus the important addition that the
control over circumstance is even more completely
in your own hands and centers in the personal, domestic, home side of your existence. If this is kept peaceful,
calm and conventional, is will prove a constant well-
spring of self-confidence and illumination.

127. NEPTUNE TRANSITS CONJUNCTION YOUR MOON

Under this transit you discover things about yourself.

You may discover, for example, that you are a
more sensational, lustful, roistering kind of individual
than you want the world to know. This knowledge may
be a burden on your conscience: it gives you a picture
of yourself that you don't like. Or you may find that
you are less ambitious, more lazy than you want
folks to know. You try to conceal this. Or you may be
greedier for money, more snobbish, more socially ambitious, or any one of a thousand things. As Neptune
transits your Moon, your attitude toward yourself is
determined. *To make your inner secrets about yourself
things that make you feel superior rather than inferior*
is the way to get the most out of this transit. Establish
yourself, in your own mind, as *more* understanding,
more charitable, *more* religious, *more* idealistic, *more*
creative, *more* original than others. Don't *tell* them

about it; hold it as a fixed idea: *do* something about it, so that they too will know it from first-hand evidence. Drive away the attitudes that are destructive of self-confidence; and then "so live that your light will shine before men" and vindicate the high dream which under this transit becomes to you an inner reality.

128. NEPTUNE TRANSITS OPPOSITION YOUR MOON

While your outer nature, the side you show the world, at this time may remain simple enough, your inner nature is a complex mechanism full of contradictions, doubts and perhaps delusions. You get fixed ideas about yourself which may not bear any time relation to reality. You may think yourself better or worse than you really are; more, or less, capable. The acid test of what you feel and think is your willingness to try to do something about it. If you think yourself bad, ineffectual, you should want to improve and should set about doing so. If you think yourself supergood, you should be eager to let the world know it. If you are unwilling to submit your feeling to the test of reality—if it is something that you save to brood over—you can rest assured that it is delusional, and you should make every effort to root it out of your thinking. Health suffers through fixed ideas. Emotional matters that at another time would pass unnoticed become unduly magnified; there is some danger of hypochondria, melancholy, depression or elation of spirit. Material and practical matters suffer because your mind is not *concentrating* on them; human relations suffer because you find yourself more absorbing than others. The best plan under such conditions is to do as much, objectively, as possible; to turn your thoughts outward, away from yourself; and to reject the temptation to crawl away by yourself with your pet private thoughts, which more likely than not are simply an escape from reality.

129. NEPTUNE TRANSITS UPPER OR LOWER SQUARE YOUR MOON

Very similar to 128, which you should read and apply. This action is not so intense as 128, but is of sufficient import, along the same line, to warrant your careful attention and self-analysis, especially if other transits in force with it make external matters difficult.

130. NEPTUNE TRANSITS CONJUNCTION YOUR MERCURY

Acuteness of sense perceptions can lead either to (1) sensationalism of a very destructive sort or to (2) a great sense of beauty and symmetry which you express intellectually and artistically in your life and your creations. (1) Your mind may become absorbed with sensory impressions, obsessed by sight, sounds, smells and especially by imaginative pictures related to sense impressions. A fixed idea, dream, daydream, can undermine efficiency, intruding itself unbidden at the most inopportune times. Danger of giving way to your mental reactions and following a fruitless, or definitely downward, path of activity. Needs rigid self-discipline. Emotions dangerous, tending to become passional and to absorb the whole attention and personality. (2) Acuteness of perceptions, sensitiveness to the outer world, if translated intellectually and creatively, leads to deep intuitions, the development of extraordinary mental and artistic powers, success through intuition in practical matters and through genuine creative arts or letters. Material gain through acute understanding of details, immediate awareness of, and reaction to, stimuli. An inspired period to be used for all it's worth.

131. NEPTUNE TRANSITS UPPER OR LOWER SQUARE OR OPPOSITION YOUR MERCURY

Calculate exactly. Confusion of the senses, inaccuracy of thought, errors of judgment due to erroneous sense impressions and improper application of logic. Tendency to wish-thinking—the habit of believing what you want to believe despite evidence; refusal to look facts in the face; escape tendencies. Danger of bad habits. In controlled, mature individuals, creative force, necessitating plenty of self-discipline to keep the mind working smoothly along progressive channels: it tends to slip off into impractical and intangible day-dreams.

132. NEPTUNE TRANSITS CONJUNCTION YOUR VENUS

Calculate exactly. Your sensitivity to emotional stimulus is increased. According to whether your nature is idealistic or physical, humane or sensual, you will react with greater intensity. Human relations will achieve added significance, bringing either great magnetism and popularity (if you're an extrovert); or a tendency to be hurt, brood, feel sorry for yourself (if you're an introvert). Habits relating to love and sex are important and tend to become fixed; emotional attitudes assumed now endure a long time. Other habits which are not at first glance related to love or the emotions at all also tend to become established. Especially in the presence of real or imagined hurt feeling, you tend to escape, and this can take a variety of forms. Hypochondria, expensive and excessive forms of relaxation, self-indulgence of one kind or another: any of these can get a grip on you, and the emotional hook-up may require some analysis on your part. You are stubborn in a curious way, having a deep sense of the infallibility of your reactions (which can, as a matter of cold fact, be pretty erroneous). Distrust your hunches unless you are an exceptionally self-controlled individual. *In its best form* (seldom achieved in full, but worth trying for), this transit leads to deep magnetism, ideal love, high creative powers, a sense of beauty and order in the world which you make a part of your own life. A universality of outlook colors experience and makes you a truly superior, charming person, with an extraordinary beauty of spirit which never deserts you if you attain it here.

133. NEPTUNE TRANSITS UPPER OR LOWER SQUARE OR OPPOSITION YOUR VENUS

Calculate exactly. Bewilderment of the emotions, touchiness due to misunderstandings and sensitiveness: a sense of knowing the unknowable, which more often than not is interpreted wrongly. Danger of self-pity; also of falling in with evil companions owing to increased sensationalism. Self-indulgence. In best form, leads to self-annihilation through service, submergence of self to the will of others, true humility. Danger of being imposed on through "softness" but also a great opportunity to touch the heights of selflessness in human relations.

134. NEPTUNE TRANSITS CONJUNCTION YOUR MARS

Your energy works automatically under the dominance of intuition. A period of great success or great failure, due, in either case, to the nature of the dream you hold, which you express with great intensity. A union is effected between *your deepest inner nature* and the *energy-expression factor* through which you externalize. If your inner nature is dark, sensational and destructive, it manifests itself here in that form. If it is shining and idealistic, master of a high dream, you accomplish wonders. To translate your hidden powers—to express your suppressed desires—is the task of this period, and in the accomplishment of this task, rest assured that you will be helped by opportunity, luck and magnetism. Whatever your deep "dream" (or nightmare!) may be, here is where it comes to light. This is a very powerful transit, leading to success, power, riches, fame—or to the exact reverse—but always leading along the path which, in your inner heart of hearts, you have trained the feet of your spirit to follow.

135. NEPTUNE TRANSITS UPPER OR LOWER SQUARE OR OPPOSITION YOUR MARS

Calculate exactly. "Runnin' wild" aspect when the worst suppressed desires come out, tempting to "self-expression" in its least progressive form. Experiences of deception, betrayal—or the illusion of them, which is worse. Needs fighting continuously. Energy runs into destructive channels as the personality is made actively aware of what is the matter with it and is forced to re-evaluate its concept of itself in relation to everyday living. Generally causes an upheaval of far-reaching consequences. The result depends on the discipline of the total nature and on the other transits in force at the time.

136. NEPTUNE TRANSITS CONJUNCTION YOUR JUPITER

A period of unparalleled opportunity, when intangibles work on your side to bring new chances for material and spiritual expansion. Do not permit your life or your viewpoint to get into a rut at this time. Your chances are best in proportion to the height of your aims and the idealism of your aspirations. Release yourself from materialistic thoughts: practical rewards will be "added unto you" as you devote yourself wholesouledly to broad social, artistic or humanitarian aims. Be ready for unusual and spectacular developments; widen your horizon to take in everything possible. *In its worst manifestation,* leads to physical excess, extravagance and self-indulgence of a particularly heady and disagreeable sort. But this will come to only the material and sensational-minded. To the average run of humanity, halfway between heaven and earth in their outlook, this is a never-to-be-repeated chance to interpret the highest of idealism in the practical realm of everyday life, so as to achieve permanence of both philosophy and security.

137. NEPTUNE TRANSITS CONJUNCTION YOUR SATURN

Calculate exactly. The ambitions (defense-conquest motives) are brought in direct contact with the deepest internal aspirations, which here are either permanently achieved or permanently submerged. This will do something lasting to your zest for achievement. *In its best form,* it releases terrific intuitive and psychic power into achievement channels. The deep, permanent psychological factors take possession of the urge-to-become, driving you either forward into success or backward into yourself if you decide that the objective struggle is too much for you. To define your aims in terms of your dream and to fit your dreams to the methods of practical worldly affairs is the dual task of the ego in this extremely important period.

138. NEPTUNE TRANSITS CONJUNCTION YOUR URANUS

Relatively few people experience this transit. Those who do have a rare opportunity to interpret their personal inner dream in terms of their true creative genius. It requires a superior mentality and spirituality to live up to this at all; to many it will pass unnoticed. To the aware it represents a period of spiritual awakening and material opportunity to put high dreams and aspirations to the test. All the deepest urge to individual expression is stimulated as psychic forces join with mental abilities and creative expression reaches a height. It makes for sensitiveness, preferably not in the touchy form, but in acute awareness to opportunity and in a keen intuition for the proper timing of individual effort along original, unusual lines.

139. URANUS TRANSITS CONJUNCTION YOUR SUN

Swift, important developments make this a highly significant period. Your attitude toward life and toward yourself undergoes sudden change as your individualism asserts itself. Abruptly shaken out of yourself, you face the world with new courage and faith in your own powers. Your idealism becomes a working reality, your creativeness a vital force. (Look to the nearest transits to the Moon for the effect this will have on your own ego and opinion of yourself.) You are given opportunity to translate your individual aims into action and language that the world understands. Your magnetism increases as you become spokesman for your most characteristic self and win the support of others to your dearest purposes. This can bring you to a pitch of realization (in love, in business) seldom equaled; it can bring you also an inner peace, acquired through self-sufficiency and an exciting sense of accomplishment. It is an aspect of dreams come true, and the satisfaction of it will depend on the *sort of dream* you have nourished. If it has been high, its realization will be a joy. If it has been a nightmare of defeat and inadequacy—if, in the past, you have blocked your aspirations with fears and never really imagined success—then this period will bring the very nightmare you have feared and have made more a part of yourself than any dream of positive accomplishment. In one way or another your creative powers are here manifest for what they are worth. By the careful interpretation of opportunity, you can make this into one of the most glowing and significant of all the periods of your life.

140. URANUS TRANSITS OPPOSITION YOUR SUN

Externalization of self, breaking of ties, sometimes the formation of new ties to replace old ones. Marriage here likely to indicate that you are marrying on impulse or perhaps to get away from some other undesirable tie. Or it may indicate marriage to an eccentric, neurotic, original or creative individual. It isn't a *good* time for marriage, because you are touchy and start married life by getting into bed on the wrong foot. Creative impulses are strong; your magnetism helps you make rapid strides, if you are controlling the purely self-centered and self-indulgent urges which are powerful. Watch nerves; put less stress on individuality and more on cooperativeness. Think less of forcing your will on others, more of understanding their wishes. If you're a genius or a great personality, this is an outstanding period of your life; if you are an ordinary mortal, you have to look out for expressing the temperament of genius without getting its results or meriting its rewards.

141. URANUS TRANSITS UPPER SQUARE YOUR SUN

Calculate exactly. Generally indicates a sudden shift in your worldly status. A change of job has far-reaching results, perhaps setting you to work at some-

thing new and different. Under best conditions, the new
occupation will be more in line with your true aims
and desires than what you leave behind. A sudden
event, looking like a setback, turns out well—"every
knock is a boost." By making the most of fast-develop-
ing opportunity, and by taking this chance to stress
what you really want in the world, you are able to better yourself. You garner the fruits of creative work, of
ideas held and ideals adhered to in the past, and may
be able to shake off a lot of drudgery as a result. Temperament works for you instead of against you, especially if you are self-controlled. If you aren't, self-indulgence makes trouble here and denies the best results
of this transit.

142. URANUS TRANSITS LOWER SQUARE YOUR SUN

Sets up unsettled domestic conditions and rebellious reactions to conditions in your personal life. Un-
dermines security if temperament rules you. If you
rule it, creative work is favored; you enliven your environment and draw inspiration from it. Frequently
will accompany removal, basic change, far-reaching
alterations in the life plan. In harmony with those
around you, you will flare out, perhaps with far-reaching results. Requires careful analysis of yourself, of
others, of your entire life program, and demands a
flexible and selfless attitude toward all these if the best
results (i.e., change leading to speedier progress) are
to accrue.

143. URANUS TRANSITS CONJUNCTION YOUR MOON

The urge to self-expression is strong and leads to
unusual, not to say unconventional, actions. In a woman, health may be a factor. In either sex, nerves become high-strung, as the personality (inner nature)
tries to live up to a very high and individualistic
standard. Discontent with things as they are leads to
rebellious and irregular actions, for the satisfaction of
the ego and of self-indulgent urges is stronger than the

desire to find the good that exists in the status quo. Idealism mounts, and if you are lucky you can discover an ideal love under this condition. If you aren't, you will simply search for it or its equivalent and wind up coming back to the home pasture anyway. This is an eye-opener for the soul, and whatever events come under it will teach you some deep and important lessons about the nature of yourself and your ideals.

144. URANUS TRANSITS OPPOSITION YOUR MOON

The urge to "express yourself" takes hold; and since expressing yourself generally means doing something you aren't supposed to do, this is likely to be a period of strange behavior. You tend to kick over the traces and run wild with whatever ideas you have been suppressing up until now. You can see your complexes and your subconscious in the cold light of day if you are sufficiently in possession of yourself to look for them. Use self-control here to direct your energies into some useful channel: remember that "being yourself" is important only when the "self" you are being is worth the effort. To be, or become, your best self as a result of this transit is to harness your magnetism, your originality and your creative talents for all time. To run wild is to accumulate a fine crop of wild oats to be mowed down and carted away later.

145. URANUS TRANSITS UPPER OR LOWER SQUARE YOUR MOON

Similar to 143 and 144 in general effect. The lower square comes seven years before the opposition (144) and starts awakening the ego to its final rebellion, implanting individuality deep in the nature. The upper square comes seven years after the opposition (144) and re-establishes the lessons learned under it. Either square represents temperament, stimulus of the creative and individualistic urges, cautions against self-indulgence, and urges that you divert your energies, your passions, your ideas into constructive and creative channels, instead of spilling them out in "expressing yourself."

146. URANUS TRANSITS CONJUNCTION YOUR MERCURY

Mental brilliance, originality and creative vigor. Sudden rush of ideas to the head. Practical, workable inventions or ideas for business progress make for sudden gain. If there is any tendency to eccentricity, this brings it out. Sharp speech leads to strife; the quick answer may be clever, but not friendly. Translation of all energy to the mental place, and away from the personal or emotional, enables you to use your mind with knifelike precision and lightning speed, for very fine results. Beware of gambles and risks, which are tempting but likely to be unsound.

147. URANUS TRANSITS UPPER OR LOWER SQUARE OR OPPOSITION YOUR MERCURY

Period of mental stimulation, eccentricity, self-assurance and self-indulgence. Quarrels, strife, resentments at first, followed by illumination, originality, inventiveness. Financial setback due to bad judgment, risks, erratic moves or desires, impractical schemes. If you're sufficiently controlled, creative originality all the way up to genius. If you're not, temperament all the way down to nonsense.

148. URANUS TRANSITS CONJUNCTION YOUR VENUS

This is likely to bring an ideal human relation, perhaps quite outside the beaten track of your life. To be worth while, it must be kept on the high plane where it begins. Ideals are paramount, and you reap here the rewards of your romantic aspirations. It can also be a period of considerable material luck and of sudden, unexpected gains and/or losses. The purely sensational will not profit much by this. But high-minded people who have kept their spirits pure and their aspirations lofty will reach new heights of understanding and happiness as their deepest natures are stimulated and rewarded.

149. URANUS TRANSITS UPPER OR LOWER SQUARE OR OPPOSITION YOUR VENUS

The aspect of bohemianism, free love, the individual seeking for salvation through love or what passes for love. Danger of breaks, quarrels, sensationalism, heartache and headache. Rebellion against conventions, loss of prestige (and money) as a result. A devil-may-care attitude which, if you have the stomach for adventure and the "one moment of rapture," can be very exciting before you wake up in the cold gray dawn of the morning after. Coleridge wrote long ago:

> The sensual and the dark rebel in vain,
> Slaves by their own compulsion. In mad game
> They break their manacles, and wear the name
> Of freedom, graven on a heavier chain.

which is a good stanza to think of once in a while when you're going through this period when you take yourself much too seriously for any good use.

150. URANUS TRANSITS CONJUNCTION YOUR MARS

Calculate exactly. Swift-moving period when energies express themselves freely and perhaps along erratic and dangerous lines. Any tendency to eccentricity or temperament comes out; quarrelsomeness mounts; temptation to force issues must be guarded against. Recklessness extends to mental, emotional and physical planes; accidents may result, and considerable care should be used in traveling, and around electricity and machinery. Individual dynamics are high and seem to attract excitement, stress and danger like a lightning rod. Revolutionary tendencies increase: some way or other, you are likely to kick over the traces, or have them kicked over for you, and start along a radically new line which may prove only temporary. Direct energies into inventive and creative rather than destructive self-indulgent channels.

151. URANUS TRANSITS UPPER OR LOWER SQUARE OR OPPOSITION YOUR MARS

Erroneous methods in contacting the world lead to loss of self-confidence. You stand in your own light. Fear supplants assurance, and when you try to assert yourself, you tend to arrogance. You "know what you mean," but you "can't say it"—and when you try, you are misunderstood. Quarrels, setbacks, stoppage of progress and a sense of frustration result; you emerge shaken and in need of rest. Few go through this period without being put in their place. It is unfortunate to have this aspect coincide with one indicating opportunity, for this will probably cause you to muff it. Lie as low as possible and make self-effacement your credo. You win by retreating. A time for passive resistance to circumstances, not for pitched battle with them. Accidents—both literal and figurative. Trace out carefully the part you have played in your own failure in this period; to learn this is to understand yourself better.

152. URANUS TRANSITS CONJUNCTION YOUR JUPITER

Response to opportunity is electric, not always well-advised or moderate, but likely on the whole to bring progress. Profit and gain through original and expansive ideas, inventions, business. If there is any natural tendency to gamble, fight it here. Dare to be original, and have the good sense to be sound. Marks a swift-moving period of personal expansion, rapid adaptability to circumstances, a keen eye for the main chance, and you should not allow it to slide by without making some major forward stride. Beware that overoptimism doesn't lead to unsound ventures, and thus to loss.

153. URANUS TRANSITS UPPER OR LOWER SQUARE OR OPPOSITION YOUR JUPITER

A period of opportunity, with a good chance that it will be misused. Conflict of big ideas within yourself may block progress temporarily, but can result in eventual clarification. Some strife with others, and a tendency to stand in your own light through stubborn if quiet adherence to some wrong course of thought or action. If you are an adventurous soul, gambling of one kind or another is a menace: "live dangerously" seems sensible even when it isn't bringing the desired results. Creativeness runs high, but may be ill directed. Material matters may suffer because distractions seem more important than routine. Can bring heavy material loss either through neglect, overoptimism, speculative ventures ill-timed and overstayed. An aspect of anarchy, revolt against what is, intellectual rather than violent, but far-reaching in its consequences to the individual and to as much of society as he influences.

154. URANUS TRANSITS CONJUNCTION YOUR SATURN

Conflict between basic forces, either mental, emotional or physical, makes a period of tension. Psychologically, this period represents an inner development when your genius (creative force, individuality, desire for self-expression) quarrels somehow with the psychic defenses you have set up against the world. It may embody run-ins with authority (parents, bosses, traffic officers, policemen). It is likely to bring out any latent "delusions of persecution" that you may have had, or to cause feelings of resentment against individuals or circumstances that you think impede the free flow of your expression. If these sensations are not brought rudely into the light of consciousness, they become delusions below the level of consciousness and cause trouble later. Sometimes, if there is no apparent psychic or mental tension, physical ailments result, perhaps of a nervous order. Since your (psychic) defenses are under the fire of your ego, your problems at this time are more internal and personal than material and should be dealt with as such. Keep your feelings before your mind for analysis: don't force them down into the dark of the subconscious or try to forget them. Hard reason must be used. On the other hand, keep reactions from breaking out in quarrelsomeness, temperament or open rebellion, and so prevent your inner strife from making trouble.

155. URANUS TRANSITS OPPOSITION YOUR URANUS

This coincides with one section of 174 (Saturn transits opposition your Saturn), which you should read in this connection. Since the two fall at once, their action will be indistinguishable one from the other. However, while 174 does things to your material progress and demands retreat on the material plane, this aspect is bringing your originality to full fruition and promising satisfaction from the development of inner and personal talents which may or may not have a material aspect. In making the necessary readjustments suggested under 174 (for age forty-two only), heed the important note of individualism mounting within you; interpret it, not in business, but in private achievement (study, writing, creative work of some sort) and seek to plan your life from here on so as to leave time and energy for the many things you have "always wanted to do, but never quite got around to." This is bound to be a period of important change, and you must approach it in full command of yourself, ready and able to follow the dictates of your intelligence, rather than of your emotions, which will be unreliable.

156. URANUS TRANSITS SQUARE YOUR URANUS

(1) The lower square falls at about the age of twenty-one and marks a period of temperament, the emergence of the individuality at the beginning of maturity. From here to Saturn's conjunction with his own place (par. 173) you fit your originality, your indi-

vidualism to the pattern of the world. Try to make this period as smooth as possible. Avoid breaks and changes resulting from temperament. Calculate exactly, and watch carefully for the developments of the exact period. They fix the pattern of your thinking and creative nature for a long time to come, and will provide a clue for your personal development for many years. (2) The upper square falls at the age of about sixty-three and should indicate the abandonment of individualism, so far as external affairs are concerned. To go through this period without "drawing in your horns" is to lose the peace of your later years. Any desire which has not been achieved by now should be abandoned—released from concentrated effort. Your mind should be allowed to dwell on personal, intellectual matters; for as a result of releasing your drive for personal vindication in the outer world, you give your accomplishments of the first sixty years a chance to work and gain recognition for you after you have, in a sense, voluntarily given up the struggle. Protect health from nerves in this period and the years that follow.

157. URANUS TRANSITS CONJUNCTION YOUR NEPTUNE

A period of great self-confidence and individualism. To those with *Neptune in Aries,* deep individualism brings its results for good or bad; fixed ideas lead to permanent shifts in mental and material dealings. The ego is very powerful and needs to be held in check with realistic considerations; the free play of the intuitions, hunches and desires can permanently undermine security, especially if fixed ideas are allowed to become dominant and take over the mind and existence. To those with *Neptune in Taurus,* same danger of fixed ideas as expressed in reading for Aries but greater chance of true inner illumination. Tendency to overstress finances, material things; to become set in notions about money, property. Some danger of delusional ideas about what you need, the state of your security, health, etc. If these are overcome, chance for deep spiritual insight, mental and creative development. To those with *Neptune in Gemini, Cancer, Leo,* this period offers unparalleled opportunity for the development, expression and application of all your deepest and most intimate dreams and desires, *if* you have learned by the time this comes along to submerge the personal, sensation-seeking self and concentrate on the permanent creative values of life.

158. SATURN TRANSITS CONJUNCTION YOUR SUN

This position brings you the results of what you have accomplished in the past. Under it *you get what you have worked for and what you deserve.* This law is so absolute that you can apply it in reverse: that is, if under this transit you get success, you can be sure you deserve it and have earned it; and if you get failure, you can be sure that for some reason or other you have it coming to you. You may have to dig deep for the reasons *why* you deserve *what,* but you will find them if you look. In its best manifestation this period sets the crown of achievement on the deserving head of effort; and thus it may mark a giddy period of riding the crest of popularity, success and accomplishment. In its worst manifestation it marks the end of a road that was aimed wrong in the first place and therefore ends, as it deserves, in defeat. It is, in any case, a *period of climaxing* when the chickens of ambition come home to roost. If they are well-fed, well-cared-for chickens, they will come home to lay the golden eggs of success and acclaim. If they are scrawny chickens that have been permitted to run wild and scratch in the neighbor's vegetable garden, they will come home to provide only the scantiest kind of dinner, if any. If the results are *good,* you must learn not to let success go to your head. Past this point you can't push your luck too far or too fast: this, remember, is a climax, and you should ease off from it. If the results have been *negative* or *bad*—if you have been, in this period, blocked, or set back on your heels —then you must revise your plans and ambitions carefully and gracefully, working toward some accomplishment that is realistic and possible, and forgetting, in so far as possible, the failure of the past. To forget, in the deep and inner sense, either the *success* or the *failure* that this transit brings is to enable yourself to go forward smoothly and gracefully into other and different accomplishments.

159. SATURN TRANSITS OPPOSITION YOUR SUN

This position brings one of the most difficult periods of your life and also, if you will understand it, one of the most fruitful in personal development. It represents a period in which the world around you seems harsh, difficult and antagonistic. You are temperamental, not easy to get along with, although you probably think yourself abused. A material setback may closely precede or accompany this period. Your vitality is low, and your urge to impress *your* personality, *your* will, *your* ideas, *your* feelings on those around you leads to strife, quarrels and separations. If you do not actually have an open break of some kind, you withdraw into yourself and separate from others in spirit. There may be some ill health, real or imagined, probably more mental and psychic than actual and physical. You are passing through a period when the ego-expressive urge is hampered both by circumstances and by your own personality. You rebel against this; and it is your rebellion, rather than externals, that makes the period difficult. You come in contact, perhaps for the first time, with certain worldly realities, certain practical problems of human relations, certain gaps in your own personality—and you fight against recognizing what you see. The result is a deepening of your character and a broadening of your personality; but while the period is going on, you will perhaps be unable to see this. You will be locked into yourself, probably feeling very sorry for the same, very much misunderstood and pushed around. It will take you some time to see that all the pushing around is being done by yourself and that you can stop when you like —by accepting what is and by learning to conform to the circumstances of the world as it is and of people as you find them. You will learn, before you are through, that the only thing you can be sure of controlling always is yourself; and that things outside you are less important than the interpretation you put on them.

Naturally introspective people, under this influence will go quickly to the bottom of the problem, will plunge, perhaps swiftly, to a depth of despair and depression, will quickly find within themselves the root of their difficulty and eliminate it once and for all. They will emerge "twice-born," with a deep knowledge of themselves that will never desert them and a newly acquired self-assurance that will stabilize their lives forever.

Those less introspective will have a more difficult time, for they will be less ready to fix the blame where it belongs: within themselves. In these people the period may last beyond the time actually consumed by the transit itself and may indeed linger for many years. These are the people who are constantly at war with their world—if not in open strife with those around them, then resentfully, within themselves, so that "life loses its zest" and becomes, not a vigorous adventure, but a tedious struggle toward a badly defined goal.

Seek from this transit to acquire self-knowledge. Learn that when *you* become the kind of person whom *you* understand and can live with happily, the entire world becomes easy to live with and you become a useful and progressive citizen of it.

160. SATURN TRANSITS UPPER SQUARE YOUR SUN

This marks a period of results, when things come to you which you have deserved by work you have done in the past. (1) It may mark a high point of prestige and income if past work has been sound. (2) It may mark a collapse of hopes if hopes have been unrealistic and if work done toward their realization has been inconsistent. If (1), then you are to be congratulated, for you have somehow caught the rhythm of things and made it work for you, and must beware in this period only of pushing your luck too far. This is a point to consolidate your gains, withdraw from further pushing, and let things take their course, which is so satisfactory. This is a peak of accomplishment, and you should be willing to realize that past a peak there is no place to go but down. Therefore make your descent willingly; gear your aims from now on toward something different from what you have accomplished in the past—never toward more of the same thing. If your income has mounted to this point, make your next aim something besides money. If power has accumulated in your hands, relinquish it; strive for something else. Make your aims following this different, less public, more personal, less material than they have been, in order that the progress already achieved may continue through being translated into another sphere of activity and ambition. If (2), you can rest assured that you have been striving along some line for which you are unsuited, or that your effort has not been consistent. Look within yourself for the seeds of the difficulty; revise your aims and your methods; make them less material, more idealistic, perhaps less grasping. Depersonalize your wishes; decrease your demands on the world and others, and increase your demands on yourself, in order to merit maximum accomplishment in the years that follow this setback.

161. SATURN TRANSITS LOWER SQUARE YOUR SUN

This marks a period of new starts. It is usually accompanied by the breaking of old ties and the acceptance of new obligations or new maturity. It can mark departure from home and the taking of one's place in the world; graduation from school and the beginning of a career; marriage, as the break from one tie and the establishment of another; a business break and a new start. It always indicates a slow period; the reorganized life is getting its foundations established along new lines that require serious personal readjustments. And because all readjustments take a good deal out of you, it may be a period of tension, strife with those around you, and resentment that things do not develop as fast as you would like them to. It is a bad period only if you expect miracles of progress, for the miracles will not come off. You cannot, by being anxious, add one cubit to your stature in this period —or one foot per hour to your speed. You have to take things as they come and moderate the pace of your desires to conform with the pace of the world. It is an excellent period if you are willing to do this. Things begun slowly and carefully, with an eye to a long plan, work out well. Ambitions aimed at with patience will be achieved in from seven to fourteen years; any ambition that won't stand the test of this length of time should be ignored. To catch the rhythm and pace of events at this time is to build truly for success of the highest sort in the long run; while to rebel and run ahead of yourself is to find exhaustion and despair and to be forced to start over again later, under less permanently helpful influences.

162. SATURN TRANSITS CONJUNCTION YOUR MOON

In this period you are highly sensitive to circumstances, and plenty goes on to make you sensitive. Your concept of yourself is assailed by events and by other people; and you are forced to see yourself, not as you fondly imagine yourself to be, but as you appear; when stripped of your defenses, you stand amid the rush and turmoil of things. The result is likely to be at first elating, then depressing, as your private, inner notions of yourself are one by one torn away. It is not a kind or easy period. Much of what comes to you seems unjust and ill deserved. Perhaps you think yourself misunderstood. In a sense you *are* misunderstood; or, to put it another way, you find, perhaps suddenly, that you are unable to project yourself as you want to. A wide gulf exists between intention and performance—between what you believe you are doing and what you actually accomplish. The result is frustration and bafflement. Yet through it all you learn deeply that, to appear as you wish to, you must take into account more than your own ideas of yourself. You must take into account the ways of the world, which may not be your ways, but which you must interpret so that, through their channels, the self you like best may truly express itself for all to see. You struggle here for comprehension, for the seal of external approval on the personality you think most truly your own; and in the disappointment and frustration you learn how to accomplish this, if not in the present, at least more satisfyingly in the future. This period is frequently accompanied by, or followed by, some physical or nervous trouble, probably resulting from psychic factors, as the physical body reflects the dissatisfaction of the mind and spirit. Be suspicious of your ailments: there's a good chance that they are methods of getting sympathy which you fall back on when all other efforts fail to get it. This is not necessarily true, for genuine illness can come at this time and often does. Seek medical advice if you feel the need, but be ready to take the doctor's word for it if he tells you there's nothing the matter that you can't cure by yourself.

163. SATURN TRANSITS OPPOSITION YOUR MOON

Emotional stress, perhaps physical or material setback. Your personality has worked toward objectifying itself, and you are now finding that you have lost something in the process. Not to feel sorry for yourself is the chief prescription for this period. What you have lost is mainly sentimentality—an attitude toward yourself better forgotten. What you gain is re-evaluation of your personal qualities, an ability to stand outside yourself, and to marshal your mental and emotional energies so that you will continuously master them in the future. You gain a certain hardness, which need not destroy your human qualities, but which will enable you to use mental, emotional and creative powers more effectively in the future. The beneficial result of this period is self-mastery through objectivity and detachment. In love, a difficult period. In material matters, likely to mark a low point. The ego is too much occupied with itself to be materially effective in the world, but learns the need of effectiveness as a result of this experience.

164. SATURN TRANSITS UPPER OR LOWER SQUARE YOUR MOON

Similar to 163, which you should read and apply to this period. The effect here is less tense than in 163. The *lower square* occurs about seven years *before* 163 and paves the way for it; the more you learn here, the more stress you take from the opposition when it comes. The upper square occurs about seven years *after* 163 and is a postgraduate course in the lessons learned at 163. Under the period covered by 164 you are able to learn by the experience of others or to help others with what you have learned by your own experience. What happens to you here or to those around you should be taken to heart and applied to yourself. The aim should be self-discovery through emotional experience: taking your whims *less* seriously, that you may take your true virtues *more* seriously.

165. SATURN TRANSITS CONJUNCTION YOUR MERCURY

Mental activity deepened and stimulated. You take life and yourself very seriously. A philosophic attitude results, more or less profound according to your own nature. An excellent period for study and hard mental work, especially in science or business routine. Creative effort can be made to go well if you are thoroughly disciplined and depend less on inspiration than on perspiration. Finances somewhat restricted; chance to get things in line through self-discipline and budgets. Gain through steady routine effort and the promotion of efficiency.

166. SATURN TRANSITS UPPER OR LOWER SQUARE OR OPPOSITION YOUR MERCURY

Deepens mental processes, provides concentrative powers for deep study and thought. Usually accompanied by some mild or acute melancholy and depression, which work and self-discipline will minimize. Loss of self-esteem likely—the thought that you're no good becomes acute. Keeping your mind on things outside yourself helps. Study, reading, writing, excellent—though creativeness and originality fail you. *Don't worry* must be your motto: also *Face the facts*. Escapism leads into bad nervous tangles. Good aspect to have while in school or college, when opportunity for study is greatest and the "cold, cold world" is not yet a reality that you have to consider. Coming later when you're out in the "cold, cold world," it indicates a period when you can return to the student state to good advantage, putting your mind on objective fact rather than on emotional concerns. Finances under tension; need for budgets, restraint, efficiency.

167. SATURN TRANSITS CONJUNCTION YOUR VENUS

Has both a practical and an emotional significance. In both planes, realities make themselves felt. This transit brings about some important, and probably permanent, revision in your emotional life and in your attitude toward it. Sometimes this is sad and heartbreaking if your love is not capable of surviving the imprint of realities. But it can establish love on a firm basis forever if its foundations are solidly on earth. Guard against sensitiveness, for the fear of being hurt through your emotions can cause you to make your own heart break; in which case self-analysis will make you understand that if "that which you feared has come upon you" it is because your fear was translated into your actions and attracted what you least wanted. *In material matters* this stabilizes your fortunes and should be used for this purpose. Extravagance must go by the board, and budgets should dominate. Financial programs inaugurated here succeed well, if slowly. Seek consolidation, rather than expansion, of possessions, income and work.

168. SATURN TRANSITS OPPOSITION YOUR VENUS

Very similar to 169. The emotional stress is likely to be greater, the revision of ideas deeper and more completely experienced. Occurring before marriage, can mean a broken engagement or attachment, frequently contributed to by worldly affairs, always heartbreaking and sometimes thought of as "fated." Occurring after marriage, often leads to the brink of divorce, if not actually into it. Financial matters, under stress, contribute to emotional upheaval.

169. SATURN TRANSITS UPPER OR LOWER SQUARE YOUR VENUS

Experience finds its mark in your heart, and some home truths about emotional matters are impressed on you. Usually accompanied by separation or break, caused by circumstances or quarrels and followed by a maturing process that enables you to revise your emotions along more practicable lines. Disappointment in others or in yourself, or both, leads you toward a saner approach to human relations. In material matters, generally calls for skimping to make both ends meet, or can accompany loss of money or security.

170. SATURN TRANSITS CONJUNCTION YOUR MARS

Restraint of energies required. Illness, especially if you try to do too much. Calls for discipline of physical and temperamental forces; your dynamics externalize badly; you may feel that your personality fails to assert itself and should not try to force your will or your ways on others. Avoid strife and excess effort; you'll feel blocked and frustrated if you don't. "Ride loose in the saddle of fate," for this is no time to fight destiny by trying to alter the normal course of events. Will power won't work effectively. Need for complete rest and withdrawal follows any serious effort to break down the resistance of things as they are. Guard health, nerves, human relations.

171. SATURN TRANSITS UPPER OR LOWER SQUARE OR OPPOSITION YOUR MARS

Individualism and energy run into obstacles, events conspire to increase responsibility, which you will at first take as a personal affront and rebel against. This won't do you any good—unless you are utterly conscienceless and willing to throw obligations to the wind. A revision of attitudes is required: you have to bring your personal urges into line with realities, and can do it in a variety of ways. Any of these will be all right, so long as it doesn't create a rebellious spirit in you. Temperament must be forced into the pattern of life as it is—and the more you have to force it, the more you can be sure that it needs to be forced.

172. SATURN TRANSITS CONJUNCTION YOUR JUPITER

Your response to opportunity is practical, and as a result you are able to make a great deal out of somewhat restricted circumstances by keeping your feet on the ground. Calm and poise should be made your way of life. What comes to you is not spectacular, but it is stable and can be made into an important cornerstone of present security and future progress. Ventures begun here have steel foundations; while older matters continued under this influence become increasingly, and more significantly, a part of your life. Expect nothing spectacular from this, but recognize it as a time of serious purpose in which apparently small opportunities can be made to grow. Start savings accounts, make long-term investments, buy property to keep.

173. SATURN TRANSITS CONJUNCTION YOUR SATURN

This transit occurs twice during the normal lifetime (three times if you live to be ninety) and at each occurrence marks very deep and important changes. Its action is always along similar lines, and its results are permanent in their effects. It increases your aware-

ness of conditions that surround you; it sensitizes you
to yourself and to the world you live in; and it forces
on you fundamental realizations of your capacities,
your limitations and your opportunities. These realizations, arising from within yourself, generally lead to
a complete revision of ideas and plans, so that by the
time the aspect is passed you are a new person, living
a new life with a deeper purpose, and aiming at a
more thoroughly comprehended goal.

At its first occurrence (age 26–30), Saturn's contact with your own Saturn (his return to his own
place in the Vitasphere) causes your mind to turn inward and to think long and deeply about yourself and
what you have already accomplished. It is the most
important period of introspection and self-analysis,
which may rise directly from yourself or may be forced
on you by circumstances. Frequently a shift in human
relations is indicated here: marriage, divorce, change
of jobs, loss of job, separation from parents, move to a
new locality, or something in the world outside you
which alters the course, direction and pace of life. It
is within yourself, however, that the major changes are
going on. You are reviewing the past, taking stock of
your aims, your accomplishments, your desires; revis-
ing deeply your notions of many things. As a result, by
the time this period is past, you find yourself a new
person. You have abandoned many old ideas—and
perhaps have struggled hard against the abandonment.
Sentimentalities disappear—or at least there will be
fine opportunities for you to rout them out if you aren't
just too soft to do it. You will stand freed, when this
transit is past, of many erstwhile inner restrictions.
You will have swept your nature clean of dead wood
and cleared the decks for action that now proceeds less
impeded by internal complexes and personal difficulties. You will, in short, have matured—"put away
childish things"—and you will be ready to take your
place in the world as an adult.

*Saturn's transit of his own place is the most im-
portant point at which free will operates in the life,
untrammeled and as free of circumstances as it ever
will be. Accept the obligations of this privilege: as-*

sume here and now the mastery over life and over yourself that is yours for the taking. You will not stand so free again. The choices you make are yours: make them wisely, for here it is that your free will in a very real sense forges your fate for a long time to come, if not indeed for the rest of your life.

This is always a period of unforgettable stress which climaxes from a year to eighteen months before the actual contact of Saturn with his own place. The tension may come from temperament, from illness—physical or nervous—which in all probability has a psychological basis and is merely the body's way of aiding and abetting the resentment of the inner man against the unpalatable necessities of life that are being impressed.

It does not pay to lay the blame at the door of circumstances. These will seem harsh; but they are only the reflection in the outer world of something within yourself that needs revision. To get the most from this transit—to be really, after its passage, one of the "twice-born" to whom life is, forever after, a different and more exciting adventure—you must shoulder the "blame" for everything that happens to you. You must realize that it is not *what happens* to you that counts, but your *reaction to it and handling of it.* As a result of this transit you will either bog down under the burden of the world (having failed to learn sufficiently from experience) or you will throw out your chest in a new pride and self-assurance and go forward to bigger and better things. You may be sure that this is an important period and that from it stems a new life, in which you are able to live more freely and more efficiently directly in proportion to the whole-heartedness with which you accept the revision of ideas now presented to you.

At its second occurrence (age 54–62), the basic factors are all similar—stress, review of the past, correction of error. Because of the age at which it occurs, the temperament reaction is likely to be less violent. Especially if the lessons of the first contact have been thoroughly learned, this period may pass without much excitement, except that your ideas of material success and security may be revised on a more realistic basis. Some ill health, also, may accompany this second visitation, which can cause an alteration of the life plan along lines readily recognizable. If, however, the lessons of the first contact were ignored or pushed down into the subconscious, then the second contact comes as a distinct shock and second revelation, and there may be hell to pay—specifically, whatever hell has remained in you throughout the years. If you have refused to be "twice-born" when you had your first chance, you'll have to take it here. Temperament, ailments rising primarily from psychic disfunctioning and maladjustments, physical woes can mark this period, which, like the first one, calls for deep, careful and honest self-analysis *first,* and a shift in material and self. The second contact of Saturn with his own place frequently marks the end of the career and should be allowed to do so. Men and women who try to push forcefully onward at this time run into insurmountwordly affairs *second* after you have mastered yourable obstacles, often losing thereby the ultimate rewards of a useful life which blow up because the individual is unwilling to heed the stop signal and goes barging through this red light. Security should be sought here, and aggressive action forsworn.

174. SATURN TRANSITS OPPOSITION YOUR SATURN

Occurs twice before the age of 70.

(1) Between the ages of thirteen and fifteen, it marks the reorganization of the personality along lines of ego justification and self-vindication. At this time the adolescent determines how he can best defend himself against the world and/or make his mark on it. By calculating this exactly, a parent can determine the important year and months to watch in the development of the child; and by correlating carefully the other transits occurring at this time, can form a total picture of the child's ego development. Sympathetic and understanding guidance at this time will do much to help the bewildered young personality find itself in the world into which it is emerging. Two main develop-

ments are possible: (a) The personality may recede into itself, i.e., give up the struggle to impress itself on the world and seek peace within. (b) The personality may find the extroverted method of self-expression and form its permanent psychological plan for impressing itself on the world aggressively. (b) is, of course, one result to be desired. Analysis along these lines of what you did and decided in this period will give you an excellent clue to your ego development and may enable you to solve some mysteries about yourself that have hitherto baffled you. Review periods in your life covered by paragraphs 173, 158, 159, 160, 161, 162, 163 and 164 in light of what you can discover about yourself in this period.

(2) Occurring between the ages of forty to forty-four, this aspect marks, generally, a turning point in the career, following which the aim should be security rather than further aggressive progress. According to the choice made when you were from thirteen to fifteen years of age, this second transit of Saturn opposite its own place will find you in a satisfactory or unsatisfactory mental and material position. Regardless of this, however, you must recede hereafter from aggressive action in the world; must fix your aims at personal, rather than material, progress; and must set your goal at security. Business changes frequently are made at this time and work out well if risks are avoided and iron-clad contracts substituted for hit-and-miss methods. Falling in the well-known "prime of life," it sometimes urges further expansion of the ego (see par. 143, which coincides with it in time). But for the best results you should be willing to start taking a more moderate and secure course than you have hitherto followed. And to be sure that you do this, examine any change you consider now primarily in light of the effect that it will have on your *security* and your *personal contentment* in years to come.

175. SATURN TRANSITS SQUARE YOUR SATURN

(1) Lower square comes seven years after the conjunction (par. 173) and should mark a period of

achievement in line with the lessons learned under the period covered by par. 173. The choices made then, if wise, have led to accomplishment; a minor cycle has been completed; and you should be moving forward smoothly toward a point of maximum attainment to be reached in about another seven years. Some shift in method—but no change in basic direction—may be indicated here. Changes, both in the material world and in thinking, are important and should be related carefully to basic goals. Some temperament needs fighting down; the personal tends to intrude over the practical and must be put firmly back in its place. (2) Upper square comes seven years after the opposition (par. 174) and should find you moving toward a revision of aims and purposes. An important change developing here introduces seven years in which more and more the answer to your problems will be found within yourself, less and less in the outer world. If the move at par. 174 was genuinely in the direction of security, as recommended, this period enables you to clinch this still further. If the move at 174 was along less stable lines, you are given a chance here to shift again toward the secure course, and should do so, no matter what sacrifices are apparently entailed. You are moving during the next seven years toward the conjunction of Saturn with his own place (par. 173) when you will be forced to eliminate the dead wood from your life. If you start that process here, you will find it less acute than if you wait until it is forced on you.

176. SATURN TRANSITS CONJUNCTION YOUR URANUS

A very touchy vibration. Read the analyses of influences coinciding with this and immediately preceding and following. Under most favorable circumstances, brings practical application of originality and genius. Under least favorable, calls forth the worst of temperament, self-indulgence, kicking over the traces. In any case, a period of tension, in which the individualist in you fights against the world for expression along one line or another. To translate this from the purely personal, egotistic plane into one of mental or artistic creation is to insure the development of your deepest individualism smoothly and progressively for a long time. To submit to its weaker side is to store up lessons that will have to be disentangled later.

177. SATURN TRANSITS CONJUNCTION YOUR NEPTUNE

The world, the flesh and the devil descend on the inner man with all their temptations. As in par. 176, observe the surrounding influences from other planets. Deepening of intuition, the practical application of truths deeply known, the profound comprehension of still deeper truths as yet unsuspected are the best results of this influence, which will lend magnetism to your nature, charm to your personality, and so attract success magically. If operating on the non-spiritual, purely materialistic plane (and it often will!), the world will seem a cold place, unsympathetic to the profound things you know; you will feel balked, frustrated, pushed back into yourself by the restraints of reality pressing in on your deeply held dreams. Since Neptune occupies the same sign for fourteen years, everyone born in this period will feel Saturn's transit over Neptune at about the same time; so the spiritual-material feelings it evokes will be the common lot of all those of about your own age. However, since each is an individual, you are able to put your own interpretation on these general influences and will do so in accordance with your ego, the nature of your psychic base, and the direction you have chosen to take in your personal development.

178. JUPITER TRANSITS CONJUNCTION YOUR SUN

Wider fields expand before you. Popularity, luck, a sense of well-being and good fellowship raise self-confidence. Chances for material progress surround you, provided that you do not use the wide fields for aimless enjoyment of life, which is very tempting. Motives are important, and basic aims. If you aren't afraid of work, and if you know that work is the only way to progress, the expanded viewpoint of this period will be a real blessing, increasing your capacity for material gain. But if you are impractical, think the world owes you a living, love ease and luxury, incline to extravagance in spending and a cavalier attitude toward earning, this will just be a pleasant and relaxed period in which you will dream great dreams and accomplish nothing. Opportunity is all around you; you have only to grasp it—but that "only" is very important. Good may drop in your lap, but *you* must hold it. Keep your eyes open; the danger is that you will relax, feel good, and wake up to find that you have slept through the biggest chances of your life.

179. JUPITER TRANSITS OPPOSITION YOUR SUN

New contacts, new modes of expression, new work, new energies and ambitions tax mind and health. But you overflow with vitality and optimism and can carry quite a load if you take care of your health and refuse to indulge your weaknesses. Partners or associates provide excitement, and also luck. Money may come in without much effort on your part—and can go out the same way. Avoid a spending spree, which you can slip into almost before you realize it. Apparently innocent indulgences mount till they are far from innocent. Human relations are glamorous; be sure they are also sound and not built on the quicksands of temperament and sensationalism. Be ready to grasp opportunity and keep your head clear so that you won't waste the chances that crowd around you.

180. JUPITER TRANSITS UPPER SQUARE YOUR SUN

Publicity and public affairs favor you and tend to go to your head. You may get careless with money, extend credit too far, and thus lay the basis for later regrets. Restraint brings you gain through important people. You profit by pull, if you are willing to use it as a stepping stone to work and honest effort. Avoid overextension of ego and authority; be content to take a back seat. Use opportunities, not to promote fame or prestige, but to build foundations on which these may rest in the future. Protect health from excess; some danger of physical setback through self-indulgence or overwork. Raises of salary come automatically, if at all, and you gain little by demanding. Rest assured that you will get no more and no less than you deserve, and that the intrusion of the ego is more likely to bring disappointment than favors.

181. JUPITER TRANSITS LOWER SQUARE YOUR SUN

New starts work out well. Plans for long activity—business, marriage, etc.—get off favorably. Home is a good base of operations; and, if other indications for this time concur, it is a good time to buy a permanent home. Extravagance in private life needs controlling, but money is probably well spent because concentrated on basic and permanent possessions and should be steered into these channels. Entertain, build self-assurance by surrounding yourself with the things and the people that make you feel relaxed and comfortable; the ego thus stimulated shines out and helps you toward advancement. Derive your satisfaction from personal pleasures rather than from public acclaim.

182. JUPITER TRANSITS CONJUNCTION YOUR MOON

You feel new self-assurance and are able to solve, within yourself, important problems that have troubled you. Little may change in the external world around you, but your attitude toward it changes. You may not be able to control what happens to you, but you achieve new dominion over your viewpoint and in this way become master of situations and of yourself. Good health contributes to good spirits and a general sense of well-being. Self-reliance and self-sufficiency are your big assets here, through which you "find yourself" significant. Allow your eyes to turn inward; define aims and desires; discover what you want from the world, in the assurance that it is to be found less in *things* than in *your approach* to them. May accompany a real "conversion of spirit" based on swift insight into yourself, and may thus mark a point at

which you turn away from false values to true ones
and start a new life, richer and happier because based
on high evaluation of essentials.

183. JUPITER TRANSITS UPPER OR LOWER SQUARE OR OPPOSITION YOUR MOON

These are periods of physical and mental excess,
generally resulting in fatigue and a necessity to take
time off and rest. Self-indulgence wears you out and requires a holiday. Good times for vacations. If you can
afford to relax (and you really can't afford *not to*), you
can enjoy life here. Be careful of excesses with money
and emotions; protect your diet. The pleasures of food
and drink are very alluring and make plenty of trouble if indulged in.

184. JUPITER TRANSITS CONJUNCTION YOUR MERCURY

You become sure of your beliefs, but that's no assurance that what you believe is right. This period
finds you stubborn and self-willed; your interpretation
of what you see and hear is very clear to you, whether
right or wrong. Nobody can tell you anything. This
can be a good or a bad period, depending on what you
tell yourself and what you encourage yourself to believe. Once you have made up your mind, you'll
stick to your course through thick and thin. If your
determined course is reasonable, you go far by sticking to it. If it is unreasonable or self-indulgent, you
will stick to it and go just as far—in the wrong direction. This can be an excellent transit when it comes
after the judgment is mature; then you gain by standing pat and following a sound course; you win popularity and progress through integrity and stick-to-it-
iveness and also through the favor of important people
who value these things. Coming before the judgment is
sound, it is touch and go whether it leads you up or
down, as you follow your own bent. Whatever it does,
it results in experience, from which, sooner or later,
you learn some important and sobering lessons. Generally indicates financial gain, or at least security.

185. JUPITER TRANSITS CONJUNCTION YOUR VENUS

A slightly felt condition, contributing mildly to social and business success and promoting good will. Sometimes accompanies marriage or engagement, but isn't enough alone to bring these about. You are sure of your emotional reactions, which may or may not lead into progressive paths. Self-will in love, less from intensity of passion than from mental firmness of purpose. Expanded romantic and social aspirations which can range all the way from high idealism to self-indulgence and social climbing. You take yourself seriously and ought to make sure that you aren't stressing superficial things. Financial gain; some danger of extravagance; expenses heavy.

186. JUPITER TRANSITS CONJUNCTION YOUR MARS

Increases opportunity and self-confidence and contributes to business success, popularity, earning power; but holds the danger of arrogance and personal excesses. Strong tendency to waste energy and to ride roughshod over obstacles and opportunity alike. You show little inclination to compromise with reality, and waste time looking for the *ideal* job, mate, friend, etc., while excellent contacts are passed up because not exactly in line with what you think you require. Self-will makes trouble and incurs losses. The great-I-am in you is dominant. A period of swift movement and considerable ego. Chance for success through ability to do things on the fly—or through sufficient self-discipline to slow down when a real opportunity comes your way. Self-indulgence dissipates benefits and is the chief thing to watch out for.

187. JUPITER TRANSITS CONJUNCTION YOUR JUPITER

Marks a twelve-year cycle and a period in which important plans and ideas are revised. May indicate big new steps, like marriage, business partnership, independent or cooperative ventures that have long-term implications. Note especially the occurrences at the twenty-fourth and thirty-sixth years, which frequently indicate the conclusion of one sort of life and the beginning of another. Opportunity accumulates, and your response to it is at its most characteristic; thus the development here suits you down to the ground. Calls for self-control, since the existence of welcome opportunity is no guarantee that you will handle it right. The knock of opportunity is at the door—but you have to open the door and concentrate on entering the guest, for the benefits that come without effort go just as effortlessly if you don't hold onto them. Note the nearby Saturn transit and make it your guide to action in order to develop the opportunity of Jupiter.

188. JUPITER TRANSITS OPPOSITION YOUR JUPITER

This occurs six years before and after 187 and marks a turning point in your career, when things begun at 187 take a new twist and plans are revised accordingly. Can be a minor peak of accomplishment in which you finally receive the encouragement to continue the line you have been following. Changes in pace and direction should be adopted only after sober thought, for what happens here is of more far-reaching significance than you are likely to realize at the moment. This influence of itself seems innocent enough, but really marks a period that you will later look back on as having indicated the course of your life for a long time to come.

189. JUPITER TRANSITS UPPER OR LOWER SQUARE YOUR JUPITER

These periods fall halfway between Jupiter's conjunction with his own place (187) and his opposition to it (188) and indicate minor shifts in emphasis in your work and life plan. Opportunities may become more numerous; or, as is the case most of the time, you will simply be busy with what you are doing, and perhaps careless of money as a result. Financial status at these periods tends to remain fixed for about three years, and you should budget ahead according to the situation you find yourself in.

190. JUPITER TRANSITS CONJUNCTION YOUR SATURN

A sobering influence which enables you to dig into your trenches of security and raise your standard of living according to the terms of your life and job as you find them. Will bring opportunity only if you are able to see it in routine channels. Not a good time for change. Under normal conditions, this will pass more or less unnoticed, except that you slowly and unobtrusively accumulate power and authority in whatever work you are doing. Coming in a period of unemployment or depression, it breaks the deadlock, providing you an opportunity to make a new start which should not be rejected because it is slow or "beneath" you.

191. JUPITER TRANSITS CONJUNCTION YOUR URANUS

Expands the ego and brings opportunity for self-expression along your most original characteristic line. Some temperament accompanies this essentially creative period; but in it you can overcome whatever obstacles stand between you and the free expression of your dominant urge. Self-assurance is high and takes a noble form. Travel may be indicated. Or "travel" in the figurative sense may send your mind ranging to new bounds of thought and philosophy. Sudden gain possibly as a gift, legacy, unearned increment, also a good deal of extravagance, the result of self-assurance. Inventive genius flourishes, and you should try to put across the original ideas that you consider most truly your own.

192. JUPITER TRANSITS CONJUNCTION YOUR NEPTUNE

Deep self-assurance causes you to believe in your emotions, your intuitions, your hunches. They're probably right, but that is no reason for you to go to extremes about them. Best result of this is a creative period; externalize your ideals, find the way to express the things you take for granted, in terms that the world will admire. In your determination to "be yourself" remember that you have several selves; and choose to be the one that will best serve your long-range purposes. Exorcise the demons of your subconscious; and at the same time call on your subconscious to support your highest aims, your most idealistic dreams. This can be a period of self-pity, spiritual debauchery and self-indulgence—or it can be a high and shining crusade for the truest vision you have ever experienced.

193. MARS TRANSITS CONJUNCTION YOUR SUN

Relate the time of this occurrence to the time of the occurrence of 203 and 204 and read the section of this paragraph that applies to you.

(1) If 193 occurs within six months of 203, then the new starts of 203 are helped greatly; your energies work smoothly, starting with whichever comes first (203 or 193) and gaining momentum as the other is reached. Your danger at 193 is temperament, temper, a tendency to feel your own importance too strongly and to get into trouble because of it. Also, unless you have the endurance of an ox, you will tire yourself as Mars transits your Sun, and fatigue is likely to lead to strife, breaks and separations. Translate your energies to work, activity, detached application to a job or task; and don't get touchy or allow personal reactions to interfere with efficiency. This can be a romantic period; your magnetism is high, and you are likely to get what you want if you moderate your demands and use more persuasion and less insistence than you want to. Intuitions can go wrong, and you need the balance of strict mental discipline to bring out the best of your energies. However, it is an excellent time to go after what you want, and in the life check-up will be found, like 203, to mark periods of important decisions and moves.

(2) If 193 occurs within six months before 204 you have to exercise considerable judgment about the

starts you make, for things begun at 193 are likely to
break down when 204 is reached. If this is your case,
you have probably made a lot of false starts in your
life—with high enthusiasm begun things that looked
glowing, and been forced by circumstances or temperament or both to abandon them shortly thereafter. This
is a difficult combination and requires a good deal of
self-education and caution. Your energies don't work
smoothly, and you have to school yourself by "main
strength and ignorance" to learn the right time to start
things and what to start. You should distrust your intuitions at 193, embark on things carefully at this
time and hold yourself flexible till after 204 is past.
Best to start new ventures at 203 and stick to them,
ignoring the temptations to changes that are offered at
both 193 and 204.

(3) If 193 comes *at the same time* with 204, this
means that your Sun and Mars are in opposition at birth,
and you have to jockey your energies very carefully
at all times. Their ebb and flow are timed so as to
leave you stalemated a good deal of the time, uncer-
tain of how to do what, and what to do when, so that
your aggressive vitality is low. You should try to start
things at 203 with a maximum of cooperativeness and
understanding of the factors involved and stick to
them doggedly. No matter how conciliatory and willing
to please you may be, you will not find other people
easy to deal with, especially when you are trying to
impress yourself and your deepest ideas on them. You
have to learn the technique of passive resistance—to
get what you want by retreat rather than by attack—
never to lose sight of your goal—and always to adhere
to what you believe even when you are making technical compromises.

194. MARS TRANSITS OPPOSITION YOUR SUN

Likely to mark periods of quarrels, strife, disagree-
ments, difficulty in getting along with people. Therefore a good time to lie low and be silent; to observe
and do your duty without argument or fuss. Conserve
strength: there is a tendency to go to extremes. Ad-
venturesomeness and romance run riot and kick up a

lot of trouble. New contacts are exciting but not necessarily of any permanent worth. If other transits indicate a generally good period, increased energy here can bring good results; under negative, or bad, transits you should lie as low as possible and avoid getting into trouble. Accidents, illness.

195. MARS TRANSITS UPPER SQUARE YOUR SUN

Increases the importance of worldly position; brings shifts in prestige, credit, standing, publicity. Contacts with superiors, with need to handle them carefully. Can be a peak of accomplishment or the collapse of hopes: it is in any case a climax, for good or bad, of career matters. You should not force issues but should rather "relax in the saddle of fate" and take what comes. Making demands, insisting, becoming arrogant, stressing your "rights" will only make trouble. Luck is with you, if you let it flow in its own channels and at its own pace; it deserts you if you try to hurry it or to force it beyond its normal bounds.

196. MARS TRANSITS LOWER SQUARE YOUR SUN

Domestic matters are important. Frequently times a move from one house (or town or locality) to another; or some important decision in the private life. New starts work out if well considered and unmotivated by temperament. Social activity increased; lots of friends around you. A good time to begin new ventures for quick completion, which have a bearing on your longer-range plans. Good time for housewives to houseclean, redecorate, etc. The home is likely to be upset, and it's wise to make the upsetting literal and to some good purpose, instead of figurative and quarrelsome.

197. MARS TRANSITS CONJUNCTION YOUR MOON

Urge to express yourself induces you to express your most temperamental self. In emotional people this marks, as it recurs every two years, some tension and inner turmoil directly related to the inner self that they are trying to express in the world. It leads to strife, unconventionality, inner discord which transfers itself to the outer world. An excellent time for a vacation or for lying low and forcing no issues. Frequently, especially in women, marks ill health; in men, ill health in the women around them, if not in themselves. Occurring at the same time with 203, a period of tremendous opportunity and magnetism, with danger of overreaching and trying to do, or get, too much. At the same time with 204 or 205, the worst of the ego nature comes out; all the complexes and suppressed desires rush to the surface and need to be put back in their place. Best result of this transit is awakened and increased self-knowledge. One of these periods in the life check-up will frequently mark a major emotional experience that you have never forgotten. The inner nature is brought rudely into contact with realities, and false notions are stripped away, frequently with great personal upheaval.

198. MARS TRANSITS UPPER OR LOWER SQUARE OR OPPOSITION YOUR MOON

Fatigue leads to strife; relax. Strife, illness, loss of grip on things. Refuse to take yourself too seriously. Go to bed and rest instead of brooding; you'll avoid strife and trouble thereby. Force no issues. Energy may find its expression in some glamorous romance which may or may not be important, depending on other long-range transits in force at the same time with this.

199. MARS TRANSITS CONJUNCTION YOUR MERCURY

Sharp wits help if you use them right, hinder if you get smart-alecky with them. Snap judgments, quick speech, sharp retorts and anger make trouble. On the other hand, keen perceptions give you the edge on others; you express yourself readily and to good effect if you keep emotions and personalities out. Sensory perceptions, powers of observation are increased. Creative powers mount; rapidity of mental processes enables you to do more than usual. Mental fatigue can result; budget time for relaxation and sleep. Any tendency to insomnia is emphasized; also to temperament, temper and self-will. Good time to sell, bad time to buy. Business is active, judgment shrewd. Sign no papers, don't commit yourself permanently; the picture changes too rapidly. Avoid strife, especially over trifles. Distrust intuitions; put deep trust in hard work and pure reason.

200. MARS TRANSITS SQUARE OR OPPOSITION YOUR MERCURY

Quick speech, thought and actions make strife and trouble. Be silent, cagey, noncommittal. The quick retort makes trouble. Wrong decisions often come in one of these periods, which recur about every six months and need careful watching. Sometimes the most casual remark results in a lasting grudge. Mountains (of trouble) grow out of molehills (of speech). Best to be silent.

201. MARS TRANSITS CONJUNCTION YOUR VENUS

Heightened emotions make romance, which is favored if you keep it within the bounds of reason and convention. Impulsive acts, with or without a future, are frequently found in these recurrent periods. Glamour surrounds your approach to life; you are susceptible to the opposite sex and they to you. Frequently fixes the time of marriage within the period of a longer transit that favors it. If the era of romance is past, this indicates an active and on the whole satisfactory social period; business progress; extravagance with money; a sudden urge to go places and do things —and perhaps a chafing at the marital bit which should not be taken too seriously. Energies work through emotions and passions, which in turn work overtime and should be gently disciplined though not entirely submerged. Often, for obvious reasons, indicates the conception of children, especially if it occurs near 203 and/or 193.

202. MARS TRANSITS SQUARE OR OPPOSITION YOUR VENUS

Social and romantic glamour leads to excesses, sometimes to strife, quarrels, separations. Minor loves and friendships break up, but important relations are merely strained; and indeed this frequently adds glamour to a deep love, intensifying its beauty. A break here, unless contributed to by some more important transit, is a sure index that the feeling wasn't very deep or important anyway. Avoid excess spending and stay away from temptation if you're interested in sticking to the conventions.

203. MARS TRANSITS CONJUNCTION YOUR MARS

A period when new starts should be made, new plans put into execution, new ideas promoted. Energies work along their most characteristic line and can be utilized to excellent advantage. Control natural impulses if you have any that get you into trouble, because now is the time when you are "being yourself" and it is your business to be your best self, not your worst. You are starting a two-year cycle and should establish the line you want to continue on for the next twenty-four months. Seek new contacts, new avenues of self-expression, new channels into which to direct talents and energies. Beware lest anger and temper—letting go because you're feeling your oats—interfere with your best development. In your life check-up you will find that these recurrent two-year periods marked with great consistency periods of important decisions, developments, activity and changes.

204. MARS TRANSITS OPPOSITION YOUR MARS

Ideas are numerous but likely to prove more bother than they are worth; thus not a good time for starting new ventures. Aim to quell restlessness, and stick to the line established about a year before, giving it perhaps some new twist, but not deviating from it in any radical particular. Temperament runs high; emotions are likely to be troublesome; self-will is an obsta-

cle. A good time to go away on a vacation. But it is a
bad time to try to get away from any established thing
permanently. In the life check-up, these periods, recurring about every two years, mark tension, stress, new
obligations connected with established things—sometimes a break or change which, in all probability, did
not work out as well as it was expected to and forced
a new start again a year or less later.

205. MARS TRANSITS UPPER OR LOWER SQUARE YOUR MARS

Period of hard work and abundant energies,
which causes no trouble unless major disruptive influences are in force. Some slight tendency to talk too
much, boast, be arrogant, but the swiftness of the pace
generally carries you through without major trouble.
If about six months *after* 203, you should not let distractions interfere with plans started then. If six months
before 203, look ahead, work toward and plan for
some major development to take place coincident with
203. Frequently marks the busy start of something
that matures at 203 and should be viewed with that in
mind. Protect health and nerves from excess; be objective and detached; and let reason rule the emotions.

206. MARS TRANSITS CONJUNCTION YOUR JUPITER

Opportunities abound, and your energies are up
to them. Optimism runs high, and you can be made
to color, and perhaps prophesy, the life for a long
time. Work is abundant and gratifying; you are popular and lucky. Be careful not to waste opportunities
through trying to do too much at once; don't spend
too much money, either, but make a point of saving.
Ought to be a period of good income, which tends to
make you openhanded and generous, perhaps to a
fault. Keep your eyes and ears open; some of the best
forward pushes of your life will come in these periods
when circumstances combine to give you the rewards
of work done in the past and to open up new doors for
the future.

207. MARS TRANSITS UPPER OR LOWER SQUARE OR OPPOSITION YOUR JUPITER

This will generally not amount to much, but periods of loss through risks or gambles or through over-enthusiasm or bad business judgment are frequently marked by it. The outlook is too enthusiastic to let sober reason dominate; but this generally brings nothing but minor extravagance. This transit might once mark some major material setback due to a combination of bad judgment and bad luck.

208. MARS TRANSITS CONJUNCTION YOUR SATURN

Good time to slow down—and if you don't do so voluntarily, you may be forced to do so by a cold or some other type of illness. Do your duties quietly and solidify the existing position in which you find yourself. Superiors need kid-glove handling; you may feel hampered and restrained in your work; your energies may be forced into a yoke that chafes. Be philosophic about taking what comes; passivity and acceptance rather than activity and aggression serve you best. You build good, substantial foundations, despite limitations; or else you kick over the traces and probably regret it later. Colds, low vitality, fatigue, nerves, system run down. Take a rest cure if you can. If you stay well, those around you may be ill, increasing your responsibilities.

209. MARS TRANSITS CONJUNCTION YOUR URANUS

Temperament, haste, anxiety, nerves require watching. These can lead to illness from fatigue and nervous exhaustion. Accidents (literal and figurative!) from excess speed, lack of care over details. Watch temperament. Accidents in the realm of human relations result from overemphasizing the ego and minimizing the other fellow's viewpoint. Inventiveness abounds; originality is in the saddle; but you can't get your best and truest ideas over to any good advantage, and simply make trouble if you "try too hard." Store them up for a later time when you express them better and when other people listen to you more readily. Look out for machinery, travel, electricity; avoid danger, be careful getting on and off trains and crossing streets.

210. MARS TRANSITS SQUARE OR OPPOSITION YOUR URANUS

Not usually important, except as a marker of temperament and minor strife. But at one of these periods some major break due to temperament—some sudden shift in the pace and direction of the life—is likely to occur. The individuality is suddenly awakened to broader horizons, greater worlds to conquer, and determined to shake off the shackles of restraint. In undisciplined persons this will mark periodic temperament, rages, rebellion and strife; also accidents and setbacks due to lack of nervous coordination. In normally disciplined individuals all but one or two of these periods should be comparatively inconspicuous. But the one or two may be memorable—and probably nothing to be proud of.

211. MARS TRANSITS CONJUNCTION YOUR NEPTUNE

Superintuition gives you uncanny insight into motives and methods of other people, but not always into your own. Practice self-analysis. Swift feeling of creative power of which you can make good use. Beware sensationalism, sentimentality, self-indulgence; fight subconscious urges, suppressed desires, and make your inner ego work for you along constructive lines. Excellent period for creative work, for impersonal use of magnetism for business ends and aims and for social popularity. You have glamour that attracts others: be sure it attracts the right kind of people and for the right reasons. The Old Adam rears his head and may require discipline.

XII

The Grand Strategy of Living

Part I: The Nature and Meaning of the Planets

The basic principle of astrology is that man can choose to develop his good and constructive qualities, rather than to indulge his bad and destructive ones;[1] and that he can choose his times for action and his times for inaction, rather than remain passive before the tides of circumstances.

Throughout this book, we have drawn our examples largely from the action of the planet Saturn, and have seen the extent to which both great and small respond to the timing of his influence as he goes through the houses and sectors of the Vitasphere. The reason we have used Saturn is not because we do not react similarly to other planets, but because Saturn, due to the pace and rhythm of his movement, is synchronized with the normal processes of worldly and visible growth. This is elaborated further on in this chapter, and elsewhere in this book.

However, it seems desirable, in preparing this new edition, to explain the relationship between the influence of Saturn, and that of the other planets, since in

---

[1] The analysis of the horoscope with respect to the qualities and capacities with which one is born is given *in extenso* in the author's other books *Heaven Knows What* and *Your Greatest Strength*. *Astrology for the Millions* is devoted mainly to the horoscope in motion, and the proper timing of initiative and passivity.

your study of your Vitasphere, you will encounter
Martian, Neptunian, Uranian, and Jupiterean influences, as well as those of Saturn, and you will want to
know how to interpret them so as to have a more
complete view of your development as shown in the
movement of your Vitasphere.

The house and sectors of the Vitasphere always
have the same meaning, of themselves. What these
sectors and their activations mean is stated briefly in
Par. 121, p. 284, and is further discussed in connection with biographical data, in Chapters VII and VIII.

In viewing the meaning of the transits of the
various planets through your Vitasphere, you must
bear in mind that the meaning of the sectors and houses
does not change. Thus, the 4th House is always *the
base of operations, the domestic environment, the parent of the opposite sex, change, the end of one phase
and the beginning of another*. Any planet going
through this House will activate these factors in your
life.

The question is, how will Uranus activate them
differently from Saturn, how will Mars differ from both
of these, what about Jupiter, and Neptune, and so
forth?

It used to be stated, or implied, in the older astrological texts, that each of the planets had a different
quality, character, or *tone,* because of something inherent in its nature. Thus Saturn might have been said
to have the *quality of iron,* hardness, weight; the *character of sobriety* or *gloom;* the *tone* of G-sharp Minor,
or of the rumble of distant thunder. Mars might have
been said to have the quality of hot steel, the character
of courage or recklessness, and the tone of an awakening bugle. Whether these attributes emanated from the
physio-chemical structure of the planets, which caused
them to emit rays of a certain quality, or from other
causes, was not clarified.

The premise seems to have been that each planet
had a quality inherent in itself, differentiating it and its
influence from that of other planets because of this
self-contained quality.

Over a long period of study, in contact with

numerous charts viewed experimentally and clinically, I have come to the conclusion that, so far as their astrological influence is concerned, the planets do not differ in inherent quality. We know from the astronomers, physicists, spectrum-analysts, and chemists that the physical structure of the planets is different, quantitatively, with respect to the percentages in which the elements are found in them and their atmospheres; and qualitatively, with respect to their stages of hotness, coolness, age, youth, formedness or non-formedness. It is possible that these differences do bear on their astrological influence.

However, consistent observation of planetary effects in a very large number of charts leads me to the conclusion that, whether or not planets differ in their inherent character, *their chief observable difference as they act in the chart is traceable directly to the difference in the rate of motion with which they pass through the vitasphere.*

I began to arrive at this conclusion through observing the alteration in effect between *Mars direct* and *Mars retrograde.* The nature, quality, character, and tone of Mars does not change because he is retrograde in motion; indeed, nothing at all happens to Mars, who goes right on moving ahead in his orbit, so far as the viewpoint of Mars is concerned. "Retrogression" is merely a statement of the earth-view—a kind of illusion we have on earth that, because of the relative rates of speed of the Earth and Mars, it appears, when they are in a certain relationship in their orbit, that Mars stands still, moves backward, stands still again, and then moves forward again—just as a freight train, moving along a track, appears to you to stand still if your car is going at exactly the same speed alongside of it. Since nothing happens to the character, etc. of Mars when he is retrograde and something does seem to alter with respect to his influence, this difference must be due to what *does* change. And what *does* change, when Mars is retrograde, is the length of time during which he remains in one portion of the zodiac, as viewed from the earth, and therefore in the individual chart.

Normally,—that is, when direct in motion and traveling at his mean rate of speed—Mars will remain in one House or portion of the chart for about six weeks. When he is retrograde, he remains there for something like eight months. This is all the difference between your neighbor who drops in for supper and goes home at 10 o'clock, and the same neighbor if she dropped in and stayed for seven and half months. The quality of the neighbor would not change . . . but there would be a difference.

The same principle is applicable to the other planets, and the differences in their influence. Once we disabuse our minds of the idea that planets differ in quality, and base our view of the chart on their differences in rates of motion, we come to grips with the basic realities of the Vitasphere, with the meaning of planetary influences in the forming of character and the timing of opportunity.

In proceeding with this view, we must divide the planets into two groups.

The first group consists of the two planets inside the earth's orbit—Mercury and Venus—and the Moon. These are the planets of the inner, subjective, and self-contained life. They operate wholly on the internal plane. They have little, if anything, to do with the impingement of experience from the outside, but indicate the view we take of experience, how it impresses us, etc. They do not have to do with *action* (except at an infantile level) but with reaction.[2]

Because Mercury and Venus remain always close to the Sun, their rhythms are merely slight variants on the solar rhythm, as viewed from the earth. The Moon's rhythm also has a relationship to the solar rhythm, since the Moon goes all the way around the zodiac in approximately the same time that the Sun, Mercury and Venus are going through one sign.

If we consider you and the house you live in as

---

[2] It is for this reason that all magazine daily guides, based on the movement or aspects of the Moon, concentrate—or should if they don't—not on "what is going to happen to you," but on how you will react to whatever does happen—that is, on what will happen *in* you.

the Sun, then Mercury, Venus and the Moon are those who inhabit the house with you, to whom you get accustomed and accept as an integral part of yourself and your life. You absorb them as you absorb early family and environmental influences. You (the Sun) live in your house with Mercury, Venus and the Moon, and they are your eyes, ears, emotions and senses with which you interpret what goes on outside the House and affects you, with and through them.

It is with the things that go on outside the House —that is to say, with Mars, Jupiter, Saturn, Uranus, Neptune and Pluto—that we are primarily concerned (a) in interpreting and understanding past experience and (b) in projecting the Vitasphere into the future.

The rates of motion of these planets are as follows:

MARS takes about two years to go around the zodiac. *This is one Mars cycle;* i.e., the space of time, about two years, that it takes Mars to go from one point in the zodiac (or chart) around the circle and back to the same point again. During this time, Mars remains in each sign about six weeks, and because of retrograde motion, will hover around one portion of the zodiac, usually a portion consisting of about 20 degrees, for about seven or eight months.

JUPITER takes about 12 years to complete the circle of the zodiac, and spends about a year in any given 30-degree area, or sign.

SATURN takes about 29 years to complete the circle of the zodiac, and spends about two and a half years in any sign, house, or 30-degree area.

URANUS takes about 84 years to complete the circle of the zodiac, and remains in any sign or house about seven years.

NEPTUNE takes nearly twice as long as Uranus, requires 165 years to complete the circle, and stays in one sign or house for about fourteen years.

PLUTO's orbit is eccentric; he requires about 248 years to complete the circle of the zodiac, and he remains for unequal periods of time in the different signs of the zodiac. He was in Taurus from 1852 till 1884 (32 years); in Gemini from 1882 till 1914 (31 years); in Cancer from 1912 till 1939 (27 years); he is in Leo from 1937 till 1957 (20 years) and will be in Virgo from 1956 till 1971 (15 years).

Now let us look at you and your Sun in your house, with respect to these different rates of motion.

In infancy, youth, and adolescence you get used to yourself and your House, and to the parents, relatives and neighbors who share it with you (Moon, Mercury, and Venus).

For a good many years, these form your world, and things outside it seem alien. For some time, you are not called on to pay much attention to them.

Gradually, however, you are forced to notice other things.

First you notice things outside yourself, but still closely related to you. Let's say that you note the comings and goings of your father (also the Sun) who leaves the house and comes back with a regular rhythm; and through this accent on *dailiness* and its recurrent cycles you become accustomed to the Sun, which is both you and your house, and the first contacts of you and your house with other outside things. You've been accustomed to your mother, brother, sister, inside the house, and also the neighbors as they come and go (Moon, Mercury, Venus). Now you get accustomed to a rhythm that links you and your House with the world outside—the daily rhythm of the *Sun,* and also its yearly, seasonal, vacation, holiday, and so-forth rhythms. All this is still intimately connected with *you,* and, though the outside world has begun to take form in the *solar rhythm,* it is still a very intimate and personal kind of "outside form."

The next step, however, is different. You are sitting in your house one evening when you become aware of a strange footfall outside, proceeding at a slower pace than any you have ever heard. This is someone new, a stranger. This is Mars (taking six weeks to go through one sign, as opposed to the Sun's accustomed 4). Not very different from the rhythm of the Sun, but enough different to let you feel that there are more things in the world than are contained within yourself. You get used to the rhythm of Mars; it is not (usually) very different from that of the Sun, and it happens every two years, so that you have a chance to accustom yourself to it before you are very old.

On top of the new rhythm of Mars, there is also the rhythm of Jupiter. He stays in the same place for a year—just as long as it takes the Sun to go around the zodiac once—and because of this equation—Jupiter in a sign = approximately one solar year—you accustom yourself to the rhythm of Jupiter, as a kind of super solar year. But the next planetary cycle does not have any such obvious relationship to anything you know about. You are perhaps not even aware of it at all till you're 14 or thereabouts, and then one evening, you hear a very slow and methodical footstep outside the window, and it stays there a long time (two and a half years) with an insistent beat that you cannot deny, and that you have some trouble synchronizing with the other rhythms. Synchronizing with Saturn is getting in step with *maturity* and it happens slowly, between the ages of 14 and 29. But then, at the age of 29 (end of the first Saturn-cycle), you begin to go through the second Saturn cycle, and, as you grow, you are more and more adjusted to it, through the use of experience, memory, and common sense (see the section on *Cycology* on page 355).

The rhythm of Saturn is the rhythm of the world. When one is attuned to the rhythm of Saturn, he is attuned to the forces that make the world move, that make for maturity, self-respect, and the ability to grow and get along in the world as it is.

Beyond the rhythms of Saturn, we come to the slow-moving planets. By applying our principle that *difference in the time-factor is the difference in influence,* you can understand why the influence of Uranus and Neptune seems so different from anything else. You have got used to the fellow who hangs around for two and a half years (Saturn); you know how to deal with his requirements, and have accustomed yourself to his habits. Then along comes this interloper Uranus, and he prowls up and down in the same place for seven years—and Neptune for fourteen!—and they do tend to get on your nerves.

These do not seem to belong to you and your House (Sun, Moon, Mercury, Venus) though by their constant presence in the vicinity, they seem to think they live there.

Neither do they seem to have any connection with the outside rhythms of daily life (Sun), its related extensions (Mars, Jupiter), nor the way of the world (Saturn).

These are new rhythms, making different demands, and the *newness* and the difference all lie in the *length* of time they remain in the same place, in your chart, and focus attention in that place.

The difference in rate of motion between the planets also bears directly on the novelty of their influence. We have seen how we early get accustomed to the solar-lunar-Mercury-Venus influence; they are repeated every year, and the Moon every month, till the *planetary memory* gets to take them for granted.

Moreover, by the time we are 29, we have experienced 14½ Mars cycles, and two and a half Jupiter cycles—that is, we have experienced a repetition of Mars in any given place, and in all places, 14 times, and we have come to know that road, so to speak, as we know the road to town, or the path to school. We can encounter surprises but if we have learned by experience, we do not stumble over the old stump that has been there since we were four and a half.

Similarly, Saturn sets up a rhythm to which we become accustomed, though it takes longer, because we are 29 before we start going over the same road again. (See *Cycology,* page 355.)

In the cases of Uranus and Neptune (and more so even in the case of Pluto) the timing of their movement presents an entirely unique experiential problem.

Uranus is generally said to be "swift, sudden and unpredictable" in his influences, and indeed it often seems to be so. Neptune is said to be "delusional" and to "encourage fantasies" and this too seems to be true.

Yet if we look beneath the surface of things, we shall discover that Uranus is less unpredictable, and Neptune less delusional than we have thought. To begin with, no planet is either unpredictable or delusioned: individuals are, or may be, under influences that are strongly felt and little understood—that is, under influences which *remain in force for so long that we act on them through panic, fear or impatience and inertia, without trying to relate them to the known forces in ourselves and our lives.*

In the case of Mars, Jupiter, and Saturn we experience similar influences repeatedly, in the course of a lifetime. We get to know, (perhaps unconsciously, in the planetary memory; perhaps consciously, if we study the Vitasphere and its cycles) *what to expect, and how to behave* when it becomes.

In the case of Uranus, however, we must live to be 84 years old to experience one full cycle, and so, to all practical purpose, we may say that most of us never experience a repetition of Uranus' influence in any given place in our charts. The same is even more strongly marked in the case of Neptune; you would have to be 165 years old to experience one full cycle, and so, unless you are the High Lama of Tibet, you have never before experienced the transit of Neptune in the place where he is now, or will be in the future.

Thus, every Uranian experience, and every Neptunian experience, seems new when it first comes to us. We seem to have no precedent to bring to bear on it, and it appears as if we must proceed by dead-reckoning. So, if what happens to us, or in us (it is much the same thing) seems strange, new, eccentric, and different, it is because we feel that "we have not passed this way before" and all the scenery, and every curve of the road seems new to us—unless we know how to relate the novelty to something *within ourselves.*

Now, a very important fact presents itself. During the first 29 years of life, you experience one full cycle of Saturn, and during these years, everything you encounter in the world is new, different, and strange. We call these growing pains, and under Saturn, we grow with relative speed, if we accept the demands of maturity. By the time you are 29, you have covered the whole road of the zodiac, with respect to Saturn, and are starting over again, and by the experience stored in the unconscious, or *planetary memory,* as well as by the more aware forms of memory and experience. We generally do not notice Uranus or Neptune too much, till we have completed one cycle of Saturn at about the age of 29. Until then, we are too busy with the rapid developments of youth (Mars, Jupiter) and of growing maturity (Saturn) to be much affected by Uranus and Neptune, except unconsciously.

With the start of the second Saturn cycle (age approximately 29) and especially at the first and second quarters of it (age approximately 35 and 42), we begin to get, unconsciously, a sense that we're going over the same ground. We begin to feel that life is just more of the same. In short, we get bored; and it is then that we start noticing the influences of Uranus and Neptune . . . and, more often than not, get into mischief.

For after the age of 29, Neptune and Uranus are activating areas that have been previously stirred by Saturn, and their problems solved . . . or not solved. But whether it was solved before or not, you may know, after the age of 29, that you have been over this area of your chart before, with Saturn, and if you will go back, in retrospect, to the time when Saturn (and also Jupiter and Mars) have been over the area inhabited by Uranus and Neptune now and in the future, you will have a clue to the *type of experience* to expect. The *duration* of the experience will be, under Uranus and Neptune, longer than it has been before; but the *nature* of the experience will be—except for the time difference—substantially the same. It is in reconciling the *similarity of the experience* with the *lengthening out of the time process* that you achieve an understanding of yourself, and of how to handle the influences of Uranus and Neptune as they come through the sectors and over the planets in your Vitasphere.

Let us clarify this with two examples.

John Q., well over 29, had experienced a cycle of Saturn, plus quite a few years in addition. He has Cancer on the cusp of his 4th House. He knows that in 1944–46, when Saturn went through this area, he experienced a certain kind of change; and he also knows, by looking through the Mars cycle, that he took a new lease on life more or less regularly as Mars went through Cancer. But then he was confused by Uranus' transit there, and worried because it lasted for so long: till 1955.

He is accustomed to the Martian rhythms, and, by keeping his head, was able to make a purposeful change when Saturn was there. But then he seemed to be in a state of "permanent revolution." He must bear in mind that the long action of Uranus is the same in nature as was that of Mars and Saturn, but it lasts longer. If he has kept this in mind, he will have made under Uranus in 4th a change similar in nature to that he made under Saturn there; if he lost his head and got impatient to bring this about too quickly, he could upset the apple cart.

This is a simple example, simply stated, but it presents the essence of the method of understanding planetary influence in your life.

Similarly, Susy Q. is a married woman, sometimes known to be (tell it not in Gath!) flirtatious. Harmlessly so, and she and her husband understand that when Mars goes over the little lady's Venus, her eyes are likely to wander for a few days. So what? Mars passes on, and Susy's crush on so-and-so passes with it. But along comes Neptune, which hangs around her Venus for a long, long time, and with it comes a crush that does not wear off. It is no different in nature from the harmless others, but it *seems* important, because the heat is on for so long. If Susy and her husband do not understand this, they can make some serious mistakes. The time-factor is everything, and it is this that we must understand, properly to evaluate the meaning of planetary influences . . . and of ourselves, as we react to them.

Seek awareness, with respect to Uranus and Neptune, by looking back to the time when Saturn activated the areas they inhabit at any time. The problem you solved, or failed to solve, when Saturn was there are the same problems you face now. Thus, as this is written (June 1950) Uranus is in Cancer, and Neptune in mid-Libra, and they will be on those signs till 1955. Recall your life when Saturn was in early Cancer (June 1944–June 1945) and when he was last in mid-Libra (1923) and you will get the psychological (and perhaps also circumstantial) connection between the long drawn-out influences of the present, and your development in those periods in the past which are thus shown to be related to them.

The trouble with Uranus and Neptune is that, though the duration of their influence is long and therefore new because of its length, it is "old stuff" with respect to the place they transit, after the 29th year of your life. You feel that you've been there before, and so you have been, superficially, at least. You are required to be there now in *depth* as well as in position. The time element requires that. What you went over "once lightly" before under Saturn . . . and even more lightly under Mars and Jupiter, more than once . . . you now have to go over "for keeps." The process is emotionally and psychologically tiring, and requires constant awareness. The tendency, under Uranus and Neptune, is to think that "enough is enough" and to break and run from the problem before it is solved. That is why Uranus is called "unpredictable" and Neptune "delusioned" . . . But the unpredictability is the result of your own impatience, and the delusions are self-imposed, if you will not become aware of the present problems in terms of *memory* and *experience,* and solve the old problem at the new level of maturity and growth with Uranus and Neptune. The tendency to impulse is merely the tendency to say "Hey! We've been over this before, and I'm not going to wait any longer; I must be on my way; I learned all about this way back when, and I'm off to a new idea!"

Every Uranian and Neptunian experience seems *new* in point of the time element, and *old* with respect to the area of your chart that is stirred. The conflict between the novelty of the time demand, and the familiarity of the type of experience, makes impatience, if you are not on guard, and traps you into what I have named "long-lasting impulses."

What is a "long-lasting impulse"? How do we

recognize it, and what can be done about it? Let us give a homely example.

One day we get angry with our neighbor, and have an almost irresistible impulse to heave a rock over the fence through his window, get him out in the yard, and beat him up. Custom, however, (which is Saturn) has taught us that this is not the way civilized people behave; we know that we should not act in heat or anger or momentary rage; so, when we get this savage rage, something automatically says no, and we refrain. We'll at least think it over. We bide our time. Three months later, we get the same urge all over again. By this time, we have been unconsciously whipping ourselves into a frenzy of righteous wrath over our neighbor. His kids trample the flowers. His wife doesn't cover the garbage pail. His dog is a nuisance, we don't like his politics, and he doesn't say hello on the bus. So, when we get the fighting urge three months later, we are convinced of the righteousness of our cause, and we are also convinced that we have been patient, and have waited. So, with the comforting thought that we have turned it over in our mind, we act. The result is precisely the same as if we had heaved the rock the first time we felt like it.

This is Uranian (and also Neptunian) in the extreme. For these planets stay around the same place for so long that there is plenty of time to "think it over" without running the risk of losing in the slightest degree the emotional ferment of the original impulse. The wily unconscious—which wants always to satisfy its savage urges and justify itself in the eyes of its conscience—is fully, though unbeknownst to your conscious mind, aware of this . . . and if you will examine your impulses and reactions closely, carefully, and with infinite honesty, in connection with the houses that Neptune and Uranus inhabit at any time, you will find that this is so. You must bring to bear on these planets and their influences all the *awareness* you can muster, *plus* all the experience derived from the planetary memory as you can stir it through following the principles set forth under *Cycology, plus* all that you can remember of what you have learned in the past, to use wisely and well the deepening process of Uranus and Neptune, as they operate on you over the years.

Part II: The Timing of Action and Passivity

The horoscope of birth shows the positions of the planets at the time of birth, and diagrams the conditions existing in the solar system at the moment of the birth of any individual. It shows the relationship of the Sun, the Moon, and the planets to the horizon and meridians (House positions) and the relationships between the Sun, the Moon and the planets themselves (the aspects).[3] This chart of birth tells, when the laws of astrology are applied to it, the environmental conditions under which the individual was born, and the effect that these have on the physical, mental, and emotional equipment with which he came into the world.

The tone of most astrological writings until very recent years—and even of many recent writings—carries the implication that this horoscope of birth—the birth chart—is something which remains forever rigid and fixed, a frozen moment in time which states forever the destiny of that which, at that moment, came to being.

Yet this is not so. The horoscope of birth is indeed the accurate picture of the solar system *at that moment,* and it is the replica of that moment in the life of the individual then born. It describes the environment into which he is born, the attitudes of his parents and those who share the environment, the worldly and material status, and the channels through which these impinge on the new life, to form a new individuality, mentally, emotionally, and morally.

But unless this individuality lives all his life in the same house—nay, in the same crib—with the same people, with the same attitudes, in the same

---

[3]The meaning of aspects as such is described in detail in *Heaven Knows What,* by Grant Lewi, published by Llewellyn Publications and Bantam Books.

material status, and without any other influences whatsoever, this natal chart begins to be impressed with other planetary influences, from the moment of birth throughout the entire life. The natal chart continues to have importance, not as a thing frozen in time, but as a starting point, a base of operations, from which moves are made, and on which is built up, in successive and never-ending layers, the structure of the whole and complete life.

For the birth-chart contains another piece of evidence, besides the evidence of the conditions that surrounded the moment of birth.

It contains, in the space-relationships between planets, and between planets and house-cusps, *a precise statement of the timing of the planetary influences in the future,* and it is in this foreknowledge that one may plan his grand strategy of living so that, by doing the right thing at the right time (and by avoiding the wrong thing at the tempting time) one may succeed and be happy.

Chart 1 illustrates this principle in its simplest form. This chart shows the Sun directly across the circle from Uranus, that is, opposed to Uranus, or in opposition to Uranus.

To have the Sun in opposition to Uranus in one's chart means something, considering this condition as an *aspect.* (See footnote 3 above.) It tells us something about the nature of the personality, character, nerve structure, etc., according to the nature of the Sun, the nature of Uranus, and the nature of the opposition (180 degrees apart) in which they fall.

But, in connection with the grand strategy of living, and with looking ahead to the future, it means something more, of equal, and perhaps of greater, importance. We know the speed of the movement of Uranus; it takes him about 84 years to complete the entire circle of the zodiac, 360 degrees. We know, therefore, that he will complete the transit of 180 degrees which separated him from the natal Sun in this chart in half this time, and that the individual born with the Sun in opposition to Uranus will experience the transit of Uranus over the place of his Sun at the age of 42. Since this is a very dynamic transit to experience at any age, we know something of particular importance about this individual who will experience it at the critical age of 42, and we know that he should gear his thinking, and the development of his neuro-emotional-mental nature to get the most from this transit when it occurs.

If we look at Chart 2, we see a picture of the Sun in square to Uranus, and in all charts the planets move in the direction of the arrow. In this chart, Uranus is 90 degrees from the Sun, and approaching it. He will transit the position of the Sun, in this chart, when the native is 21; therefore this native, instead of waiting till he is 42 to experience this influence, will get it

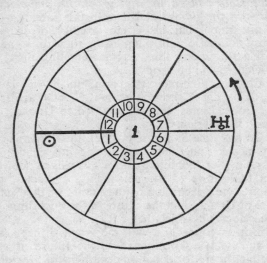

relatively early in his life. Similarly, the native of Chart 3, whose Uranus is also in square to the Sun, but from the other side, will experience the transit of Uranus over his Sun at the age of 63, which is quite late in life, and has for this reason a meaning of its own.

Seen in this light, the chart of birth becomes a great deal more than the picture of a moment of frozen time. It becomes, properly interpreted, the potential time-table of an entire life, the timing of which is precisely indicated in the space-relationship of the planets as shown in the birth-chart, plus the time-factor as we know it to exist because the planets move at certain rates of speed and because there are tables (ephemerides) which show *where* they will be *when*.

Let us define the transit of Uranus over the Sun, briefly and succinctly, as that time when your attitude toward life and toward yourself undergoes sudden change as individualism asserts itself . . . You are given an opportunity to translate your individual aims into action and language that the world understands, which can bring you to a pitch of realization seldom equalled.

Now, to know when this is going to happen is of the utmost importance. If one knows it will happen when he is 21 he will (if he wishes to live by plan, for

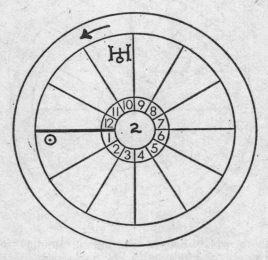

success, and not merely by guess and by golly, for con-fusion) do all in his power to develop, by the time he is 21, something in himself and his background worthy to take advantage of this opportunity.

If one knows it will happen when he is 42 (the dangerous age, anyway!) he will have different things to think about.

And if he knows that it won't happen till he is 63, he will watch very carefully his individualistic urges around that age, since at that age, this exciting transit probably holds as many pitfalls as opportunities, and needs a very special kind of handling.

This principle, of seeing in the chart the grand strategy of living, has numerous applications. In the preceding examples of influences between the Sun and Uranus, we have dealt with the timing of an influence that is, in the main, subjective: that is, it has to do with the Sun, which is the ego; with Uranus, another phase of the ego; and with their coming together. Thus the things to expect under these influences are things which take place mainly within the individual (as opposed

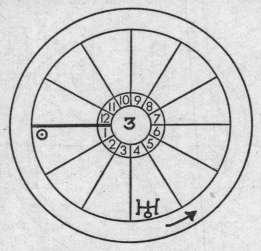

to those which happen in the surrounding world, events, opportunities, etc.). In one sense, the entire chart and everything that happens in it, pictures only the subject side of life; and nevertheless, some influences in the chart are much more closely related to outside influences than others, and in connection with events, opportunities, and the like, the application of the grand strategy of living to practical purposes is of the utmost importance.

The objective, outside-world phase of planetary influence is seen and felt most strongly in connection with the movements of Saturn, and in connection with the movement of all the planets through the houses and house sectors. Let us apply the principles of the grand strategy to the development of opportunity and events in the practical world.

Chart 4 shows a birth-position of Saturn on the cusp of the 1st House (Ascendant), moving (as always) in the direction of the arrow. We know that it takes Saturn about 28 years to complete the circle of the zodiac.

This means that it will take him a quarter of this time to complete his transit of a quarter of the circle,

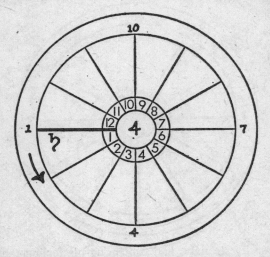

or 7 years. Thus, when this native is about 7, Saturn will reach the cusp of his 4th House (4) and will experience some change of location or alteration in domestic environment that will give him the child-time equivalent of a new start for better or for worse; when he is 14, Saturn will come into the 7th House (7) and the adolescent will be in the presence of an expanding world and expanding opportunity; when he is 21, Saturn will come to the cusp of his 10th House (10) and an early, perhaps premature, "success" will be achieved, leading, perhaps, to the need for a total revision of the life when Saturn returns to his own place when this native is 28.

This is to say that anyone who has Saturn rising at birth will, unless someone is consciously aware of what is ahead, probably experience an early environmental shake-up (at age 7) that will lead to premature participation in the world, and to premature success requiring, perhaps, some later back-tracking.

Note, now, the difference in timing of Chart 5, with Saturn in the 7th House at birth. This Saturn comes to the 10th cusp when the child is 7, building his sense

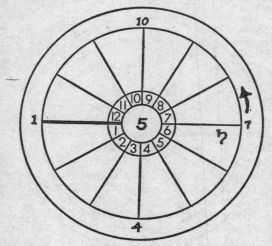

of security strongly, and cementing his feeling that he has a place in the world; at adolescence, age 14, Saturn is on his ascendant, difficult, but consistent with adolescence. By the time Saturn comes to the 4th cusp (age 21) this individual has his feet well under him, and the break with infantile security, dependency, comes when the native is mature enough to handle it, and to reach for the transit of Saturn over its own place in the 7th House, at the age of 28, where maturity is confirmed in marriage (7th House).

These are elementary examples. Life and the horoscope chart are both complicated by the presence of numerous planets, all of which must be interpreted and evaluated. Yet the principle that the *timing of influences proceeds from the natal space relationships* between (a) planets and each other and (b) planets and house cusps and angles remains the rock on which all fruitful chart analysis and projection must be founded.

Part III: Cycology

"A definite and precise system, by which anyone can examine a particular period in the past, in the assurance that he will there discover wisdom about a particular period in the present or the future."

from THE ASTROLOGER magazine, June 1949.

If you are motoring through strange country and a native tells you "The next five miles are just like the piece you went through four miles back," you know what to expect and how to drive.

Life is constantly running through stretches that are "like the piece you went through two, or four, or six, or thirty years back." This is because the planets move in circles. Mars will go around forever, so far as we can tell, and he will *always* follow the same path, which is defined by the zodiac. He will march from Aries to Taurus to Gemini, and so on to the end, and then we will start all over again. In the course of a life that lasts 70 years, Mars will go over the same areas 35 *times,* and each time he repeats the same, or very similar, astrological influences. We ought to be able to learn something from this *repetition of planetary experience,* and indeed we can.

Looking at this from your viewpoint, it means that every two years, approximately, you are living under the same type of Mars influence, as related to the place he recurrently transits. Experience teaches us, who have watched individual charts and individual reactions over a long period of time, that you tend to repeat the same kind of experiences—mistakes, fortunate choices, whatever—each time Mars goes through a given area. Psychologists have also noted repetitions in human behavior, for good or ill, but it has remained for astrologers to indicate the planetary relationship, and so enable you to utilize the experience of the past for the guidance of the present and future, according to a definable timetable. We have found that it is possible to have "advance information" about the kind of period that is coming up, and to prepare for it—*by knowing what kind of things have happened to you, or in you, at similar past periods.*

The type of guidance and help you can get from the application of this knowledge is probably the most important that astrology has to offer. It is important because it enables you to draw on *your own knowledge of yourself* in the past, for *your guidance in present and future.* You have always used this kind of knowledge so far as the seasons are concerned: for example, experience tells you to lay in coal for the winter, and so forth. However, you are probably not so aware of the "seasons of the planets," yet they exist, and preparation for them is as important to your emotional, material, and psychological health as the laying in of coal is for your physical comfort in cold weather.

Tables of the places of Mars, Jupiter, Saturn, Uranus, and Neptune are given elsewhere in this book, from 1870 to 1999. You can therefore look backward over your life and study your reactions and experiences for any time from 1870 to the present; and you can look ahead until 1999.

The best way to use *cycology* is to select, from your past experience, some event or series of events and find out, in the planetary tables, where Mars was at that time. You may also relate it to Saturn, Jupiter, Uranus, or Neptune, but we are here going to follow through a typical Mars-cycle type of recurrence, as an example of how to "look back in order to look forward." This is the story of Jane Doe, who, just as school ended in 1943, fell for the star of the high school ball team, Dick Roe, and got her heart broken. She finds in the Mars table that in June of 1943, Mars was in Aries (the table shows him there between 5/29 and 7/8), which includes her time of romance and subsequent unhappiness. Of itself, that might mean something or nothing, but there's another step, and when Jane takes it, she is startled and amazed. For when Mars was *next* in Aries (5/4 to 6/12, 1945) . . . why, that was the next time she saw Dick again, after June, 1943, and the whole unhappy plot was repeated. She never did see Dick again; but the next time Mars was in Aries (4/13 to 5/22, 1947) she went all out trying to be president of the College class, and got set back on her heels; and the next time (in 1949) she almost got engaged . . . but something happened . . . By now, Jane knows that she'd better be wary of her emotions and desires when Mars is in Aries, and she will approach March 2–April 9, 1951 with her guard up.

Cyclic recurrences of this sort are going on all the time, on the relatively short cycle of Mars, and also on the longer cycle of Saturn. It is an invaluable guide to "judging the future by the past," to avoid the repetition of error, and to spot periods that have been fortunate in the past, to be ready to cash in on them in the future. There are people whose "luck is in" about every two years, and the cycle of Mars is a probable explanation. To take advantage of good periods, and to avoid bad ones, the application of this cycology is of inestimable importance in understanding your Vitasphere and yourself in the past, the present, and the future.

Supplemental Material

Note—Additional *Astrology for the Millions* Horoscope blanks can be purchased in pads of 100 at a price of $3.00 each (1977 price).

Ask your dealer, or write:
LLEWELLYN PUBLICATIONS
P.O. Box 43383
St. Paul, MN 55164

JUPITER	MARS
Transits this sign in the year (fill in below) For this time in your life, Par.No. below applies	Transits this sign in the year (fill in below) For this time in your life, Par.No. below applies
178	193
179	194
180	195
181	196
182	197
183	198
183	198
183	198
184	199
	200
	200
	200
185	201
	202
	202
	202
186	203
	204
	205
	205
187	206
188	207
189	207
189	207
190	208
191	209
	210
	210
	210
192	211

After you have filled in the columns under Neptune, Uranus and Saturn, and checked your life against their transits, you will want to go ahead and check special periods and special events by the transits of Jupiter and Mars, according to the directions on page 279.

To use the Jupiter and Mars columns most satisfactorily, trim the edge of the chart with a pair of scissors, right up to the left-hand edge of the Jupiter column.

TO CHECK JUPITER'S TRANSITS fold back the Jupiter column along its right-hand line—the one separating it from the Mars column. This brings it into position on the other side of the chart, and enables you to use the needed data there in connection with Jupiter's transits.

TO CHECK MARS' TRANSITS leave the Jupiter column folded under as above, and fold back the Mars column along its right-hand edge. This brings it into place for use with the data on the other side of the chart.

REMEMBER that Mars and Jupiter move in comparatively rapid cycles, and should be used chiefly for checking special periods within the larger cycles of Neptune, Uranus and Saturn.

After you have worked with this chart awhile, you may find it convenient to copy it, increasing the size. Or you may find, after you have studied the chart awhile, that you can check transits by inspection of the tables of planets' places without the need for entering all the data in the chart every time. As you become more proficient, you will find new angles and new possibilities in the data in this book, and become more and more adept at reading the charts and checking the lives of those you come in contact with.

BIRTH POSITION OF THE PLANETS IN MY VITASPHERE	TABLE FOR MAKING A LIFE CHECKUP AND-10 YEAR FORECAST	Fill in proper sign from tables on page 276	NEPTUNE Transits this sign in the year (fill in below)	NEPTUNE For this time in your life, Par.No. below applies	URANUS Transits this sign in the year (fill in below)	URANUS For this time in your life, Par.No. below applies	SATURN Transits this sign in the year (fill in below)	SATURN For this time in your life, Par.No. below applies
MY SUN is in the sign .... Par.No.......	Conj. falls in			123		139		158
	Opp. falls in			124		140		159
	Sq.U. falls in			125		141		160
	Sq.L. falls in			126		142		161
MY MOON is in the sign .... Par.No.......	Conj. falls in			127		143		162
	Opp. falls in			128		144		163
	Sq.U. falls in			129		145		164
	Sq.L. falls in			129		145		164
MY MERCURY is in the sign .. .. Par.No.......	Conj. falls in			130		146		165
	Opp. falls in			131		147		166
	Sq.U. falls in			131		147		166
	Sq.L. falls in			131		147		166
MY VENUS is in the sign .... Par.No.......	Conj. falls in			132		148		167
	Opp. falls in			133		149		168
	Sq.U. falls in			133		149		169
	Sq.L. falls in			133		149		169
MY MARS is in the sign .... Par.No.......	Conj. falls in			134		150		170
	Opp. falls in			135		151		171
	Sq.U. falls in			135		151		171
	Sq.L. falls in			135		151		171
MY JUPITER is in the sign .... Par.No.......	Conj. falls in			136		152		172
	Opp. falls in					153		
	Sq.U. falls in					153		
	Sq.L. falls in					153		
MY SATURN is in the sign .... Par.No.......	Conj. falls in			137		154		173
	Opp. falls in							174
	Sq.U. falls in							175
	Sq.L. falls in							175
MY URANUS is in the sign .... Par.No.......	Conj. falls in			138				176
	Opp. falls in					155		
	Sq.U. falls in					156		
	Sq.L. falls in					156		
MY NEPTUNE is in the sign .... Par.No.......	Conj. falls in					157		177
	Opp. falls in							
	Sq.U. falls in							
	Sq.L. falls in							
If you know your birth hour, you can fill in this section by following the directions on page 274. If you don't know your birth hour, ignore this	Ascendant					122		121
	Obscure Period					122		121
	4: Rise being					122		121
	7: Emergence					122		121
	10: Climax					122		121

JUPITER	MARS
Transits this sign in the year (fill in below) For this time in your life, Par.No. below applies	Transits this sign in the year (fill in below) For this time in your life, Par.No. below applies
178	193
179	194
180	195
181	196
182	197
183	198
183	198
183	198
184	199
	200
	200
	200
185	201
	202
	202
	202
186	203
	204
	205
	205
187	206
188	207
189	207
189	207
190	208
191	209
	210
	210
	210
192	211

After you have filled in the columns under Neptune, Uranus and Saturn, and checked your life against their transits, you will want to go ahead and check special periods and special events by the transits of Jupiter and Mars, according to the directions on page 279.

To use the Jupiter and Mars columns most satisfactorily, trim the edge of the chart with a pair of scissors, right up to the left-hand edge of the Jupiter column.

TO CHECK JUPITER'S TRANSITS fold back the Jupiter column along its right-hand line—the one separating it from the Mars column. This brings it into position on the other side of the chart, and enables you to use the needed data there in connection with Jupiter's transits.

TO CHECK MARS' TRANSITS leave the Jupiter column folded under as above, and fold back the Mars column along its right-hand edge. This brings it into place for use with the data on the other side of the chart.

REMEMBER that Mars and Jupiter move in comparatively rapid cycles, and should be used chiefly for checking special periods within the larger cycles of Neptune, Uranus and Saturn.

After you have worked with this chart awhile, you may find it convenient to copy it, increasing the size. Or you may find, after you have studied the chart awhile, that you can check transits by inspection of the tables of planets' places without the need for entering all the data in the chart every time. As you become more proficient, you will find new angles and new possibilities in the data in this book, and become more and more adept at reading the charts and checking the lives of those you come in contact with.

BIRTH POSITION OF THE PLANETS IN MY VITASPHERE	TABLE FOR MAKING A LIFE CHECKUP AND 10 YEAR FORECAST	Fill in proper sign from tables on page 276	NEPTUNE		URANUS		SATURN	
			Transits this sign in the year (fill in below)	For this time in your life, Par.No. below applies	Transits this sign in the year (fill in below)	For this time in your life, Par.No. below applies	Transits this sign in the year (fill in below)	For this time in your life, Par.No. below applies
MY SUN is in the sign .... Par.No.......	Conj. falls in			123		139		158
	Opp. falls in			124		140		159
	Sq.U. falls in			125		141		160
	Sq.L. falls in			126		142		161
MY MOON is in the sign .... Par.No.......	Conj. falls in			127		143		162
	Opp. falls in			128		144		163
	Sq.U. falls in			129		145		164
	Sq.L. falls in			129		145		164
MY MERCURY is in the sign .. .. Par.No.......	Conj. falls in			130		146		165
	Opp. falls in			131		147		166
	Sq.U. falls in			131		147		166
	Sq.L. falls in			131		147		166
MY VENUS is in the sign .... Par.No.......	Conj. falls in			132		148		167
	Opp. falls in			133		149		168
	Sq.U. falls in			133		149		169
	Sq.L. falls in			133		149		169
MY MARS is in the sign .... Par.No.......	Conj. falls in			134		150		170
	Opp. falls in			135		151		171
	Sq.U. falls in			135		151		171
	Sq.L. falls in			135		151		171
MY JUPITER is in the sign .... Par.No.......	Conj. falls in			136		152		172
	Opp. falls in					153		
	Sq.U. falls in					153		
	Sq.L. falls in					153		
MY SATURN is in the sign .... Par.No.......	Conj. falls in			137		154		173
	Opp. falls in							174
	Sq.U. falls in							175
	Sq.L. falls in							175
MY URANUS is in the sign .... Par.No.......	Conj. falls in			138				176
	Opp. falls in					155		
	Sq.U. falls in					156		
	Sq.L. falls in					156		
MY NEPTUNE is in the sign .... Par.No.......	Conj. falls in					157		177
	Opp. falls in							
	Sq.U. falls in							
	Sq.L. falls in							
If you know your birth hour, you can fill in this section by following the directions on page 274. If you don't know your birth hour, ignore this	Ascendant					122		121
	Obscure Period					122		121
	4: Rise being					122		121
	7: Emergence					122		121
	10: Climax					122		121

JUPITER	MARS
Transits this sign in the year (fill in below) For this time in your life, Par.No. below applies.	Transits this sign in the year (fill in below) For this time in your life, Par.No. below applies.
178	193
179	194
180	195
181	196
182	197
183	198
183	198
183	198
184	199
	200
	200
	200
185	201
	202
	202
	202
186	203
	204
	205
	205
187	206
188	207
189	207
189	207
190	208
191	209
	210
	210
	210
192	211

After you have filled in the columns under Neptune, Uranus and Saturn, and checked your life against their transits, you will want to go ahead and check special periods and special events by the transits of Jupiter and Mars, according to the directions on page 279.

To use the Jupiter and Mars columns most satisfactorily, trim the edge of the chart with a pair of scissors, right up to the left-hand edge of the Jupiter column.

TO CHECK JUPITER'S TRANSITS fold back the Jupiter column along its right-hand line—the one separating it from the Mars column. This brings it into position on the other side of the chart, and enables you to use the needed data there in connection with Jupiter's transits.

TO CHECK MARS' TRANSITS leave the Jupiter column folded under as above, and fold back the Mars column along its right-hand edge. This brings it into place for use with the data on the other side of the chart.

REMEMBER that Mars and Jupiter move in comparatively rapid cycles, and should be used chiefly for checking special periods within the larger cycles of Neptune, Uranus and Saturn.

After you have worked with this chart awhile, you may find it convenient to copy it, increasing the size. Or you may find, after you have studied the chart awhile, that you can check transits by inspection of the tables of planets' places without the need for entering all the data in the chart every time. As you become more proficient, you will find new angles and new possibilities in the data in this book, and become more and more adept at reading the charts and checking the lives of those you come in contact with.

BIRTH POSITION OF THE PLANETS IN MY VITASPHERE	TABLE FOR MAKING A LIFE CHECKUP AND 10 YEAR FORECAST	Fill in proper sign from tables on page 276	NEPTUNE		URANUS		SATURN	
			Transits this sign in the year (fill in below)	For this time in your life, Par.No. below applies	Transits this sign in the year (fill in below)	For this time in your life, Par.No. below applies	Transits this sign in the year (fill in below)	For this time in your life, Par.No. below applies
MY SUN is in the sign .... Par.No........	Conj. falls in			123		139		158
	Opp. falls in			124		140		159
	Sq.U. falls in			125		141		160
	Sq.L. falls in			126		142		161
My MOON is in the sign .... Par.No........	Conj. falls in			127		143		162
	Opp. falls in			128		144		163
	Sq.U. falls in			129		145		164
	Sq.L. falls in			129		145		164
My MERCURY is in the sign .. .. Par.No........	Conj. falls in			130		146		165
	Opp. falls in			131		147		166
	Sq.U. falls in			131		147		166
	Sq.L. falls in			131		147		166
My VENUS is in the sign .... Par.No........	Conj. falls in			132		148		167
	Opp. falls in			133		149		168
	Sq.U. falls in			133		149		169
	Sq.L. falls in			133		149		169
My MARS is in the sign .... Par.No........	Conj. falls in			134		150		170
	Opp. falls in			135		151		171
	Sq.U. falls in			135		151		171
	Sq.L. falls in			135		151		171
My JUPITER is in the sign .... Par.No........	Conj. falls in			136		152		172
	Opp. falls in					153		
	Sq.U. falls in					153		
	Sq.L. falls in					153		
My SATURN is in the sign .... Par.No........	Conj. falls in			137		154		173
	Opp. falls in							174
	Sq.U. falls in							175
	Sq.L. falls in							175
My URANUS is in the sign .... Par.No........	Conj. falls in			138				176
	Opp. falls in					155		
	Sq.U. falls in					156		
	Sq.L. falls in					156		
My NEPTUNE is in the sign .... Par.No........	Conj. falls in					157		177
	Opp. falls in							
	Sq.U. falls in							
	Sq.L. falls in							
If you know your birth hour, you can fill in this section by following the directions on page 274. If you don't know your birth hour, ignore this	Ascendant					122		121
	Obscure Period					122		121
	4: Rise being					122		121
	7: Emergence					122		121
	10: Climax					122		121